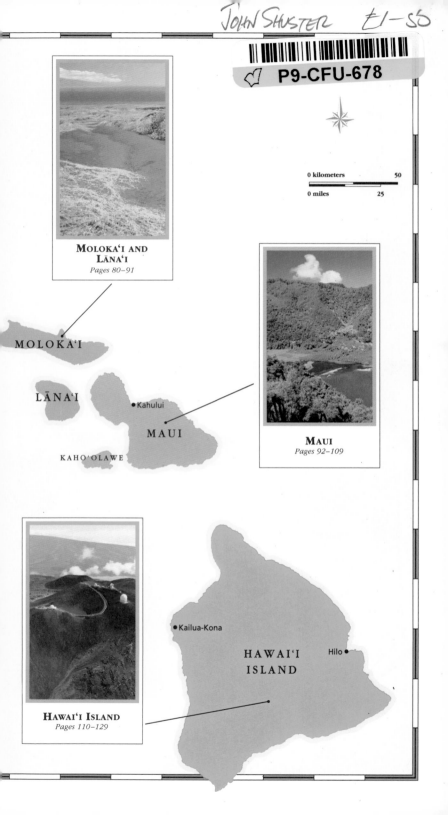

JOHN SHUSTER $1-50

P9-CFU-678

0 kilometers   50
0 miles   25

**MOLOKA'I AND
LĀNA'I**
Pages 80–91

MAUI
Pages 92–109

MOLOKA'I

LĀNA'I

●Kahului

MAUI

KAHO'OLAWE

HAWAI'I ISLAND
Pages 110–129

●Kailua-Kona

HAWAI'I
ISLAND

Hilo ●

LEON WASSERMAN

EYEWITNESS *TRAVEL GUIDES*

HAWAII

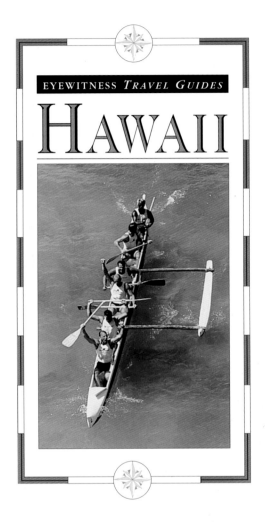

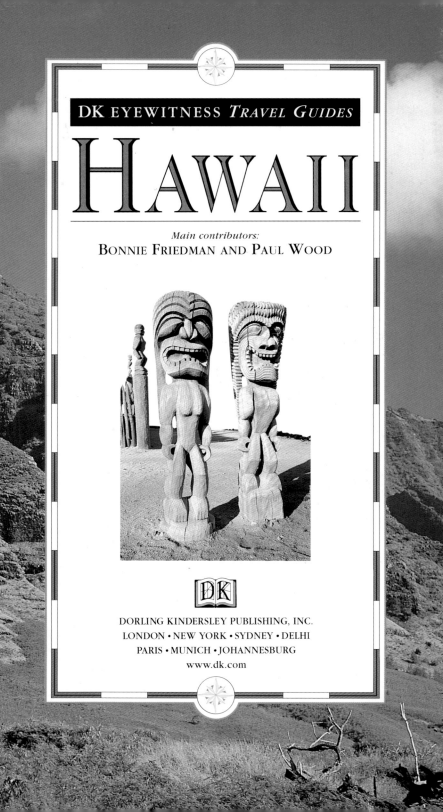

DK EYEWITNESS *TRAVEL GUIDES*

HAWAII

Main contributors:
BONNIE FRIEDMAN AND PAUL WOOD

DORLING KINDERSLEY PUBLISHING, INC.
LONDON • NEW YORK • SYDNEY • DELHI
PARIS • MUNICH • JOHANNESBURG
www.dk.com

DORLING KINDERSLEY PUBLISHING, INC.

www.dk.com

PROJECT EDITOR Helen Townsend
ART EDITOR Anthony Limerick
EDITOR Freddy Hamilton
DESIGNERS Tessa Bindloss, Tim Mann
US EDITORS Mary Sutherland, Michael Wise
MAP CO-ORDINATORS Emily Green, David Pugh

PICTURE RESEARCH Ellen Root
DTP DESIGNER Ingrid Vienings

CONTRIBUTORS
Gerald Carr, Bonnie Friedman, Rita Goldman, Clemence McLaren,
Melissa Miller, Alex Salkever, Stephen Self, Greg Ward, Paul Wood

PHOTOGRAPHERS
Rob Reichenfeld, Mike Severns

ILLUSTRATORS
Robert Ashby, Richard Bonson, Gary Cross, Chris Forsey,
Stephen Gyapay, Claire Littlejohn, Chris Orr & Associates,
Robbie Polley, Mike Taylor, John Woodcock

Reproduced in Italy by Flying Colours, Verona
Printed and bound by L. Rex Printing Company Limited, China

First American Edition, 1998
4 6 8 10 9 7 5

Published in the United States by
Dorling Kindersley Publishing, Inc.,
95 Madison Avenue, New York, New York 10016
Reprinted with revisions 1999, 2000, 2001

Copyright © 1998, 2001 Dorling Kindersley Limited, London

Library of Congress Cataloging-in-Publication Data
Hawaii. -- 1st American ed.
    p.   cm. -- (Dorling Kindersley travel guides)
Includes index.
ISBN 0-7894-2750-8
1. Hawaii -- Guidebooks.   I. Series.
DU622.H325 1998   97-35006
919.6004'41 -- dc21   CIP

Hawaiian words and place names have been spelled throughout the
book with glottal stops and macrons to facilitate pronunciation and
as a mark of respect to Hawaiian culture. For a detailed guide to
pronunciation, see page 208. Floors are referred to in American
usage; i.e., the "first floor" is at ground level.

Waikīkī Beach and Diamond Head

CONTENTS

INTRODUCING HAWAI‘I

**Ali‘iōlani Hale, the state judiciary
building in Honolulu**

◁ Beautiful, lush Mākaha ("ferocious") Valley on O‘ahu's remote Wai‘anae Coast

The rugged, sharply incised Nā Pali Coast on Kaua'i's North Shore

SURVIVAL GUIDE

HONOLULU AND WAIKĪKĪ

Historic cape made with the feathers of thousands of birds

HAWAI'I ISLAND BY ISLAND

Dancer at the Polynesian Cultural Center at Lā'ie, O'ahu

Yellow *'ilima*, a Hawaiian hibiscus relative and O'ahu's official flower

Geological diagram of the Hawaiian Islands
(see pp10–11)

INTRODUCING
HAWAI'I

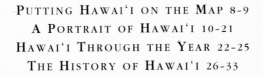

Putting Hawai'i on the Map

HAWAI'I IS AN ISOLATED ARCHIPELAGO in the middle of the Pacific Ocean and is one of the United States. It consists of eight main islands covering 6,425 sq miles (16,650 sq km). Most visitors arrive in Honolulu, the state capital, and travel to the other islands by inter-island flights or cruises.

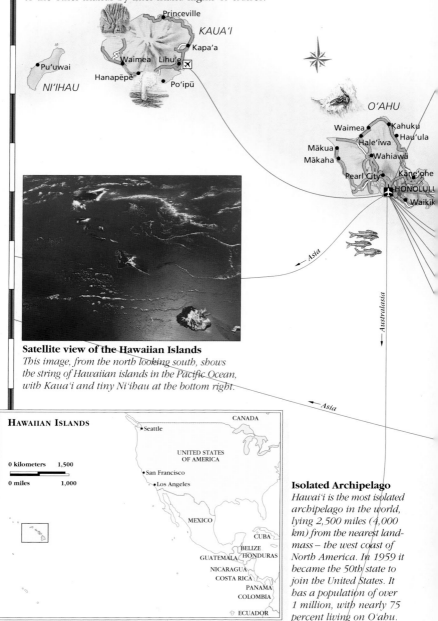

Princeville

KAUA'I

Kapa'a

Pu'uwai
Waimea Līhu'e
Hanapēpē
Po'ipū

NI'IHAU

O'AHU

Waimea
Kahuku
Hau'ula
Hale'iwa
Mākua
Wahiawā
Mākaha
Pearl City
Kāne'ohe
HONOLULU
Waikīkī

← Asia

Australasia ↓

← Asia

Satellite view of the Hawaiian Islands
This image, from the north looking south, shows the string of Hawaiian islands in the Pacific Ocean, with Kaua'i and tiny Ni'ihau at the bottom right.

HAWAIIAN ISLANDS

CANADA
Seattle

UNITED STATES
OF AMERICA

0 kilometers   1,500

0 miles   1,000

San Francisco
Los Angeles

MEXICO

CUBA
BELIZE
GUATEMALA HONDURAS
NICARAGUA
COSTA RICA
PANAMA
COLOMBIA
ECUADOR

Isolated Archipelago
Hawai'i is the most isolated archipelago in the world, lying 2,500 miles (4,000 km) from the nearest land-mass – the west coast of North America. In 1959 it became the 50th state to join the United States. It has a population of over 1 million, with nearly 75 percent living on O'ahu.

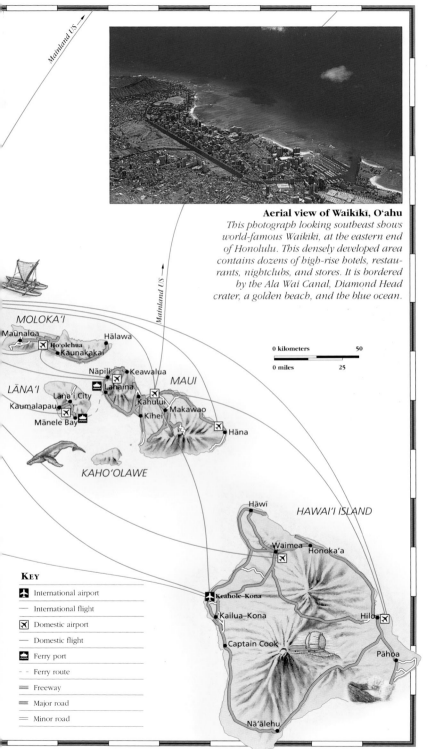

Aerial view of Waikīkī, Oʻahu
This photograph looking southeast shows world-famous Waikīkī, at the eastern end of Honolulu. This densely developed area contains dozens of high-rise hotels, restaurants, nightclubs, and stores. It is bordered by the Ala Wai Canal, Diamond Head crater, a golden beach, and the blue ocean.

Mainland US

Mainland US

MOLOKAʻI
Maunaloa
Hoʻolehua
Kaunakakai
Hālawa

Nāpili
Keawalua
Lahaina
MAUI
LĀNAʻI
Lānaʻi City
Kahului
Kaumalapau
Makawao
Mānele Bay
Kīhei
Hāna

KAHOʻOLAWE

0 kilometers   50
0 miles   25

Hāwī
HAWAIʻI ISLAND

Waimea   Honokaʻa

KEY

✈	International airport
—	International flight
☒	Domestic airport
—	Domestic flight
⛴	Ferry port
- -	Ferry route
▬	Freeway
▬	Major road
═	Minor road

Keahole–Kona
Kailua–Kona
Hilo
Captain Cook
Pāhoa

Nāʻālehu

Formation of the Hawaiian Islands

THE HAWAIIAN ISLANDS are the tips of a large chain of volcanoes stretching almost 3,100 miles (5,000 km) from Hawai'i Island to the Aleutian Trench in the north Pacific. Most are now underwater stumps, fringed by coral reefs, but many were once great shield (dome-shaped) volcanoes. The oldest, northernmost volcano is slowly disappearing into the Aleutian Trench. The youngest volcano – Kīlauea – today spews out basaltic lava, creating new land on Hawai'i Island. This cycle of destruction and creation, driven by the conveyor-belt movement of the Pacific plate over a stationary hot spot of magma, has been occurring for 70 million years.

Moloka'i's sea cliffs (see pp86–7) constitute the back wall of giant landslide scars formed when half of the Wailau shield volcano slumped into the sea. Marine erosion keeps the cliffs steep by undercutting the bases.

The areas of undulating ocean floor are deposits of giant landslides. Little is known about them because they sit in deep water, and their precise age of formation is unknown.

O'AHU

KAUA'I

NI'IHAU

Kaua'i's amazing Waimea Canyon (see pp144–5) is carved into the Wai'ale'ale shield volcano. The layers of lava flows that created the volcano are visible. Large canyons of this nature are typical of Hawaiian volcanoes in their late erosional stage.

Stretching almost halfway along O'ahu, the spectacular Nu'uanu Pali (cliffs) formed when a large section of the Ko'olau shield volcano slumped into the sea.

Ocean floor

The Pacific plate moves northwesterly at a rate of 2–3.5 in (5–9 cm) a year.

CONVEYOR BELT

As it moves, the Pacific plate – the huge slab of earth's crust underlying the Pacific Ocean – rides over a stationary hot spot (mantle plume) that feeds heat and basaltic magma toward the surface. Mauna Loa, Kīlauea, and the "new" underwater volcano Lō'ihi, are presently over the hot spot. As the plate moves to the northwest, volcanoes are gradually pulled off the hot spot while new volcanoes grow in their place.

O'ahu's Hanauma Bay (see p76) is a late-stage volcanic crater, one of several forming a line of cones, craters, and vents caused by an eruption at least 10,000 years ago. The ash cones are the result of explosive interaction of rising magma with sea water. Either the bay's present shape is due to breaching of the crater wall or, more likely, the wall was never complete.

Maui's Haleakala *(see pp106–7), in its erosional,
middle to late stage, is Hawai'i's only active shield
volcano outside Hawai'i Island. Its last lava eruption
was in 1790. Young cones and lava flows occur in and
around the misnamed crater – actually an erosional
depression formed where two large valleys coalesced.*

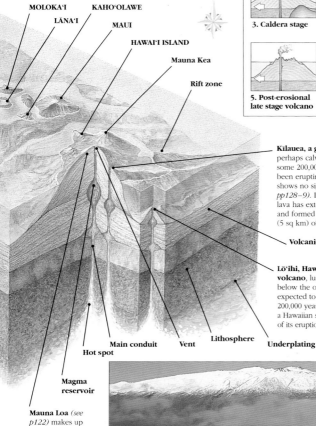

MOLOKA'I · KAHO'OLAWE
LĀNA'I
MAUI
HAWAI'I ISLAND
Mauna Kea
Rift zone

Main conduit · Vent · Lithosphere · Underplating
Hot spot
Magma
reservoir

Mauna Loa *(see
p122)* makes up
over one-half
the volume of
Hawai'i Island.

VOLCANO LIFE CYCLE

Shield volcanoes form while over a
hot spot. As they move off it, volcanic activity decreases and erosion
begins. Late stage volcanoes occur
from a magma source deeper than
the hot spot. Eventually volcanoes
disappear under the ocean surface.

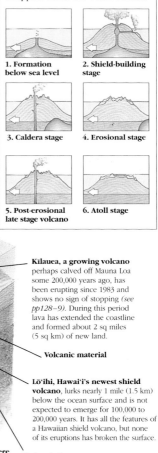

**1. Formation
below sea level**

**2. Shield-building
stage**

3. Caldera stage

4. Erosional stage

**5. Post-erosional
late stage volcano**

6. Atoll stage

Kīlauea, a growing volcano
perhaps calved off Mauna Loa
some 200,000 years ago, has
been erupting since 1983 and
shows no sign of stopping *(see
pp128–9)*. During this period
lava has extended the coastline
and formed about 2 sq miles
(5 sq km) of new land.

Volcanic material

**Lō'ihi, Hawai'i's newest shield
volcano,** lurks nearly 1 mile (1.5 km)
below the ocean surface and is not
expected to emerge for 100,000 to
200,000 years. It has all the features of
a Hawaiian shield volcano, but none
of its eruptions has broken the surface.

Hawai'i Island's Mauna Kea *(shown here) and Mauna Loa, a pair of giant
shield volcanoes, are hard to distinguish at their base beneath the sea. Mauna
Kea (see p122) is older, in its post-shield stage with many smaller cones, giving it
a rough appearance. Bulkier Mauna Loa's mass is so heavy that it has depressed
the ocean floor. Together they make up the earth's largest single volcanic structure.*

Flora of the Hawaiian Islands

PRIOR TO HUMAN SETTLEMENT, the location of the Hawaiian islands in the middle of the Pacific Ocean was a natural barrier to the colonization of plants from other parts of the world. In prehistoric times, fewer than 300 immigrant flowering plant species – seeds borne by wind, carried by birds, or drifting on the ocean – colonized the islands. Extreme isolation produced a limited flora in comparison with continental floras; for example, Hawai'i has only three native orchids out of a worldwide family of 20,000 species. Some species evolved into new forms able to exploit a wide variety of habitats. Thorns and other defensive adaptations have largely been lost in Hawaiian plants as they conferred no advantage in a flora isolated from natural predators. As a result, native flora is unique, with 89 percent of its flowering species found only in Hawai'i.

Koa *is one of the most important forest trees in the Hawaiian islands. The largest specimens can attain heights of over 115 ft (35 m), and their huge trunks were used by Hawaiians to make voyaging canoes.*

Grasses are found in virtually all vegetation zones, occasionally as the dominant species. In dry, lowland areas *pili* grasslands provided thatching material for early Hawaiians (*see p57*). About 150 native and naturalized species of this important and large family occur in Hawai'i.

'Ōhi'a lehua, *probably the most common tree in the Hawaiian flora, occurs from near sea level to elevations of 7,200 ft (2,200 m). It is also one of the most variable, with mature forms ranging from a few inches in bog habitats to 80 ft (24 m) or more in forest habitats. Epiphytes and a tree fern understory also characterize wet 'ōhi'a lehua forests.*

Iliau, a relative of the silversword

Hibiscus, *a favorite flower, is represented here by koki'o, one of seven native species and hundreds of ornamental varieties and hybrids in Hawai'i.*

Palm trees imported from Polynesia

Bougainvillea imported from Brazil

Pōhuehue, a typical beachfront plant

Naupaka *is a dune-binding shrub with distinctive "half" flowers. Ocean currents have dispersed its buoyant fruits throughout the Pacific Basin. Scientists believe that two separate colonizations account for eight endemic species growing in a variety of upland habitats.*

'Ākala, *or native Hawaiian raspberries, appear to have lost an unnecessary defense mechanism (thorns in this case) that was present in their continental ancestors.*

The silversword, or 'ahinahina *(see p107), occurs on Maui and Hawai'i Island in alpine desert habitats to elevations of over 12,000 ft (3,650 m). This species, together with the bog greensword and 25 other shrubs, trees, and a liana, actually evolved in the Hawaiian islands from one single ancestral immigrant.*

VEGETATION ZONES

Alpine vegetation, *a sparse array of shrubs dominated by silverswords and* kūpaoa, *occurs at 9,850–11,150 ft (3,000–3,400 m). A harsh, dry zone, it may freeze at night.*

Subalpine communities *occur in a relatively cool, dry zone from about 5,575–9,850 ft (1,700–3,000 m). Vegetation varies from grassland or shrubland to stunted trees.*

Mamane tree, found in subalpine areas

TYPICAL ISLAND

The diversity of Hawaiian flora can be seen on this hypothetical island. At coast level native shrubs and imported palm trees exist, gradually giving way to lowland shrubs and trees of increasing stature as rainfall increases. Bog vegetation may develop on flat, poorly drained areas. Above 6,000 ft (1,850 m), and at lower elevations in leeward areas, a dramatic reduction in rainfall usually results in sparse, low vegetation.

Montane dry areas *are characteristic of leeward slopes at an elevation of 1,650–8,850 ft (500–2,700 m). Vegetation varies from dry grasslands to dry forests with a canopy 10–65 ft (3–20 m) high.*

Montane wetlands, *in areas of high rainfall at elevations of 3,950–7,200 ft (1,200–2,200 m), include wet herblands, sedgelands, shrublands, bogs, and forests with canopies up to 130 ft (40 m) high.*

Raised hummocks of oreobolus

The greensword, a close relative of the silversword, is found in summit bogs of West Maui and at mid-elevations mostly in windward East Maui.

Tropical plants *from around the world thrive in Hawai'i. This lush planting on O'ahu includes giant aroids and bananas. Alien plants pose a real threat to native species by displacing them and preventing their regeneration.*

Lowland and coastal communities *include a diverse array of dry, medium, and wet herb, grass, shrub, and forest vegetation occurring below 5,000 ft (1,500 m) elevation.*

Voices of Hawai'i

David Malo

ANCIENT HAWAI'I produced a wealth of oral literature and myth, which was passed down from generation to generation. A 12-letter alphabet, the smallest in the world, was developed by the missionaries in the early 19th century. Notable literary visitors wrote accounts of the islands and completed other works during their stays. Today, a new generation of Hawaiians is creating modern native literature, while maintaining a profound respect for the myths and chants that perpetuate the old ways of Hawai'i.

The demigod Maui fishing the Hawaiian islands out of the sea

ORAL TRADITION

THE ORAL TRADITIONS of pre-contact Hawai'i played a vital role in island life. The literature, committed to memory, was often chanted to the accompaniment of music and dance. There were *oli* (instructional chants), *mo'olelo* (legends and narratives), *mele* (lyric poetry), and *'ōlelo no'eau* (proverbs). The *kāhuna* (priests) composed and recited poetry to preserve history, genealogies, and the knowledge of traditional crafts. *Haku mele* (master poets) often composed verses for special occasions, such as the birth of an *ali'i* (royal) child; such songs were considered sacred.

19th-century image of Kū

The *haku mele* took advantage of the fact that many words sound alike, building on repetitions and word play. The similarity of words was not considered accidental; if a sea creature's name matched that of a geographical feature, these phenomena were considered *kino*, manifestations of the same spiritual force.

The most famous creation chant, the *Kumulipo*, tells of life and the islands growing up gradually, on their own initiative. The progenitors of humans were the male *Wākea* (the Heavens) and the female *Papa* (the Earth). Hawaiians venerated four main gods: Kāne (light, life, water), Lono (productivity of the land), Kū (war, courage), and Kanaloa (sea). Each had numerous manifestations, all with names, and their deeds were visible in everyday life.

Stories tell of Pele, the fiery-tempered volcano goddess who migrated from *Kahiki* (Tahiti, or simply the distant homeland) seeking a dry place for her eternal fires. Tracing the geological evolution of the islands, she resided first on Kaua'i and then O'ahu before settling for a time in Maui's Haleakalā Crater. She now lives in Hawai'i Island's Kīlauea Caldera (*see pp128–9*).

Myths are told of Pele's entire clan, especially of her jealous relationship with Hi'iaka, her beautiful younger sister and the goddess of *hula*. Pele's opponent in many stories is the shape-shifting pig-man Kamapua'a, a carnal, violent manifestation of Lono. Representing the productivity of the mountains and fields, his unending quest is to tame and fertilize the destructive goddess of lava. A cinder cone near Hāna on Maui is called Ka Iwi o Pele, or Pele's bones (*see p109*), because the two titans met there for a cataclysmic battle.

Other stories tell of Maui, the Prometheus of Hawaiian mythology, who brought fire to the human race, lifted the roof of the heavens, slowed the speed of the sun, and fished the islands out of the sea with a magic hook.

EARLY RECORDS

THE FIRST written words about Hawai'i are found in the logbooks and journals of the early visitors. Thomas Manby, on an expedition in 1791, wrote candidly of the seamen's amorous relations with Hawaiian women and gave a humorous portrait of Kamehameha I's first sight of a cow – startled, the great warrior knocked over half his retinue fleeing for his life.

The first missionaries kept more restrained records. The Reverend Hiram Bingham, leader of the first mission in

An 1834 edition of *Ka Lama Hawaii* (The Hawaiian Luminary)

1820, set the pattern with his *Missionaries versus Man-of-Warsmen*. Within 14 years of their arrival the missionaries had created a Hawaiian alphabet, translated the Bible, established a printing press, and put out the first Hawaiian language newspaper, *Ka Lama Hawaii*.

Native oral tradition was suppressed but never lost during this time. Traditional songs *(mele)* passed through the filter of hymns *(himeni)* and the introduction of the guitar and *'ukulele* to emerge as "Hawaiian music." King Kalākaua (1874–91) started a renaissance of Hawaiian culture by calling for a revival of the *mele*, chants, and *hula*. In the same era, scholarly converts such as Samuel M. Kamakau and David Malo wrote invaluable records of life in precontact Hawai'i.

Portrait of Robert Louis Stevenson by Girolamo Piero Nerli (1892)

LITERARY VISITORS

IN THE OPENING chapter of Herman Melville's *Moby Dick*, Ishmael says, "I love to sail forbidden seas and land on barbarous coasts." This urge to explore exotic realms was an echo of that felt by Ishmael's creator and many other writers, and in the 1800s the lure of the South Seas was particularly strong. In 1843, Melville himself spent four months in Hawai'i, working in a Honolulu bowling alley and beachcombing in Lahaina.

Jack and Charmian London on Waikiki Beach in 1915

Following in Melville's footsteps, the 31-year-old Mark Twain explored the islands in 1866 as a correspondent for the *Sacramento Union*. While touring, he wrote a series of *Letters from the Sandwich Islands* and later put several chapters about Hawai'i in his book *Roughing It*. Though he never visited again, he wrote that "no other land could so lovingly and so beseechingly haunt me, sleeping and waking, through half a lifetime, as that one has done."

In 1889, the Scottish writer Robert Louis Stevenson dined with King David Kalākaua. Suffering from tuberculosis, the author of *Treasure Island* traveled the South Seas from 1888 until his death in 1894. In Hawai'i he befriended the royal family, studied the language, and visited Kalaupapa leprosy colony *(see pp86–7)*. Stevenson worked at fever pitch during his five-month visit, finishing *The Master of Ballantrae*, conceiving his novel *The Wrecker*, roughing out a collection of sketches about Hawai'i called *The Eight Islands*, and writing numerous poems and letters. Two of his best stories, "The Bottle Imp" and "The Isle of Voices," were also penned here.

Jack London arrived in Honolulu aboard his yacht *Snark* in 1907. The islands became his second home, the

place where he wrote some of his most famous works, including *The Call of the Wild* and *White Fang*. He was the first literary figure to call himself a *kama'aina* (native). His two volumes of island-set stories, *On The Makaloa Mat* and *The House of Pride*, angered the local establishment by depicting racial snobbery and the cruelty of official responses to leprosy.

HAWAI'I CALLS

TWENTIETH-CENTURY tourism produced a new mythology, casting the islands as a "paradise" filled with relaxed, *'ukulele*-strumming natives. A surge of interest in 1916 stimulated songs such as "Oh, How She Could Yacki Hacki Wicki Wacki Woo (That's Love In Honolu)." A second wave in the 1930s prompted a string of Hollywood Waikīkī fantasies, including the 1936 film *Honolulu*, which turned *hula* into a form of tap dance.

Today, the Hawai'i Visitors and Convention Bureau continues to romanticize Hawai'i. However, island-born writers such as Oswald A. Bushnell and Milton Murayama are creating a wealth of native literature. With support from local intellectuals, many now write in pidgin, the hybrid language that evolved on the plantations so that different ethnic groups could communicate. The stories of Lois-Ann Yamanaka, for example, have received international acclaim.

Wild Meat and the Bully Burgers, a novel by Lois-Ann Yamanaka

Hula and Hawaiian Music

Traditional 'uli'uli rattle

HULA BEGAN, it is believed, as a form of religious ritual to honor the ancient gods and chiefs while providing entertainment for the ruling classes. The traditional *hula kāhiko* was accompanied only by the human voice through chants *(oli)* or song *(mele)*, and by percussion instruments. In the early 19th century the missionaries tried to abolish *hula* but succeeded only in driving it underground. King Kalākaua, the Merrie Monarch, encouraged the revival of *hula* in the late 19th century, giving rise to the modern *hula 'auwana*. This style was influenced by Western music and clothing – women wore, and still do, long-sleeved, floor-length dresses *(holokū)*. The 1930s ushered in the "Sweet Leilani" era when dancers in cellophane skirts and flower *lei* greeted the ocean liners bringing tourists to Honolulu. Today *hula* enjoys great respect.

This 19th-century engraving *is a European interpretation of a native woman with traditional tattoos dancing* hula noho *(sitting hula) in a* kapa *skirt.*

The earliest **hula** *was, some say, the domain of men, although there is no documented evidence. However, there has been a great resurgence of male* hula *in recent years.*

Knee-length *ti*-leaf skirts are worn in *hula kāhiko*. The flat leaves rustle with the dancers' movements.

Dog-tooth leg ornaments, *or* kūpe'e niho 'ilio, *were traditionally worn exclusively by male dancers. Only four teeth from each dog were used, and it took nearly 3,000 dogs to make some ornaments.*

The **'uli'uli** is a small gourd containing seeds and fitted with a handle. It is often decorated with feathers.

The **ipu heke** *is a percussion instrument made of two gourds. It is the most common accompaniment for* hula kāhiko. *The* kumu *(teacher) here is wearing a dried* ti-leaf *cape, which originally would have functioned as a raincoat.*

The standing **pahu** ***drum*** *is traditionally made from a section of coconut tree covered with shark skin, played with the hands. Pahu are often used in conjunction with the smaller* pūniu – *a drum made of coconut, lashed to the chanter's right thigh and played with a thong of braided fiber.*

WHERE TO ENJOY HULA AND MUSIC

Merrie Monarch Festival (p25)
Kodak Hula Show (p180)
Polynesian Cultural Center (p78)
Moloka'i Ka Hula Piko (p22)
Prince Lot Hula Festival (p23)
Na Mele O Maui (p24)

Pu'ili are made of bamboo; one end is a handle and the other is split into a narrow "fringe" that makes a rattling sound.

*This group of **kūpuna** (respected elders) dressed in* mu'umu'u *are singing and playing instruments that typically accompany* hula 'auwana – 'ukulele, *guitar, and standing bass. The* ipu heke *and* 'uli'uli *lying in the foreground are used for* hula kāhiko.

The **'ukulele** *is one of many instruments brought to Hawai'i by immigrants, in this case the Portuguese. It is integral to contemporary Hawaiian music.*

Flower lei are not authentic to *hula kāhiko*; dancers traditionally wear fern anklets and bracelets.

Maui's Keali'i Reichel *is a well-known chanter, hula dancer, singer, composer, and teacher dedicated to the preservation of the culture.*

HULA KĀHIKO

This old form of *hula* is shown here with contemporary twists. The *ti*-leaf skirts, *pū'ili*, and *'uli'uli* are traditional, while the plumeria flower *lei* and colorful fabric tops are modern. Visitors can see this combined style of old and new elements on all the Hawaiian islands.

THE REVIVAL OF HULA AND HAWAIIAN MUSIC

Today *hula kāhiko* is pursued by hundreds of students performing the same chants and using the same instruments as their ancestors, and *hula 'auwana* is more popular than in King Kalākaua's time. *Hula's* connection to Hawaiian music is inextricable. The "music" accompanying traditional dancers took the form of musical poetry – chants and song. When Western musical influence became widespread, *hula* embraced it in the *'auwana* style. In the early 19th century missionaries brought sober hymns to Hawai'i, and increased sea traffic brought musicians from Europe and Asia with their varied secular music. The era from 1900 to the Hawaiian Renaissance of the 1970s saw an explosion of *hapa haole* – Hawaiian music influenced by ragtime, Tin Pan Alley, and even orchestrations from films and television shows. The instruments brought by immigrants – *'ukulele*, Hawaiian guitar, standing bass, piano – were stirred into the musical pot. The ongoing Hawaiian Renaissance has brought an enthusiastic revival of early Hawaiian music.

Child dancing hula kāhiko

Traditional Hawaiian Crafts

WHAT WE CONSIDER crafts today – woven baskets, feather *lei* (garlands), *poi* (taro paste) pounders, wooden bowls – were integral to the lives of ancient Hawaiians. They were made with care from readily available sources, such as coconut fronds, feathers of the *mamo* bird, local stone, and native *koa* wood. Many crafts are still made in the old, precontact ways. Even the ancient, almost lost art of beating and printing *kapa* (bark cloth) is undergoing a revival. Traditional implements are often favored over the modern, but certain tools have been updated. For instance, metal needles for stringing *lei* have replaced those made from coconut palm frond midribs. Not all crafts are indigenous. The missionaries introduced quilting, an art that is still passed from generation to generation *(see p56)*. Both the ancient and modern crafts are time-consuming pursuits requiring patience and skill – not unusual attributes among Hawaiians.

Netting *was the most efficient method of fishing in old Hawai'i. The best nets were made with a netting needle and mesh gauge, using cord from the* olonā *shrub.*

These two wooden bowls, connected by a human figure crowned with feathers, were probably used by an ali'i *(chief) for* poi *(taro paste) or* 'awa *(a ceremonial drink).*

THE STARBUCK CAPE

This superb 19th-century *'ahu'ula* (cape) with a unique geometric pattern was made with the feathers of thousands of birds, which were released after giving up just a few feathers each. It was probably given to Captain Starbuck by Kamehameha II, who with his wife sailed to London on the captain's ship in 1824.

Feathers were arranged by size, tied together at the quills, and attached to the net with *olonā* thread.

KAPA CLOTH

Common garments (*'a'ahu*) in ancient Hawai'i were made of *kapa* (bark cloth). The *wauke* (paper mulberry tree) produced the best cloth, which was pounded with wooden *kapa* beaters. Using dyes from native plants in every imaginable hue, bamboo implements were used to stamp patterns on the cloth. Today *kapa* is still made for certain ceremonies and is highly regarded for its variety of textures and beautiful, intricate designs.

Decorating *kapa* cloth

This late 18th-century **pe'ahi** *(fan) is made out of coconut leaves, human hair, cordage, and dyes. Fans with this distinctive shape were probably used exclusively by the* ali'i *(chiefs).*

Gourds with tubular necks were used in ancient Hawai'i to hold drinking water. It is believed that dyes created with infusions of bruised leaves, bark, or black mud were used to make the dark patterns on gourd bowls and water containers. Gourds of different shapes and sizes were also used as percussion instruments (see pp16–17).

Two-ply cord made from the bark of the *olona* shrub was used in the net foundation and the fasteners.

The irregular black shapes are made from the feathers of the *'ō'ō* bird. Black feathers were rarely used.

The red background was made from the feathers of the *'i'iwi* bird.

The '*ō'ō* bird also provided the bright yellow feathers.

HAWAIIAN LEI

Lei are wreaths or garlands, made of flowers, leaves, shells, ivory, or feathers, which are worn around the neck. They range from simple strings of blossoms to complex woven garlands of native leaves and plants. *Lei* have always been important symbols of affection in Hawai'i and are bestowed frequently with a kiss. They are worn by everyone with pride on Lei Day *(see p22).*

Woman with colorful flower *lei*

Stone **poi** *pounders* were used to grind taro (see p109), a vital food source, into poi (a thick paste eaten with the fingers). It was heavy work, done by men who sat at a wooden pounding board, which was moistened with water, and mashed the cooked taro.

TRADITIONAL BRAIDING

In ancient Hawai'i, braiding or weaving was an important method of creating everyday objects, such as floor coverings, sleeping mats, pillows, baskets, and fans. *Lauhala* – the large leaves *(lau)* of the pandanus tree *(hala)* – were one of the most common materials. Sedge grass, including the coveted fine sedge *makaloa*, and certain palms were also used. The most extraordinary sleeping mats were made of *makaloa* on the island of Ni'ihau. In preparing the leaves for braiding, the weaver had to be careful because their edges and spines were sharp. Today, coconut palm fronds are commonly woven into hats and baskets. Generally speaking, the tighter the weave, the more valuable the item.

Coconut frond hat

Stiff, sharp leaves used as braiding material

Surfing in Hawai'i

Sign for Hale'iwa, O'ahu's surf town

Past and present, surfing has occupied an honored place in Hawaiian culture. Though its exact origins are unclear, *he'e nalu* (wave sliding) has been practiced here for centuries. The sport was dominated by the *ali'i* (chiefs), who had their own surf breaks that commoners were not permitted to enjoy; Kamehameha the Great himself was an avid wave rider. In the 19th century the sport went into decline after the missionaries discouraged it. A revival started in the early 20th century when Waikīkī became an international playground. Today the islands remain the ultimate place to surf.

Hawaiian surfers ride the waves in this 19th-century engraving. In ancient times, entire villages flocked to the beach when the surf was up.

The face of the wave, just before it breaks, is where the energy is most concentrated.

Duke Kahanamoku, shown here with fellow surfers in front of the Moana Hotel c.1915, was the father of modern surfing (see p53). The Duke was a gifted surfer and the epitome of the carefree Waikīkī Beach life in the early 20th century.

The surfer keeps knees bent and arms out for balance and to control speed and movement.

Most modern surfboards *are made of lightweight fiberglass and range in length from 6–12 ft (2–4 m). They usually have three fins attached to the underside of their tails, though longer boards may only have one.*

Long boards may be wide for riding gently sloped waves, like those of Waikīkī, or narrow for riding steep, very large waves, like those of Waimea Bay.

Fins add stability and maneuverability. They come in different shapes and sizes. In big waves, the fin would be backward and in small waves, it would be forward.

BANZAI PIPELINE

This spectacular wave on O'ahu's North Shore shows an expert surfer engulfed in a tube of water. He must maintain an exact position inside the "barrel" or risk being thrown over the "falls."

Short boards, the most maneuverable boards, are used for steep small- to medium-size waves. They are more difficult to stand on than long boards.

Boogie boards are small foam boards coated with fiberglass used to surf steep waves, often in shallow water. Riders lie flat on the boards and kick with fins to gain enough speed to catch the waves.

O'ahu's North Shore *sees towering waves from October to April, when storms sweep across the North Pacific producing powerful swell lines. Waimea Bay (above) has always been known for the largest waves that can be surfed.*

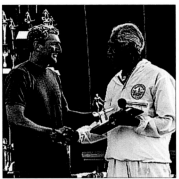

In the 1960s *daredevil surfers like American Mike Doyle, seen here with Duke Kahanamoku, came to Hawai'i in search of challenging surf. They found it on Oahu's North Shore, which soon became the surfing capital of the world.*

The wave breaks just behind the surfer, creating a cascade of spray and foam.

Recent developments *in surfing include the use of foot straps for aerial tricks, exotic board shapes, and towing by jet skis to surf giant waves.*

TRIPLE CROWN OF SURFING

Every year for three weeks in late November to mid-December O'ahu's North Shore is transformed into a surf carnival. During this time the Triple Crown of Surfing, the world's most prestigious series of surfing contests, takes place at Banzai Pipeline and Sunset Beach near Waimea, and at Ali'i Beach Park in Hale'iwa (see p78). Giant waves and spectacular rides create a level of excitement and performance found almost nowhere else in surfing. The contests attract surfers from around the globe for competitions that often decide the world championship. The highlight is the PipeMasters at the Banzai Pipeline – the most coveted title in surfing. Live commentary makes the events accessible even to spectators watching surfing for the first time, and there is usually plenty of good food to add to the enjoyment of the experience.

Winners of O'ahu's famous Triple Crown, which is contested on waves bigger than 20 ft (6 m)

HAWAI'I THROUGH THE YEAR

CONTRARY TO POPULAR BELIEF, Hawai'i does have distinct seasons but only two: summer and winter. To residents, the distinctions are clear. It is summer if the mango tree in the garden is weighed down with fruit, or the intoxicating aroma of white ginger wafts in the air. Sudden rains or storms mean the onset of winter, as do the big waves that surfers eagerly await. Residents

Statue decorated for King Kamehameha Day

in the cooler upcountry areas of Kaua'i, Maui, and Hawai'i Island spend Christmas Eve gathered around the fireplace. A fair generalization for visitors is that May to October is hot and dry; November through April is slightly cooler and wetter. Happily for visitors, though, there are very few days during the year when Hawai'i's fine beaches do not beckon.

SUMMER

BY MAY the winter rains have ceased and summer bursts into life all over the Hawaiian islands with blooming flowers and myriad festivals. **Lei Day** takes advantage of the abundance of beautifully scented flowers, with everyone young and old donning a flowered garland. Hawai'i's oldest state holiday, **King Kamehameha Day**, dates back to 1872; there are many celebrations on all the islands to honor the great chief who united Hawai'i (see p29). All summer long there are cultural, music, and food festivals, as well as great sports competitions, from big rodeos to outrigger canoe races and the grueling **Ironman Triathlon**. The summer draws to a close with the grandest of all annual parties, the **Aloha Week Festivals**.

MAY

Lei Day (May 1), all islands. Everyone is adorned with at least one of these traditional Hawaiian garlands; lei-making contests are held on the islands of O'ahu and Kaua'i.
Moloka'i Ka Hula Piko (3rd Sat), Pāpōhaku Beach County Park (see p89), Moloka'i. This celebration of the birth of hula features music, dancing, food, and traditional crafts.
Ho'omana'o Challenge (late May), Kā'anapali (see p100), Maui. An outrigger canoe race to Waikīkī. **Memorial Day** (last Mon), all islands. This national holiday commemorates those soldiers who have lost their lives in battle.

JUNE

Aloha State Games (1st two weekends), throughout O'ahu, held every two years. Next scheduled for June 2000.
Maui Chamber Music Festival (1st week), Kapalua (see p100), Maui. Chamber music is performed by accomplished conductors and musicians from all over the US at this upscale resort.
King Kamehameha Day (Jun 11 and surrounding days), all islands. This state holiday is celebrated with parades, hula and chant performances, crafts festivals, and much more. The biggest celebration is held at the Neal Blaisdell Center in Honolulu (see p183).
O-Bon Festivals (late Jun to end Aug), all islands. At every Buddhist temple in Hawai'i, Japanese Bon dancers honor their ancestors. There are spectacular floating lantern ceremonies in Lahaina, Maui, (Jul) and at Honolulu's Ala Wai Canal (Aug).

Dancers at the traditional Buddhist O-Bon Festival in Honolulu

JULY

Pu'uhonua O Hōnaunau Cultural Festival (weekend closest to Jul 1), Pu'uhonua O Hōnaunau National Historical Park (see pp116–17), Hawai'i Island. A royal court and traditional crafts demonstrations.
Makawao Rodeo (weekend closest to Jul 4), Makawao (see p105), Maui. Hawai'i's biggest rodeo, where paniolo (see p121) demonstrate their skill.
Parker Ranch Rodeo (weekend closest to Jul 4), Waimea

Crowd-pleasing bull-riding at the annual Makawao Rodeo

AVERAGE NUMBER OF SUNNY DAYS PER MONTH

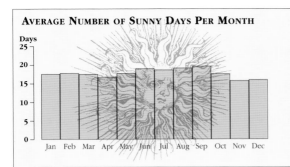

Days
25 —
20 —
15 —
10 —
5 —
0 —

Jan Feb Mar Apr May Jun Jul Aug Sep Oct Nov Dec

Sunshine Chart
Hawai'i has few days without at least some sunshine, with leeward (southwest) coasts being, on the whole, sunnier than windward (northeast) ones. Blue skies and warm days are thus a fairly consistent feature, except at higher altitudes, which are often misty. The chart gives the number of days per month with little or no cloud cover, averaged across the islands.

(see p120), Hawai'i Island. Set in the ranching heartland.
Prince Lot Hula Festival (3rd Sat), Moanalua Gardens, O'ahu. Local *hālau hula* (*hula* schools) honor Prince Lot (Kamehameha V) with both the ancient and modern styles.
Kōloa Plantation Days (late Jul), Kōloa, Kaua'i. A parade and other celebrations commemorate one of the first sugar plantations in Hawai'i.

AUGUST

Hawaiian International Billfish Tournament (late Jul to early Aug, or 1st half of Aug), Kailua-Kona (see p114), Hawai'i Island. World's leading international marlin fishing tournament, drawing fishermen and fans from everywhere.
Hawaiian Slack Key Guitar Festival (mid-Aug), Honolulu. This uniquely Hawaiian guitar tuning is used in performances by the state's best guitarists.

SEPTEMBER

Aloha Week (mid-Sep to late Oct), all islands. Dozens of music and dance events, craft fairs and demonstrations, floral parades, delicious food, and even a royal ball make up this grandest of Hawai'i's annual celebrations. The festival begins on O'ahu and continues on each of the other main islands, lasting a week on each island.
A Taste of Lahaina (weekend closest to and before Sep 15), Lahaina (see pp96–9), Maui. Hawai'i's biggest culinary festival draws a crowd of about 30,000 people to sample the best in fresh island fare.

Traditional costumes and flower-decked float at an Aloha Week parade

Bankoh Nā Wahine O Ke Kai (late Sep), Hale O Lono, Moloka'i. The most important women's outrigger canoe race of the year; finishes on O'ahu.

OCTOBER

Talk Story Festival (2nd weekend), Ala Moana Park, the McCoy Pavilion, O'ahu. This festival features storytellers who describe traditional lore and contemporary tales of Hawai'i.
Ironman Triathlon (Sat closest to full moon), Kailua-Kona (see p114), Hawai'i Island. The ultimate physical challenge for the 1,250 participants, this race combines a 2.4-mile (3.8-km) swim with a 112-mile (180-km) bike ride before finishing with a grueling 26-mile (42-km) marathon.
Bankoh Nā Moloka'i Hoe (mid-Oct), Hale O Lono, Moloka'i.

More than 50 men's teams from around the world compete in this outrigger canoe race to O'ahu. It has become the most important annual event in the sport.
Aloha Classic Windsurfing Championships (late Oct to early Nov), Ho'okipa Beach (see p108), Maui. This event is a contest between the best of the big wave sailors from all around the world.
Halloween Mardi Gras of the Pacific (Oct 31), Lahaina (see pp96–9), Maui. The streets are closed to all traffic for this rollicking Halloween party.

Start of the Ironman Triathlon in Kailua-Kona

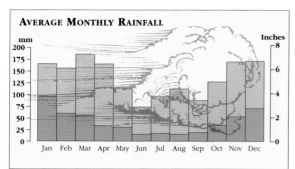

AVERAGE MONTHLY RAINFALL

mm		Inches
200		8
175		
150		6
125		
100		4
75		
50		2
25		
0		0

Jan Feb Mar Apr May Jun Jul Aug Sep Oct Nov Dec

Rainfall Chart
This two-tiered chart gives average figures for all of Hawai'i. The dark blue indicates rainfall on the sheltered, leeward coasts, while the light blue indicates the higher rainfall on the exposed windward coasts. The winter months, from November through April, receive the most rainfall, while the summer months, May to October, receive the least.

WINTER

IN ANCIENT HAWAI'I, winter was the time of Lono, the god of agriculture and peace *(see p14)*. Lono made himself known with extreme weather that could change from minute to minute. Traditionally, wars were concluded by the onset of winter, and it was time for the people and the land to rest from the year's labors.

November, December, and January are the most unpredictable months, but Hawaiian winters are generally mild, and there are many sports and cultural events. The remarkable **Triple Crown of Surfing** displays feats of great skill and courage, while the **Mauna Kea Ski Meet and Hawai'i Ski Cup** draws skiers to the snow-covered slopes. Winter ends with the famous **Merrie Monarch Festival** of *hula*.

NOVEMBER

Kona Coffee Cultural Festival *(2nd week)*, Kona district *(see p115)*, Hawai'i Island. With parades, arts and crafts, gourmet tasting, and a coffee-picking contest, the Kona district pays homage to the bean that made it famous.

Float at the Kona Coffee Cultural Festival

Hawai'i International Film Festival *(early to mid-Nov)*, all islands. Dozens of screenings, workshops, and symposia starting on O'ahu, and then running concurrently on the other islands. Except for some films on O'ahu, screenings are free.

Triple Crown of Surfing *(late Nov to mid-Dec)*, North Shore *(see p78)*, O'ahu. The world's most prestigious surfing competition, which spans three weeks *(see p21)*, waves and weather permitting.

Thanksgiving Day *(4th Thu)*, all islands. National holiday celebrated with family feasts.

Mission Houses Museum Annual Christmas Fair *(last weekend in Nov)*, O'ahu. An open-air market features artists and craftspeople showing and selling Christmas-related handicrafts.

DECEMBER

Honolulu City Lights and Festival of Trees *(early Dec to early Jan)*, Honolulu. A must-see display of lights and one-of-a-kind trees, all created by employees of different county and city departments.

Nā Mele O Maui *(1st weekend)*, Kā'anapali *(see p100)*, Maui. Cultural celebration of music, *hula*, arts, crafts, and food to help preserve the knowledge and love of Hawaiian traditions.

Honolulu Marathon *(2nd Sun)*, Honolulu. One of the most popular and scenic marathons in the US, it stretches 26 miles (42 km) from the

Aloha Tower to Kapi'olani Park, drawing 15,000 runners.

Christmas *(Dec 25)*, all islands. National holiday.

Aloha Bowl *(Dec 25)*, Aloha Stadium, O'ahu. A double-header college football event with the Aloha Bowl followed by the O'ahu Bowl .

Lion dancer at the Narcissus Festival in Honolulu's Chinatown

JANUARY

Narcissus Festival *(Jan–Mar, lasting 12 weeks)*, all islands. This celebration of the Chinese New Year features lion dances, fireworks, a coronation ball, and traditional food. Honolulu's Chinatown *(see pp46–7)* hosts the best parties.

Ka Moloka'i Makahiki *(late Jan)*, Kaunakakai *(see p84)*, Moloka'i. Week-long cultural festival beginning with a fishing contest in outrigger canoes. There are traditional Hawaiian games, sports, *hula*, and music.

Hula Bowl *(3rd weekend)*, War Memorial Stadium, Maui. College football with all-stars from around the US.

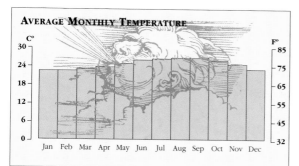

AVERAGE MONTHLY TEMPERATURE

C°   F°
30   85
24   75
18   65
12   55
6   45
0   32

Jan Feb Mar Apr May Jun Jul Aug Sep Oct Nov Dec

Temperature Chart
Hawai'i has consistently warm temperatures year round, with little variation between summer and winter. The coastal areas are warmest, particularly the leeward coasts, which are more sheltered from wind and rain. The upcountry and mountainous areas can be much cooler, with a marked difference in the mornings and evenings.

Sony Open in Hawai'i
(mid-Jan), Wai'alae Golf and Country Club, O'ahu. Major tournament on the PGA tour.

FEBRUARY

Cherry Blossom Festival
(late Jan or early Feb to Mar or early Apr), all over O'ahu. Japanese festival with tea ceremonies, cooking and flower arranging demonstrations, *mochi*-pounding, and traditional Taiko drumming.
Great Aloha Cultural Festival *(early Feb)*, Waimea Valley and Adventure Park *(see p 78)*,O'ahu. A reenactment of an ancient celebration heralding the traditional "season of peace."
NFL Pro Bowl *(early Feb)*, Aloha Stadium, O'ahu. NFL stars play a post-season game. Reserve tickets early.

The annual NFL Pro Bowl game at O'ahu's Aloha Stadium

MARCH

Mauna Kea Ski Meet and Hawai'i Ski Cup *(Feb or Mar, depending on snow)*, Mauna Kea *(see p122)*, Hawai'i Island. International event held on Hawai'i's highest mountain.

Enthusiasts with their kites at the Hawaii Challenge Kite Festival

Hawaii Challenge Kite Festival *(early Mar)*, Kapi'olani Park, Honolulu. A colorful event displaying a vast array of kites takes place in this park at the edge of Waikīkī.
Lahaina Whalefest *(early Mar)*, Lahaina *(see pp96–9)*, Maui. Celebration of the beloved mammal that spends winters in Maui's coastal waters *(see p101)*, with lectures, dives, and whale watching activities.
Prince Kūhiō Day *(Mar 26)*, all islands. Holiday in celebration of Hawai'i's first delegate to the US Congress and a well-liked "people's prince." There are ceremonies at the Federal Building in Honolulu.

APRIL

Easter Sunrise Service *(Easter Sun)*, National Memorial Cemetery of the Pacific *(see p59)*, Honolulu. An inspiring ceremony held at "Punchbowl" crater with views of the city.
Merrie Monarch Festival *(week starting Easter Sun)*, Hilo *(see pp124–5)*, Hawai'i Island. This week-long Hilo festival honoring King David

Kalākaua culminates with the "Olympics" of *hula*. Plan well in advance for this extremely popular event, as tickets sell out almost immediately.

PUBLIC HOLIDAYS
New Year's Day (Jan 1)
Martin Luther King Day (3rd Mon in Jan)
Presidents' Day (3rd Mon in Feb)
Prince Kūhiō Day (Mar 26)
Memorial Day (last Mon in May)
King Kamehameha Day (Jun 11)
Independence Day (Jul 4)
Admission Day (3rd Fri in Aug)
Labor Day (1st Mon in Sep)
Columbus Day (2nd Mon in Oct)
Election Day (1st Tue in Nov)
Veterans' Day (Nov 11)
Thanksgiving Day (4th Thu in Nov)
Christmas Day (Dec 25)

THE HISTORY OF HAWAI‘I

SPANNING LESS THAN 2,000 YEARS, *Hawaiian history is one of the briefest in the world, with much of it shrouded in legend. And yet it equals the world's best for bloodshed, irony, and heroism. Hawai‘i has had to adapt to waves of invasion and immigration, and now supports one of the world's most ethnically diverse cultures.*

The islands were formed by volcanic eruptions in the Pacific Ocean, more than 2,500 miles (4,000 km) from the nearest landmass. Life on the isolated Hawaiian archipelago evolved from wind-borne spores and seeds, corky fruits that drifted in the sea, and the occasional hardy bird blown off course by a storm. Sea creatures had difficulty reaching the islands, as the North Pacific currents push life-rich plankton away from Hawai‘i. As a result, the unspoiled island ecosystem consisted of thousands of unique species that evolved by adapting to the new environment.

Ancient petroglyph from Hawai‘i Island

The Polynesians, whose culture was established in the island clusters of Samoa and Tonga between 2,000 and 1,500 BC, possessed a remarkable seafaring technology. They traveled in twin-hulled voyaging canoes that carried up to 100 passengers plus planting stocks of crops (taro, coconut, sweet potato, banana) and pairs of domesticated animals (pigs, dogs, and chickens). These explorers colonized the Society Islands (Tahiti) and the Marquesas Islands in the first century AD. Around AD 300 the Marquesans dared the 3,000-mile (5,000-km) ocean crossing to discover the Hawaiian islands. Archaeologists have based this date on excavations of habitation sites at Waimānalo (O‘ahu), Hālawa Valley (Moloka‘i), and Ka Lae (Hawai‘i Island). Hawaiian ancestral chants, which were rigorously preserved in oral tradition, carried family lines back further, to the first century.

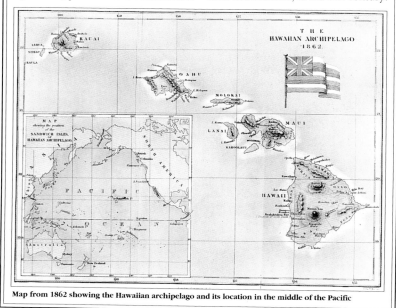

Map from 1862 showing the Hawaiian archipelago and its location in the middle of the Pacific

◁ **Early Hawaiians gathered around a thatched *hale* (house)**

KĀNAKA MAOLI ("REAL PEOPLE")

The early Hawaiians established an advanced, spiritual culture. Dedicated farmers and stone-builders, they were the first to alter a landscape that had evolved in isolation for millions of years.

Hawaiian men dancing in front of a crowd

They divided the land into *ahupua'a*, pie-shaped wedges running from the mountaintop to the sea, providing each district with access to the full range of island resources. They also built monumental *heiau* (temples) and some of the largest irrigation systems in Polynesia.

Life centered on the *'ohana* (extended family) of 250 to 300 people, in which everyone from *keiki* (child) to *kupuna* (grandparent) was vital to the whole. Cultural values included *aloha 'āina* (love of land), *laulima* (cooperation), and *pa'ahana* (hard work).

INVASION OF THE ALI'I

During the 12th and 13th centuries, new waves of Polynesian settlers came from the Society Islands (Tahiti). According to oral tradition, the invasions were cruel and bloody. Casting themselves as reformers of a weakened Polynesian race, they established a rigid class system with themselves as

Traditional *ali'i* attire, as worn in the 13th century

ali'i (chiefs) who regulated the lives of the *maka'āinana* (commoners) through the harshly enforced *kapu* system. Derived from the Tahitian term "taboo," *kapu* designated any activity that was forbidden because it interfered with the apportionment of *mana* (supernatural power). Women, for example, were forbidden to eat with men. Commoners could not touch the clothes or shadows of the nobility, or lift their heads higher than the chiefs'. Punishment for infractions was quick and fatal, and the *ali'i* rededicated temples as *luakini heiau*, for human sacrifice.

The chief figure in this reform was the Tahitian priest Pā'ao, who probably made several journeys between the two archipelagos. He established a line of *kuhina nui* (high priests) and brought a chief named Pili, probably from Samoa, to consolidate political power. For unknown reasons, these voyages ceased after the 13th century.

CONTACT

Although British sea captain and explorer James Cook is credited with the "discovery" of Hawai'i in 1778, convincing evidence suggests that Spanish ships preceded him by more than 200 years. In the mid-16th century, Spanish galleons made annual voyages across the Pacific between their colonies in Mexico and recently established bases in the Philippines. In 1542 a fleet commanded by Ruy Lopes de Villalobos and led by Portuguese navigator Joao Gaetano stumbled onto islands they named the Isla de Mesa group. Navigators were ordered not to mention

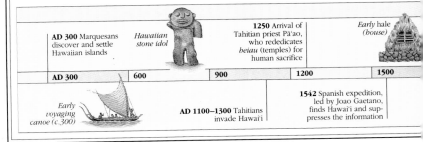

AD 300 Marquesans discover and settle Hawaiian islands	*Hawaiian stone idol*		1250 Arrival of Tahitian priest Pā'ao, who rededicates *heiau* (temples) for human sacrifice	*Early hale (house)*
AD 300	**600**	**900**	**1200**	**1500**
Early voyaging canoe (c.300)		**AD 1100–1300** Tahitians invade Hawai'i	**1542** Spanish expedition, led by Joao Gaetano, finds Hawai'i and suppresses the information	

the islands in their logs for fear that knowledge of them would fall into British hands. In 1742, the British burst into the Pacific with their man-of-war *Centurion*, commanded by Lord Anson, and captured a Spanish galleon in its annual crossing. They seized its treasure and a chart showing the Isla de Mesa group; Cook must have had a copy of that chart.

Confrontation at Kealakekua Bay, Hawai'i Island, in 1779

The timing of Cook's arrival at Hawai'i Island's Kealakekua Bay constitutes one of history's oddest ironies. His ships the *Resolution* and *Discovery* appeared at the height of the annual *makahiki* festival honoring the Hawaiian god of agriculture, Lono. The British ships bore a startling resemblance to Hawaiian prophecies that said that one day Lono would return on a floating island. Much to Cook's surprise, the Hawaiians greeted him with reverence beyond anything he had experienced in the Pacific.

All went well until his departure in February 1779, when a storm snapped a mast, forcing Cook back to Kealakekua Bay. By now the Hawaiians surmised that the *haole* (Westerners) were less than divine, and a series of squabbles, including the killing of a chief, escalated into violent confrontation over a stolen boat. Cook was knifed to death in the fray.

Other explorers followed, including Frenchman La Pérouse in 1786, the first Westerner on Maui. Four years later, American Simon Metcalf ordered the slaughter of dozens of Maui natives in the Olowalu Massacre. In 1792 British captain George Vancouver introduced cattle, goats, and sheep to Hawai'i. Within a generation of "discovery," domestic animals had begun to denude the forests, and imported diseases were killing large numbers of Hawaiians.

KAMEHAMEHA THE GREAT

An ambitious chief from Kohala (Hawai'i Island), Kamehameha could claim a direct kinship to the powerful chief Pili, who lived 500 years earlier. A skilled warrior and shrewd opportunist, he managed to quell centuries of internecine warfare by systematically conquering each of the islands. In 1790 he demoralized the Hawai'i Island chiefs by constructing Pu'ukoholā Heiau *(see p119)* and sacrificing his key rival on its altar. In 1795 he stormed Maui, terrifying the enemy with cannon plundered from an American ship. O'ahu fell the same year after bloody fighting along the Nu'uanu *pali* (cliffs). Twice he tried to invade Kaua'i, but storms turned back his fleet. Kamehameha then invited chief Kaumuali'i to visit him on O'ahu.

Kamehameha the Great, ruler from 1795 to 1819

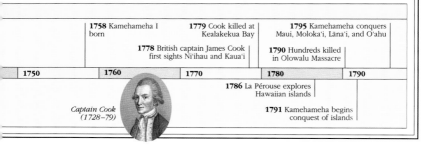

	1758 Kamehameha I born	1779 Cook killed at Kealakekua Bay	1795 Kamehameha conquers Maui, Moloka'i, Lāna'i, and O'ahu	
		1778 British captain James Cook first sights Ni'ihau and Kaua'i	1790 Hundreds killed in Olowalu Massacre	
1750	1760	1770	1780	1790
			1786 La Pérouse explores Hawaiian islands	
	Captain Cook (1728–79)		1791 Kamehameha begins conquest of islands	

Through threats and rewards, he forced the chief to cede Kaua‘i, and Hawai‘i became a united kingdom in 1809.

When the old conqueror died in 1819, he left a leadership void that his son Kamehameha II was unable to fill. The

Mid-19th-century painting of an enormous whale effortlessly destroying a whaling boat

drunken youth was coerced that same year to abandon the strict *kapu* system. The crucial moment came when he shared a meal with women – his mother Keōpūolani and his father's favorite wife, Ka‘ahumanu. This act of *‘ai noa* (free eating) was taken as a symbolic deed that invalidated all traditional rules. Thus the kingdom was reduced to a class of leaders with no precise set of laws.

MISSIONARY YEARS

The American Board of Foreign Missions provided relief just six months later. On April 19, 1820, the brig *Thaddeus* landed in Kailua Bay *(see p114)* carrying 23 Congregationalists, the first of 12 such groups to come to Hawai‘i over the next three decades. In 1823 the second group established a church in Lahaina, Maui, which was by now the whaling capital. The missionaries had running battles with rowdy whalers. They also baptized

Missionary preaching to Hawaiians on Kaua‘i, 1840

Keōpūolani, the dying queen mother, who commanded her people to embrace Christianity.

Kamehameha II had bankrupted the kingdom by now, despite stripping the native forests to sell Hawaiian sandalwood to China. To distract himself from his problems, he and his wife sailed to England where they arrived unannounced and unrecognized. Instead of meeting King George IV as they had hoped, they both contracted measles and died of the disease in July 1824. This misfortune left Kamehameha III, the king's 11-year-old brother, to rule. Power, however, was wielded by the formidable regent, Queen Ka‘ahumanu. By the time of her death eight years later, Ka‘ahumanu had engineered the peaceful conversion of the entire kingdom to Christianity.

THE RISE OF AMERICAN BUSINESS

Generally speaking, the missionary children showed a greater appetite for commerce than for religion. They and other Western entrepreneurs began to experiment with agribusiness ventures, particularly plantation-style production of sugar. In 1832 Kamehameha III leased land in Kōloa, Kaua‘i for this purpose.

The king's unenviable job was to push ancient Hawai‘i into the Western-dominated world. Guided by his *haole* (Western) advisors, he developed a constitution in 1840. Then, needing an infusion of revenues for the monarchy and maintaining that the *maka‘āinana* (commoners) deserved to own land, he announced the Great *Mahele* (land division) in 1848. This released millions

Kamehameha III (1814–54)

1809 Kaua‘i joins united Hawaiian Kingdom	1820 First missionary party arrives in Kailua-Kona		1840 Kamehameha III proclaims Hawai‘i's first constitution 1825 Kamehameha III becomes king, with Ka‘ahumanu as regent	
1800	**1810**	**1820**	**1830**	**1840**
A blubber pot used in the whaling trade	1819 Kamehameha I dies; Kamehameha II discards *kapu* system. Whaling commences		1825 Sugar and coffee plantations begun on O‘ahu	1842 US recognizes independence of Hawaiian Kingdom

Sugar plantation workers gathered around a steam plow in the mid-19th century

of acres for sale to private owners. Ironically, the *maka'āinana* possessed a weak understanding of "owning" land, and most of the deeds went to Western planters. For the next 100 years, sugar ruled the Hawaiian economy.

Large plantations required a labor force willing to endure long hours, poor pay, and cruel treatment, and native Hawaiians, demoralized by social change and crippling foreign plagues, largely declined. Instead, the planters began importing contract laborers, first from China in 1852. Later recruitments drew from the Portuguese islands of Madeira and the Azores, Japan, Puerto Rico, Korea, and the Philippines. As workers finished their contracts, a great number assimilated into island life. Many Chinese married into Hawaiian families. The Portuguese came, with their families, intent on settling. Other workers, particularly Japanese men, saw little incentive for returning to their former lives of hardship; they opted to

pioneer lands leased in the Hawaiian wilderness, eventually writing home for brides and family members to join them. By 1900, over half the population of Hawai'i was of Japanese origin.

THE ENDANGERED MONARCHY

After Kamehameha III's death in 1854, a succession of short-lived rulers did what they could for the rapidly dwindling native population. Kamehameha IV and his wife Queen Emma established Queen's Medical Center to help stave off the effects of contagious disease on Hawaiians. Kamehameha V issued a new constitution in 1864 that strengthened the power of the monarchy, and introduced laws to protect the rights of foreign laborers. Lunalilo ruled only a year. By 1873 high tariffs on sugar were causing the planters to talk openly of annexation to the US. In 1874 David Kalākaua took the throne. Called the "Merrie Monarch," he initiated a cultural renaissance by promoting a revival of the *hula* and ancient chants, spending lavishly to build 'Iolani Palace *(see p43)*, and planning a Polynesian empire with Hawai'i as its capital. The tide of history, however, had turned against him. Pressure applied by armed *haole* planters forced the king to secure a reciprocity treaty with the US. It eliminated tariffs on Hawaiian sugar, creating an economic dependency on agribusiness and US imports. In 1887 a league of planters forced Kalākaua to sign the Bayonet Constitution, which restricted the power of the monarchy.

Queen Kapi'olani and Princess Lili'uokalani, wife and sister of Kalākaua, visiting the White House in 1887

1848 Kamehameha III proclaims Great *Mahele.* Imported diseases kill 10,000 Hawaiians *Father Damien (1840–89)*		**1866** Leprosy patients taken to Moloka'i's Kalaupapa Peninsula		**1876** H.P. Baldwin completes Hāmākua Ditch, bringing wide-scale sugar production to Maui. Reciprocity Treaty with US	
1850	**1860**	**1870**	**1880**	**1890**	
1863 Kamehameha IV dies		**1874** Kalākaua ascends the throne		**1887** Royal power curtailed by Bayonet Constitution	
45 Seat of government moves m Lahaina to Honolulu	**1864** Kamehameha V issues constitution strengthening the monarchy	**1873** Lunalilo reigns for a year			

The king's sister Lili'uokalani took the throne in 1891 and attempted to broaden constitutional powers, but was deposed in 1893 by the all-white "Committee of Safety" backed by illegally requisitioned American troops. Queen Lili'uokalani turned to the United States government for justice. President Grover Cleveland examined the facts and demanded that the queen be restored. However, the Provisional Government, led by missionary son Sanford P. Dole, refused.

Hula dancers accompanied by musicians at Waikiki, with Diamond Head in the background (c.1920)

THE STOLEN KINGDOM

The Provisional Government established itself as the Republic of Hawai'i in 1894, but its clear intention was to be absorbed into the United States. Cleveland refused to annex the pirated kingdom, but his successor McKinley did so gladly in 1898. In 1900, Hawai'i became a US territory. The territorial government was largely an oligarchy of white Republicans who controlled every aspect of island life from their positions as directors of Hawai'i's five main agribusiness companies. Attempts to unionize plantation labor in the

1930s were firmly squelched. Ironically, it took the threat of Japanese invasion to force democracy on the nearly feudal institutions of territorial Hawai'i.

On December 7, 1941, Japanese bombers crippled US military installations on O'ahu, sinking or severely damaging 18 battleships at rest in Pearl Harbor, destroying or disabling nearly 200 aircraft, and killing more than 2,000 officers and men. Within 24 hours, Hawai'i's government was replaced by a military one that stayed in power throughout World War II. Five years of direct federal involvement forced territorial leaders to adopt more democratic methods. After the war, a strike – violent, but ultimately effective – shut down the plantations for 79 days. At the same time, Hawai'i's underclass began wielding the power of the ballot, and soon the children of the plantation camps were being swept into positions of political power. In 1959 the US Congress offered to make Hawai'i the 50th state of the union, and a majority of citizens voted to accept, led by a strong endorsement from the Japanese population.

Celebration of the US annexation of Hawai'i in 1898

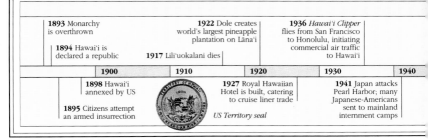

	1893 Monarchy is overthrown			1922 Dole creates world's largest pineapple plantation on Lāna'i		1936 *Hawai'i Clipper* flies from San Francisco to Honolulu, initiating commercial air traffic to Hawai'i	
	1894 Hawai'i is declared a republic	1917 Lili'uokalani dies					
1900		**1910**		**1920**		**1930**	**1940**
	1898 Hawai'i annexed by US			1927 Royal Hawaiian Hotel is built, catering to cruise liner trade		1941 Japan attacks Pearl Harbor; many Japanese-Americans sent to mainland internment camps	
	1895 Citizens attempt an armed insurrection		*US Territory seal*				

Japanese bombing of US naval base at Pearl Harbor in 1941, bringing the United States into World War II

The invention of air travel has changed Hawai'i perhaps more than any other imported technology, not only because it turned O'ahu into the center of US military defense in the Pacific but also because it opened the door for mass tourism. Commercial flights had begun in the 1930s with Pan Am's *Hawai'i Clipper*, but it was the introduction of jet travel in 1959 that brought the world to the islands. Suddenly, Hawai'i, especially Waikiki, was an affordable four-and-a-half hour flight from the US mainland. Hotel development and population growth hit O'ahu first; by 1959 more than half the people in the state lived in Honolulu. Soon the large agribusiness landholders on all islands began diversifying. During the 1960s, the development of West Maui's Kā'anapali as a resort community signaled a new era for island economy. Whereas the plantations were once the driving economic force, many of the great sugar and pineapple fields now lay fallow, and Hawai'i's fortunes began to rise and fall with the moods of tourism and the price of real estate.

Anniversary of the monarchy's overthrow (1993)

At the same time, some 140,000 resident Hawaiians have started taking political action to reclaim autonomy in their ancient homeland. During the 1970s, Hawaiians began demanding the release of Kaho'olawe from the grip of the US military, which had been using the island for target practice for 50 years. A renewed interest in Hawaiian culture, language, and crafts culminated in 1976 with the building of the *Hōkūle'a* – the first authentic voyaging canoe to be built in over 500 years *(see p45)*. In 1993 the US government apologized for any complicity in the wrongful overthrow of the monarchy, and the "nation of Hawai'i" began a movement to reestablish its own sovereignty.

Today the Hawaiian islands support a population of over 1 million, with Hawaiians accounting for 12.5 percent, and each year over 6 million tourists visit. The island chain accommodates one of the most ethnically diverse and tolerant populations in the world, where over 15 entrenched cultures jostle for position with an embattled heritage. No matter where you go in the islands, however, Polynesian roots grow very close to the surface.

The crowded golden sand of Waikīkī Beach, Hawai'i's most popular visitor destination

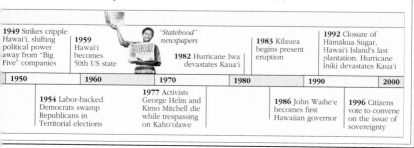

1950	1960	1970	1980	1990	2000
1949 Strikes cripple Hawai'i, shifting political power away from "Big Five" companies	**1959** Hawai'i becomes 50th US state	*"Statehood"* newspapers	**1983** Kīlauea begins present eruption	**1992** Closure of Hāmākua Sugar, Hawai'i Island's last plantation. Hurricane Iniki devastates Kaua'i	
		1982 Hurricane Iwa devastates Kaua'i			
	1954 Labor-backed Democrats swamp Republicans in Territorial elections	**1977** Activists George Helm and Kimo Mitchell die while trespassing on Kaho'olawe	**1986** John Waihe'e becomes first Hawaiian governor	**1996** Citizens vote to convene on the issue of sovereignty	

HONOLULU AND WAIKĪKĪ

Honolulu and Waikīkī at a Glance

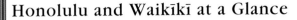

HAWAI'I'S CAPITAL CITY has two focal points, the historic and business district of Downtown Honolulu and the world-famous resort of Waikīkī. The downtown area first gained prominence as a trading port in the early 19th century. Waikīkī, by contrast, was still a swamp when its first luxury hotel went up in 1901. With Honolulu's best beach, however, the resort's success was guaranteed.

Chinatown (see pp46–7) *is a lively district. The streets are lined with exotic emporia, religious shrines, and seedy bars.*

'Iolani Palace (see p43) *was built in 1882 and served as home for Hawai'i's last two monarchs, King Kalākaua and Queen Lili'uokalani.*

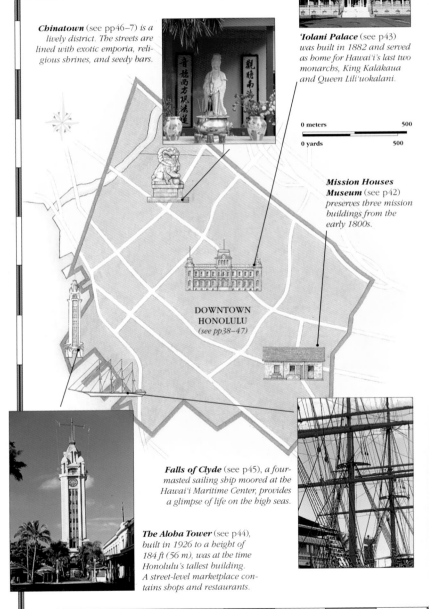

Mission Houses Museum (see p42) *preserves three mission buildings from the early 1800s.*

0 meters 500

0 yards 500

DOWNTOWN HONOLULU
(see pp38–47)

Falls of Clyde (see p45), *a four-masted sailing ship moored at the Hawai'i Maritime Center, provides a glimpse of life on the high seas.*

The Aloha Tower (see p44), *built in 1926 to a height of 184 ft (56 m), was at the time Honolulu's tallest building. A street-level marketplace contains shops and restaurants.*

◁ **Joggers in 'Ainamoana State Recreation Area with Ala Wai Yacht Harbor behind it**

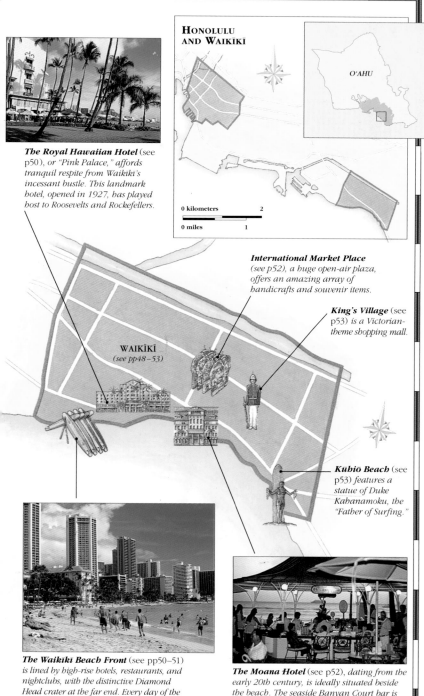

The Royal Hawaiian Hotel (see p50), or "Pink Palace," affords tranquil respite from Waikīkī's incessant bustle. This landmark hotel, opened in 1927, has played host to Roosevelts and Rockefellers.

HONOLULU AND WAIKĪKĪ

O'AHU

0 kilometers 2

0 miles 1

International Market Place (see p52), a huge open-air plaza, offers an amazing array of handicrafts and souvenir items.

King's Village (see p53) is a Victorian-theme shopping mall.

WAIKĪKĪ (see pp48–53)

Kūhiō Beach (see p53) features a statue of Duke Kahanamoku, the "Father of Surfing."

The Waikīkī Beach Front (see pp50–51) is lined by high-rise hotels, restaurants, and nightclubs, with the distinctive Diamond Head crater at the far end. Every day of the year this 2-mile (3-km) stretch of golden sand attracts sun-seekers by the thousands.

The Moana Hotel (see p52), dating from the early 20th century, is ideally situated beside the beach. The seaside Banyan Court bar is the perfect spot for sipping cocktails while watching glorious sunsets over the ocean.

DOWNTOWN HONOLULU

Seal on the gates of the State Capitol

ONCE a fishing village called Kou, Honolulu was described in the 1820s as "a mass of brown thatched huts looking like haystacks." In the course of that century, however, it became a vital port of call for fur traders and whaling vessels visiting O'ahu, and in 1866 the novelist Mark Twain commented that every step in the city revealed a new contrast. This is no less true today. In a relatively small and compact area, downtown Honolulu manages to squeeze together towering skyscrapers, Japanese shrines, New England-style missionary houses, a cathedral, a royal palace, former opium dens, strip joints, and fish markets.

This bustling capital has a strong ethnic mix, and the downtown streets mirror the diversity. Hawaiian businessmen in three-piece suits, children in school uniforms, and Samoans in bright sarongs mingle in harmony.

SIGHTS AT A GLANCE

Historic Streets and Buildings
Aloha Tower Marketplace ⑧
Chinatown pp46–7 ⑩
Fort Street Mall ⑦
'Iolani Palace ④
State Capitol ⑤

Museums and Galleries
Hawai'i Maritime Center ⑨
Mission Houses Museum ③

Cathedrals and Churches
Kawaiaha'o Church ②
St. Andrew's Cathedral ⑥

Monuments
King Kamehameha Statue ①

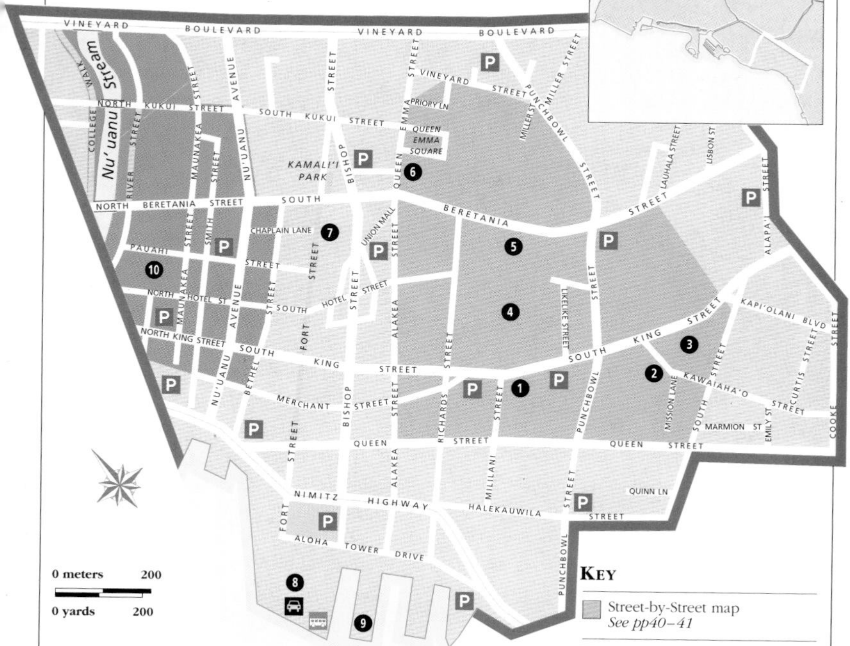

KEY

	Street-by-Street map See pp40–41
	Street-by-Street map See pp46–7
🚌	Main bus terminal
🚕	Taxi stand
P	Parking
	Pedestrian street

GETTING THERE

Downtown Honolulu is 3 miles (5 km) *'Ewa* (to the west) of Waikīkī. From Waikīkī, take *TheBus* 2, 13, 19, 20, or 47 westbound, or the Aloha Tower Trolley or Waikīkī Trolley. For more details, see inside back cover.

◁ **The King Kamehameha Statue, draped with dozens of *lei* in celebration of Kamehameha Day (June 11)**

Street-by-Street: Capitol District

'Iolani Palace crest

T HE ARCHITECTURAL CONTRASTS in this compact area mirror Hawai'i's cultural medley and trace its fascinating history. A short walk takes you from clapboard missionary homes to a sophisticated, Victorian-style palace where Hawaiian kings hosted lavish parties and the last queen of the islands was imprisoned. This majestic survivor of the island monarchy soon gives way, though, to a nearby symbol of 20th-century democracy – one of the few domeless state capitol buildings in the United States.

The 'Iolani Barracks were built in 1871 to house royal soldiers.

Chinatown
(see pp46–7)

Old YWCA building

★ 'Iolani Palace
The only royal residence in the United States, 'Iolani ("Royal Hawk") Palace was completed in 1882. The interior has an elegant koa-wood staircase ❹

Hawaiian Electric Company building

The Royal Bandstand, set in the shaded grounds of 'Iolani Palace, was built for the coronation of King Kalākaua in 1883. It is still used for official functions.

Post Office

King Kamehameha Statue
The king's bronze statue stands proudly in front of Ali'iolani Hale ❶

RICHARDS STREET

SOUTH KING STREET

MILILANI STREET

QUEEN STREET

PUNCHBOWL ST

Waterfront

STAR SIGHTS

★ **'Iolani Palace**

★ **Kawaiaha'o Church**

★ **Mission Houses Museum**

Ali'iolani Hale, or "House of the Heavenly King," was designed as a palace and built in 1874. It was never put to its intended use, however, and now houses the Supreme Court.

St. Andrew's Cathedral
Built in 1867, this cathedral features a large window of vivid stained glass **6**

Washington Place, a Georgian-style frame house built in 1846, is now the official residence of the Governor of Hawai'i.

LOCATOR MAP
See Street Finder map 1

Eternal Flame War Memorial

State Capitol
The design of this unique building represents the formation of Hawai'i's volcanic islands **5**

The Statue of Queen Lili'uokalani commemorates Hawai'i's last monarch, who took the throne in 1891 but was deposed by the "Committee of Safety" just two years later *(see p32).*

LILI'UOKALANI

★ Kawaiaha'o Church
Prior to the completion of this New England-style church in 1842, missionaries used to preach from thatched huts on the same site. Sunday services are conducted here in both English and Hawaiian **2**

Kawaiaha'o Cemetery

SOUTH BERETANIA STREET

PUNCHBOWL STREET

SOUTH KING STREET

KAWAIAHA'O STREET

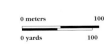

0 meters   100

0 yards   100

KEY

Suggested route

★ Mission Houses Museum
This excellent museum is housed in three buildings, including a printing house, erected by missionaries between 1821 and 1841 **3**

Bronze statue of the king, his hand extended in a gesture of welcome

King Kamehameha Statue ❶

Corner of King St & Mililani St.
Map 1 B3. 2, 13.

KAMEHAMEHA THE GREAT, who ruled the islands from 1795 to 1819, is Hawai'i's most revered monarch. This Hawai'i Island chief turned the islands from chiefdoms riddled by internecine warfare into a respected monarchy. As a young warrior, Kamehameha met illustrious foreigners, including Captain Cook in 1778. He soon grasped the importance of Western technology and incorporated ships and cannons into his conquest of the warring chiefs. After consolidating the kingdom, Kamehameha I turned his attention to looking after his people.

With its gold-leaf feathered helmet and cloak, the bronze statue in front of Ali'iōlani Hale is one of the most famous sights in Hawai'i. The original statue was lost in a storm, and this replica was unveiled by King Kalākaua in 1883. The original was recovered by divers the same year and erected in Kapa'au *(see p120)*.

Kawaiaha'o Church ❷

957 Punchbowl St. **Map** 1 B3. (808) 522-1333. 2, 13. 8am–4pm daily. public hols. by appt.

THIS IMPOSING EDIFICE is a monument to Hawai'i's missionary days. With the collapse of the old Hawaiian religion around 1820 – shortly after Kamehameha I's death – the missionaries soon gained influential converts, including the formidable Ka'ahumanu, the king's favorite wife. In earlier thatched churches on the site, the Reverend Hiram Bingham preached to as many as 2,000 penitent Hawaiians, who would attend in what one missionary wife described in 1829 as "an appalling state of undress." With their first exposure to Western clothing, some wore just a shirt and others only a top hat. By the time the present church was built in 1842, the women wore decorous *mu'umu'u* (long dresses), and most worshipers sported shoes, a habit encouraged by the planting of thorn-shedding *kiawe* trees.

King Lunalilo's Gothic-style mausoleum

The church's New England-style architecture is softened by the coral-block construction. The upper gallery has 21 portraits of the Hawaiian monarchs and their families, most of whom were baptized, married, and crowned here.

Outside are two cemeteries for missionaries and their early converts, and a mausoleum where King Lunalilo is buried. Apart from Kamehameha I, whose bones were hidden so that no one could steal his *mana* (spiritual power), most of the other royalty lie in the Royal Mausoleum *(see p58)*.

Mission Houses Museum ❸

553 South King St. **Map** 1 C3.
(808) 531-0481. 2, 13. 9am–4pm Tue–Sat. public hols. first floor only.

THIS BUCOLIC ENCLAVE of the past contains the oldest timber frame house in Hawai'i, a testament to the persuasive powers of the New England missionaries. In 1821, one year after their arrival, Kamehameha II allowed Reverend Bingham to build a Christian house with clapboards shipped from New England, and to establish Hawai'i's first printing press. A more elegant house followed, part of which contains a replica press. The interiors have been lovingly preserved. Especially interesting are the clothes worn by the missionaries, including long underwear.

The missionaries were so good at converting the rowdy whalers and Sandwich Island heathens that in 1825 a Russian visitor described Honolulu as follows: "streets deserted, games prohibited [and] singing, dancing [and] riding horseback on Sundays all punishable offenses."

Elegant coral-block house at the Mission Houses Museum

South façade of ʻIolani Palace, with steps up to the main entrance

ʻIolani Palace ❹

King St & Richards St. **Map** 1 B3.
📞 *(808) 522-0832.* 🚌 *2, 13.*
🕐 *9am–2:15pm Tue–Sat.* ● *Jan 1, Jul 4, Thanksgiving, Dec 25.* 📷 🚫
♿ 📷 *compulsory.*

KING DAVID KALAKAUA was inspired by English Victorian architecture when he commissioned this royal residence on the site of an earlier palace. Drawing heavily on sugarcane profits, Hawaiʻi's "Merrie Monarch" tried to re-create the pomp and circumstance of the English court in the palace's luxurious interiors.

The only royal palace in the US, ʻIolani ("Royal Hawk") Palace served that function for just 11 years. Kalakaua took up residence in 1882, followed by his sister, Liliʻuokalani, who reigned for only two years before the monarchy was overthrown in 1893 (see p32).

The palace became the seat of government, and in 1895, Liliʻuokalani was imprisoned here for nine months. The first governor used Kalakaua's bedroom as his office, and the legislature met in the chambers downstairs. After the government moved to the Capitol building, the palace became a set for Jack Lord's office in the television series *Hawaii Five-0*. Fans will recognize the arched floor-to-ceiling windows and beautiful golden oak shutters. Children under five are not admitted to the palace.

The grounds make a pleasant place for a stroll. The barracks of Kalakaua's royal guard, which date from 1871, serve as a gift shop and visitor center.

The grass near Kalakaua's coronation bandstand makes an ideal picnic spot, and every Friday at noon – except in August – the Royal Hawaiian Band gives a free concert.

State Capitol ❺

Beretania St & Richards St. **Map** 1 B2.
📞 *(808) 586-0178.* 🚌 *2, 13.*
🕐 *7:45am–4:30pm Mon–Fri.*
● *public hols.* ♿ 📷 *by appointment.*
Washington Place ● *to the public.*

CROSSING BENEATH the canopy of banyans from ʻIolani Palace to the back of Hawaiʻi's State Capitol is a trip from old to new, from Victorian monarchy to contemporary crossroads of the Pacific.

America's youngest state boasts the most imaginative statehouse, its architecture symbolizing Hawaiʻi's majestic environment. The building rises from a reflecting pool just as the islands rise from the blue Pacific. Fluted columns, suggesting lofty palms, circle the veranda, and two volcano-shaped chambers contain the houses of the legislature. At the rear, by the Capitol veranda, stands a statue of Queen Liliʻuokalani, clutching the music to "Aloha ʻOe," a famous ballad she composed. The words mean "may you be loved or greeted." The statue is often decked with flower *lei*. In front of the building stands a modern statue of Father Damien (see p87) by Marisol Escobar.

Across Beretania Street ("British" street in Hawaiian), is the **Eternal Flame**, a memorial to World War II soldiers. Farther down the street, visitors can look through the fence at **Washington Place**, Hawaiʻi's oldest continuously occupied dwelling. Now the governor's mansion, this Georgian-style frame house was built by John Dominis, Queen Liliʻuokalani's father-in-law, in 1846. After her release from imprisonment in the palace, the queen lived out her days in this house.

The Eternal Flame, a war memorial across from the State Capitol

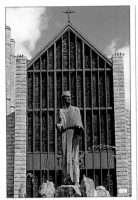

St. Andrew statue at the cathedral

St. Andrew's Cathedral **6**

229 Queen Emma Square. **Map** 1 B2.
 (808) 524-2822. 2, 13.
 6:30am–6pm daily.

THE OLDEST Episcopal edifice in Hawai'i, St. Andrew's was built as an Anglican cathedral in 1867. Alexander Liholiho (Kamehameha IV), Hawai'i's most Anglophile king, brought the Anglican religion to Honolulu following a trip to England during which he was enchanted by English church rituals. His wife Queen Emma, the granddaughter of Englishman John Young, an advisor of Kamehameha the Great, was baptized by the first Anglican clergymen to arrive in the islands.

Detail of stained glass at St. Andrew's

After the death of the king in 1863, Emma traveled to England to raise funds and to find an architect for the cathedral. Her husband's brother and successor, Kamehameha V, laid the cornerstone four years later. Much of the stone was imported from England, although the arched walkways are more suggestive of Gothic churches in France.

The congregation changed its allegiance to Episcopalian when Hawai'i became an American territory in 1898.

The latest addition to the cathedral, a new wing that incorporates a wall of stained glass, was consecrated in 1958. In front of it stands a statue of St. Andrew, who appears to be preaching to fish rising from a surrounding pool. The carved message reads "Preach the Gospel to every creature."

Fort Street Mall **7**

Fort St. **Map** 1 A3. 2, 13.

THIS STREET was named after the former Kekuanohu fort. Kamehameha I decided to build a harbor fort after he fought off a Russian bid to colonize the islands in 1816. John Young, the king's advisor, supervised the work, and the whitewashed walls stood until 1857. According to early documents, the stronghold also functioned as a prison. By the 1860s the adjacent street was a thriving business center, with a dressmaker, milliner, hardware store, and lumberyard. Some small shops remain today, but the four-block street has been turned into a pedestrian mall. At the *mauka* end (toward the mountains) is **Our Lady of Peace**, an austere Catholic cathedral built of coral in 1843. Father Damien (*see p87*), the "Martyr of Moloka'i," was ordained here in 1864. Opposite is the contemporary **Hawai'i Pacific University** building. Eating places nearby reflect the university's international student body – Vietnamese, Korean, Chinese, French gourmet, and even a Filipino-Polish restaurant. Midway down the mall, the benches are often occupied by retired Filipino grandpas who spend their time people watching, strumming *'ukulele*, and chatting away in Tagalog. The mall affords interesting views both *mauka* and *makai* (toward the sea).

View down Fort Street Mall, lined with diverse eating establishments

Aloha Tower Marketplace **8**

Pier 9, Honolulu Harbor. **Map** 1 A3.
 (808) 566-2337. 19, 20, 47.
 9am–9pm Mon–Thu, 9am–10pm Fri & Sat, 9am–6pm Sun.
Observation Deck 9am–sunset daily. **Navatek I** Pier 6. (808) 848-6360.   main deck only.

ORIGINALLY KNOWN AS the "Gateway to Fort Street," the Aloha Tower was constructed in 1926, in the days when tourists arrived by steamship.

View of Honolulu Harbor and the Falls of Clyde from the Aloha Tower

Locals flocked to the tower and terminals to sell *lei* to the arriving passengers, dance the *hula*, dive for coins, and partake vicariously of the excitement of travel only few could afford. Departing passengers threw multicolored streamers from the decks while the Royal Hawaiian Band played the famous and much loved ballad, "Aloha 'Oe *(see p43)*.

Standing ten stories high, with four clocks facing the four points of the compass, what was once Honolulu's tallest building is now dwarfed by gleaming skyscrapers. An elevator carries visitors to an observation deck, which delivers a 360° view of Honolulu Harbor and the mountains.

Today the tower is the hub of a tasteful complex that houses upscale stores, and restaurants offering sheltered outdoor seating, perfect for sunset-watching. A food court sells Asian and Pacific regional cuisine as well as Italian and New York deli fare. A microbrewery, Gordon Biersch *(see p166)*, offers nouvelle cuisine and free beer tasting in wonderful open-air surroundings only feet away from visiting ships. Local musicians play Hawaiian and contemporary music throughout the complex.

Clock face at the top of the Aloha Tower

Cruise liners still pull up at the pier, as do working ships from all over the world. Some naval vessels welcome visitors free of charge during designated hours. Sightseeing vessels run harbor tours, and **Navatek I** offers whale-watching cruises from January to April.

Hawai'i Maritime Center ❾

Pier 7, Honolulu Harbor. **Map** 1 A4.
📞 (808) 536-6373. 🚌 *19, 20, 47.*
🕐 *8:30am–5pm daily.* ⬤ *Dec 25.*
📷 ♿

THIS MULTIMILLION-dollar museum devoted to the maritime history of Hawai'i opened in 1988. In an airy building that is full of light reflected off the water, antique canoes hang from the rafters, as does a suspended skeleton of a humpback whale *(see p101)*. Other exhibits trace the exploits of Polynesian navigators, from their earliest voyages of discovery up to contemporary voyages on modern-day oceangoing canoes. An interactive exhibit allows visitors to navigate virtually a double-hulled voyaging canoe under star-filled skies.

Maritime display featuring an antique wooden surfboard

Anchored next to the building is the restored **Falls of Clyde**. This 266-ft (80-m) iron-hulled vessel, built in Scotland in 1878, is the world's last surviving full-rigged four-masted sailing ship. She became part of the Matson Navigation Line in 1898, ferrying passengers and cargo from Hilo to San Francisco, flying the Hawaiian flag and then the American. The restoration gives a glimpse of the tough, cramped life of a working sailor. Visitors may walk along the decks and look into the cargo holds.

Another important vessel, the **Hōkūle'a**, is moored here when not voyaging out at sea. This is a modern replica of an ancient Polynesian canoe.

THE HŌKŪLE'A

Hawai'i's first modern reconstruction of an ancient sailing canoe, the *Hōkūle'a* sailed to Tahiti and back in 1976 without radar or compass. This feat proved that the first Hawaiians arrived in these islands thanks to their mastery of celestial navigation, rather than by chance, and helped to spark off a full-blown renaissance of Hawaiian culture.

Ancient navigators were carefully chosen as infants for a lifelong training to read the stars, ocean currents, and flights of birds. Because this knowledge had been lost to modern Hawaiians, the *Hōkūle'a* relied on a Micronesian, Mau Pialug, to steer that first voyage. Over the years he has passed on his wisdom to a young Hawaiian, Nainoa Thompson, who, with Hawai'i's Polynesian Voyaging Society, is training a new generation in the ancient arts of canoe building and navigation. Since 1976 the society has sponsored further voyages of rediscovery.

The *Hōkūle'a* ("Star of Joy") at sea with billowing sails

Street-by-Street: Chinatown

HAWAI'I'S FIRST CHINESE arrived on merchant ships in 1789, followed in 1852 by large numbers who came to work on O'ahu's sugar plantations. On completion of their contracts, many gravitated to downtown Honolulu to build restaurants, herb shops, and clubhouses. Chinatown also developed a flourishing opium trade. A fire in 1886 destroyed the area, and in 1900 another was started by health officials to wipe out bubonic plague. By this time Chinese immigration was a divisive political issue, and some believe the fire was intended to ruin the area. However, Chinatown rose from the ashes and today is a thriving community.

★ Izumo Taisha Shrine
The oldest Japanese Shinto shrine in Hawai'i, this was built in 1923 without nails. Facing the Nu'uanu Stream is a traditional gate.

Footbridge

Nu'uanu Stream

COLLEGE WALK

RIVER STREET

NORTH

Dr. Sun Yat-sen (1866–1925), the Chinese statesman who became the first president of the Republic of China, is honored with this statue next to the Nu'uanu Stream. On the other side of the stream is a statue of Jose Rizal (1861–96), a Filipino hero.

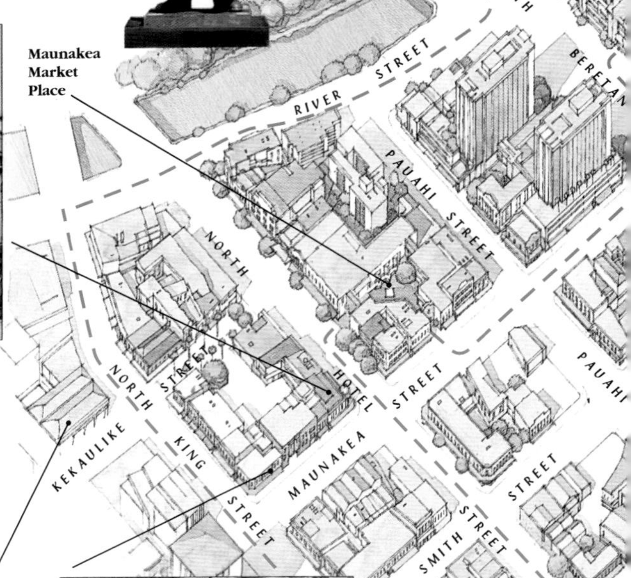

Maunakea Market Place

RIVER　STREET

NORTH

PAUAHI STREET

BERETAN

The Wo Fat building, with its pagoda-style roof, was once a landmark Chinese restaurant. Mr. Wo Fat, a baker, opened the original establishment in the 1880s. The present pink building dates from 1936.

NORTH　KING　STREET

KEKAULIKE

HOTEL　STREET

MAUNAKEA　STREET

SMITH　STREET

PAUAHI

STREET

At O'ahu Market you can haggle for fresh fish, exotic fruits and vegetables, and delicacies such as pigs' heads.

★ Open-Air Markets
Chinatown's abundant open-air markets sell everything from duck and salmon heads to fresh ginger.

Waterfront

0 meters	100
0 yards	100

STAR SIGHTS

★ **Izumo Taisha Shrine**

★ **Open-Air Markets**

★ **Hawai'i Theatre**

Foster Botanical Gardens

Kuan Yin Temple

DOWNTOWN HONOLULU

LOCATOR MAP
See Street Finder, map 1

The Lum Sai Ho Tong Temple is a small Taoist temple above a store, where members of the Lum clan worship.

Chinese Cultural Plaza contains shops and a stage where Chinese dances and plays are performed.

★ **Hawai'i Theatre**
This newly renovated Art Deco theater on the edge of Chinatown has elaborate plasterwork on the exterior and also boasts an elegant interior.

At the entrance to Chinatown sit two marble lions. They were donated by Honolulu's sister city, Kaohsiung in Taiwan, in honor of the 200th anniversary of Chinese settlement in Hawai'i.

KEY

— — — Suggested route

Chinatown ⑩

Map 1 A2. ⨻ 2, 13. 🛈 HVCB, Waikiki, (808) 924-0266. 🎎 Chinese New Year (early Jan-Mar). **Foster Botanical Gardens** 50 N Vineyard Blvd. **Map** 1 A1. 📞 (808) 522-7065. ⨻ 4. 🕐 9am–4pm daily. 🌑 Jan 1, Dec 25. 🎟 ♿ 📷

THIS EXOTIC neighborhood is full of colorful flower *lei* (garlands worn around the neck) stands, open markets with hanging ducks and tropical fish, herbal medicine shops displaying dried snakes and rats, trendy art galleries, and acupuncture and tattooing emporia. There are also less salubrious saloons with topless dancing, especially on Pauahi and North Hotel streets, downtown Honolulu's red light district – the legacy of World War II soldiers on leave.

The twin lions on Bethel and North Hotel streets, the gateway to Chinatown from the adjacent business district, are symbols of a major rejuvenation project. Many buildings, such as the Hawai'i Theatre, have been beautifully restored.

Visitors to Chinatown may be lucky enough to witness a Chinese wedding with full percussion orchestra and a prancing lion dance. At the Maunakea Market Place, you can sample food from all over Asia, and the noodle shops along River Street are much favored by local residents.

At the edge of Chinatown, the **Foster Botanical Gardens** are an oasis of tranquillity in the heart of a fast-paced city. They contain some protected trees and a prehistoric plant exhibit. The gift shop sells plants that can be sent home.

Chinese herbalist in a North King Street shop weighing his goods

WAIKĪKĪ

WAIKĪKĪ WAS A nondescript place of taro patches and fish ponds when Kamehameha I, the chief who united the Hawaiian islands, landed here to launch an invasion in 1795 *(see p29)*. After conquering the chiefs of O'ahu, he built a bungalow facing the ocean, not far from the present Royal Hawaiian Hotel. Now Waikīkī has one of the world's famous beaches, a sliver of people-packed sand against the backdrop of Diamond Head crater.

Waikīkī's "golden mile" of glass and concrete skyscrapers is a hectic hodgepodge of Western, Asian, and Pacific

Waikiki Trolley sightseeing bus

cultures bustling with some 65,000 tourists a day. The streets are packed with T-shirt vendors, sunburned honeymooners, Japanese matrons with Christian Dior bags, and barefoot boys carrying surfboards on their bikes. Local people strum 'ukulele at beachfront bars, music throbs from nightclubs, and Hare Krishnas chant on the streets.

The turquoise water is dotted with swimmers and multicolored inflatables. Beyond them, outrigger canoes cut swaths through the ranks of surfers, and farther out, red and yellow sailboats bob on the horizon.

SIGHTS AT A GLANCE

Historic Hotels
Moana Hotel ❸
Royal Hawaiian Hotel ❶

Shopping Areas
International Market Place ❷
King's Village ❹

Beaches
Kūhiō Beach ❺

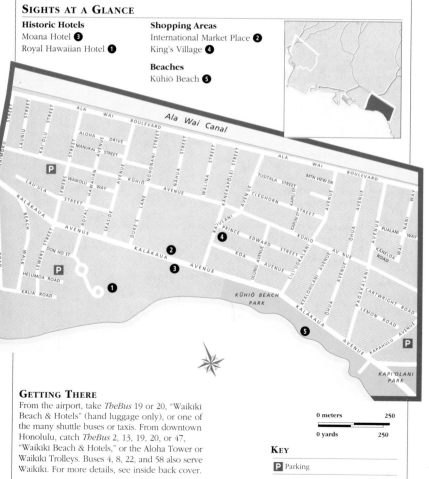

GETTING THERE
From the airport, take *TheBus* 19 or 20, "Waikiki Beach & Hotels" (hand luggage only), or one of the many shuttle buses or taxis. From downtown Honolulu, catch *TheBus* 2, 13, 19, 20, or 47, "Waikiki Beach & Hotels," or the Aloha Tower or Waikiki Trolleys. Buses 4, 8, 22, and 58 also serve Waikiki. For more details, see inside back cover.

| 0 meters | 250 |
| 0 yards | 250 |

KEY

🅿 Parking

◁ **Vacationers relaxing on the terrace of Waikīkī's "Pink Palace" – the Royal Hawaiian Hotel**

Beachfront façade of the Royal Hawaiian Hotel, known to countless tourists as the "Pink Palace"

Royal Hawaiian Hotel ❶

2259 Kalākaua Ave. **Map** 4 D5.
📞 *(808) 923-7311.* 🚌 *many buses.*

A N OASIS in the high-rise surroundings of Waikīkī, the Royal Hawaiian Hotel occupies 10 acres of land in a former coconut grove where Kamehameha V built a summer cottage in the 1870s. Some of the hotel's palms are thought to survive from that period. Paths meander across emerald green lawns under cathedral-size banyan trees to arrive at this Spanish-Moorish-style gem, known affectionately as the "Pink Palace." Almost every-

thing here is coral pink, from the rooftop cupolas and cascading flowers to the towels, telephones, and carpets.

When it opened in 1927, the Royal Hawaiian Hotel was hailed by the *Honolulu Star-Bulletin* as "the finest resort hostelry in America." It soon became famous for its rollicking parties and was patronized

Waikīkī Beach Front

T HIS WORLD-FAMOUS SANDY BEACH actually encompasses several individually named, smaller beaches stretching 2.5 miles (4 km) from the Hilton Hawaiian Village *(see p154)* to Diamond Head. The whole beach is open to the public.

Thousands of tourists *flock to Waikīkī Beach daily to sunbathe on the golden sand, swim in the sheltered water, and surf the gentle waves.*

The coral-pink Royal Hawaiian Hotel is a pocket of luxury at the west end of the beach (see p153).

Outrigger Waikīkī
(see p153)

The Sheraton Waikīkī Hotel's Hanohano Room, on the 30th floor, offers stupendous views, especially at sunset *(see p153)*.

Royal Hawaiian Shopping Center

The International Market Place is a popular center for vacation souvenirs *(see p52)*.

Hawai'i Visitors and Convention Bureau

Sheraton Surfrider
(see p153)

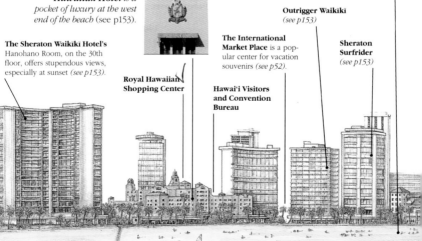

by the wealthy and fashionable. Some well-heeled guests even brought along their own servants and Rolls Royces.

The Depression of the 1930s slowed business down, and during World War II the hotel was leased to the US Navy as a center for rest and recreation for sailors in the Pacific Fleet. After refurbishment, the hotel was reopened in 1947.

The aura of Hollywood glitz still lingers. On the beach, the "beautiful people" can be seen tanning and attracting all sorts of local commerce – aging hippies with pet parrots selling photographs, beach boys offering surfing lessons, and sand artists seeking donations for their elaborate sculptures.

Behind the hotel, covering three city blocks, is the **Royal Hawaiian Shopping Center**. This modern arcade contains dozens of upscale shops, boutiques, and fast-food places.

EARLY TOURISM IN WAIKĪKĪ

Prior to the development of tourism, Waikīkī was a swampy marshland, consisting mainly of taro patches *(see p109)* and rice paddies. The land was reclaimed in the early part of the 20th century; large areas were filled in and the Ala Wai Canal was dug to drain the area by diverting streams from the hills above Waikīkī to the sea. Tourism began gradually around 1901 with the building of the Moana Hotel, the area's first deluxe hotel, which included a wooden pier that extended 300 ft (90 m) into the sea. Tourism accelerated in the 1920s with the opening of the Royal Hawaiian Hotel, which entertained a glamorous crowd of movie stars and millionaires.

A view toward the gracious Moana Hotel in April 1920

Kūhiō Beach and the waves of Waikīkī make a fitting backdrop for this statue of Duke Kahanamoku, the beloved Father of Surfing who popularized the royal pastime (see p53).

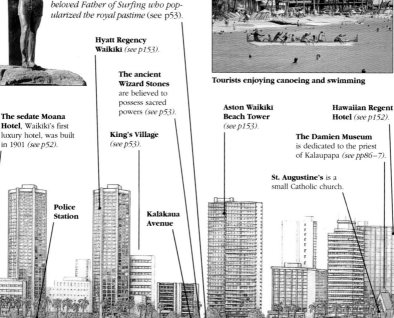

Tourists enjoying canoeing and swimming

Hyatt Regency Waikīkī *(see p153).*

The ancient Wizard Stones are believed to possess sacred powers *(see p53).*

The sedate Moana Hotel, Waikīkī's first luxury hotel, was built in 1901 *(see p52).*

King's Village *(see p53).*

Aston Waikīkī Beach Tower *(see p153).*

Hawaiian Regent Hotel *(see p152).*

The Damien Museum is dedicated to the priest of Kalaupapa *(see pp86–7).*

St. Augustine's is a small Catholic church.

Police Station

Kalākaua Avenue

The imposing façade of the Moana Hotel, the "First Lady of Waikīkī," restored to its original splendor

International Market Place ❷

2330 Kalākaua Ave. **Map** 4 E5.
((808) 971-2080. **many buses.**
(9am–11pm daily. **(**

SITUATED ACROSS the street from the Royal Hawaiian Shopping Center (see p51), the open-air International Market Place occupies a city block between Kalākaua and Kūhiō Avenues. This theme-park shopping plaza is a labyrinth of food stalls (on the Kūhiō Avenue side) and souvenir-crammed carts. Choose from shell sculptures, funky cigarette lighters, and racks of identical chains and watches, or pick up an "island" candle or silk flower lei – often manufactured in Korea, unfortunately.

Typically vivid Hawaiian shirt on sale at International Market Place

Elsewhere in the market, visitors can watch local sculptors at work, ship home a painted coconut, have their fingernails painted with tropical scenes, or even consult the on-site palm reader. They can have their pictures taken in grass skirts, with green and red parrots, in front of a waterfall, or next to a fiberglass wave.

Just like the wave, this shopping plaza is plastic Polynesia at its worst, but it is a good, central place to shop for T-shirts and colorful island wear. Bargaining is de rigueur, and it is always wise to

Souvenir plate at International Market Place

check the prices of similar merchandise around the market. When the going gets too hot, you can rest in the shade of the huge banyan tree in the middle. If you get lost, follow the yellow stripe on the floor to get back to the street.

Moana Hotel ❸

2365 Kalākaua Ave. **Map** 4 E5.
((808) 922-3111. **many buses.**
(daily. **((**

THE VENERABLE, colonial-style Moana, Waikīkī's oldest hotel, opened in 1901 to cater to an international steamship crowd. It became famous for gala events, attended by chic

movie stars and dashing polo players. In 1920, during the Moana's heyday, the Prince of Wales stayed at the hotel and was given outrigger canoe and surfing lessons from local hero Duke Kahanamoku.

An award-winning restoration project, begun in 1986, returned the hotel to something approaching its original look. To retain authenticity, restorers used original drawings and templates that were found in the hotel basement. Memorabilia now on display throughout the hotel include a 1905 guest register, photos of famous visitors, and monogrammed woolen swimsuits that were issued to guests in the 1930s. There are free daily tours.

Although the Moana is now run by the Sheraton chain and has been renamed the Sheraton Moana Surfrider (see p153), the hotel's quiet luxury still seems a world away from brash and bustling Kalākaua Avenue, just outside the grand entrance. On a front porch bedecked with rocking chairs, visitors are greeted with lei by South Seas beauties dressed in Victorian attire. The nostalgic lobby is decorated with period furniture and huge vases of anthuriums, while over on the ocean side, guests are served high tea on the airy veranda.

King's Village ❹

131 Ka'iulani Ave. **Map** 4 E4.
☎ (808) 944-6855. 🚌 many buses.
🕐 9am–11pm daily. ♿

K ING'S VILLAGE IS a cobble-
stone shopping mall that
recreates the period of David
Kalākaua, ruler of the islands
from 1874–91. Kalākaua was
the last Hawaiian king and is
known as the Merrie Monarch,
thanks to his revival of the
hula, which had been banned
by the missionaries as a "lewd
and lascivious dance." As the
first Hawaiian monarch to
travel the world, Kalākaua was
particularly impressed with the
British Empire and modeled
'Iolani Palace *(see p43)* and
his guards' uniforms on what
he saw in Victorian London.

King's Village itself consists of mock 19th-century
shops selling souvenirs,
clothing, jewelry, and
fabrics. There are various
food stalls and an English
pub, the Rose and Crown.
Local street artists gather
here at night to provide
impromptu entertainment.

Every day at 6:15pm the
center puts on a changing-
of-the-guard ceremony, set
against the backdrop
of a Victorian-style
Burger King! This is
followed three nights
a week by a *hula* show that
demonstrates both ancient and
modern styles *(see pp16–17)*.

Lifeguard keeping watch over water activities at Kūhiō Beach

**Changing of the
guard at King's Village**

The area where King's Village
and the Princess Ka'iulani and
Hyatt hotels now stand was
once a royal estate called
'Āinahau, famous for its
lush gardens and flocks
of peacocks. Here, in a
grass hut, Robert Louis
Stevenson told tales of
England and Scotland to
Ka'iulani, a half-Scottish,
half-Hawaiian princess
who was next in line to
the Hawaiian throne.
Later, distressed by the
US annexation of Hawai'i
(see p32), Stevenson left
the islands, heading far-
ther into the Pacific,
to Samoa. Princess
Ka'iulani died in
1899 at the age of
23, some say from a broken
heart caused by the loss of her
beloved land.

Kūhiō Beach ❺

Map 4 F5. 🚌 many buses.

W IDE KŪHIŌ BEACH stretches
eastward from Duke
Kahanamoku's statue in central
Waikīkī. Near the statue are
four sacred boulders, known
as the **Wizard Stones**, that
represent healers who came
from Tahiti before the 16th
century. The healers are said
to have passed their powers
to the stones before returning
home. The beach is a calm
haven amid Waikīkī's swirling
crowds. It is often rich in local
color – grandmas in *mu'umu'u*
(long, loose dresses) string *lei*
garlands and weave coconut
fronds, locals play back-
gammon, and *hula* schools
entertain in the evenings.

DUKE KAHANAMOKU

Duke Kahanamoku (1890–1968) first swam into
fame at the 1912 Olympics, when he broke the
world record for the 100-yard freestyle. It was
as the father of modern surfing, though, that
"the Duke" really made his name. He popularized the Hawaiian pastime, called *he'e nalu*
(wave sliding), by giving demonstrations in the
US, Europe, and Australia, and has been credited with putting Hawai'i on the map almost
single-handedly. Back home, the popular hero
was sheriff of Honolulu and unofficial good-
will ambassador. When he danced the *hula*
with Queen Elizabeth, the photos were cap-
tioned "royalty dancing with royalty." At his
funeral in 1968, 10,000 people turned out to
see his ashes scattered in the seas off Waikīkī.
His statue on Kūhiō Beach, always draped with
lei from devoted fans, stands with its back to
the sea. Some say it should be turned around
so that the Duke can face his beloved ocean.

**Sports hero Duke Kahanamoku receiving an
award from Mayor Hylan of New York in 1920**

GREATER HONOLULU

THE LANDSCAPE around Honolulu and Waikīkī is dominated by the peaks of the Ko'olau Range. Here, wild boar roam freely and hiking trails lead to waterfalls splashing into mountain pools. Set in these wooded hills, the Lyon Arboretum offers the chance to marvel at Hawai'i's botanical heritage, while nearby, the Queen Emma Summer Palace provides respite from the city heat, just as it did for the Queen herself back in the 1850s.

Closer to the city, the extinct craters of Diamond Head and Punchbowl stand guard. Kapi'olani Park, which sprawls beneath Diamond Head's

Rhinoceros at Honolulu Zoo

famous profile, is home to the Honolulu Zoo and Waikīkī Aquarium. The National Memorial Cemetery of the Pacific, in Punchbowl Crater, contains the graves of thousands of US war dead, and the horror of war is also remembered to the west, at Pearl Harbor. Here, on the site of the infamous 1941 attack, visitors tour the memorials and pay their respects to those who died.

Many of Honolulu's museums and galleries are situated on the outskirts of the city. Most significant among them is Bishop Museum, which houses the world's finest collection of Hawaiian and Polynesian artifacts.

SIGHTS AT A GLANCE

Museums and Galleries
Bishop Museum pp56–7 ❶
Honolulu Academy of Arts ❻
The Contemporary
  Museum ❼

Historic Buildings
Queen Emma
  Summer Palace ❹

Parks and Gardens
Kapi'olani Park ❾
Lyon Arboretum ❽

Cemeteries and Memorials
National Memorial Cemetery
  of the Pacific ❺
O'ahu Cemetery ❷
Pearl Harbor ❿
Royal Mausoleum ❸

KEY

▨	Main sightseeing areas
▨	Urban area
▨	Military/restricted area
✈	Airport
═	Freeway
═	Major road
═	Minor road

0 kilometers   5

0 miles   3

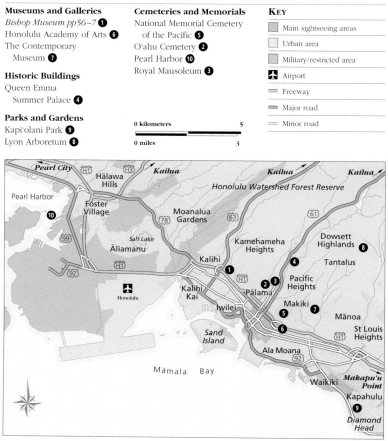

Bishop Museum ❶

Princess Bernice Pauahi Bishop

CONSIDERED THE WORLD'S finest museum of Polynesian culture, Bishop Museum was created as an American businessman's farewell to his beloved wife. When Princess Bernice Pauahi, the last royal descendant of Kamehameha the Great *(see p29)*, died in 1885, she left all her family heirlooms to her husband, Charles Bishop. Her cousin, Queen Emma, died shortly afterward and bequeathed her own Hawaiian artifacts to Bishop. He immediately set about building a home for the priceless collection, and Bishop Museum opened in 1892. Designated the "State Museum of Natural and Cultural History," it has over a million Pacific artifacts, plus millions of specimens of regional fauna and flora.

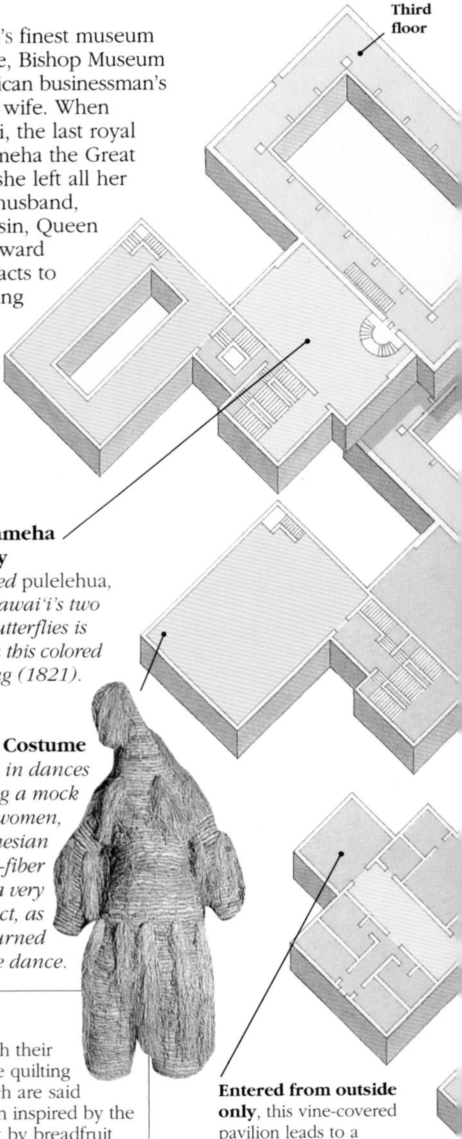

Third floor

Kamehameha Butterfly
Also called pulelehua, *one of Hawai'i's two native butterflies is shown in this colored engraving (1821).*

KEY

- Hawaiian Hall
- Polynesian Hall
- Natural History exhibits
- Hawaiian Vestibule
- Kāhili Room
- Nonexhibition space

★ Tamate Costume
Worn in dances involving a mock chase of women, this Melanesian shredded-fiber costume is a very rare artifact, as most are burned after the dance.

TRADITIONAL HAWAIIAN QUILTS

The Hawaiians' style of quilting reflects both their own tradition with *kapa* (bark cloth) and the quilting methods of missionaries. The designs, which are said

to have been inspired by the shadow cast by breadfruit leaves on a piece of cloth, often honor the Hawaiian monarchy or depict the natural beauty of the islands. The habit of stitching Hawaiian flags into quilts began in 1843, when a British admiral ordered all flags destroyed.

At Bishop Museum you can see a fine collection of old quilts and also watch quilting demonstrations.

Traditional Hawaiian quilt

Entered from outside only, this vine-covered pavilion leads to a shell collection.

STAR EXHIBITS

- ★ **Akua Hulu Manu**
- ★ *Pili-grass Hale*
- ★ **Tamate Costume**

★ Pili-grass *Hale*
The timbers of this full-sized hale (traditional house), thatched with pili grass, were brought from Kauaʻi in 1902. It sits on a platform to discourage dampness, has woven floor mats and a low doorway.

VISITORS' CHECKLIST

1525 Bernice Street. ☎ (808)
847-3511. 🚌 2. ◻ 9am–5pm
daily. ● Dec 25. 🈺 ♿ 🎁 🖥
📷 Daily craft demonstrations,
music & dance performances.
Planetarium ◻ 11:30am, 1:30
& 3pm daily.

Second floor

★ Akua Hulu Manu
Made of feather-covered basketry, this late 18th-century image of Kūkāʻilimoku (Kamehameha the Great's family war god) was discovered in a cave.

Kū, the War God
This large sacred image of the war god Kū, carved from ʻōhiʻa wood, dates from the early 19th century. It probably came from a heiau (temple) on Hawaiʻi Island.

First floor

Hawaiian crafts and demonstations

Fern Stem Top Hat
A Hawaiian adaptation of Western fashion, this top hat was made in the early 19th century from local ferns.

Planetarium

MUSEUM GUIDE

The Hawaiian Hall has three floors: the first covers traditional Hawaiian culture – including a replica heiau – and the Kamehameha family collection; the second and third floors deal with 19th-century history and Hawaiʻi's ethnic groups. Artifacts from the whole Pacific region can be seen in the Polynesian Hall, while the Kāhili Room displays treasures of Hawaiʻi's monarchy. Other parts of the complex include the Castle Building, which houses traveling exhibitions, the Hall of Discovery, which highlights aspects of the collection, a planetarium, and a library.

Castle Building

Main entrance

Three tiers of galleries overlooking the heart of the impressive Hawaiian Hall

Tombstones at Oʻahu Cemetery, established in 1844

Oʻahu Cemetery ❷

2162 Nuʻuanu Avenue. 📞 (808) 538-1538. 🚌 4. 🕐 6:30am–6pm daily. 📷 only 5 or 6 times a year.

Oʻahu cemetery (1844) was one of the first cemeteries established in Hawaiʻi. It was created to bury foreigners who did not belong to Kawaiahaʻo Church (see p42), including members of prominent 19th-century missionary and merchant families. The cemetery is still in use, and many notable people of Asian, European, and Hawaiian descent are buried here. Among them are A.J. Cartwright, the "father of baseball"; Martha Root, spokesperson for the Bahaʻi faith; and several of Hawaiʻi's governors. Veterans of the Civil War who settled in Hawaiʻi are laid to rest here, as are casualties of the bombing of Pearl Harbor on December 7, 1941 (see p32).

Royal Mausoleum ❸

2261 Nuʻuanu Avenue. 📞 (808) 587-2590. 🚌 4. 🕐 8am–4:30pm Mon–Fri. 🌑 public hols. except Mar 26 & Jun 11.

A few hundred yards from Oʻahu Cemetery is the Gothic-influenced Royal Mausoleum, enclosed by a wrought-iron fence with gold crowns on each post. The final resting place of the kings and queens of Hawaiʻi, and their families, their bodies lie in tombs placed about the lawns.

Only two royal names are missing from this sanctuary: Kamehameha the Great (1758–1819), who was buried in the traditional way – in secret, his whereabouts unknown to this day – and Lunalilo (1835–74), who is buried in the grounds of Kawaiahaʻo Church (see p42) in downtown Honolulu. Other people buried at the Royal Mausoleum include John Young, the English advisor to Kamehameha the Great, and Charles Bishop, the founder of the Bishop Museum (see pp56–7). The original mausoleum building (1865) is now a chapel. The interior is made entirely of rich, dark koa-wood.

Queen Emma Summer Palace ❹

2913 Pali Highway (Hwy 61). 📞 (808) 595-3167. 🚌 4. 🕐 9am–4pm daily. 🌑 public hols. 📷 🚫 🎫

Built in the 1840s, this airy retreat in the Nuʻuanu Valley was used as a summer home by Queen Emma and her husband, Kamehameha IV, to escape from the heat of Honolulu. More modest than its name implies, it is a unique combination of Greek Revival architecture and local touches, such as the long lānai (porch). The house initially belonged to Emma's uncle, John Young II, who left it to her in 1850.

Set in extensive gardens, it is still a cool oasis surrounded by huge trees, some planted by the royal family over 100 years ago. The mango trees planted at their wedding in 1856 are now 100-ft (30-m) tall and still bear fruit. The tamarind tree was planted by the couple's only son, Prince Albert, who died soon afterward, at the age of four.

The building houses many of the royal couple's personal belongings, including valuable period pieces, jewelry, household items, and artifacts from their Hawaiian heritage. Among the beautiful koa-wood furniture is the couple's large bed and their son's cradle, famous for its wave design.

The gift shop is run by the Daughters of Hawaiʻi, a group of women descended from missionary families, who rescued the house from demolition in 1913, restored it and then reopened it two years later. They also give daily tours to groups of ten or more.

The elegant façade of Queen Emma Summer Palace

The Honolulu Memorial at the National Memorial Cemetery of the Pacific

National Memorial Cemetery of the Pacific ❺

2177 Pūowaina Drive. **Map** 1 C1.
[(808) 566-1430. 📷 15, then short
walk. ◯ Mar–Sep: 8am–6:30pm
daily; Oct–Feb: 8am–5:30pm daily.

LOOMING ABOVE downtown
Honolulu is Punchbowl, an
extinct volcanic crater. Within
it lies a 116-acre US military
cemetery, dedicated in 1949.
By 1991 the plot was filled to
capacity with over 33,000
graves, nearly half of them for
World War II dead, including
victims of the Pearl Harbor
attack in 1941 (see p32).
There are also casualties from
the Korean War (1950–3) and
the Vietnam War (1964–75).
Dominating the grounds is
the **Honolulu Memorial** (dedicated in 1966), which consists
of a chapel, marble slabs bearing the names of over 28,000
soldiers missing in action, and a
staircase topped by **Columbia**,
a huge memorial statue. South
of here a short walk leads to a
great viewpoint over the city.

Honolulu Academy of Arts ❻

900 S Beretania St. **Map** 2 D2.
[(808) 532-8700. 📷 2, 13.
◯ 10am–4:30pm Tue–Sat; 1–5pm
Sun. ● public hols. 🖼 ♿ Ward
Ave Gate. ✔

FOUNDED IN 1927 by Mrs.
Charles Montague Cooke,
a missionary descendant, the
light, airy Academy has 30 galleries displaying a permanent
collection of Asian, European,
American, and Pacific works.
It has an outstanding array of
Asian art, including Chinese
jades and bronzes, Korean ceramics, and the James Michener
Collection of Japanese prints.
European art on display
includes the Kress Collection
of Italian Renaissance paintings
as well as works by Dürer,
Rembrandt, Van Gogh, Monet,
and Picasso. Among American
works on display are paintings
by Winslow Homer and Mary
Cassatt. The Pacific Collection
includes a range of artifacts
from Micronesia, Papua New
Guinea, and Hawai'i. There are
also official illustrations from
the first Western expeditions to
Hawai'i, 19th-century scenes of
the islands, and works by contemporary Hawaiian artists.
The Academy also has a
well-stocked shop, a gourmet
café, and six unique garden
courtyards with sculptures and
fountains that make welcome
retreats from the noisy city.

The Contemporary Museum ❼

2411 Makiki Heights Drive. [(808)
526-0232. 📷 15. ◯ 10am–4pm
Tue–Sat; noon–4pm Sun. ● public
hols. 🖼 ♿ ✔

HONOLULU'S ONLY museum
dedicated to modern art,
TCM started life in the downtown News Building. It moved
to the present site in 1988,
when the *Honolulu Advertiser*
donated this luxurious estate
as a permanent home. The
house, a mixture of Asian and
Western architectural elements,
was built in 1925 for Mrs. C.M.
Cooke, the founder of the
Honolulu Academy of Arts,
and has great views of the city.
TCM has a permanent collection of sculptures, ceramics,
paintings, prints, photos, and
videos by national and international artists, spanning the
years from 1940 to the present.
There are also numerous temporary exhibitions. The **Cades
Pavilion** displays *L'Enfant et
les Sortilèges* (1983), David
Hockney's walk-through instal-
lation based on his set for
Ravel's opera, staged by New
York's Metropolitan Opera.
The beautiful estate that surrounds the museum features
innovative sculpture, huge
trees, sloping lawns, orchids,
bromeliads, and a path that
encourages meditation as it
winds among grottoes
designed by a local minister
turned landscape gardener.
The Contemporary Café, set
in a secluded corner, offers
delicious food (see p167).

Part of Hockney's *L'Enfant et les Sortilèges* at The Contemporary Museum

Lyon Arboretum ⓼

3860 Mānoa Rd. 📞 *(808) 988-0464.*
🚌 *5.* 🕐 *9am–3pm Mon–Sat.*
🔴 *public hols.* **Donation.** ☑

ONLY A SHORT DRIVE from busy Waikīkī, this serene, wooded retreat is an ideal tonic for the weary sightseer. Short, verdant trails wind through the trees and reveal botanical delights at every turn.

Founded in 1918 in an effort to reforest land made barren by cattle grazing, the Lyon Arboretum is now home to over 5,000 plant species, both native and introduced. It is nationally recognized as a center for the conservation of Hawaiian plants, and its 194 acres support over 80 endangered and rare species. These include the state flower, *ma'o hau hele* (a yellow hibiscus), and the tree gardenia, *nānū*, whose scientific name, *Gardenia*

brighamii, honors W.T. Brigham, the first director of the Bishop Museum *(see pp56–7)*. The arboretum now features around 600 varieties of palm, more than any other botanical garden in the world.

A substantial part of the arboretum is open to the public; the rest is set aside for research. The on-site hybridization program has provided the gardeners of the world with more than 160 new cultivars, including hybrids of hibiscus, ginger, and rhododendron.

There are three quiet memorial gardens and an aromatic spice and herb patch near the main building. A little farther away, the Beatrice H. Krauss Ethnobotanical Garden displays plants that have been used by native Hawaiians as medicine, food, and building materials.

View of Kapi'olani Park from Diamond Head

Kapi'olani Park ⓽

Map 4 F5. 🚌 *4, 8, 19, 20, 47.*
🔴 *daily.* 🐾 **Zoo** 151 Kapahulu Ave.
📞 *(808) 971-7171.* 🕐 *9am–4:30pm daily.* 🔴 *Jan 1, Dec 25.* 🎫 🔱
Aquarium 2777 Kalākaua Ave.
📞 *(808) 923-9741.* 🕐 *9am–5pm daily.* 🔴 *Dec 25.* 🎫 🔱

THIS 200-ACRE expanse of green offers a 2-mile (3-km) jogging path, tennis courts, barbecues, and special areas for softball, archery, and

---

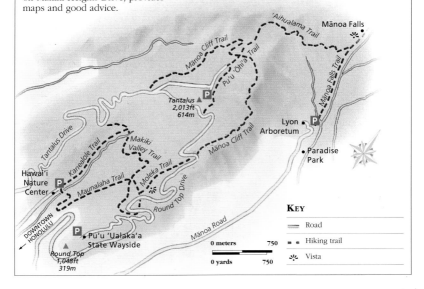

HONOLULU'S MAKIKI-TANTALUS TRAILS

Forming a loop around lush Makiki Valley 3 miles (5 km) north of Waikīkī, Round Top Drive and Tantalus Drive offer fine views of the city. The trails that lace between the roads delve deep into the rain forest and teem with bird life and exotic flora. Weekday mornings are quietest, but weekend hikes run by the Sierra Club or Nature Conservancy *(see p191)* are informative and tackle the more challenging areas. On any hike, be well prepared: dress for comfort, wear sturdy shoes, bring a flashlight and plenty of water and food, and stick to the main trails. Most importantly, never hike alone. The Hawai'i Nature Center, off Makiki Heights Drive, provides maps and good advice.

View from Pu'u 'Ōhi'a Trail

'Aihualama Trail
Mānoa Falls
Mānoa Cliff Trail
Pu'u 'Ōhi'a Trail
Mānoa Falls Trail
Tantalus ▲ 2,013ft 614m
Lyon Arboretum
Tantalus Drive
Makiki Valley Trail
Mānoa Cliff Trail
Paradise Park
Kanealole Trail
Moleka Trail
Hawai'i Nature Center
Maunalaha Trail
Round Top Drive
DOWNTOWN HONOLULU
Pu'u 'Ualaka'a State Wayside
Mānoa Road
Round Top 1,048ft 319m

KEY

═══	Road
▪ ▪	Hiking trail
☆	Vista

0 meters   750
0 yards   750

kite-flying. It is the site of crafts fairs, celebrations, and the popular Kodak Hula Show (see p180). The show can be seen on three mornings a week from stands beside the Waikīkī Shell outdoor amphitheater.

The north end of the park is devoted to **Honolulu Zoo** whose highlight is an extensive African savanna section. On Sunday mornings, local artists display their works on the zoo fence facing Monsarrat Avenue.

The **Waikīkī Aquarium**, on the southwest side, features the usual sea life as well as a special exhibit on the endangered Hawaiian monk seal and a hands-on tide pool. The aquarium also organizes reef walks, some specially for children.

The park acts as a gateway to **Diamond Head**. To see the extinct volcano, either take the scenic circle drive to Diamond Head lighthouse, whose lawn is a favorite spot for tourist weddings and sunset watching, or you can hike to the summit from a parking lot in the crater. Entrance to the crater is marked by a sign on Diamond Head Road, the continuation of Monsarrat Avenue. The trail is quite steep, but the sweeping view is worth the hour-long ascent. Part of the hike involves climbing a staircase in a tunnel; take a flashlight if you are claustrophobic.

Pearl Harbor ⑩

7 miles (11 km) NW of downtown Honolulu. 🚌 20, 47. **USS Arizona** 1 Arizona Memorial Drive. 📞 (808) 422-0561. ⏰ 7:30am–5pm daily. ⦿ Jan 1, Thanksgiving, Dec 25. ♿ 🎥
USS Bowfin 11 Arizona Memorial Drive. 📞 (808) 423-1341. ⏰ 8am–5pm daily. ⦿ Jan 1, Thanksgiving, Dec 25. 🎥 ♿ museum only.
USS Missouri and Battleship Missouri Memorial 11 Arizona Memorial Drive. 📞 (808) 973-2494. ⏰ 9am–5pm daily. 🎥 🎥

Oₙₑ OF THE WORLD's best natural harbors, Pearl Harbor was a major reason for Honolulu's becoming the

The white-marble USS *Arizona* Memorial in Pearl Harbor

capital of Hawai'i. In the time of Kamehameha the Great, the inlet supported oysters that were farmed for their pearls. Later, the port was crucial for whalers, trade with China, and both the sugar and pineapple industries. Leased to the US in 1887 as part of a trade treaty, it was first used militarily in 1898 Spanish-American War, for ships fighting near Guam and the Philippines. Today it houses modern warships, military museums, and memorials.

A huge Galapagos tortoise at Honolulu Zoo

Most significant among these is the **USS Arizona Memorial**, perched above the sunken ship of that name. The ship went down with hundreds of its crew during the Japanese attack on December 7, 1941 that brought the US into World War II. For many people the visit to this site is a pilgrimage, so appropriate dress is requested.

On busy days tickets may all be allocated by 1pm, and there is often a wait of up to 2 hours for the boat to the offshore memorial. It is best to get your ticket first and then browse in the museum, which features details of the attack and histories of the ships, planes, and personnel involved, both US and Japanese. It offers a balanced and personal view of the participants. Near the ticket desk is a panel describing the volunteers for the day. They are usually Pearl Harbor survivors and are available to answer questions and share their stories. Ceremonies are held here on important days.

Another place to visit during a day at Pearl harbor is the nearby award-winning **USS Bowfin Submarine Museum and Park**, a tribute to the role of the submarine in war and peacetime security. The museum covers the history of submarines, beginning with the first attempt to buid one in 1776. Visitors can view the inner workings of a Poseidon missile, and they can also inspect control panels from retired submarines and see how the crew whiled away their time in cramped quarters.

The USS *Bowfin* submarine is moored nearby and is open for public viewing. The park itself contains a memorial to the crews of the 52 US submarines lost in World War II.

The most recent addition to the Harbor is the **USS Missouri** and the **Battleship Missouri Memorial**. On September 2, 1945, General MacArthur, aboard this ship, accepted the Japanese surrender that ended World War II. Check the website for additional information: (www.ussmissouri.com).

The crew's tightly packed bunks inside the USS *Bowfin* submarine

STREET FINDER

THE MAP REFERENCES given for sights, shops, and entertainment places in Honolulu and Waikīkī refer to the four pages of maps in this section. The key map below shows the area of the city that is covered, with the two major sightseeing districts color-coded red. All the principal sights mentioned in the text are marked as well as useful information such as transit stations, parking lots, tourist offices, and post offices; a full list is given in the key. Map references are also given in the Travelers' Needs section for the hotels *(see pp152–4)* and restaurants *(see pp166–9)* in Honolulu and Waikīkī.

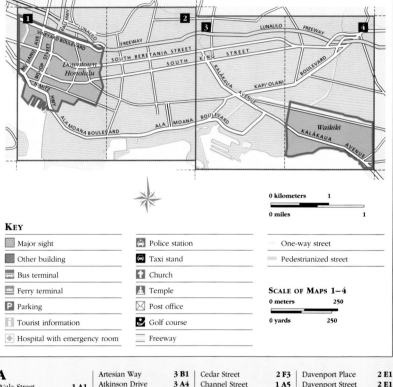

KEY

Major sight	Police station
Other building	Taxi stand
Bus terminal	Church
Ferry terminal	Temple
Parking	Post office
Tourist information	Golf course
Hospital with emergency room	Freeway
	One-way street
	Pedestrianized street

SCALE OF MAPS 1–4

0 meters 250
0 yards 250

A

'A'ala Street	1 A1
'Ahana Street	3 A2
'Āhui Street	1 C5
'Ākala Lane	2 F2
Akoko Street	2 F2
Ala Moana Boulevard	1 B4 & 3 A4
Ala Wai Boulevard	3 B4
Alakea Street	1 A3
Alapa'i Street	1 C3
Alder Street	2 F3
Alexander Street	3 B1
Algaroba Street	3 B2
Aloha Drive	4 D4
Aloha Tower Drive	1 A3
'Alohi Way	2 E3
'Āmana Street	3 A3
Artesian Street	3 B1

Artesian Way	3 B1
Atkinson Drive	3 A4
Auahi Street	1 B4
Avon Way	2 D1

B

Barron Lane	1 B1
Beach Walk	4 D4
Bethel Street	1 A3
Beverly Court	2 E2
Bingham Street	3 B1
Birch Street	2 F3
Bishop Street	1 A3
Bowers Lane	1 B2

C

Captain Cook Avenue	1 C2
Cartwright Road	4 F5
Cary Circle	2 D3

Cedar Street	2 F3
Channel Street	1 A5
Chapin Street	2 D3
Chaplain Lane	1 A2
Church Lane	4 E2
Citron Street	3 B2
Clark Street	3 A1
Clayton Street	2 D3
Cleghorn Street	4 E4
College Walk	1 A1
Cooke Street	1 C5
Coolidge Street	4 D2
Coral Street	1 B5
Coyne Street	3 B1
Cummins Street	2 D4
Curtis Street	1 C3

D

Date Street	3 C2

Davenport Place	2 E1
Davenport Street	2 E1
Dewey Court	3 C5
Dole Street	3 A1
Don Ho Street	4 D5
Dudley Street	3 C4
Dudoit Lane	3 C4

E

'Ekela Avenue	4 F3
Elm Street	2 E3
Elsie Lane	3 A2
Emerson Street	2 D1
Emma Lane	1 B2
'Ena Road	3 B4
Enos Lane	3 A1
Ernest Street	2 E2
Evelyn Lane	3 B1

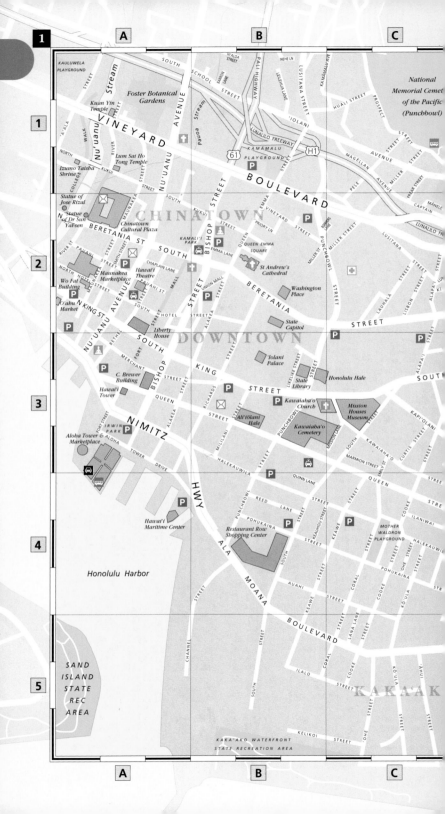

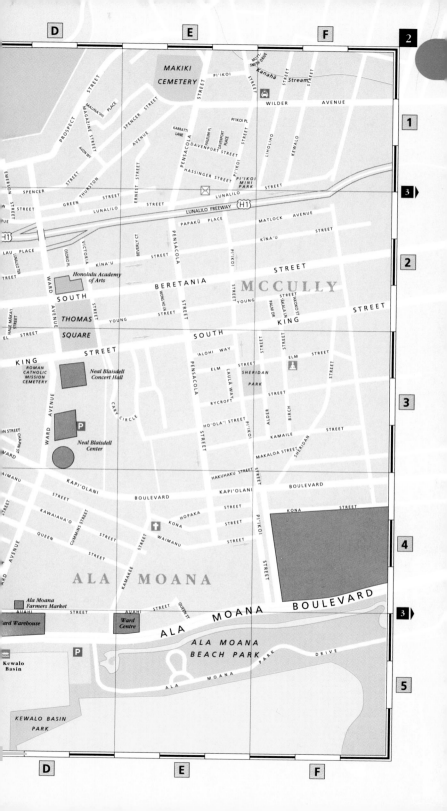

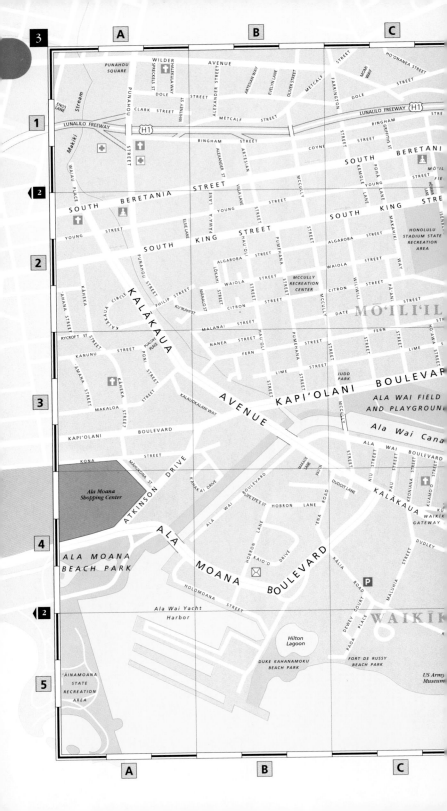

HAWAI'I ISLAND BY ISLAND

The Hawaiian Islands at a Glance

THE HAWAIIAN ISLANDS OFFER an outstanding array of natural beauty spots and places of cultural interest. The landscape is incredibly diverse, from beach-fringed coastal shores to lush, grassy uplands and alpine summits. Visitors may experience volcanic eruptions, see world-class surfing, explore the fascinating cultural heritage of Polynesia, or simply relax in the sea and sun.

Princeville (see p139), *a resort community on Kaua'i's lush North Shore, is a favorite with golfers for its excellent courses.*

KAUA'I
(see pp130–47)

NI'IHAU

0 kilometers   50

0 miles   25

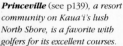

O'AHU
(see pp72–9)

Honolulu and Waikiki

Kaua'i's Na Pali Coast
(see pp142–3) *features stunning, sharply incised cliffs, slender beaches, and deep blue seas. Enthusiastic hikers can see the scenery up close by following the rugged Kalalau Trail.*

Waimea Bay on O'ahu's North Shore (see p21) *is home to some of the world's biggest waves. Expert surfers flock here from around the world to demonstrate their skill and courage in front of appreciative onlookers.*

The Polynesian Cultural Center (see p78) *in Lā'ie on O'ahu's windward shore displays Polynesian heritage. Through dances and craft demonstrations, visitors witness the traditional cultures of Tonga, Hawai'i, Samoa, Tahiti, Fiji, the Marquesas, and New Zealand.*

◁ **Makapu'u Beach on southeast O'ahu, backed by the peaks of the Ko'olau Range**

Kalaupapa National Historical Park (see pp86–7) *commemorates the more than 8,000 victims of leprosy who suffered and died on this remote Moloka'i peninsula, and the saintly work of Father Damien who tended the sick. He was buried in the garden of St. Philomena.*

Wailea Beach *is one of a string of beautiful sheltered beaches on East Maui's leeward coast (see p103). Visitors flock here to relax on the golden sands and in the calm coastal waters, and to take advantage of the ideal swimming, snorkeling, and diving conditions.*

MOLOKA'I
AND
LĀNA'I
(see pp80–91)

MAUI
(see pp92–109)

KAHO'OLAWE

Maui's sheltered coastal waters are home to wintering whales.

Mauna Kea, snow-capped for part of the year, is Hawai'i's tallest mountain.

Hawai'i Volcanoes National Park (see pp128–9), *with its active East Rift Zone, is the site of both spectacular fire cones and lava flows. Billowing steam plumes, such as this one at Lae'apuki at sunrise, form when fiery lava enters the ocean.*

HAWAI'I ISLAND
(see pp110–29)

Pu'uhonua o Hōnaunau National Historical Park (see pp116–17), *an ancient place of refuge, provides a unique glimpse into traditional Hawaiian culture and its laws.*

O'AHU

THE THIRD LARGEST *island in the archipelago with an area of 600 sq miles (1,550 sq km), O'ahu was born of two volcanoes that formed the Wai'anae Mountains to the west and the Ko'olau Range to the northeast. Three-quarters of Hawai'i's million residents live here, mostly in the greater Honolulu area or nestled in the deep valleys that cut between the mountains. This island also receives the largest number of visitors.*

O'ahu was conquered in 1795 by Kamehameha the Great, whose forces chased rival chiefs Kai'ana and Kalanikūpule and their men back into Nu'uanu Valley, forcing them off a precipice at the top. Kai'ana was killed outright, and though Kalanikūpule escaped, he was later captured and sacrificed by the great king. The battle was an important victory in Kamehameha's campaign to unify the islands *(see pp29–30)*.

In the 1800s, farmers began growing pineapples in the highlands, and by the middle of the century sugar-cane plantations had become big business. Workers came from China, Japan, Portugal, and elsewhere – the origin of Hawai'i's ethnic diversity. But in recent years, as both the sugar and pineapple industries have declined, much of central O'ahu has been given over to malls and nondescript housing complexes, crammed together on expensive acreage. Some residents now link tourism with overdevelopment and the resultant threat to ancestral lands. Many local people live in relative poverty.

Beautiful scenery, however, is never far away. From Wahiawā the road rolls through undulating fields of pineapple down to the bohemian North Shore surfing town of Hale'iwa. From here to Makapu'u Point on O'ahu's southeast corner, the narrow highway skirts a chain of green velvet, mist-draped mountains. Islets dot the turquoise sea as you pass seaside villages and one deserted beach after another. Along the way are fruit stands, sparkling waterfalls, and Buddhist temples. In the west, the old town of Waipahu is a living museum of plantation history, and the arid Wai'anae Coast offers perfect sunsets and a chance to see an unspoiled slice of Hawaiian life.

Traditional dancing at the Polynesian Cultural Center in Lā'ie, a popular tourist attraction

◁ Fearless surfers riding the record-breaking waves of Waimea Bay, on O'ahu's legendary North Shore

Exploring O'ahu

Hawai'i's most visited island, O'ahu has much to offer besides the clamor of humanity in Honolulu, Waikīkī, and the central 'Ewa plain. The rest of the island is amazingly rural, with large areas of sugarcane fields and rain forest where wild boar still roam. It is easy to escape into O'ahu's spectacular scenery as jungle-clad roads and trails transport you from the high-rises of Honolulu. The Wai'anae Mountains and the Ko'olau Range form the backbones of the island, while tropical beaches line the shimmering coast. The snorkelers' paradise of Hanauma Bay and the world-class surf breaks on the North Shore draw the crowds, but the Wai'anae Coast is peaceful. Cultural attractions range from the popular Polynesian Cultural Center to the tranquil Byodo-In Temple.

Byodo-In Temple, a Buddhist shrine

Sights at a Glance

- Byodo-In Temple ❸
- Dole Plantation ❽
- Hale'iwa ❼
- Hanauma Bay ❶
- Hawai'i's Plantation Village ❾
- *HONOLULU & WAIKĪKĪ pp34–67*
- Ka'ena Point ⓫
- Makapu'u Point ❷
- Polynesian Cultural Center ❺
- Sacred Falls State Park ❹
- Wai'anae Coast ❿
- Waimea Valley Adventure Park ❻

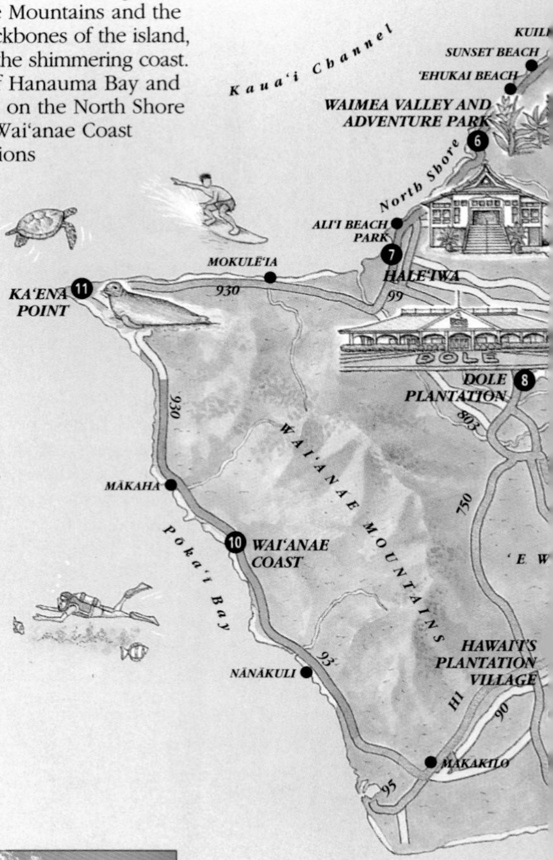

See Also

- ***Where to Stay*** p155
- ***Where to Eat*** p169

Sheltered Hanauma Bay, a favorite with snorkelers

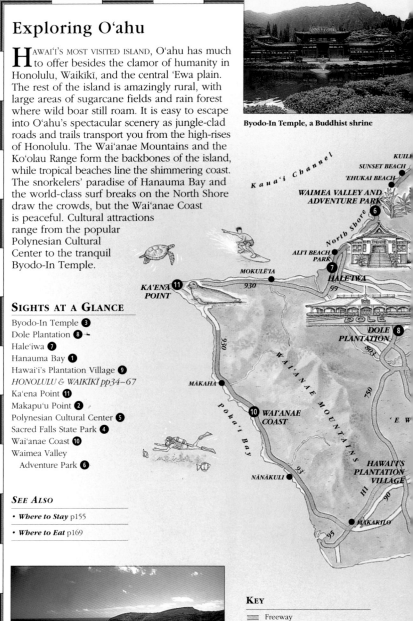

Key

- Freeway
- Major road
- Minor road
- Dirt or four-wheel-drive road
- Scenic route
- River or stream
- Vista

TOP RECREATIONAL AREAS

The places shown here have been selected for their recreational activities. Conditions, especially those of the ocean, vary depending on the weather and the time of year, so exercise caution and, if in doubt, stay out of the water or seek local advice.

	Swimming	Snorkeling	Diving	Body-Surfing	Windsurfing	Hiking	Horseback Riding	Golf
Ala Moana Beach County Park	●			■				
Ali'i Beach Park	●			■				
Diamond Head				■	●	■		
Hanauma Bay		■	●					
Ka'ena Point						■		
Kahuku and Kuilima	●						●	■
Kailua Beach County Park	●				●			
Koko Head Crater						■		
Makapu'u Point				■				
Mānoa Falls						■		
Maunawili						■		■
Mokulē'ia	●			■		■		
North Shore		■	●	■	●	■	●	
Sacred Falls State Park	Park is closed indefinitely							
Tantalus						■		
Wai'anae Coast	●	■	●	■		■		■
Waikiki	●	■		■				
Waimānalo	●		●	■			●	

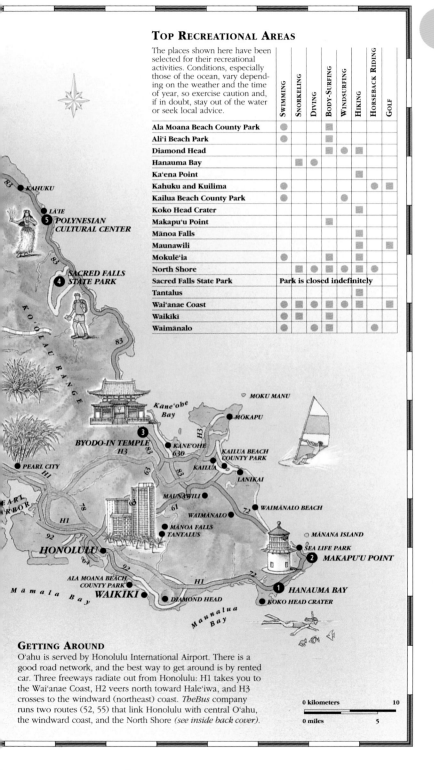

KAHUKU

LA'IE
5 POLYNESIAN CULTURAL CENTER

KO'OLAU RANGE

4 SACRED FALLS STATE PARK

MOKU MANU

Kāne'ohe Bay

MOKAPU

3 BYODO-IN TEMPLE
KĀNE'OHE
H3
630
KAILUA BEACH COUNTY PARK

PEARL CITY
KAILUA
LANIKAI

MAUNAWILI
WAIMĀNALO
WAIMĀNALO BEACH

MĀNOA FALLS
TANTALUS

MĀNANA ISLAND

SEA LIFE PARK
2 MAKAPU'U POINT

HONOLULU

ALA MOANA BEACH COUNTY PARK
WAIKIKI
DIAMOND HEAD

1 HANAUMA BAY
KOKO HEAD CRATER

Māmala Bay

Maunalua Bay

PEARL HARBOR

GETTING AROUND

O'ahu is served by Honolulu International Airport. There is a good road network, and the best way to get around is by rented car. Three freeways radiate out from Honolulu: H1 takes you to the Wai'anae Coast, H2 veers north toward Hale'iwa, and H3 crosses to the windward (northeast) coast. *TheBus* company runs two routes (52, 55) that link Honolulu with central O'ahu, the windward coast, and the North Shore *(see inside back cover)*.

0 kilometers 10

0 miles 5

Trained dolphins performing graceful maneuvers at Sea Life Park

Hanauma Bay ❶

Honolulu Co. Kalaniana'ole Highway
(Hwy 72), 10 miles (16 km) E of Waikiki.
▐ (808) 396-4229. 🅿 ◯ Wed–
Mon. 🎫

SNORKELING IN this sheltered
bay is like swimming in a
gigantic aquarium with over
400 species of fish, some of
which exist only here. A sandy-
bottomed hole in the reef is
perfect for first-time snorkelers.
To get away from the other
snorkelers, try swimming with
flippers. Fish-feeding, once a
popular tourist activity, is no
longer allowed. To avoid the
crowds, visit early in the
morning. On the east side is a
natural phenomenon called
the **Toilet Bowl**, a hole in the
reef that fills and empties
from below.

Makapu'u Point ❷

Honolulu Co. Kalaniana'ole Highway
(Hwy 72), 14 miles (23 km) E of Waikiki.
🚌 Sea Life Park.

IT IS WORTH STOPPING at the
lookout below the Makapu'u
lighthouse for humbling views
of sky and sea, with rock islets
artistically arranged. You can
watch the action on nearby
Makapu'u Beach, a pocket
cove that boasts the island's
best body-surfing waves. Local
kids make the wave-hopping
look easy, but it requires precise timing to avoid being
dragged onto the rocks.

Hiking trails lead upward
into black mountains, but you
do not need to climb beyond
the first 100 ft (30 m) or so for

spectacular photos. Hikers can
continue to the hang-glider
launch site at 1,250 ft (380 m)
and watch the intrepid fliers.

Facing Makapu'u Beach, the
educational **Sea Life Park**
features a huge Hawaiian reef
tank and regular extravaganzas
performed by penguins, sea
lions, and dolphins.

🐳 Sea Life Park
41-202 Kalaniana'ole Hwy (Hwy 72).
▐ (808) 259-7933. ◯ daily. 🎫 ♿

Byodo-In Temple ❸

Honolulu Co. 47-200 Kahekili
Highway (Hwy 83), Kāne'ohe. ▐
(808) 239-8811. 🚌 on Kahekili Hwy
(Hwy 83), then 10-min walk. ◯ daily.
● Dec 25. 🎫 ♿

THIS REPLICA OF a 900-year-
old Japanese temple cannot
be seen from the highway. The
only marker is a Hawai'i
Visitors and Convention
Bureau sign for a historic
sight. Once you turn into
the Valley of Temples –
a nondenominational
cemetery – the road winds
into the valley to reach
this hidden treasure, its
walls red against fluted,
green cliffs. After crossing the curved vermilion
footbridge, you can ring a
three-ton bell to assure
long life and to receive the
blessings of the Buddha.
Remove your shoes before
entering the shrine, where
a 9-ft (3-m) gold and lacquer Buddha presides.

Visiting the temple just
before sunset provides a
tranquil experience. You

will not be able to see the
Buddha (the temple closes at
4pm), but the profound silence
will be punctuated only by
the singing of birds. The sun
setting behind the cliffs gives
off pink and mauve hues, and,
if you are lucky, you may
have the scene all to yourself.

Sacred Falls State Park ❹

Honolulu Co. Kamehameha Hwy (Hwy
83), 18 miles (29 km) NW of Kāne'ohe
(between Punalu'u and Hau'ula).
▐ State Parks Office, (808) 587-0300.
● indefinitely.

ANOTHER TOURIST attraction
that is not well marked,
the 1,400-acre Sacred Falls
State Park is almost a mile (1.5
km) north of Pat's at Punalu'u
(a seaside condo and restaurant). The park was closed in
May of 1999 because of a
landslide that killed eight
hikers. Conditions have
always been dangerous at this
park due to the possibility of
flash flooding from the many
streams and waterfalls.

Should the park reopen in
the next year, hikers reaching
the end of the very muddy
2-mile (3-km) trail will no
doubt find the verdant canyon
of trees and the 80-ft (24-m)
waterfall and mountain pool
worth the effort. There is an
old Hawaiian legend that tells
of a *mo'o* (an enchanted lizard)
that lives deep inside this pool.

The beautifully crafted Buddha, centerpiece of the Japanese Byodo-In Temple

Beaches of Southeast O'ahu

FROM MAKAPU'U POINT at the southern tip to the commuter suburbia of Kāne'ohe, O'ahu's southeast coast features a range of delightful beaches, with free access to the public. Waimānalo Beach offers lazy swimming in calm seas, Lanikai Beach is exclusive and quiet, and the tree-lined community of Kailua has extensive beach facilities. To discourage break-ins in the area, do not leave items of value in your car.

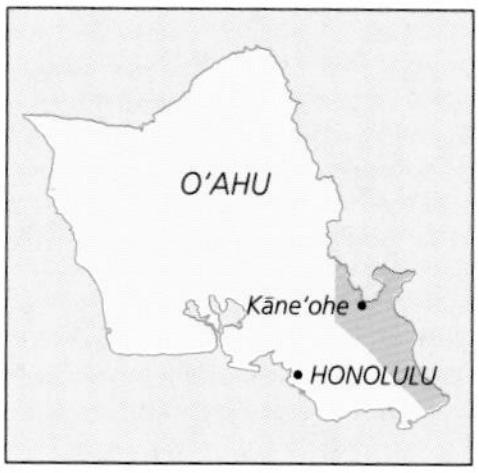

Kāne'ohe Bay, protected by the state's only barrier reef, is rich in marine life. The Coral Queen, a glass-bottomed boat, offers tours of the bay. Kāne'ohe itself is a bedroom town for the local military base.

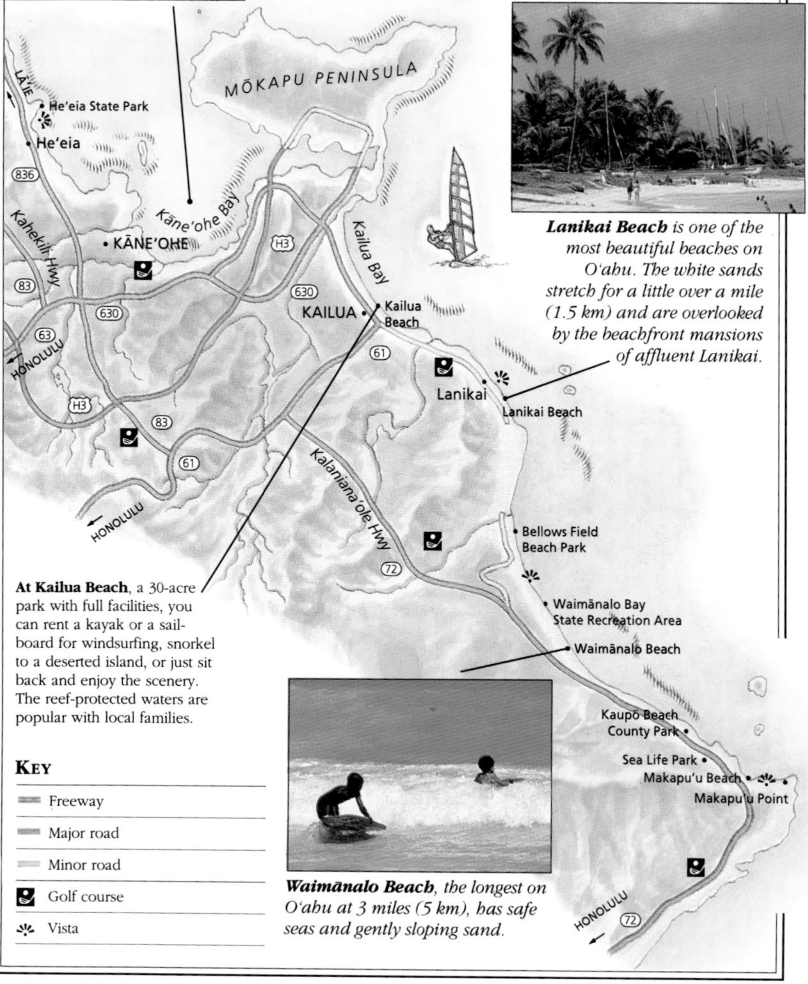

O'AHU

Kāne'ohe •

• HONOLULU

0 kilometers   4

0 miles   2

Lanikai Beach is one of the most beautiful beaches on O'ahu. The white sands stretch for a little over a mile (1.5 km) and are overlooked by the beachfront mansions of affluent Lanikai.

MŌKAPU PENINSULA

LA'IE

• He'eia State Park

• He'eia

836

Kahekili Hwy

Kāne'ohe Bay

• KĀNE'OHE

83

630

63

HONOLULU

H3

H3

83

61

HONOLULU

Kailua Bay

H3

630

KAILUA   • Kailua Beach

61

Lanikai

Lanikai Beach

Kalaniana'ole Hwy

• Bellows Field Beach Park

• Waimānalo Bay State Recreation Area

• Waimānalo Beach

72

Kaupō Beach County Park •

Sea Life Park •

Makapu'u Beach •

Makapu'u Point

At Kailua Beach, a 30-acre park with full facilities, you can rent a kayak or a sailboard for windsurfing, snorkel to a deserted island, or just sit back and enjoy the scenery. The reef-protected waters are popular with local families.

KEY

═══ Freeway

═══ Major road

═══ Minor road

⛳ Golf course

☀ Vista

HONOLULU

72

Waimānalo Beach, the longest on O'ahu at 3 miles (5 km), has safe seas and gently sloping sand.

Polynesian Cultural Center ⑤ √

Honolulu Co. 55-370 Kamehameha Highway (Hwy 83), Lā'ie. ☎ *(808) 293-3333.* ☐ ☐ *Mon–Sat.* ● *Thanksgiving, Dec 25.* ▨ ♿

THE VILLAGE OF Lā'ie was founded by Mormon missionaries in 1864 after a failed attempt to settle on the island of Lāna'i. Lā'ie now contains a Mormon temple, a branch of Brigham Young University, and a 42-acre educational theme park known as the Polynesian Cultural Center.

At the Center, students from all over the Pacific demonstrate crafts and dancing in seven Polynesian "villages": Tongan, Hawaiian, Samoan, Tahitian, Fijian, Maori, and Marquesan. The instruction, whether it be Tongan drumming or Samoan fire-making, is delivered in almost continuous minishows, and audience participation is encouraged. The major musical spectaculars have casts numbering well over 100. The afternoon show, the **Pageant of the Long Canoes**, presents legends from all the islands with singing, dancing, and martial arts performed on double-hulled canoes.

For people interested in Pacific cultures, the Center is worth the hefty admission price. However, some critics question the authenticity of the exhibits and shows – not all the "islanders" in the villages are the real thing. Despite this, the PCC remains Hawai'i's most popular paid attraction, with 900,000 visitors a year, and regular shuttle buses connect the Center with Waikīkī.

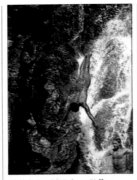

Cliff-diving in Waimea Valley

Waimea Valley Adventure Park ⑥

Honolulu Co. 59-864 Kamehameha Highway (Hwy 83), Waimea. ☎ *(808) 638-8511.* ☐ ☐ *daily.* ▨ ♿

WAIMEA VALLEY is a botanical paradise. Paths meander through 36 different gardens featuring thousands of well-labeled, and often very rare, tropical plants. Thirty species of birds, including peacocks and *nēnē* geese, roam freely through excavated sites of village houses and fishing shrines from the valley's original settlement.

The valley also boasts superb cliff-diving shows. World-class high divers execute their feats from as high as 62 ft (19 m) above a 45-ft (14-m) waterfall, thus perpetuating a tradition in which warriors challenged each other to cliff dives to prove their bravery. Also featured are ancient Hawaiian games and healing arts, a show on the evolution

of *hula*, and tours of the gardens and of a *hale kahiko* (ancient house). The attached Adventure Park offers more active forms of entertainment: all-terrain vehicle rides, horseback riding, mountain biking, and kayaking.

ENVIRONS: Set above Waimea Bay at an elevation of 300 ft (90 m), **Pu'u O Mahuka Heiau State Monument** offers fine views. Here the ruins of three sacred rock terraces make up the largest *heiau* (temple) on O'ahu. Ironically called "hill of escape" in Hawaiian, this was once a site of human sacrifice.

∩ Pu'u O Mahuka Heiau State Monument

Off Pūpūkea Road, half a mile (800 m) E of Kamehameha Hwy (Hwy 83), just N of Waimea.

Hale'iwa ⑦

Honolulu Co. ⩕ 2,500. ⬜ ℹ HVCB, Waikīkī, (808) 924-0266. ☒ O-Bon Buddhist Festival (Jul or Aug).

ONCE A PLANTATION town and more recently a hippie hangout, Hale'iwa is now the hub for the North Shore surfing community. Graced by local color from these subcultures, the town has a single main street with art galleries, boutiques, general stores, restaurants, and coffee shops. Tin-roofed **Matsumoto's** is the best place to try a Hawaiian specialty known as shave ice (thinly shaved ice flavored with exotic syrups and toppings, such as adzuki beans).

Matsumoto's shave ice

Flanking a picturesque boat harbor are well-appointed public beaches. **Ali'i Beach Park** is famous for big waves and surfing contests *(see p21)*, but the adjacent **Hale'iwa Beach Park**, protected by a breakwater, is one of the few North Shore spots where it is usually safe to swim in winter.

The town's biggest event, the O-Bon Festival, is held every summer at a seaside Buddhist temple. It involves folk dancing and the release of thousands of floating lanterns into the sea, a truly enchanting sight.

Dancers performing aboard a canoe at the Polynesian Cultural Center

ENVIRONS: Driving west from Hale'iwa, you pass a former sugar plantation at Waialua and arrive at **Mokulē'ia**, where polo fields border on empty, white-sand beaches. Here you can spend a pleasant afternoon watching parachutists from nearby Dillingham Airfield float down across the surf like clouds of colorful butterflies.

Dole Plantation ❽

Honolulu Co. 64-1550 Kamehameha Highway (Hwy 99), 2 miles (3 km) N of Wahiawā. 📞 *(808) 621-8408.* 🚌 *Wahiawā.* ☐ *daily.* ● *Dec 25.* ♿

Interior of the Chinese Cookhouse at Hawai'i's Plantation Village

T HE DOLE CANNERY, built by James Dole in 1903 next to his Wahiawā pineapple plantation, was at that time the world's largest fruit cannery. In 1907 operations moved to Honolulu, but recently closed due to stiff competition from Asia. The original Dole Cannery in Wahiawā now functions as a distribution warehouse.

Dole's famous company logo

Across from the warehouse is Dole Plantation – a gift shop selling a range of pineapple products and a demonstration garden showing the different stages of the fruit's growth.

Nearby is the **Del Monte Pineapple Variety Garden**, where a self-guided tour takes in decorative bromeliads and various pineapple species, including the smooth cayenne, Hawai'i's commercial variety.

❧ Del Monte Pineapple Variety Garden

Junction of Hwy 99 & Hwy 80. 📞 *(808) 621-1215.* ☐ *daily.*

Hawai'i's Plantation Village ❾

Honolulu Co. 94-695 Waipahu Street, Waipahu. 📞 *(808) 677-0110.* 🚌 *Waipahu.* ☐ *Mon–Sat.* ● *public hols.* 📷 ♿

T HIS THREE-MILLION-DOLLAR re-stored village portrays over 100 years of sugar plantation culture, from 1840 to 1943. It shows how plantation owners segregated workers along strict ethnic lines and how, in spite of this, a common pidgin language developed *(see p15).*

The village contains some recreated buildings from the major ethnic groups that worked the plantations, from the Korean, Puerto Rican, and Japanese homes to a Japanese bath-house and a Shinto shrine. Personal objects placed in the houses give the impression that the occupants have just left. The small on-site museum runs informative walking tours.

Wai'anae Coast ❿

Honolulu Co. 🚌 *Nānākuli, Wai'anae and Mākaha Beach.* 🛈 *HVCB, Waikīkī, (808) 924-0266.*

W ITH NO SOUVENIR stands and very few restaurants, O'ahu's sunny leeward coast is home to a population of native Hawaiians and other Pacific islanders. One of the coast's prettiest beaches is **Pōka'ī Bay**, where a breakwater shelters an aquamarine lagoon with sand as soft as cloth under your feet.

Farther northwest is **Mākaha Beach**, a surf break famous for its 30-ft (9-m) waves. In lush Mākaha Valley is the restored **Kāne'ākī Heiau**, with thatched houses and *ki'i* (carved idols). It was used as a war *heiau* (temple) by Kamehameha I. Mākaha means "ferocious," and the valley was once notorious for bandits. The area still has a reputation for car break-ins; camping is not advised.

⋔ Kāne'ākī Heiau

Off Mākaha Valley Rd. ☐ *Tue–Sun.*

Ka'ena Point ⓫

Honolulu Co. Beyond end of Farrington Highway (Hwy 930), 7 miles (11 km) N of Mākaha.

O 'AHU'S WESTERN extremity, Ka'ena Point has a stark, mountainous coastline and spectacular sunsets. A hot but relatively easy 2-mile (3-km) trail leads to the point. Leave nothing of value in your car.

Legend tells that the rock off the point is a chunk of Kaua'i that the demigod Maui pulled off when he was trying to unite the two islands. On clear days Kaua'i can be spotted to the north. You may also see rare monk seals, green turtles, and humpback whales *(see p101).* The world's highest waves slam against the rocks here. So far no one has been suicidal enough to surf them. The point can also be reached from the road's end in Mokulē'ia. The two roads do not connect.

Ka'ena Point, reached by the exposed trail in the foreground

MOLOKA'I AND LĀNA'I

THE SMALL ISLAND OF *Moloka'i tends to be overlooked by vacationers scurrying between O'ahu and Maui. Far less developed for tourism than its neighbors, Moloka'i is the place to get away from it all, and most visitors are enchanted by its gentle pace. Across the Kalohi Channel to the south lies the smaller island of Lāna'i. This former pineapple plantation is now an exclusive tourist destination.*

Moloka'i is part of a volcanic duo consisting of two extinct, adjacent volcanoes that were once, along with Lāna'i and Kaho'olawe, attached to Maui. Its higher eastern peak, at some 5,000 ft (1,500 m), is topped by dense rain forest. The north shore is lined by the world's highest, steepest sea cliffs and indented by vast green valleys. The sheltered southern slopes traditionally held the bulk of the inhabitants, who planted crops along the coastline and raised fish in artificial enclosures just offshore. The western volcano, Mauna Loa, has been eroded to a smooth, rounded monolith, which receives so little rain that it is technically desert. Until recently this end of Moloka'i was barely populated, but since the 1970s, thanks to guaranteed sun and beaches like vast Pāpōhaku, it has been the site of what little development Moloka'i has seen.

Despite repeatedly falling to invading armies from O'ahu, Maui, and Hawai'i Island, Moloka'i acquired a reputation for great spiritual power. Partly thanks to that sense of mystery and isolation, the Kalaupapa Peninsula was set aside in the 1860s as a leprosarium. The work of the Belgian priest Father Damien in tending its exiled patients became famous, and pilgrims now flock to the peninsula from all around the world.

Lying in the rainshadow of Moloka'i and Maui, Lāna'i is now almost wholly owned by the Castle & Cooke Corporation, and its luxury resorts have begun to shift the economy and lifestyle of the people from agriculture to tourism. Visitors will find an open, sun-baked terrain, spectacular sea cliffs, unpopulated beaches, and the haunting remains of ancient native Hawaiian settlements.

Moloka'i's isolated Kalaupapa Peninsula, backed by the world's highest sea cliffs

◁ Native *kauna'oa* vine growing along Polihua Beach on Lāna'i's northern shore

Exploring Moloka'i and Lāna'i

MOST OF MOLOKA'I'S accommodations are in the resort of Kaluako'i at the island's sunnier west end. Kaluako'i offers a golf course and wonderful beaches. Kaunakakai, on the south coast, has a few charming hotels and most of the island's restaurants. No visitor should miss a drive along the flower-decked south coast to Hālawa Valley or a trip to Kalaupapa National Historical Park, backed by the north shore's huge sea cliffs. Lāna'i, Moloka'i's smaller and drier neighbor to the south, has luxury hotels, deserted beaches, and ancient ruins. Most residents live in the island's one small town, Lāna'i City.

SIGHTS AT A GLANCE

Hālawa Valley **3**
Kalaupapa National Historical
  Park pp86–7 **4**
Kaluako'i **8**
Kamakou Rain Forest **5**
Kaunakakai **1**
Kualapu'u **6**
Lāna'i pp90–91 **10**
Maunaloa **9**
Mo'omomi Beach **7**

Tours

A Tour of East Moloka'i **2**

The yellow sands of Polihua Beach on Lāna'i's remote north coast

TOP RECREATIONAL AREAS

The places shown here have been selected for their recreational activities. Conditions, especially those of the ocean, vary depending on the weather and the time of year, so exercise caution and, if in doubt, stay out of the water or seek local advice.

	SWIMMING	SNORKELING	DIVING	BODY-SURFING	WINDSURFING	HIKING	HORSEBACK RIDING	GOLF
Dixie Maru Beach	●	■						
Hālawa Valley	●			■				
Hulopo'e/Mānele Bay (Lāna'i)	●	■	●					■
Kalaupapa Nat'l Historical Park						■	●	
Kamakou Rain Forest						■		
Kawa'aloa Bay	●			■				
Kawākiu Bay	●	■						
Kepuhi Bay	●				●		●	■
Kō'ele (Lāna'i)						■	●	■
Mo'omomi Beach	●	■						
One Ali'i Beach Park	●							
Pāpōhaku Beach						■		
Twenty-Mile Beach	●	■						

KEY

▬	Major road
▭	Minor road
▭	Dirt or four-wheel-drive road
▬	Scenic route
--	Trail
≈	River, stream, or lake
- -	Ferry route
☆	Vista

SEE ALSO

- **Where to Stay** pp155–6
- **Where to Eat** p169

KALAUPAPA NATIONAL HISTORICAL PARK 4

ʻALAʻAU STATE PARK

KAUHAKŌ CRATER

KUALAPUʻU 6

3 *HĀLAWA VALLEY*

5 *KAMAKOU RAIN FOREST*

K AA II

KAPUĀIWA COCONUT GROVE

1 *KAUNAKAKAI*

ONE ALIʻI BEACH PARK

2 *A TOUR OF EAST MOLOKAʻI*

TWENTY-MILE BEACH

450

Pailolo Channel

The road to Kalawao on Kalaupapa Peninsula, with ʻŌkala Island and Molokaʻi's northern cliffs behind

Kalohi Channel

GETTING AROUND

Neither Molokaʻi nor Lānaʻi has public transportation, so renting a car is essential. Car rental firms operate at Molokaʻi's Hoʻolehua airport and in Lānaʻi City. A 12-mile (19-km) drive west of Hoʻolehua gets you to Kaluakoʻi, while Hālawa Valley is 35 miles (56 km) east, on a road that steadily narrows beyond Kaunakakai. Lānaʻi is best explored in a four-wheel-drive vehicle since the island has only 30 miles (48 km) of paved road and more than 100 miles (160 km) of red-dirt "pine roads" and rocky trails to the sea.

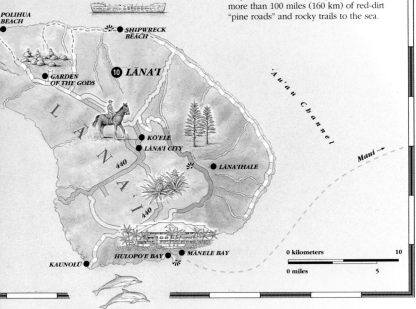

POLIHUA BEACH

SHIPWRECK BEACH

10 *LĀNAʻI*

GARDEN OF THE GODS

L A A N N A A II

KŌʻELE

LĀNAʻI CITY

LĀNAʻIHALE

440

440

ʻAuʻau Channel

Maui →

HULOPOʻE BAY

MĀNELE BAY

KAUNOLŪ

| 0 kilometers | | 10 |
| 0 miles | | 5 |

Kaunakakai ❶

Maui Co. 🏙 *2,700.* 🚹 *Ala Malama St and Kamehameha V Hwy (Hwy 450), (808) 553-3876.* 📷 *Ka Moloka'i Makahiki (cultural festival; late Jan).*

THE MAIN TOWN on Moloka'i, Kaunakakai was built at the end of the 19th century as an administrative center and port for the local sugar plantations. During the 1920s, pineapple production took over from sugar, but these days commercial agriculture has all but

Ala Malama Street, Kaunakakai's main street

disappeared from the island, and Kaunakakai looks its age. The wooden boardwalks of its principal thoroughfare, Ala Malama Street, are lined with false-fronted stores, such as the **Kanemitsu Bakery**, famous throughout the islands for its sweet Moloka'i bread. Dotted along the same street, homey diners reflect Moloka'i's broad ethnic mix *(see p169).* At the eastern end, tiny **St. Sophia's Church** is all but obscured behind an African tulip tree with its orange blossoms.

About half a mile (800 m) from the town center, the long stone jetty of of **Kaunakakai Harbor** juts out into the ocean. It was built in 1898 with rocks taken from a destroyed *heiau* (temple). To the ancient Hawaiians this place was known

as Kaunakahakai, or "beach landing." A break in the coral reef made it a natural place from which to launch canoes. The harbor is often busy with local fishermen and divers.

During the 1860s, Chief Kapuāiwa, who later became King Kamehameha V, had a home near here. Its remains can still be seen just west of the road leading to the jetty.

ENVIRONS: Chief Kapuāiwa was also responsible for planting the soaring palms of the **Kapuāiwa Coconut Grove**, sandwiched between the highway and the ocean 2 miles (3 km) west of Kaunakakai. Well over 1,000 in number, the trees are a majestic sight when silhouetted against the setting sun. Visitors should take care, however, not to stand in the way of falling nuts. Opposite the grove is Kauanakakai's **Church Row**, a set of small wooden chapels belonging to different sects.

A Tour of East Moloka'i ❷

THE COASTAL HIGHWAY that nestles beneath the peaks of eastern Moloka'i is among the most beautiful drives in Hawai'i. Ancient sites and picturesque churches lie tucked away amid tropical flowers and luxuriant rain forest, while the slopes of West Maui are visible across the water. Few people live here now, so the villages often feel like ghost towns.

Old gas pump en route

The road finally twists to a halt at ravishing Hālawa Valley, one of Hawai'i's most stunning "amphitheater" valleys.

Fishing boats and yachts in Kaunakakai Harbor

KEY

▬ Tour route

🔆 Vista

TIPS FOR DRIVERS

Tour length: 55 miles (88 km) round trip.
Stopping-off points: Allow a full day to visit the ancient fish ponds and pretty churches, to have a picnic at Twenty-Mile Beach or One Ali'i Beach Park, and even to fit in a hike through Hālawa Valley.

Kaunakakai

Kamehameha V Highway 450

One Ali'i Beach Park ①
At One Ali'i Beach Park, the small expanse of lawn, scattered with coconut palms, is ideal for picnics and also provides a perfect launching point for kayak trips. One Ali'i is a modern misspelling of the ancient Hawaiian name Oneali'i, meaning "Royal Sands."

St. Joseph Church ②
Built in 1876 by Father Damien *(see p87),* this tiny church was painted a dazzling white in 1995 to celebrate the return of the priest's right hand to Kalaupapa. His statue, permanently garlanded with fresh *lei,* stands in the colorful garden.

Hālawa Valley ❸

Maui Co. End of Kamehameha V Highway (Hwy 450), 27 miles (43 km) E of Kaunakakai. ⊞ *Kaunakakai, (808) 553-3876.*

HAWAI'I'S ORIGINAL Polynesian settlers were established in beautiful Hālawa Valley by AD 650, and for over 1,000 years they grew taro *(see p109)* in an elaborate network of terraced fields. The ruins of nearly 20 ancient *heiau* (temples), including two dedicated to human sacrifice, lie hidden in the undergrowth on both sides of the valley. Hālawa was all but abandoned after the 1946 tsunami, but a new generation of farmers grows taro now.

Visitors get their first glimpse of Hālawa from an overlook near mile marker 26. Though its farthest reaches are often obscured by mountain mists, the dramatic shoreline lies spread out 750 ft (230 m) below. The placid, unhurried

Waterfall in Hālawa Valley, seen from a roadside overlook

meanderings of the main stream as it approaches the ocean are in sharp contrast to the roaring surf just ahead.

The highway switchbacks down the hillside, reaching the valley floor at a quaint wooden chapel. A little farther along, the road ends at a low ridge of dunes, knitted together by

naupaka, a white-flowered creeper. Surfers launch themselves into the waves from the small gray beach just beyond.

In summer, visitors wade across the river mouth to reach a nicer beach on the far side; in winter it's safer to follow the dirt road that curves from beside the chapel. Shaded by imposing palm trees and sheltered from the full force of the sea by a stony headland, the beach makes an utterly idyllic place to swim.

A difficult but spectacular two-hour trail, which involves wading through the stream, leads through the rain forest to the 250-ft (75-m) **Moa'ula Falls** at the head of the valley. Hawaiians claim that the pool at its base is home to a *mo'o* or giant lizard. Hikers traditionally throw a *ti* leaf onto the water before swimming; if it sinks, the *mo'o* is lying in wait. Unfortunately, protracted land disputes have often closed the trail in recent years.

Hālawa Valley ⑦
With its soaring walls, lush vegetation, and shimmering waterfalls, Hālawa Valley is regarded as the most scenic spot on Moloka'i.

0 kilometers 5

0 miles 3

Twenty-Mile Beach ⑥
This thin strip of pristine sand at mile marker 20 is shaded by overhanging trees. Sheltered from the open ocean, it's great for snorkeling, but beyond the reef the sea can be dangerous.

'Ili'ili'ōpae Heiau ⑤
This huge structure, Hawai'i's second largest *heiau* (temple), witnessed human sacrifices in the 18th century. It is on private land, but hikers can follow the five-minute trail that runs inland halfway between mile markers 15 and 16.

'Ualapu'e Fish Pond ③
Of the 50 or so ancient fish ponds that line Moloka'i's southeast coast, 'Ualapu'e, just after mile marker 13, is one of the largest. Created by erecting a stone wall on top of a submerged reef, it encloses a vast area of shallow ocean and was used to raise mullet for the chief's table.

Our Lady of Sorrows ④
Father Damien took his first short break from Kalaupapa in 1874, to build the church of Our Lady Of Sorrows at 'Ualapu'e. Below lush mountain slopes, its red-tiled roof is shaded by the tousled coconut palms that surround it.

Kalaupapa National Historical Park ❹

A local stone landmark

MILLIONS OF YEARS after Moloka'i emerged from the sea, a volcanic afterthought created the remote Kalaupapa peninsula *(see pp10–11)*. In 1865, when the imported disease of leprosy seemed to threaten the survival of the Hawaiian people, the peninsula was designated a leprosy colony. Bounty hunters rounded up those with even minor skin blemishes to be exiled at the original settlement of Kalawao. In the beginning, food and medicine were in short supply, and condemnation to the peninsula was seen as a death sentence. The settlement eventually relocated to the more sheltered Kalaupapa. The last patients arrived in 1969, when the policy of enforced isolation ended. The park now serves as a permanent memorial.

View from Pālā'au State Park
Sealed off from the rest of Moloka'i by a mighty wall of cliffs, this remote peninsula was an obvious choice for a leprosy colony.

★ **Kalaupapa**
All of the peninsula's residents, consisting of aging patients who chose to live out their lives here and state and federal employees, live on its sheltered western side in the village of Kalaupapa. It has three churches and a bar – Elaine's Place.

The Moloka'i Light from Kalaupapa Lighthouse was one of the most powerful in the Pacific when it was built in 1908.

Kalaupapa airstrip

SS Ka'ala, wrecked in 1932, remains a rusting hull stranded on the reef just offshore.

The Damien Monument, a Celtic cross, was paid for by public donations in England (1890) and erected in 1893.

★ **Kalaupapa Trail**
Hikers and mule riders alike pick their way down the 26 switchbacks of this precipitous trail, enjoying stupendous views during the 2-mile (3-km) journey.

Pālā'au State Park
(see p88)

PHALLIC ROCK

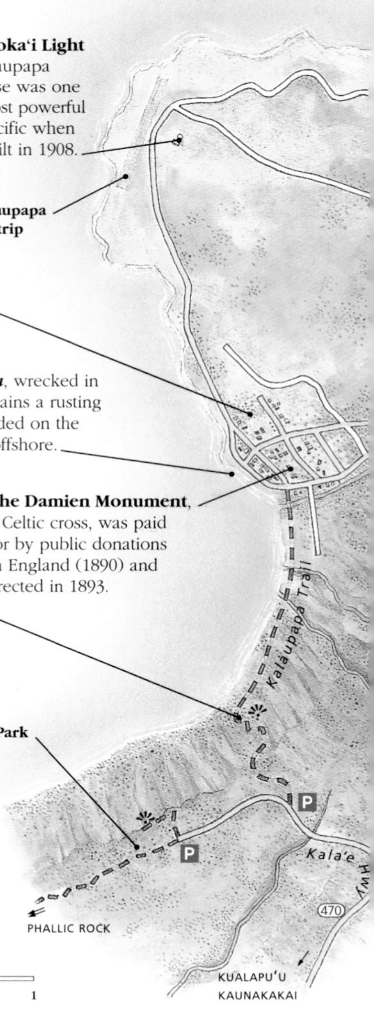

STAR FEATURES
★ Kalaupapa
★ Kalaupapa Trail
★ St. Philomena Church

0 kilometers   1

0 miles   1

Kalaupapa Trail

Kala'e

P

470

Kala'e Hwy

KUALAPU'U
KAUNAKAKAI

Offshore Islands
From the peninsula's exposed eastern side, small islands can be seen poking out of the sea next to staggering 2,000-ft (600-m) cliffs – the tallest sea cliffs in the world.

VISITORS' CHECKLIST

Maui Co. Reached by foot or mule on Kalaupapa Trail: trailhead on Hwy 470, 3 miles (5 km) N of Kualapu'u, between the mule stables and Kalaupapa Overlook. ✈ *from Ho'olehua, Moloka'i or Honolulu.* 🚌 🚶 *compulsory. Damien Tours, (808) 567-6171. Book well in advance. Visitors must be 16 years of age or older. For Molokai Mule Ride, (808) 567-6088, book well in advance.*

★ St. Philomena Church
The church was shipped from Honolulu in 1872 and later modified by Father Damien, whose grave lies nearby. In 1936 his body was returned to Belgium, but his right hand was later reinterred here.

Ancient Hawaiians used to jump off Leinaopapio Point for fun, with palm leaves as parachutes.

Judd Park

Kalawao, the original settlement on the exposed side of the peninsula, had a peak population of 1,174 in 1890, but was abandoned in 1932.

Kauhakō Crater, what's left of the volcano that formed the peninsula, has an 800-ft (245-m) deep lake at its center.

KEY

══	Minor road
═	Dirt or four-wheel-drive road
▪▪	Hiking trail and mule track
🅿	Parking
☆	Vista

FATHER DAMIEN (1840–89)

Joseph de Veuster, born in Belgium, went to Hawai'i as a Roman Catholic missionary in 1864, and was ordained as Father Damien at Our Lady of Peace *(see p44)* in Honolulu. In 1873, he volunteered to serve the original leprosy colony of Kalawao, on the isolated Kalaupapa Peninsula. Hailed as a hero by the Honolulu press, he embraced his destiny willingly. He built hospitals, churches, and homes with his bare hands and nursed patients without fear for his own life. Father Damien finally succumbed to leprosy in 1889. The dedication of the "Martyr of Moloka'i" won him universal acclaim. His beatification by the Pope as the "Blessed Damien" in 1995 was one of the last steps on the road to eventual sainthood.

Father Damien statue in Honolulu

Path through the dense vegetation of the Kamakou Rain Forest

Kamakou Rain Forest ❺

Maui Co. Reached by four-wheel-drive road E of Maunaloa Hwy (Hwy 460), 4 miles (6.5 km) NW of Kaunakakai.
🅷 *Kaunakakai, (808) 553-3876.*

T HE REMOTE mountain-top ridges of eastern Moloka'i preserve one of the least spoiled tracts of rain forest in Hawai'i. It is reached by four-wheel-drive vehicle or mountain bike on a rutted dirt road.

This region saw its one brief flurry of activity early in the 1800s, when native Hawaiians were sent up here in search of sandalwood to sell to foreign merchants *(see p30)*. Near the top of the island's central ridge is a grooved depression in the shape of a ship's hold. This so-called **Sandalwood Boat** was where the cut logs were piled.

The higher you climb, the wetter and lusher the forest becomes, and the more the road deteriorates. Native fauna and flora increasingly predominate, with colorful *'ōhi'a* trees erupting amid vivid green foliage. Ten miles (16 km) in, superb views open out all the way to the north shore valleys. Here, Waikolu Lookout stands above the 3,700-ft (1,150-m) drop of Waikolu Valley.

Just beyond, the Pēpē'ōpae Trail climbs along a wooden walkway through otherwise impenetrable rain forest. Every tree is festooned with hanging vines and spongy moss, while

orchids glisten in the undergrowth. This misty wonderland is the last refuge of endangered birds like the Moloka'i thrush *(oloma'o)* and Moloka'i creeper *(kākāwahie)*. After crossing an eerie, windswept bog, the trail traverses a series of gulches to emerge at an astonishing overlook above Pelekunu Valley.

Kualapu'u ❻

Maui Co. 🅟 *1,700.* 🅷 *Kaunakakai, (808) 553-3876.*

T HE FORMER plantation village of Kualapu'u is now home to Moloka'i's first coffee plantation, whose products can be tasted at the friendly, roadside espresso bar. Two miles (3 km) northeast of town, the **RW Meyer Sugar Mill** preserves the remains of the area's short-lived dabble in the sugar business. The mill machinery, now beautifully restored, was in use for just 11 years from 1878 to 1889. It now forms part of the adjoining **Moloka'i Museum**

RW Meyer Sugar Mill, the smallest in Hawai'i

and Cultural Center, an interesting little collection of artifacts that illustrates the island's varied history.

ENVIRONS: Four miles (6.5 km) northeast of Kualapu'u, Kala'e Highway (Hwy 470) comes to an end at **Pālā'au State Park**, which combines superb views over the Kalaupapa Peninsula *(see pp86–7)* with a legendary site. Stop at the viewpoint to gaze eastward along the awesome cliffs to Kalaupapa village and beyond. From the vista's parking lot a hiking trail leads through the forest to **Phallic Rock**. As ancient legend has it, women who sleep beneath this outcrop will wake up pregnant. Its lifelike appearance is in part the work of human hands.

🏛 **Moloka'i Museum and Cultural Center**
Kala'e Highway (Hwy 470). 🅲 *(808) 567-6436.* ⭘ *Mon–Sat.* ⬤ *public hols.* 💷 🅖

Phallic Rock in Pālā'au State Park

Mo'omomi Beach ❼

Maui Co. At the end of Mo'omomi Rd, 5 miles (8 km) NW of Ho'olehua.

M O'OMOMI BEACH, the only stretch of Moloka'i's north shore accessible to casual visitors, belongs very much to the drier western end of the island. The coastline here is made up of ancient sand dunes that have become lithified (turned to rock). The area is rich in the bones of flightless birds, which may have been hunted to extinction by the early Polynesian settlers. A 5-mile (8-km) dirt road from Ho'olehua

The dirt road serving Moʻomomi Beach

leads to Moʻomomi Bay, a surfing and fishing beach popular with local residents. The beach makes a good starting point for seaside walks.

Kaluakoʻi ❽

Maui Co. Off Maunaloa Hwy (Hwy 460), 5 miles (8 km) NW of Maunaloa. 🛈 *Kaunakakai, (808) 553-3876.* 🎭 *Molokaʻi Ka Hula Piko (May).*

THE GENTLE SLOPES of Mauna Loa, Molokaʻi's western volcano, have always been far too arid to sustain a significant human presence. The island's west coast was known to the ancients as Kaluakoʻi, "the adze pit," for its valuable basalt deposits. This area had a population of just one person in the 1970s. Since then, it has become Molokaʻi's only resort, home to a large hotel, condo complexes, and a golf course.

ENVIRONS: The island's most spectacular expanse of sand, broad **Pāpōhaku Beach** starts about a mile (1.5 km) down the coast. Colossal waves render the beach unsafe for swimming, so it is often empty, with a splendid sense of romantic isolation.

Every May, **Pāpōhaku Beach County Park** hosts the Molokaʻi Ka Hula Piko festival, which celebrates the birth of *hula* with music and dance. There are *hālau hula* (*hula* schools), contemporary musicians, and local crafts. Lectures and storytelling take place across the island in the week before the festival.

Beyond Pāpōhaku's southern end, secluded **Dixie Maru Beach** offers sheltered swimming and good snorkeling.

Maunaloa ❾

Maui Co. 🏘 *400.* 🛈 *Kaunakakai, (808) 553-3876.*

WHEN THE **Molokaʻi Ranch** specialized in cattle and pineapples, tiny Maunaloa, on the flanks of the mountain, was the quintessential Hawaiian plantation village. From wooded groves, the timber-frame houses of its farm workers and *paniolo (see p121)* faced right across the ocean to Waikiki.

Since the 1970s, the ranch has switched to tourism and real estate, and in 1996 it bulldozed almost all of Maunaloa's old homes. However, a few homespun businesses, including **The Village Grill** and the **Big Wind Kite Factory**, still survive on the main street.

Molokaʻi Ranch now offers luxury camping and various outdoor activities, including the so-called **Paniolo Round-Up**, which provides rodeo lessons for would-be cowpokes. The professional cowboys often stage unscheduled rodeos.

Molokaʻi was renowned in ancient times as *Molokaʻi pule oʻo* (Molokaʻi of strong prayers), the home of powerful priests and sorcerers. Dreaded "poison-wood gods" lived in the forests above Maunaloa; a sliver of wood cut from their favored trees could kill any foe. However, the *ʻohiʻa* woods nearby played a more benign role in Hawaiian legend. Here the goddess Laka learned the *hula* and taught it to humans. This claim to be the birthplace of *hula* is disputed, however. Keʻē Beach on Kauaʻi boasts the same distinction *(see p141).*

Molokaʻi Ranch
Maunaloa Hwy (Hwy 460). 🎬 *(808) 552-2791.* 🔵 *daily.*

Golfer at the beach resort of Kaluakoʻi on Molokaʻi's western shore

Lāna'i ⑩

THIS SUN-BAKED ISLAND was formerly the world's largest pineapple plantation, owned by the Dole Company, but in 1991 it underwent an historic conversion. In that year, Lāna'i's new owner, the Castle & Cooke Corporation, opened two luxury resorts and reemployed the island's small population of farm workers as hotel staff. This identity shift left most of the island open for freewheeling exploration of its many beaches, cliffs, and ancient ruins.

Colorful Lāna'i City house backed by Cook Island Pine trees

Exploring Lāna'i
This relatively low island is topped by the Lāna'ihale ridge. The heart of the island, rural Lāna'i City, is perched below the ridge at an elevation of 1,600 ft (490 m). Roads, more often dirt than paved, radiate outward to reach the coast at a few remote, beautiful spots.

Lāna'i City
Home to virtually all of the island's 2,500 residents, Lāna'i City offers a firsthand experience of the classic Hawaiian plantation town. Built in the early 1920s to house Dole's mostly Filipino laborers, this friendly town centers on rectangular **Dole Park**. The park is lined with frontier-style shops and the **Hotel Lāna'i**, a vintage wooden inn *(see p156)*.

At the northeast corner of the town, on the site of the former headquarters of Lāna'i Ranch (1874–1951), is **The Lodge at Kō'ele** *(see p156)*. This award-winning resort offers respite from the island's coastal heat. The attractions here include an 18-hole golf course, an orchid house, stables, and manicured grounds. The fine restaurant is open to the public.

⋔ Luahiwa Petroglyphs
Off Hō'ike Rd, 2 miles (3 km) S of Lāna'i City, near the water tower on the ridge. The broad, softly hazy expanse of Pālāwai Basin is actually the remains of Lāna'i's extinct and worn-down volcanic crater. Its eastern wall bears one of Hawai'i's richest collections of petroglyphs. Visible from quite a distance, a cluster of 34 black boulders stands out against a steep red hillside dotted with dry white patches of *pili* grass. Some of these stones were thought to possess the *mana* (sacred power) of the rain gods Kū and Hina. Starting at least 500 years ago, Hawaiians decorated them by carving enigmatic figures representing humans and dogs. More recent images of horses, surfers, and leashed dogs were carved by students from Maui's Lahainaluna School during the 1870s. The petroglyphs are best viewed early or late, when the sun is not overhead.

🏊 Mānele and Hulopo'e Bays
End of Mānele Rd (Hwy 440), 8 miles (13 km) S of Lāna'i City.
Together, these adjacent bays form a marine life conservation district, home to Hawaiian spinner dolphins. Mānele Bay is Lāna'i's only small boat harbor. The misleadingly named **Mānele Bay Hotel** *(see p156)* spreads over the hillside above Hulopo'e Bay, the island's best swimming and snorkeling spot. The resort, even with its interior opulence, fragrant gardens, and cliff-edge golf course, manages to harmonize with its savage location. The bay is off-limits to all boats except those of Maui's oldest sailing excursion company, **Trilogy**. Camping is permitted here.

Between the bays lies **Pu'u Pehe**, or Sweetheart Rock. According to legend, lovely Pehe was kept by her jealous husband in a nearby cave until one day, while he was away, she drowned in a storm. He buried her on this rock island and then jumped to his death.

Pu'u Pehe, or Sweetheart Rock, in the waters off Mānele Bay

⋔ Kaunolū
Kaunolū Trail, a dirt track off Kaupili Rd, which leaves Mānele Rd (Hwy 440) 4.5 miles (7 km) S of Lāna'i City.
Few sites evoke the drama of ancient Hawaiian life like the ruins of this seldom-visited fishing village, abandoned in the mid-19th century. The rough drive to this naturally fortified cliff top, with its dizzying views of Lāna'i's southern coast, takes a full hour from Lāna'i City and requires a four-wheel-drive vehicle.

The early Hawaiians excelled in the art of building with un-mortared stone, and here at

The beautifully maintained grounds of The Lodge at Kō'ele in Lāna'i City

LĀNA'I'S COOK ISLAND PINE TREES

Groves of Cook Island Pine, which give the island its characteristic look, were planted in the early 1900s by New Zealander
George C. Munro, the manager of what was then the Lāna'i
Ranch. Freshwater is Lāna'i's most precious resource, and
Munro realized that these trees increase the island's water-
drawing capacities. Mountain mists collect in the trees' tightly
leaved branches and drip onto the thirsty ground – on a good
day, as much as 40 gallons (150 liters) of water per tree.

An impressive row of Cook Island Pines at The Lodge at Kō'ele stables

VISITORS' CHECKLIST

Maui Co. 🚶 2,500. ✈ 4 miles
(6.5 km) SW of Lāna'i City.
🚢 Mānele Bay. 🏢 P.O. Box
700, (808) 565-7600. 🎎 Aloha
Week (mid-Oct).

Kaunolū you can see several
well-preserved examples, including the stone platform of
the large **Halulu Heiau** on
Kaunolū Bay's west side. On
the east side there is a cliff-side
platform that was once the
home and fishing retreat of
Kamehameha the Great. There
are also ruins of a canoe house
and a large fishing shrine.

One way in which ancient
Hawaiians showed their bravery was by cliff-jumping, and
just west of Kaunolū Bay there
is a suicidal diving platform. At
Kahekili's Leap, the former
chief of Maui, Kahekili, proved
his mettle by hurling himself
more than 60 ft (18 m) down
– clearing a 15-ft (4.5-m) wide
outcrop of rocks – into water
just 10 ft (3 m) deep.

🎎 The Munro Trail
Turn off Mānele Rd (Hwy 440) 5 miles
(8 km) S of Lāna'i City.
This pine-studded drive along
the volcanic ridge of Lāna'ihale,

whose summit reaches 3,370 ft
(1,050 m), offers sensational
views of five of the Hawaiian
islands. Because the Kō'ele end
of the road can be alarmingly
muddy, best taken downhill,
the drive should begin at the
other end. At the concrete
stripe on Mānele Road just
after the Pālāwai Basin, turn
left onto a dirt road and then
follow the most worn track
up the hill. Allow at least two
hours by jeep for this rugged
20-mile (32-km) jaunt.

🎎 Garden of the Gods
Polihua Rd, 6 miles (10 km) NW of
Lāna'i City.
The Garden of the Gods is a
visual oddity, a reddish lunar
landscape dotted with boulders
made of compacted sand. They
range in color from reds and
oranges to browns and blues,
and the effect is most intense at
sunset, when the rocks seem
to glow. This peculiar dry and
rocky landscape is reached by

an easy 30-minute drive along
a dirt road from Kō'ele, which
passes through a hunting zone
for axis, or spotted, deer and
native dryland forest.

Continuing on, the road to
the island's northern tip gets
rougher, ending at long, wild
Polihua Beach. At this remote
strand, one hour from Kō'ele, a
visitor's footprints may be the
only ones of the day. The ocean
currents can be dangerous.

**Strange rust-red rock formations
at the Garden of the Gods**

🎎 Shipwreck Beach
Keōmuku Rd (Hwy 430), 8 miles
(13 km) NE of Lāna'i City.
Lāna'i's northern shore is lined
with an 8-mile (13-km) stretch
of beach that takes its name
from the rusting hulk of a
World War II supply ship that
is wrecked on the reef. Many
other ships have come to harm
in these shallow, hazardous
waters, including an oil tanker
that is visible 6 miles (10 km)
up the beach. To reach the
beach, follow Keōmuku Road
(Hwy 430) until the asphalt
ends; then take the dirt road
on the left that rambles over
sandy ground for about a mile
(1.5 km). From here, a beachcomber's trek offers isolation
and beautiful views of Maui
and Moloka'i – a day's hike
northward will bring you to
Polihua Beach. Off Shipwreck
Beach is an extensive reef, but
swimming is dangerous here.

Shipwreck Beach, with the hulking 1940s wreck in the distance

MAUI

THE SECOND LARGEST HAWAIIAN *island, Maui is sparsely populated, supporting less than a tenth of the state's population. The land is verdant with sugarcane and pineapple, sprawling cattle ranches, and rain forests that descend mountain slopes to the sea. The 120 miles (195 km) of shoreline invite a host of ocean activities, from swimming, snorkeling, and diving, to world-class windsurfing.*

Maui was formed by the convergence of two volcanoes at the isthmus known as the Central Valley. The green 5,788-ft (1,764-m) West Maui Mountains are the eroded slopes of a single extinct volcano, while East Maui is composed of Haleakalā, an enormous 10,023-ft (3,055-m) dormant volcano crowned by a lunar landscape.

The earliest inhabitants are thought to have arrived from the Marquesas Islands around the 4th century AD. The areas around Lahaina, the Central Valley, and Hāna were the first to be settled. Maui was split into rival chiefdoms until the 14th century, when Pi'ilani conquered the island. This Maui chief built the massive temple of Pi'ilanihale Heiau, whose ruins are near Hāna. In 1795 Kamehameha I conquered Maui in his quest to unite the Hawaiian Islands and in 1800 established his royal seat at Lahaina.

Jean-François de Galaup, Comte de La Pérouse, was the first European to set foot on Maui, in 1786. Other foreigners followed during the 1800s, including missionaries, whalers, and contract laborers from Europe and Asia who came to work the growing sugar plantations. The communities they established retained the character of their homelands and created a multicultural heritage that is celebrated today in local holidays, customs, and food.

Visitors will see a varied landscape, from Kula's rolling farmland, where proteas and sweet onions are grown, to the arid, eroded crater of Haleakalā and the lush, tropical vegetation on the windward coast. If you want to soak up the sun, the leeward coast offers white-sand beaches and calm waters that are home to humpback whales.

Windsurfers at Ho'okipa Beach County Park near Pā'ia, on Maui's north shore

◁ A view of Honomanū Bay from the road to Hāna

Exploring Maui

MAUI IS COMPOSED of two volcanoes connected by the Central Valley, the island's population hub and the site of several attractions, including the Bailey House Museum. The West Maui Mountains are actually a single, extinct volcano that time has carved into steep canyons, accessible at just a few places, such as 'Iao Valley. A road skirting the mountain's southern flank leads to historic Lahaina and the coastal resorts of Kā'anapali and Kapalua. Haleakalā, a dormant volcano capped by a huge crater, makes up the larger region of East Maui. Its outer slopes are covered with cattle ranches and fields of sugarcane and pineapple. The lush windward coast in the north features the plantation town of Pā'ia, Ho'okipa Beach – a windsurfers' mecca – and the little town of Hāna. The popular leeward coast enjoys a sunnier climate and calmer ocean.

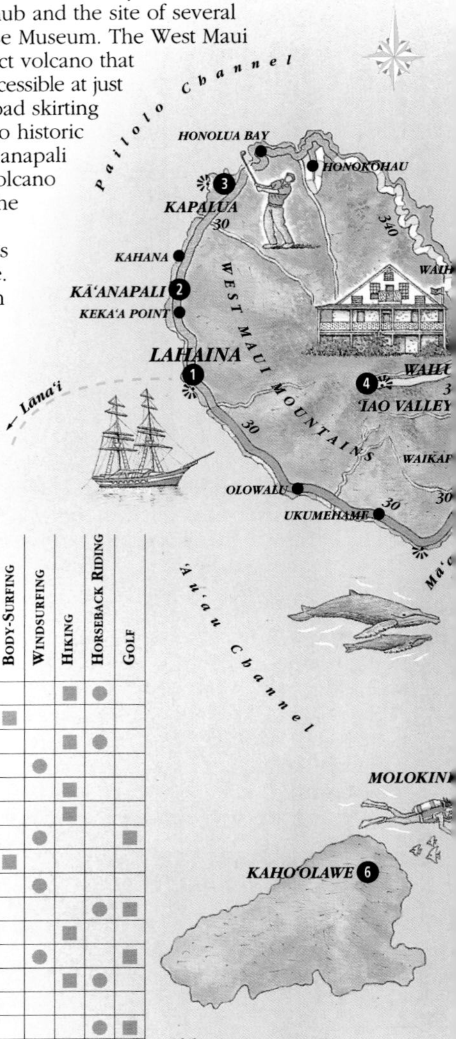

TOP RECREATIONAL AREAS

The places shown here have been selected for their recreational activities. Conditions, especially those of the ocean, vary depending on the weather and the time of year, so exercise caution and, if in doubt, stay out of the water or seek local advice.

	SWIMMING	SNORKELING	DIVING	BODY-SURFING	WINDSURFING	HIKING	HORSEBACK RIDING	GOLF
Haleakalā National Park						■	●	
Hāmoa Bay	●	■		■				
Hāna	●					■	●	
Ho'okipa Beach County Park					●			
Hosmer Grove						■		
'Iao Valley						■		
Kā'anapali and Keka'a Point	●	■	●		●			■
Kahana				■				
Kanahā Beach County Park	●				●			
Kapalua and Honolua Bay	●	■	●				●	■
Ke'anae Peninsula						■		
Kīhei	●	■	●		●			■
La Pérouse Bay		■	●			■	●	
Lahaina	●	■	●					
Mākena	●	■	●				●	■
Molokini		■	●					
'Ohe'o Gulch and Kīpahulu	●			■		■	●	
Olowalu		■	●					
Pā'ia	●		●	■				
Polipoli Springs Recreation Area						■		
Spreckelsville	●				●			
Ukumehame	●	■	●	■				
'Ulupalakua							●	
Wai'ānapanapa State Park	●	●				■		
Waihe'e	●					■	●	■
Waikapū								■
Wailea	●	■	●					■

HONOLUA BAY
HONOKŌHAU
③
KAPALUA
30
KAHANA
WEST MAUI
KĀ'ANAPALI ②
KEKA'A POINT
WAHI
②
WAIH
LAHAINA ①
④
'IAO VALLEY
MOUNTAINS
30
WAIKAP
OLOWALU
UKUMEHAME
30
Pailolo Channel
'Au'au Channel
Lana'i
MOLOKINI
KAHO'OLAWE ⑥

0 kilometers ———————— 10
0 miles ———— 5

KEY

▨	Major road
▨	Minor road
⊟	Dirt or four-wheel-drive road
▨	Scenic route
≈	River or stream
⚡	Vista

**'Iao Needle, marking the confluence of
two streams in the lush 'Iao Valley**

GETTING AROUND

Maui's main airport is in Kahului, but smaller
airports serve Hāna and Kapalua. Major resorts
offer guests free shuttle services to and from the
airport and around the resort, but most people
explore Maui with a rental car or by tour. There
is no widespread public transit system. Some
roads are tortuous, and progress can be slow.
Many highways have bicycle lanes, and tour
companies will take you to the top of Haleakalā
to bike back down. Stables offer horseback
tours all over the island. Ferry services run
between Maui and Lāna'i several times a day.

SEE ALSO

- **Where to Stay** pp156–9
- **Where to Eat** pp170–73

(Map of Maui with labeled locations)

ANAHA BEACH COUNTY PARK — PĀ'IA **11** — HO'OKIPA BEACH COUNTY PARK — SPRECKELSVILLE — KAHULUI — PU'UNENE — MAKAWAO **9** — A TOUR OF UPCOUNTRY MAUI **8** — HOSMER GROVE — KULA — KIHEI — HALEAKALĀ NATIONAL PARK **10** — SCIENCE CITY — WAILEA — POLIPOLI SPRINGS RECREATION AREA — 'ULUPALAKUA — KENA — LA PÉROUSE BAY — THE ROAD TO HĀNA **12** — KE'ANAE PENINSULA AND WAILUA VALLEY **13** — WAILUA — WAI'ANAPANAPA STATE PARK — HĀNA **14** — 'ĀLAU ISLAND — HĀMOA BAY — 'OHE'O GULCH — KIPAHULU — KAUPO — NORTH SHORE — 360 — 'Alenuihaha Channel — 'Au'au Channel — Kealaikahiki Channel

**A secluded swimming spot on the
rocky coast of the Ke'anae Peninsula**

Street-by-Street: Lahaina ❶

STROLL THE STREETS of Lahaina, and you follow in the footsteps of scoundrels and kings. Until 1845 this small harbor town was the capital of the Kingdom of Hawai'i. By the mid-19th century, during the peak of the whaling era, it had a reputation as a rowdy port-of-call. Missionaries sometimes struggled to maintain control over the town and the souls of its inhabitants. Today, it is one of the most popular visitor attractions on Maui. Front Street, lined with pioneer-style homes and storefronts, is evocative of Lahaina's past. The Lahaina Restoration Foundation has restored a number of historic sites, and a wealth of history can be found within a small area.

Statue outside Pioneer Inn

Front Street, once the haunt of boisterous sailors after women and whiskey, now offers souvenir shops and colorful street stalls.

MISSIONARY HOME
of
THE REV. DWIGHT BALDWIN
1834
Museum Open Daily

Wo Hing Temple

Masters' Reading Room

★ Baldwin Home
Maui's oldest Western-style dwelling, dating from the 1830s, has been faithfully restored with period furnishings, including several original pieces.

Hawai'i's first coral-stone house, owned by Reverend Richards, was built on this site in 1827 and then fired upon by angry sailors as a reaction to missionary zeal.

DICKENSON STREET

FRONT STREET

MARKET ST

PAPELEKANE STREET

The Hauola Stone was believed by ancient Hawaiians to calm and heal.

★ Carthaginian II
This square-rigged ship is a meticulously created replica of a 19th-century brig. Below decks, it features a floating museum devoted to the whale trade.

★ Pioneer Inn
Built in 1901 by an Englishman, the Pioneer Inn was the first hotel to open in Lahaina. It remains a hotel to this day and is a favorite landmark in the town.

LAHAINA'S TRAGIC PRINCESS

Hawaiian culture once sancti-
fied royal marriages between
siblings; such alliances kept
bloodlines pure and ensured
offspring great *mana* (power).
Ancient custom was cast aside
with the arrival of Christianity,
however. When Nahi'ena'ena
and her brother Kauikeaouli
(later Kamehameha III) fell
in love, they were separated.
Nahi'ena'ena still managed to
bear their son, who lived only
hours. Sick in body and soul,
she died soon afterward.

Nahi'ena'ena, who died at 21

VISITORS' CHECKLIST

Maui Co. 🏛 9,500. ⛴ *Lahaina
Harbor.* ℹ *648 Wharf St,
(808) 667-9193.* 🎭 *A Taste of
Lahaina (food festival; mid-Sep);
Halloween Mardi Gras of the
Pacific (Oct 31).*

0 meters		100
0 yards		100

Lahaina Courthouse is
home to the Lahaina Arts
Society, which stages free
exhibitions in the old cells.

HALE STREET

LUAKINI STREET

FRONT STREET

PRISON STREET

CANAL STREET

**Chapel in the
prison grounds**

Hale Pa'ahao, or "Stuck-in-
Irons House," was the new
prison built in the 1850s with
bricks from the Lahaina Fort.

Lahaina Fort was
built in the 1830s to
jail rowdy whalers, but
dismantled 20 years
later. A small part has
been reconstructed.

Lahaina's banyan tree, with
many separate trunks, is over
a century old. The tree is so
large that special events,
including arts and crafts fairs,
are held beneath its branches.
The square is named after it.

Exploring Lahaina

FRONT STREET IS the hub of Lahaina. A low seawall opens up nearly a block of the street to scenic views of the sea and nearby islands, and makes strolling an old-fashioned pleasure. Whether you visit the historic Baldwin Home, learn about whales on the *Carthaginian II*, or shop in the town's colorful stores, Lahaina offers a variety of interesting diversions. On most evenings, live music spills into the street from restaurants and bars.

Lahaina Harbor, against a backdrop of the West Maui Mountains

🏯 Baldwin Home

Front Street. 📞 *(808) 661-3262.*
🔵 *daily.* ⚫ *Jan 1, Dec 25.* 🎞 ♿
🎫 *compulsory.*

The four original rooms of this historic home were built in 1834 by the Reverend Ephraim Spaulding. The coral and stone walls were 24 in (60 cm) thick, perhaps a measure to minimize the sounds of revelry outside. At the height of the Pacific whaling trade, tensions often ran high between the seamen who frequented the port's brothels and grog shops and the missionaries who sought to establish Christian faith and law in the islands.

The Reverend Dwight Baldwin and his wife came to Hawai'i from the US in the early 1830s and were assigned to Lahaina's Waine'e Church. When Spaulding fell ill around 1836 the Baldwins moved into his house. As the family grew – to an eventual total of eight children – so did their home. A second-story dormitory was added in 1849, apparently to protect the daughters from the town's rowdier elements.

The first floor is open to the public. Many of the furnishings, which were donated by

the Baldwin family, date from the 1850s. Original pieces include an 18th-century sewing box, rocking chairs, and a four-poster bed made out of *koa* wood. Among the acquisitions is a quilt with a Hawaiian-flag design (*see p56*), a gift to a Captain Born from Hawai'i's last queen, Lili'uokalani.

The two-story house next door was built around 1834 – the same time as the Baldwin Home – and was used for various mission purposes. It takes its name, the **Masters' Reading Room**, from the second floor, which was designed to offer "suitable reading rooms for the accommodation of Seamen who visit Lahaina, as well as a convenient place of retirement from the heat and unpleasant dust of the market."

The Baldwin Home, set in a shady garden

The Reading Room, once housing the Lahaina Restoration Foundation, has been preserved in its original state but is closed to the public.

🏛 Carthaginian II

Opposite 658 Wharf St. 📞 *(808) 661-8527.* 🔵 *daily.* ⚫ *Jan 1, Dec 25.* 🎞

To enter this museum, you literally walk the plank! Docked permanently beside the lighthouse near the small-boat harbor, the *Carthaginian II* discloses its treasures to the gentle rocking of the sea.

The ship is in fact a 1920s' German schooner that was transformed in the 1970s to look like the kind of small freighter that brought cargo, Americans, and whalers to the islands in the 1800s. Replica or not, with its handcrafted masts it looks very impressive. The soulful sounds of recorded whale songs emanating from beneath the deck provide an appropriate ambience.

The museum in the ship's hold is worth seeing if you have not yet visited other Hawaiian museums devoted to whales and the whale trade. There is a small theater showing a film on humpback whales that includes remarkable close-up shots. Also here is a 19th-century whaleboat, with a recorded commentary and more whale songs.

🏯 Pioneer Inn

658 Wharf St. 📞 *(808) 661-3636.* ♿

Lahaina's best-known hotel was built by an Englishman called George Freeland. He had originally emigrated to Canada, where he joined the Mounties, but ended up in Lahaina in 1900, having pursued a criminal all the way to Maui. Freeland did not catch the fugitive, but stayed here, fell in love with a Hawaiian woman, and, in 1901, built a hotel.

Pioneer Inn is a hotel to this day, on land still owned by the Freeland family. It has been renovated but retains many of the original features. These include whaling memorabilia and a list of house

SCRIMSHAW – THE WHALERS' ART

Life aboard a 19th-century whaling ship had its moments of excitement, but these were the exception. For the average sailor, whaling meant months of boredom, bad food, and low pay. To pass the time, sailors made scrimshaw from whale ivory – carving and etching into the surface of whale teeth and bones. Their "dot-to-dot" technique involved puncturing the surface with a knife or sail needle, applying a mixture of soot and oil, and polishing the ivory with shark's skin. The results were often exquisite works of art.

Decorative scrimshaw made from whale bones

A scrimshander might just decorate the ivory, or else carve it into something useful, such as spoons or gun handles. Scrimshaw fetched a high price then and still does today, in stores along Lahaina's Front Street and at Kā'anapali's Whalers Village (*see p100*).

aid societies to help maintain ties with the homeland. One such was the Wo Hing Society, founded in 1909, which built the Wo Hing Temple in 1912.

As a museum, the temple provides a good insight into the local Chinese community. There are artifacts as well as a shrine; the altar is replenished with fresh offerings every day.

A separate cookhouse serves as a theater, showing old films about Hawai'i made by American inventor Thomas Edison in 1898 and 1906.

🏛 Hale Pa'i

End of Lahainaluna Road. **(** (808) 667-7040. ◯ Mon–Fri. ● Jan 1, Dec 25. ♿ 🎦

The "house of printing" is situated on the grounds of the oldest high school west of the Rocky Mountains – the former Lahainaluna Seminary. When missionaries arrived in Hawai'i they lost no time in trying to convert the locals to Christianity, as well as teaching them to read.

The Lahainaluna Seminary was set up in 1831, and in 1834 the missionaries added the Hale Pa'i. Originally a thatched hut, the printing house was later replaced with a sturdier building made of stone and timber.

In 1982, the Hale Pa'i became a museum, tracing the history of the written word in Hawai'i. There is a working replica of the original printing press and facsimiles of early Hawaiian printing.

rules in the rooms, forbidding tenants from burning the beds and womanizing. You do not need to be a guest to explore the shopping arcade or enjoy the popular bar and grill overlooking the harbor.

🚺 Lahaina Courthouse

649 Wharf St. **(** (808) 661-0111. ◯ daily. ● Jan 1, Dec 25. ♿

Completed in 1859, the Lahaina Courthouse on Wharf Street originally contained a governor's office, a customs house, a post office, a courtroom, and a jail. It was built with stones from the earlier courthouse and palace that were destroyed by gale-force winds in 1858.

Here too is the Lahaina Visitor Center, which sells souvenirs and other goods. Archive photos in the hallway give a glimpse of how the place once looked. The galleries of the Lahaina Arts Society are located in the Lahaina Center, 900 Front St.

🚺 Hale Pa'ahao

Prison & Waine'e streets. ◯ daily. ● Jan 1, Dec 25. ♿

Sailors and missionaries who arrived in the islands in the 18th and 19th centuries introduced Hawaiians to a host of new vices – and to codes of conduct unfamiliar to them.

This jail, whose name means "Stuck-in-Irons House," was built by convicts in the 1850s, using coral stone taken from the town's demolished fort.

It was used to incarcerate foreigners and natives alike for crimes ranging from murder to riding horses on the Sabbath or violating fish taboos.

A high stone wall encloses a grassy yard and the jailhouse. Visitors can peek into one of the cells, where a "convict" (actually a mannequin lying on a straw mattress) talks about 19th-century prison life.

Hawaiian papers in Hale Pa'i

🏛 Wo Hing Temple

858 Front St. **(** (808) 661-5553. ◯ daily. ● Jan 1, Dec 25.

The Chinese were among Hawai'i's earliest immigrants. They came to work on the plantations, but many later moved into commerce. The Chinese often formed mutual

Taoist altar in the shrine room of the Wo Hing Temple

Locals demonstrating their courage at Keka'a Point (Black Rock)

vessel, which shows the cramped and dismal living quarters aboard ship.

West Maui's most unusual means of transportation is the **Lahaina Kā'anapali & Pacific Railroad**, whose steam locomotives chug the 6 miles (10 km) between Lahaina and Kā'anapali. Steam engines were used in Hawai'i from the late 1800s to carry both sugarcane and plantation workers, but, by the 1950s, trucks had replaced the trains. Now the "Sugarcane Train" rides again, taking passengers along the same route as that used in earlier times. The scenic ride passes fields of cane and rises to cross the impressive Hāhākea Trestle for a view of the ocean and the West Maui Mountains.

Whalers Village and Whalers Village Museum
2435 Kā'anapali Parkway. (808) 661-4567. daily.
Lahaina Kā'anapali & Pacific Railroad
Lahaina Station: Limahana Place. **Kā'anapali (Pu'ukoli'i) Station:** off Pu'ukoli'i Road. (808) 667-6851. daily.

Kā'anapali ❷

Maui Co. 600. Suite 1B, 2530 Keka'a Drive, (808) 661-3271. Maui Onion Festival (early Aug), Na Mele O Maui (Dec).

NESTLED BETWEEN a 3-mile (5-km) beach and a pair of golf courses, Kā'anapali is Maui's largest resort. Despite all the hotels, the town maintains a sense of community by staging events like Na Mele O Maui ("the songs of Maui"), a celebration of Hawaiian culture, and the Maui Onion Festival, which honors the local crop.

Keka'a Point, better known as Black Rock, towers above long, white Kā'anapali Beach and overlooks one of the best snorkeling spots in Maui. Two centuries ago, when Maui chief Kahekili sought to encourage his troops, he would leap into the ocean from Black Rock. This involved spiritual, not physical, danger since it was believed that the dead jumped into the spirit world from here.

At the heart of Kā'anapali is **Whalers Village**, an upscale shopping center with many stores, restaurants, and bookstores. In addition to the shopping experience here, the Whalers Village Museum explores in unhappy detail the demise of the whale through the whaling trade. Displays include tools and weapons used in whaling, old photographs, models of whaling ships, and products made from the carcasses. Even more fascinating is the insight given into a young whaler's life by letters, diaries, and official accounts. There is also an amazing life-size reconstruction of the inside of a whaling

Kapalua ❸

Maui Co. 400. Lahaina, (808) 667-9193. Kapalua Wine & Food Symposium (Jul), Earth Maui Nature Summit (date changes annually).

TWENTY MINUTES' drive north of Kā'anapali lies Kapalua, West Maui's second planned resort, whose two luxury hotels and 54 championship fairways

One of the pristine bays that line the coast at Kapalua

are surrounded by a series of exquisite crescent bays and a pineapple plantation that carpets the lower slopes of the West Maui Mountains.

Two of the bays, **Honolua** and **Mokulē'ia**, have been designated marine life conservation districts, where divers and swimmers keep company with reef fish and sea turtles. The golf courses are Audubon Society-approved bird sanctuaries, and the environmentally sensitive lands above the resort are under the stewardship of the Nature Conservancy. It is not surprising therefore that Kapalua is the site of the Earth Maui Nature Summit, an annual three-day event that introduces the public to a wide variety of hands-on ecological activities.

The resort also hosts a PGA golf championship in January, with prize money in excess of $1 million, and a wine and food symposium that attracts vintners, chefs, and connoisseurs from around the world.

'Iao Valley ❹

Maui Co. 🚹 HVCB, Wailuku, (808) 244-3530.

ABOVE THE TOWN of Wailuku, the 'Iao Valley Road leads into the West Maui Mountains, winding beneath sheer cliffs as it follows a river hidden by trees. As the road begins to climb, the air becomes cooler, and traffic noise is replaced by

the green of 'Iao Valley, one of Maui's most sacred and historic sites. At one time, the bones of kings were buried here. In this valley in 1790, equipped with Western knowledge and weaponry, the forces of Kamehameha the Great trapped and annihilated those of Kahekili, the last independent chief of the island.

In a beautiful setting, about 2 miles (3 km) up the valley from Wailuku, you'll find **Kepaniwai Heritage Gardens**, a lovely county park frequented by local families – there are shaded picnic tables and a kids' wading pool. Scattered about the park are smaller-than-life models that reflect the architectural styles brought to the islands by various ethnic and racial groups. A thatched Hawaiian *hale* (house), a Portuguese dwelling with its outdoor oven, a simple Japanese home, and a prim New England cottage are some of the structures in the park that reflect Hawai'i's people – immigrants from the four corners of the world.

Adjacent to the gardens, the **Hawai'i Nature Center** offers hikes and other outdoor activities for young and old. "Mud Scientists," "Tremendous Trees," and "Slugfest" are a few of the hands-on educational offerings for budding scientists as

Statue of Japanese workers at Kepaniwai Heritage Gardens

young as three years old. In 1997, the center opened a new building called the 'Iao Valley Interactive Science Arcade, an innovative museum featuring games and displays that serve to educate visitors about the plant and animal life that has reached these islands. The museum explains why certain species evolved as they did, and how to help protect the fragile ecology of the island chain.

The paved road ends at **'Iao Valley State Park**, at the foot of 'Iao Needle, a pinnacle of rock that towers 1,200 ft (365 m) above the valley floor. The Needle is a hard, volcanic rock that remained behind when softer rocks around it eroded away. Trails continue into the valley, but this is one of the wettest places on Earth, and hiking here can be dangerous when heavy rains create flash-flood conditions.

🌺 **Kepaniwai Heritage Gardens**
'Iao Valley Road. 📞 (808) 270-7389.
⬜ daily. ♿

🍴 **Hawai'i Nature Center**
'Iao Valley Road. 📞 (808) 244-6500.
⬜ daily. ● Jan 1, Thanksgiving, Dec 25. 🎫 ♿

🏞 **'Iao Valley State Park** End of 'Iao Valley Road, 3 miles (5 km) W of Wailuku. ⬜ daily.

HUMPBACK WHALES

Once the hub of the Pacific whaling trade, Maui County is today an official sanctuary for humpbacks. The whales spend the winter here, bearing their young in the warm, shallow waters. Newborns are 10–12 ft (3–4 m) long and weigh a svelte 1–2 tons. Adults may reach 45 ft (14 m) in length and weigh 30 to 40 tons. In the mating season, males produce a hauntingly beautiful "song" – a series of whistles, groans, creaks, and screeches that are thought to help establish territory or attract females. Although regulations forbid boats from moving too close, these intelligent creatures may approach a boat, as passengers on Maui's whale-watching cruises are often thrilled to discover.

The unforgettable sight of a humpback whale breaching

Wailuku ❺

Maui Co. 🚶 *11,000.* ✈ 🛈 *HVCB, 1727 Wili Pā Loop, (808) 244-3530.*

Tucked into the foothills of the West Maui Mountains, Wailuku was in ancient times a royal center and the scene of many battles. Today it is a county seat and, along with its more commercial neighbor, Kahului, comprises the largest community on Maui. It has an intriguing mix of architectural styles, with several notable buildings clustered along High Street. These include **Wailuku Library**, whose main building was designed by Hawaiian architect C.W. Dickey, the old **Wailuku Courthouse**, and **Kaʻahumanu Church**.

🏛 Bailey House Museum

2375A Main St. 🕻 *(808) 244-3326.* ☐ *Mon–Sat.* ● *Jan 1, Thanksgiving, Dec 25.* 🈂
Headquarters of the Maui Historical Society, this museum is a time capsule of mission life in 19th-century Hawaiʻi. From 1837 to 1849, the building housed the Wailuku Female Seminary, where New England missionary Edward Bailey and his wife, Caroline, taught. When the seminary closed, Bailey bought the house.
Today, the museum has a large collection of Hawaiian artifacts, including *kapa* (tree bark) cloth, stone utensils, carvings, *lei* (neck garlands) made of shells, feathers, and even teeth, and Bailey's paintings of Maui.

Carving at Bailey House Museum

🏛 Alexander and Baldwin Sugar Museum

3957 Hansen Rd, Puʻunēnē, 3 miles (5 km) SE of Wailuku. 🕻 *(808) 871-8058.* ☐ *Mon–Sat.* ● *Jan 1, Thanksgiving, Dec 25.* 🈂 🕎
Across from the Puʻunēnē Sugar Mill, built in 1902 by Alexander and Baldwin *(see p105)* and still functioning, the old supervisor's residence has been transformed into a museum about the industry that dominated Hawaiʻi's economy for more than half a century. It features narrated displays, a model of a cane-crushing mill, artifacts, and archival photos.

Cultivated grounds of the Maui Tropical Plantation and Country Store

🍂 Maui Tropical Plantation and Country Store

1670 Honoapiʻilani Hwy (Hwy 30), 2 miles (3 km) S of Wailuku. 🕻 *(808) 244-7643.* ☐ *daily.* 🈂 *tram only.* 🕎
Some of the tropical plants displayed here, such as banana, coconut, breadfruit, and taro, were brought to the Hawaiian islands by the ancient Polynesians. Others were introduced more recently, such as orchids from Africa, papaya from South America, starfruit from Southeast Asia, and macadamia nuts from Australia. An open-air tram tour circles about half of the plantation's 112 acres, giving information on plant origins and cultivation. Various plants are sold in the shop.

🔺 Halekiʻi-Pihana Heiau State Monument

From Waiehu Beach Rd turn inland into Kūhiō Place, then left into Hea Place. ☐ *daily.*
Important religious and civic affairs were conducted here, at the most significant precontact *heiau* (temples) in the Central Valley. Halekiʻi ("House of Images") was probably a compound for chiefs. During religious ceremonies, *aliʻi* (royalty) would reside in thatched houses whose walls are still visible on the temple's eastern face.
  A reconstructed section of wall is all that remains of Pihana ("Fullness"), a *luakini heiau* (for human sacrifice). Kamehameha I conducted a sacrifice here after his victory in ʻĪao Valley in 1790 *(see p101).*

Kahoʻolawe ❻

Maui Co. No general access.

A dry, uninhabited island less than 11 miles (18 km) long, Kahoʻolawe has at different times been host to exiled convicts, sheep and goats who eroded the soil, and the United States Navy, who used it for target practice. In the 1970s, native Hawaiians began a campaign to regain the island, and in 1994 the US ceded it to the state of Hawaiʻi. Hundreds of ancient sites have been found here, and although access is strictly limited, Hawaiians have begun to reclaim their heritage.

Molokini ❼

Maui Co. 🚢 *from Māʻalaea Harbor.* 🛈 *HVCB, Wailuku, (808) 244-3530.*

An almost completely submerged volcano, Molokini rises just 160 ft (50 m) above the sea. The exposed rim is rocky and barren, but below the surface this marine reserve teems with pelagic (open sea) fish that are comfortable with people, thanks to the many boats that anchor here for snorkeling and scuba diving.

The tiny island of Molokini, a favorite spot for underwater exploration

East Maui's Leeward Coast

FROM THE SMALL harbor town of Māʻalaea to the solidified lava flows of La Pérouse Bay, East Maui's leeward coast is a playground for activities in, on, and near the water. Haleakalā's towering bulk shelters the region from trade winds and rain, while the proximity of neighboring islands and shallow waters create generally mild ocean conditions. All the beaches on Maui are public, and these along East Maui's leeward coast are particularly fine for swimming, snorkeling, scuba diving, and kayaking.

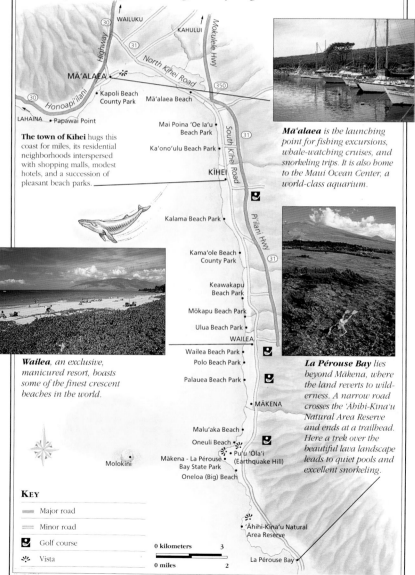

The town of Kihei hugs this coast for miles, its residential neighborhoods interspersed with shopping malls, modest hotels, and a succession of pleasant beach parks.

Māʻalaea is the launching point for fishing excursions, whale-watching cruises, and snorkeling trips. It is also home to the Maui Ocean Center, a world-class aquarium.

Wailea, an exclusive, manicured resort, boasts some of the finest crescent beaches in the world.

La Pérouse Bay lies beyond Mākena, where the land reverts to wilderness. A narrow road crosses the ʻĀhihi-Kīnaʻu Natural Area Reserve and ends at a trailhead. Here a trek over the beautiful lava landscape leads to quiet pools and excellent snorkeling.

WAILUKU
KAHULUI
Highway 30
31
North Kihei Road
350
MĀʻALAEA
Honoapiʻilani 30
Kapoli Beach County Park
Māʻalaea Beach
LAHAINA • Papawai Point
Mai Poina ʻOe Iaʻu Beach Park
Kaʻonoʻulu Beach Park
South Kihei Road 31
KĪHEI
Kalama Beach Park
Kamaʻole Beach County Park
31
Keawakapu Beach Park
Mōkapu Beach Park
Ulua Beach Park
WAILEA
Wailea Beach Park
Polo Beach Park
Palauea Beach Park
MĀKENA
Maluʻaka Beach
Oneuli Beach
Puʻu ʻÕlaʻi (Earthquake Hill)
Mākena - La Pérouse Bay State Park
Oneloa (Big) Beach
Molokini
ʻĀhihi-Kīnaʻu Natural Area Reserve
La Pérouse Bay
Mokulele Hwy
Pʻiilani Hwy

KEY

▬▬	Major road
▬▬	Minor road
🏌	Golf course
☀	Vista

0 kilometers   3

0 miles   2

A Tour of Upcountry Maui ⑧

Sign outside the Tedeschi Winery

Bᴇᴛᴡᴇᴇɴ ᴍᴀᴜɪ's coastal towns and the mountaintop wilderness of Haleakalā, the air is cool, scented by eucalyptus groves that give way to the rolling hills of 'Ulupalakua and Haleakalā ranches. Here, roads wind through long stretches of countryside and often ascend into cloud banks, meanwhile offering stupendous views of Central Maui, the West Maui Mountains, and the surrounding island-dotted seas. While the scenery alone is worth the drive, any bend in the road can reveal a surprising bit of history – a European-style winery, a park paying homage to Chinese immigrants, or a church shaped like the Queen of Portugal's crown.

Baldwin Avenue ⑧
From Makawao to the coast at Pā'ia, this scenic road makes a pleasant drive and is used by bicycle tours descending from Haleakalā National Park (*see pp106–107*).

HĀN

• Pā'ia
(390)

⑧

Hāna Highway

(36)

WAILUKU

Haleakalā Highway

(37)

Pukalani •

ᴏᴏᴋᴀᴘᴜ

①

(37)

Kula Highway

②

③

④

Church of the Holy Ghost ①
Built in the mid-1890s by Maui's Portuguese community, this Catholic church has an octagonal shape based on a crown worn by Queen Isabella of Portugal. Inside, opposite an exquisite wood and gold altar, sits a replica of a crown given to the church by Portugal.

Keōkea ②
Little Keōkea has a colorful church and charming country stores. Beyond it, the road twists through pasture-land offering expansive views of West Maui and the islands of Lāna'i, Moloka'i, Kaho'olawe, and tiny Molokini.

Sun Yat-sen Memorial Park ③
In this now overgrown park, stone lions guard the statue of the revolutionary Dr. Sun Yat-sen, first president of the Republic of China (1911), whose brother was among the many Chinese immigrants who settled in Keōkea. Sun Yat-sen hid his family here during the Chinese Revolution (1911–12).

Tedeschi Winery ④
Set in the heart of 'Ulupalakua Ranch, this winery has picnic tables under grand old trees. The tasting room is in a cottage once used by King Kalākaua.

Rolling hills and open spaces,
typical upcountry landscape

TIPS FOR DRIVERS

Tour length: *48 miles (77 km).*
Stopping-off points: *Plan half
a day to accommodate a tour of
Tedeschi Winery, a walk through
Kula Botanical Gardens, and a
stroll around Makawao. There
are good restaurants in Makawao,
Hāli'imaile (north of Makawao),
and Pukalani (see pp170–72);
alternatively, there are various
good picnic spots along the way.*

Bronco-riding at the Makawao
Rodeo, an annual extravaganza

Hui No'eau Visual Arts Center ⑦

Set in charming grounds, the Arts Center occupies a 1917 mansion designed for the Baldwin family by C.W. Dickey. A gallery and gift shop feature pieces by local artists, and the various art classes welcome visitors on a drop-in basis.

KEY

▨ Tour route

═ Other roads

🌿 Vista

0 kilometers   5

0 miles   3

Small Upcountry Farms ⑥

Proteas and sweet Maui onions are the principal crops here. Several walk-through farms and gardens admit visitors and sell cut proteas.

*HALEAKALĀ
NATIONAL PARK*

Kula Botanical Gardens ⑤

These lush, cool gardens display hydrangeas, proteas, and other delights. There is also a collection of the world's most poisonous plants.

Makawao ⑨

Maui Co. 🏘 *5,500.* ℹ *HVCB, Wailuku, (808) 244-3530.*
🎪 *Makawao Rodeo (Jul 4).*

THE FALSE-FRONT wooden buildings, the annual rodeo, and the cattle ranches that surround the town give Makawao a distinctly Old West flavor. It has been a cowboy town since the mid-19th century, but recently the *paniolo (see p121)* have been making way for an "alternative" culture catering to a growing artistic community.

Trendy art galleries showing local creations cluster around the crossroads at the town center. Glassblowing can be seen throughout the day at **Hot Island Glass** on Baldwin Avenue. Alternatively, you can sit in a café to watch town life go by, or stroll into **Komoda Store and Bakery** (also on Baldwin Avenue) for pastries and old-Maui ambience.

HENRY PERRINE BALDWIN

Maui's verdant "lawn" of cane fields is due largely to the vision of H.P. Baldwin (1842–1911), the son of prominent Lahaina missionaries. In 1876, he and his partner S.T.

"HP" (right) and associate at
Hāmākua Poko Mill in 1898

Alexander trumped their sugar competitors by digging the Hāmākua Ditch, an innovative 17-mile (27-km) irrigation system that carried up to 40 million gallons (150 million liters) of upcountry water a day to their dry fields east of Pa'ia. "HP" went on to develop a highly profitable sugar company and build modern Maui's top business power (Alexander & Baldwin). In effect, he ruled Maui during its transition from monarchy to annexation *(see pp31–2).*

A glassblower demonstrating his
skills at Hot Island Glass

Haleakalā National Park ⑩

THE LAND MASS of East Maui is really the top of an enormous shield volcano that begins more than 3 miles (5 km) below sea level. Haleakalā ("House of the Sun") last spewed molten lava some 200 years ago and is still considered to be active, although not currently erupting. Its summit depression is 7.5 miles (12 km) long and 2.5 miles (4 km) wide, formed by erosional forces acting on volcanic rock. This natural wonder is preserved as part of the national park, which includes Kīpahulu Valley and 'Ohe'o Gulch on the coast *(see p109)*. In under two hours, motorists drive from sea level to the 10,023-ft (3,055-m) summit, rising from one ecosystem to the next while temperature and oxygen level fall dramatically.

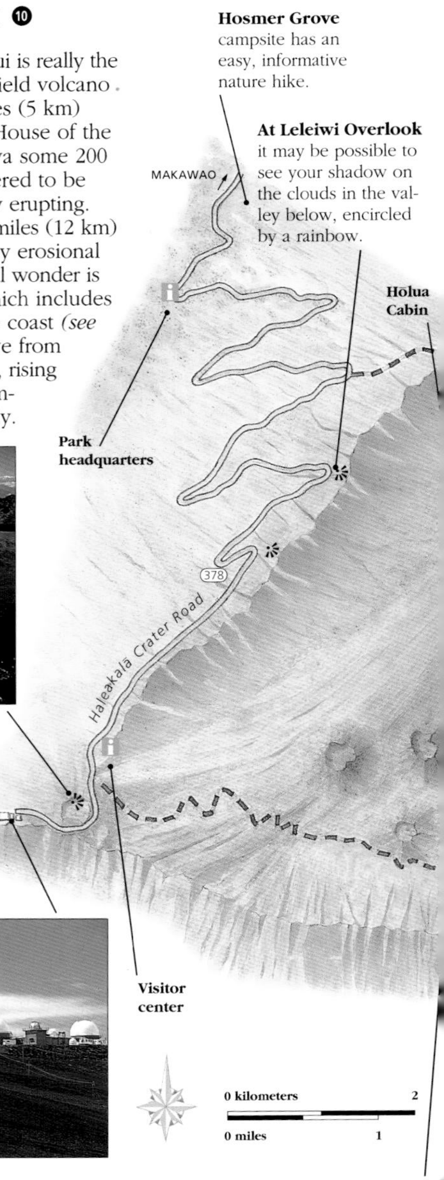

Nēnē living on Haleakalā

Hosmer Grove
campsite has an easy, informative nature hike.

At Leleiwi Overlook
it may be possible to see your shadow on the clouds in the valley below, encircled by a rainbow.

MAKAWAO

Hōlua Cabin

Park headquarters

Haleakalā Crater Road

378

Visitor center

★ **Pu'u 'Ula'ula Summit**
Standing on Pu'u 'Ula'ula (Red Hill) is a breathtaking experience because of both the altitude – this is the highest point on Maui – and the view of the entire volcano. A glassed-in shelter provides relief from the bitterly cold winds.

Science City
This off-limits, science fiction-style cluster of research stations is set in the summit's lunar landscape. Data gathered here help scientists to map the movements of the Earth's crust.

0 kilometers 2
0 miles 1

STAR FEATURES

★ **Pu'u 'Ula'ula Summit**

★ **Silversword Loop**

★ **Sliding Sands Trail**

Summit Depression
At one time, Haleakalā was much higher than it is now. Water eroded the peak, formed the basin you see today, and drained away through two huge gaps in the rim. Later volcanic activity filled in the valley floor and created the cinder cones.

Halemau'u Trail

This trail incorporates switchbacks and sharp drops, plus fine views, often to the ocean. The hike from the trailhead on Haleakalā Crater Road to Hōlua Cabin and back is a good but tough day trip.

★ Silversword Loop

The Haleakalā Silversword, one of the world's rarest plants, thrives here under the most hostile conditions the volcano can offer: hot days, cold nights, and porous ash soil. The soft silvery hairs on its incurved leaves protect the plant from sunlight and draft. It takes up to 50 years to flower, when it raises a spectacular spike of purplish flowers.

Pele's Paint Pot is a surreal landscape of brightly colored ashes.

KO'OLAU GAP

mau'u Trail

Halemau'u Trail

ding Sands Trail

Sliding Sands Trail

KAUPŌ GAP

Kaupō Trail

Palikū Cabin

KEY

=== Minor road

– – Hiking trail

🔆 Vista

★ Sliding Sands Trail

The only way to really appreciate Haleakalā's scale and varied terrain is to descend 3,000 ft (900 m) into the volcano. The 10-mile (16-km) Sliding Sands Trail takes you from the visitor center through scenery that ranges from a barren cinder desert to an alpine shrubland.

Kapalaoa Cabin

One of three primitive cabins in the volcano – so popular that you must enter a lottery to win a reservation.

Windsurfers at Hoʻokipa Beach County Park

Pāʻia ⓫

Maui Co. 👥 *2,100.* ℹ *HVCB, Wailuku, (808) 244-3530.*

TODAY, PĀʻIA IS a bohemian beach town with offbeat stores, an international surfing reputation, and good, rustic restaurants. Back in the 1930s, though, this little sugar town was the island's biggest population center. The sugar mill that supported the town is still in business, located on Highway 390, a mile (1.5 km) south-east of Pāʻia's only traffic light. The **Mantokuji Buddhist Temple**, just east of town beside Hāna Highway (Hwy 36), speaks eloquently of those who came to work the plantations.

ENVIRONS: To the west of town, **HA Baldwin Beach County Park** is good for bodysurfing and popular with locals. Ten minutes east of Pāʻia on Hāna Highway is the world-famous windsurfing spot, **Hoʻokipa Beach County Park**. Unique conditions allow windsurfers to perform spectacular aerial maneuvers over the breaking waves. This is not a swimming beach, but with five surf breaks it is certainly a spectators' spot, especially in the afternoon when the wind blows strongly.

Keʻanae Peninsula and Wailua Valley ⓭

Maui Co. ℹ *HVCB, Wailuku, (808) 244-3530.*

BETWEEN MILE MARKERS 16 and 20, drivers cross an area deemed by the state a "cultural landscape." The star attraction, the ancient *loʻi* or taro ponds, can be seen from overlooks at mile markers 17 and 19. It is said that the Keʻanae Peninsula was just lava rock until the local chief, jealous of his neighbors in Wailua, sent people to bring soil down from the hills.

Wailua's Catholic church, **Our Lady of Fatima**, was built in 1860 with coral washed up by storms. The story goes that the coral was first hoarded by Protestants, but that in punishment for their selfishness, new storms swept the rocks away and then returned them on the Catholic side of the valley.

The Road to Hāna ⓬

Mile marker

NOT UNTIL 1926 did the "Hāna Belt Road" connect the rest of Maui to its rain-forested eastern shores. The drive itself is pure fun, somehow being as suited to Jeeps as to convertible BMWs. The road is notoriously twisting and narrow, and road-handling commands every second of your attention. At the same time, the scenery demands that you stare in awe. This is one of the earth's rainiest coasts; the terrain is sliced with waterfalls and gulches choked with tropical vegetation.

Waikamoi Ridge Trail ①
An unmarked but obvious rest stop between mile markers 9 and 10 offers a picnic area, barbecues, and an easy nature walk. On the trail, labels identify the flora, which includes species of eucalyptus and bamboo.

Honomanū Bay ②
This dramatic bay with its rocky, black-sand beach is a popular surfing spot, but swimming in the turbulent waters can be risky.

KEY

| Tour route |
| Other road |
| Vista |

Keʻanae Arboretum ③
These public gardens just before mile marker 17 provide a close-up look at working taro fields as well as a pleasant trail amid a variety of tropical flora from around the world.

Hāna

Maui Co. ⚑ 700. ✈ ℹ HVCB,
Wailuku, (808) 244-3530. ⛵ East
Maui Taro Festival (Mar/Apr).

OFTEN CALLED Hawai'i's most
Hawaiian town, Hāna
continues to lag lazily behind
the tempo of modernity, and
everyone here seems to think
that this is just fine. Its perfect
round bay and dreamy climate
have made Hāna a prized
settlement since time
immemorial. Kings of Maui
and Hawai'i Island fought to
possess the district, using
Ka'uiki Head, the large cinder
cone on the right flank of the
bay, as a natural fortification.
A cave at the base of the cone
was the birthplace of Queen
Ka'ahumanu (see p30).

Tiny **Hāna Cultural Center**
presents a *kauhale* (residential
compound) in the precontact
style once unique to this area.
Exhibited artifacts give a sense
of local history. **Wānanalua**

TARO IN HAWAI'I

The purplish-gray root (corm) of
Colocasia esculenta was the staff
of life in ancient Hawai'i. It was
believed that taro and humans
had the same parents and that the
gods had ordered the plant to care
for humans, its siblings. This it did
by providing nutrition, mostly in
the form of *poi*, a pounded paste.
It also acted as a symbol of the
ideal *'ohana* (family): the plant
grows in clumps of *'ohā* (stems),
with the younger stems, like children, staying near the older core.

**The taro plant, a traditional
source of food in Hawai'i**

Church, beside Hāna Highway
(Hwy 360), was constructed
from blocks of coral in 1838.
Missionaries built it on top of
an existing *heiau* (temple),
thus symbolizing the triumph
of Christianity over paganism.

Sugar cultivation took root
in Hāna in the 1860s and con-
tinued until 1944, when San
Francisco capitalist Paul Fagan
closed the mill and converted

the area to cattle. Three years
later he built Hotel Hāna-Maui
on a plot once used by early
missionaries. Today, Fagan's
influence is still felt, and his
large memorial cross looms
on the hillside above the bay.

🏛 **Hāna Cultural Center**
Uakea Road. 📞 (808) 248-8622.
◯ daily. ● Jan 1, Thanksgiving,
Dec 25. 🎫 ♿

Hāna Gardenland ④
now closed for
renovation, these
botanical gardens have
orchids, anthuriums, and
other exotic plants.
Nearby is the beautifully
preserved Pi'ilanihale
Heiau, Hawai'i's largest
ancient temple.

Wai'ānapanapa State Park ⑤
Plan a stop here to explore sea
caves, rocky cliffs, the black-
sand beach, and the ancient
"King's Trail," which follows
the spectacular coastline
from here to Hāna.

Ka Iwi o Pele ⑥
This large cinder cone beyond mile marker 51 is the site
of mythical struggles involving Pele, the goddess of
volcanoes. Nearby, the excellent Kōkī and Hāmoa
beaches face the waters where Maui the demigod
is said to have fished the islands out of the sea.

'Ohe'o Gulch ⑦
The pools in this lovely
stream are perfect for
swimming, but beware
of sudden flooding.
A 2-mile (3-km) trail
leads through a forest
to Waimoku Falls, one of
Maui's highest waterfalls.

**Palapala Ho'omau
Congregational Church** ⑧
The famous US aviator, Charles
Lindbergh, is buried at this beauti-
fully preserved 1864 church, along
with fellow flyer Sam Pryor.

Hāna ●

Pi'ilani Highway

TIPS FOR DRIVERS

Tour length: 70 miles (110 km)
round trip.
Stopping-off points: Start early,
allowing a day for the drive. There
are no gas stations from Pā'ia to
Hāna, where most facilities close
at dusk. Hāna has a few restaurants (see p170) and hotels (see
p156); there are camping facilities
at Wai'ānapanapa State Park
(permit required) and 'Ohe'o Gulch
(very basic). For tours of Pi'ilanihale
Heiau, phone (808) 248-8912.

HAWAI'I ISLAND

To UNDERSTAND FULLY THE CULTURE *and spirit of the Hawaiian islands, travelers must venture to the island of Hawai'i itself– commonly called "the Big Island." This is the site of some of the earliest* Polynesian settlements as well as the last heiau *(temple) to be built. Here, Captain Cook met his demise, Kamehameha the Great rose to power, and the first Christian missionaries set foot on Hawaiian soil.*

Being a relatively young island (a million years old, compared with Kaua'i's five million) not yet ringed with sandy beaches, Hawai'i has wisely placed its tourist-industry focus on the preservation of cultural sites. An amazing number of these are accessible to the traveler.

Spreading over 4,035 sq miles (10,450 sq km), Hawai'i Island is more than twice the size of all the other islands combined. Its bulk includes the earth's most massive mountain, Mauna Loa, which rises over 30,000 feet (9,150 m) from its base on the sea floor and is still growing. It also includes the state's tallest peak, the often snow-capped Mauna Kea, and three other mountains: Hualālai, which blocks the moist trade winds from dry north Kona; Kohala, the soft hump of the Waimea area's northern ranch lands; and Kīlauea, the most active volcano on earth. A new mountain called Lō'ihi, currently forming 20 miles (32 km) off the southeast coast, should emerge from the sea thousands of years from now. Hawai'i Island's great bulk offers travelers the chance to see a variety of ecosystems, from alpine heights to barren desert.

Today, with only ten percent of the state's population, the Big Island is one of Hawai'i's sleepiest, most scattered communities. Hilo, its main town, was pushed into the economic background by devastating tsunamis in 1946 and 1960, and in the 1990s the island's sugar industry collapsed. Now tourism plays a big role, especially in sunny Kona. Visitors will find a land of open space, quiet towns, and a population that is friendly in the traditional Hawaiian way.

Paniolo (Hawaiian cowboys) at the Parker Ranch in the Waimea area

◁ **A cluster of astronomical domes on Mauna Kea, Hawai'i Island's tallest mountain**

Exploring Hawai'i Island

BOTH EAST AND WEST Hawai'i Island provide good bases for touring. Hilo is well situated for excursions to the Hāmākua Coast, Mauna Kea, the Puna district, and Hawai'i Volcanoes National Park – a highlight on any visitor's itinerary, with Kīlauea Caldera and its active lava rifts. Hilo itself is charming but very rainy, averaging 130 in (330 cm) per year. Travelers who prefer their days bone dry head for Kailua-Kona on the island's burgeoning west side. From here there is access to the South Kohala resorts to the north, the Parker Ranch country of Waimea, Kona coffee country to the south, and many well-preserved ancient sites, including Pu'uhonua O Hōnaunau.

Traditional canoe at Pu'uhonua O Hōnaunau National Historical Park

Top Recreational Areas

The places shown here have been selected for their recreational activities. Conditions, especially those of the ocean, vary depending on the weather and the time of year, so exercise caution and, if in doubt, stay out of the water or seek local advice.

	Swimming	Snorkeling	Diving	Body-Surfing	Windsurfing	Hiking	Horseback Riding	Golf
Ahalanui Beach Park	●							
'Anaeho'omalu Bay	●	■	●	■	●			
Hāpuna Bay	●	■	●	■				■
Hawai'i Volcanoes National Park						■		
Hilo	●	■	●				●	■
Honoka'a								■
Ho'okena	●	■						
Ka Lae						■		
Kahalu'u Beach County Park	●	■	●					
Kailua-Kona	●	■	●	■			●	■
Kalōpā State Recreation Area						■		
Kapa'au						■		
Kawaihae Harbor					●			
Kealakekua Bay	●	■	●				●	
Kekaha Kai State Park	●	■	●	■				
Kolekole Beach County Park	●							
Lapakahi State Historical Park	●	■	●					
Mauna Kea						■	●	
Mauna Lani	●	■		■			●	■
Pāhala								■
Pepe'ekeo Scenic Drive						■		
Puakō		■						
Punalu'u Beach County Park	●	■	●					
Pu'uhonua O Hōnaunau	●	■	●					
Spencer Beach County Park	●	■	●	■				
Volcano Village								■
Waikoloa							●	■
Waimea							●	
Waipi'o Valley	●					■	●	

HĀWĪ **11**
KAPA'AU
LAPAKAHI STATE
HISTORICAL PARK **10**
KOHALA MOUNTAIN ROAD **1**
KAWAIHAE HARBOR
PU'UKOHOLĀ HEIAU
NATIONAL HISTORIC SITE **9**
SPENCER BEACH COUNTY PARK
HĀPUNA BAY **8**
PU
MAUNA LANI **7**
WAIKOLOA COAST **6**
WAIKOL
'ANAEHO'OMALU BAY

19

190

MAKALAWENA

KEKAHA KAI **5**
STATE PARK

NORT
KON

KAILUA-KONA **1**

KAHALU'U BEACH
COUNTY PARK

KEALAKEKUA BAY **2**

PU'UHONUA
O HŌNAUNAU
NATIONAL
HISTORICAL
PARK

HO'OKEN **3**

PU'UHONUA
O HŌNAUNAU **4**

11

SOU
KO

270

See Also

KEY

▭	Major road
▭	Minor road
▭	Dirt or four-wheel-drive road
▭	Scenic route
▭	River or stream
☀	Vista

SIGHTS AT A GLANCE

'Akaka Falls State Park ⑲
Hāmākua Coast ⑱
Hāpuna Bay ⑧
Hawai'i Volcanoes National Park pp128–9 ㉘
Hāwī ⑪
Hilo pp124–5 ㉑
Ho'okena ③
Ka Lae ㉗
Kailua-Kona ①
Kapa'au ⑫
Kapoho ㉓
Ka'ū District ㉖

Kealakekua Bay ②
Kekaha Kai State Park ⑤
Kohala Mountain Road ⑬
Lapakahi State Historical Park ⑩
Mauna Kea ⑰
Mauna Lani ⑦
Pāhoa ㉒
Pepe'ekeo Scenic Drive ⑳
Puna Lava Flows ㉔
Pu'uhonua O Hōnaunau National Historical Park pp116–17 ④
Pu'ukoholā Heiau National Historic Site ⑨
Saddle Road ⑯
Volcano Village ㉕
Waikoloa Coast ⑥
Waimea ⑭
Waipi'o Valley ⑮

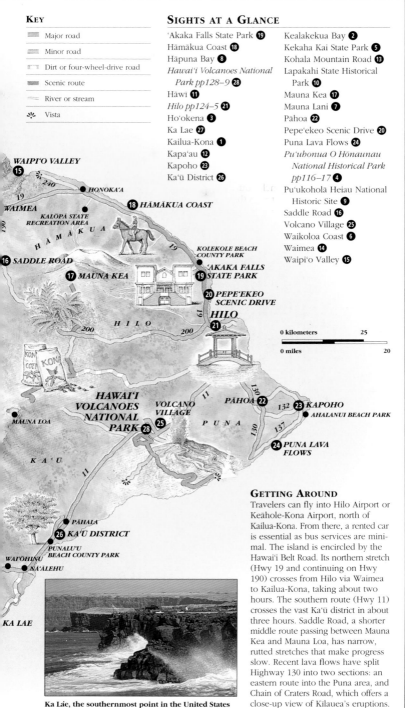

WAIPI'O VALLEY ⑮
HONOKA'A
WAIMEA
KALŌPĀ STATE RECREATION AREA
HĀMĀKUA
⑯ **SADDLE ROAD**
⑱ **HĀMĀKUA COAST**
KOLEKOLE BEACH COUNTY PARK
'AKAKA FALLS STATE PARK ⑲
⑰ **MAUNA KEA**
PEPE'EKEO SCENIC DRIVE ⑳
HILO
⑳ ㉑
HILO
KONA COFFEE
HAWAI'I VOLCANOES NATIONAL PARK ㉘
VOLCANO VILLAGE ㉕
PĀHOA ㉒
㉓ **KAPOHO**
AHALANUI BEACH PARK
MAUNA LOA
PUNA
KA'U
㉔ **PUNA LAVA FLOWS**

0 kilometers   25
0 miles   20

PĀHALA
㉖ **KA'Ū DISTRICT**
PUNALU'U BEACH COUNTY PARK
WAI'ŌHINU
NĀ'ĀLEHU

KA LAE

Ka Lae, the southernmost point in the United States

GETTING AROUND

Travelers can fly into Hilo Airport or Keāhole-Kona Airport, north of Kailua-Kona. From there, a rented car is essential as bus services are minimal. The island is encircled by the Hawai'i Belt Road. Its northern stretch (Hwy 19 and continuing on Hwy 190) crosses from Hilo via Waimea to Kailua-Kona, taking about two hours. The southern route (Hwy 11) crosses the vast Ka'ū district in about three hours. Saddle Road, a shorter middle route passing between Mauna Kea and Mauna Loa, has narrow, rutted stretches that make progress slow. Recent lava flows have split Highway 130 into two sections: an eastern route into the Puna area, and Chain of Craters Road, which offers a close-up view of Kīlauea's eruptions.

The colorful interior of St. Benedict's Painted Church in Hōnaunau

Kailua-Kona ❶

Hawaiʻi Co. 🏹 *9,500.* ⛴ 🏢
🚻 *Big Island VB, West Hawaiʻi (808)
886-1655.* 🏃 *Ironman Triathlon
(Oct: Sat closest to full moon).*

KAILUA-KONA'S tourist strip
along oceanfront Aliʻi
Drive does little to obscure
several vivid reminders of
Hawaiian history. Built out
into Kailua Bay is **Ahuʻena
Heiau**, an ancient temple
dedicated to the god Lono. It
was restored by Kamehameha
the Great, whose residence
was next to the *heiau* (temple).
Adjoining it is **King Kamehameha's Kona Beach Hotel** –
the lobby has numerous
Hawaiian artifacts: tools, handicrafts, and a feather cape.
   In 1820, the first party of
missionaries landed at Kailua-
Kona. They built the original
Mokuʻaikaua Church on Aliʻi
Drive. The present lofty, gran-
ite church dates from 1837.
A modest museum at the rear
offers a scale model of the
missionaries' brig, *Thaddeus.*
Across the street, **Huliheʻe
Palace** was built at the same
time of similar rough-stone
construction. In 1885, King
Kalākaua plastered and beauti-
fied the little building, which
now serves as a permanent
museum. It provides a candid
look at the lifestyle of the
monarchy in its heyday.
   Kailua-Kona, so named to
distinguish it from Kailua on
Oʻahu, is synonymous with
sportfishing. Charter boats
offer year-round opportunities
to fish for marlin and other
ocean giants. In October the
town is overrun by endurance
athletes who compete in the
grueling Ironman Triathlon.
The sunny coastline is dotted
with small beaches good for
swimming, snorkeling, and
diving. **Kahaluʻu Beach**, 4.5
miles (7 km) south of Kailua,
provides snorkelers with the
island's finest natural aquarium.

🏛 **Mokuʻaikaua Church**
75-5713 Aliʻi Drive. 📞 *(808) 329-
0655.* ⭕ *daily.* ♿
🚻 **Huliheʻe Palace**
75-5718 Aliʻi Drive. 📞 *(808) 329-
1877.* ⭕ *daily.* ● *public hols.* 📷

Kealakekua Bay ❷

Hawaiʻi Co. Nāpōʻopoʻo Road, 4 miles
(6 km) S of Captain Cook. 🚌 *Captain
Cook.* 🚻 *Big Island VB, West
Hawaiʻi, (808) 886-1655.*

IN 1778, CAPTAIN COOK sailed
into this deep, protected
bay, "discovering" Hawaiʻi. He
was honored as the returning
Hawaiian god Lono, but less
than a month later was killed
here *(see p29)*. **Hikiau Heiau**,
where Cook was honored, is
at the road's end. A monument marks where he died.
   The bay, a State Marine Life
Preserve with an abundance
of fish, sea turtles, and spinner
dolphins, offers excellent diving, snorkeling, and kayaking.

ENVIRONS: The bay sits at the
heart of Kona coffee country,
with its rustic farms and mills.
In the town of **Kealakekua**,
the **Kona Historical Society**
gives interpretive tours of its
headquarters in the 1870s-vin-
tage **Greenwell Store** and of
neighboring **Uchida Farm**, a
restored 1930s coffee farm.
The entire district, from the
artists' colony of Hōlualoa in
the north to Hōnaunau in the
south, invites exploration. In
Hōnaunau, **St. Benedict's
Painted Church** is brightly
illuminated with biblical scenes
executed by a Belgian priest
in the early 20th century.

🚻 **Kona Historical Society**
81-6551 Māmalahoa Hwy (Hwy 11).
📞 *(808) 323-2005.* ⭕ *Mon–Fri.*
● *public hols.* **Donation** ♿
🏛 **St. Benedict's
Painted Church**
Painted Church Road, off Hwy 160
near mile marker 1. 📞 *(808) 328-
2227.* ⭕ *daily.* ♿

Hoʻokena ❸

Hawaiʻi Co. 🚻 *Big Island VB, West
Hawaiʻi, (808) 886-1655.*

IN 1889, WHEN AUTHOR Robert
Louis Stevenson asked to
see a classic Hawaiian village,
King Kalākaua sent him to
Hoʻokena. In those days, the
town had churches, a school,
a courthouse, and a pier from
which cattle were shipped to
market in Honolulu. Today,
besides weather-beaten houses
and beach shacks, only lava
walls and the ruined pier
survive as reminders.
   The center of life, then as
now, is beautiful **Kauhakō
Bay** with its gray-sand beach
backed dramatically by long
cliffs. The water teems with
sea life, and there is excellent
snorkeling and diving. The
surf can be rough, and foot
protection is recommended.

Hoʻokena's Kauhakō Bay, lined
with a beach of gray sand

Kona Coffee

FOR OVER a century the upward slopes of the Kona district have been home to the United States' only coffee-growing region. The massive bulk of Mauna Loa, an enormous shield volcano *(see p122)*, creates a localized weather pattern that favors the crop. Sunny mornings are followed by cloudy, humid afternoons that often drench the rich, volcanic soil with rain. Over 500 independent small farms cultivate this world-class, gourmet coffee, producing a crop of about 2 million pounds (900,000 kg) a year. Roadsides are dotted with cafés, mills, and farms, and the Hawai'i Visitors and Convention Bureau in Kailua-Kona offers a driving map of the area. Every year, in the second week of November, the district celebrates its coffee with the Kona Coffee Cultural Festival.

HOW COFFEE IS HARVESTED

Coffee beans grown in the rich soil of the Kona district are picked by hand, ensuring only the best beans go into making coffee.

"Kona snow" is the local term for the white, fragrant spring flowers. The first Coffea arabica plants were introduced to the area in 1828 by the American missionary Samuel Ruggles.

Coffee cherries ripen in waves, from August until March, so they must be laboriously hand-harvested. The cherries start out green in color and turn red as they ripen.

A kuriba (pulping mill) separates the flesh of the cherry from its hard, parchment-covered bean. After soaking and washing, beans in the "wet parchment" stage are left to dry in the sun.

A hoshidana is a drying deck with a wheeled cover that is rolled over the beans whenever the mountain rains move in. Beans are raked three or four times a day for up to two weeks.

Milling removes two outer layers from the hard beans – the tough parchment and the filmy "silver skin." Raw beans, called green coffee, are then graded and ready for roasting.

IMMIGRANT WORKERS

The success of Kona's coffee owes as much to its people as to its weather. In the late 19th century, after decades of control by the large plantations, the crop began to be cultivated tenaciously on small-scale family farms. Many of these farmers were Japanese immigrants who fled slavelike conditions on the plantations to work their own farms. Today, their descendents continue the coffee tradition.

Kona coffee beans are known throughout the gourmet coffee world for their rich, highly aromatic flavor. The roasting process brings out the flavor: beans that are roasted longer and at higher temperatures are darker with a more intense taste. Additional flavorings, such as chocolate or macadamia nuts, may be added immediately after roasting.

Roasted coffee beans

Pu'uhonua O Hōnaunau National Historical Park ❹

From the 11th century on, social interactions were regulated by the *kapu* (taboo) system *(see p28)*. Violent death was the consequence of infractions, which ranged from stepping on a chief's shadow to women eating bananas. Lawbreakers could escape punishment, however, by reaching a *pu'uhonua* (place of refuge). The greatest of these was at Hōnaunau, a 6-acre temple compound dating from the 16th century that offered absolution to all who managed to run or swim past the chief's warriors. The sanctuary was stripped of power in 1819, after the fall of the *kapu* system. Partially restored, it now provides a glimpse into precontact Hawai'i.

Heleipālala Fish Ponds
These two ponds were stocked with fish reserved for the royal table.

Hālau
Thatched A-frame structures were used for storage and as work sheds.

Worker in a field

Animals in enclosure

Keone'ele Cove was the royal canoe landing, making it *kapu* to all commoners. Today it is one of the island's best snorkeling spots.

Papamū
This carved stone board was used to play kōnane, *a Hawaiian game similar to checkers.*

Outrigger canoes

★ **Hale O Keawe Heiau**
The pu'uhonua's spiritual power resided in this temple compound, built in 1650. Now reconstructed, the heiau *(temple) once held the bones and therefore the* mana *(sacred power) of great chiefs.*

STAR FEATURES

★ **Hale O Keawe Heiau**

★ **The Great Wall**

Wooden Ki'i
These carved images of gods outside Hale O Keawe Heiau are copies based on drawings and descriptions of the originals.

ʻĀleʻaleʻa Heiau predates the 16th-century Great Wall. It served as the focus of spiritual power until the construction of Hale O Keawe.

A reconstructed sailing canoe with passengers

VISITORS' CHECKLIST

Hawaiʻi Co. Hwy 160, off Hawaiʻi Belt Rd (Hwy 11). 📞 *(808) 328-2326.* 🕐 *7:30am–8pm Mon–Thu, 7:30am–11pm Fri–Sun.* ♿ **Visitor Center** 🕐 *7:30am–5:30pm. Daily orientation talks.*

★ **The Great Wall**
This superb example of dry-stone wall, built around 1550, separated the puʻuhonua *from the palace area inland. It is 10 ft (3 m) high and 17 ft (5 m) wide.*

The old *heiau* may have been built by the Tahitian priest Pāʻao in the 13th century *(see p28).* It is now in ruins, destroyed by either tsunamis or large storm waves.

0 meters	50
0 yards	50

The Keōua Stone was a favorite resting spot of Keōua, a high chief of Kona district.

A RECONSTRUCTION

This is an artist's impression of the *puʻuhonua* when the ruling chief of the district lived here along with his court and attendants. Some elements have been reconstructed by the National Park Service, and visitors may see artisans at work.

Exposed Peninsula of Black Lava
The peninsula's jagged shoreline made it diffi-cult for kapu-*breakers to approach from the sea.*

Green sea turtle swimming in the waters off the beach at Makalawena

Kekaha Kai State Park ❺

Hawai'i Co. Off Queen Ka'ahumanu Highway (Hwy 19), 9 miles (14 km) N of Kailua-Kona. 📞 Division of State Parks, (808) 974-6200. ⏲ Thu–Tue.

NORTH OF KAILUA, the road runs through barren lava fields, the aftermath of an 1801 eruption of Mount Hualalai. In places, road and landscape are distinguishable only by their relative smoothness. The state park, with its picnic shelters and sinuous beach of salt-and-pepper sand, is an oasis in this distorted wasteland. It is an excellent spot for swimming, snorkeling, diving, and, when the conditions are right, surfing.

Just before the park entrance, a dirt road on the right leads 1.5 miles (2.5 km) to isolated **Makalawena**, a beautiful beach with dunes and coves for snorkeling. Turtles, dolphins, and seals frequent these waters, as well as whales.

Waikoloa Coast ❻

Hawai'i Co. W of Queen Ka'ahumanu Highway (Hwy 19), 24 miles (39 km) N of Kailua-Kona. 🛈 Big Island VB, West Hawai'i, (808) 886-1655.

WAIKOLOA BEACH resort has built itself around one of this coast's best family recreational areas, coconut-rimmed **'Anaeho'omalu Bay**. The beach at "A-Bay" is calm, with a gradual, sandy bottom. Watersports equipment, including kayaks and sailboats, can be rented from the beach hut, and lessons in windsurfing and scuba diving are offered. Boat dives and cruises are also available.

From the beach, coastal trails lead to fish ponds, caves, and natural pools in which salt and fresh water mix to form unique ecosystems.

A short walk north of the beach is **Hilton Waikoloa Village** (see p160), a 62-acre fantasy resort built in 1988 at a cost of $360 million. Silent monorails and canal boats provide transportation around the resort. Visitors can view the impressive art collection and explore the artificial beach, lagoon, and waterfall. You can even stop for lunch by the dolphin pool, where both guests and visitors can swim with the resort's trained dolphins.

Hilton Waikoloa Village
425 Waikoloa Beach Drive. 📞 (808) 886-1234. ⏲ daily. &

Mauna Lani ❼

Hawai'i Co. Off Queen Ka'ahumanu Highway (Hwy 19), 25 miles (40 km) N of Kailua-Kona. 🛈 (808) 885-6677.

THE VAST RESORT at Mauna Lani includes two luxury hotels, a couple of award-winning golf courses, several tennis courts, and small, white-sand beaches. It also encloses sites of cultural importance. **Kalāhuipua'a Trail** – a 20-minute hike, usually through blazing sunshine – winds past petroglyphs, lava tubes, and ancient habitation sites, ending at several ancient fish ponds. A coastal trail from here leads about a mile (1.5 km) south to **Honoka'ope Bay**, a sheltered spot for swimming and snorkeling.

Petroglyph figure

At the northern end of the resort, a somewhat shorter hike leads to the **Puakō Petroglyphs**, one of the largest concentrations of these mysterious carvings left in Hawai'i. The trail ends up at a large expanse of crusty red lava plates engraved with more than 3,000 symbols that were carved between AD 1000 and 1800. The hike is shady. Wear sturdy shoes.

Hāpuna Bay ❽

Hawai'i Co. Off Queen Ka'ahumanu Highway (Hwy 19), 7 miles (11 km) N of Waikoloa Coast.

AN EXPANSE OF white sand, both broad and deep, makes Hāpuna Bay the most popular beach on Hawai'i Island. With its clean, sandy bottom, the bay offers excellent swimming, snorkeling, and diving conditions. When the

Vacationers enjoying the lagoon at Hilton Waikoloa Village

Traditional ceremony at Pu'ukoholā Heiau National Historic Site

waves are active, surfers and body-boarders flock here, and it is generally a good spot for beginners to acquire some wave-riding skills. The water should be approached with caution, however; strong currents have resulted in several drownings. On the beach, **Hāpuna Harry's** rents snorkel sets and boogie boards, and posts life guards throughout the day. **Hāpuna Beach State Recreation Area**, which surrounds the beach, has cabins for overnight stays, as well as picnic tables and a snack bar.

About 1 mile (1.5 km) north of the bay, accessed via the Mauna Kea Beach Hotel, is the lovely, crescent-shaped **Kauna'oa Beach**, with fine conditions for swimming and snorkeling most of the year.

☆ Hāpuna Beach State Recreation Area
Around Hāpuna Beach. 🔾 *Division of State Parks, (808) 974-6200.* ⏱ *daily.*

Pu'ukoholā Heiau National Historic Site ⑨

Hawai'i Co. Off Akoni Pule Hwy (Hwy 270), 1 mile (1.5 km) S of Kawaihae. 🔾 *(808) 882-7218.* ⏱ *daily.* 🔾 *visitor center only.*

I N 1790, KAMEHAMEHA I had reached an impasse in his drive to unify the island chain. On the advice of an oracle, he undertook the construction of **Pu'ukoholā Heiau**, dedicated to Kūkā'ilimoku, his family war god, and destined to become the last such temple ever built. For the dedication ceremonies, the crafty king invited his rival Keoua, the chief of Ka'ū. As Keoua stepped out of his canoe, he was slaughtered and carried to the new altar to serve as its first sacrifice.

Today, the massive monument stands undamaged on a hilltop overlooking Kawaihae

Bay. Below it are the ruins of **Mailekini Heiau**, built for Kamehameha's ancestors. A third *heiau*, **Haleokapuni**, dedicated to shark gods, is believed to lie submerged in the waters below. Sacrifices left here would soon have become shark fodder. An easy trail runs down past the first two *heiau* from the visitor center.

Immediately south of the *heiau* is **Spencer Beach County Park**, a popular spot for camping, snorkeling, and diving. The clean white beach and calm waters make it an excellent area for children.

Lapakahi State Historical Park ⑩

Hawai'i Co. Off Akoni Pule Hwy (Hwy 270), 12 miles (19 km) N of Kawaihae. 🔾 *(808) 974-6200.* ⏱ *daily.* ⬤ *public hols.*

T HE RUINS of this large settlement provide a glimpse into the daily life of an old Hawaiian fishing village. Established in the 14th century, the village was inhabited for 500 years – until a falling water table and changing economic conditions caused the natives to abandon their homes.

The thatched walls and roofs are gone, but the lava foundations, *hālau* (canoe sheds), *kū'ula ko'a* (fishing shrines), and a *kōnane* stone board-game remain undamaged. The surrounding waters are a marine conservation area.

The popular white-sand beach at Hāpuna Bay, on Hawai'i Island's south Kohala Coast

Kapa‘au's Tong Wo Society building, part of Hawai‘i's immigrant heritage

Hāwī ⓫

Hawai‘i Co. 🏠 950. 🛈 Big Island VB,
West Hawai‘i, (808) 886-1655.

THE TOWN OF HĀWĪ had its
heyday during the era of
"King Cane," when five sugar
plantations brought prosperity
to Kohala, the island's northern
district. After the mills closed
in 1975, Hāwī was
left to dwindle to
its present size.
These days it is a
pleasant town to
wander through,
with its wooden
sidewalks and
brightly painted
storefronts. Hāwī's
relaxed charm and
grassy, windswept
surroundings now
attract a new breed of citizen –
the town has a health-food
store and a few trendy eateries.

A traditional *hale* (grass
hut) at Mo‘okini Heiau

ENVIRONS: Reached by a rutted dirt road, lichen-covered
Mo‘okini Heiau is one of the
oldest temples on the islands,
possibly dating from the 5th
century AD. In 1250 it was rededicated as a *luakini heiau*
(for human sacrifice). Today
this massive *heiau* is a remote
and peaceful ruin.

⋔ **Mo‘okini Heiau**
Off Akoni Pule Highway (Hwy 270) at
mile marker 20, then left at airfield.

Kapa‘au ⓬

Hawai‘i Co. 🏠 1,100. 🛈 Big Island
VB, West Hawai‘i, (808) 886-1655.

THE SMALL TOWN of Kapa‘au
contains the original statue
of Kamehameha the Great, a
much-photographed replica
of which stands in front of

Ali‘iōlani Hale in Honolulu *(see
p42)*. A large boulder labeled
Kamehameha Rock can be
found on the roadside heading
east of town. Legend has it that
the big chief once carried it to
prove his strength; whole road
crews have failed to move it
since! Nearby, the intricately
painted **Tong Wo Society**
building is the last of its kind
on Hawai‘i Island.
Immigrant Chinese
communities once
relied on clubs
like this to provide
social cohesion.

ENVIRONS: At the
end of Highway
270, a lookout
focuses the gaze
on idyllic **Pololū
Valley**. Isolated
by lush canyon walls, the
valley's wide floor meets the
ocean at a black-sand beach.
It is a 20-minute walk down
the steep trail to the beach.

Kohala Mountain Road ⓭

Hawai‘i Co. Highway 250.

THE 20-MILE (32-KM) drive
from Hāwī to Waimea
follows the western ridge of
low, worn Kohala Mountain.
This is ranch land, and the
scenic drive gives views of

elegant ranch houses, cattle
and horses grazing in deep
grass, and occasional panoramas of the north Kohala Coast.
   Parker Ranch is the largest
operation in this area, and, in
fact, the largest privately
owned cattle ranch in the
United States. Its origins date
right back to the early years
of Western discovery and a
young American adventurer
named John Palmer Parker.
In 1809, Parker befriended
Kamehameha I and eventu-
ally married one of the king's
granddaughters. He established
a small dynasty that shaped the
history of the Kohala district.
Today, the ranch covers a
tenth of the island and supports 50,000 head of cattle.

Waimea ⓮

Hawai‘i Co. 🏠 6,000. ✈ 🏠
🛈 BIVB, West Hawai‘i, (808) 886-
1655. 🤠 Parker Ranch Rodeo (Jul 4).

WAIMEA'S SETTING amid
sprawling pasture land
at a cool elevation of 2,700 ft
(820 m) is a startling contrast to
Hilo's rain forest and the Kona
Coast's lava flats. By Hawai‘i
Island standards, Waimea is a
large, modern town. The best
evidence of this is the **Keck
Observatory Center**, on the
edge of town, where visitors
are given a video introduction
to the world's most powerful
telescopes *(see p123)*.
   In the middle of town, the
Parker Ranch Visitor Center
offers a short video and an elo-
quent collection of artifacts
that tells the history of *paniolo*
(cowboy) culture and provides
an insight into the tempestuous
and influential Parker family.
   The **Historic Parker Ranch
Homes** include Puopelu, a
ranch house with a Regency
interior and a respectable collection of European art,

The façade of Puopelu, one of the Historic Parker Ranch Homes

PANIOLO CULTURE

When George Vancouver brought eight cattle to Hawai'i Island in 1794, the sight of the huge beasts sent the natives running in terror. Fifty years later, herds of wild cattle had become such a scourge that Kamehameha III hired three Mexican *vaqueros* (cowboys) to control them. The *vaqueros* introduced their own customs, which evolved into the tradition of the *paniolo* (from *español*). They also brought the guitar and the funda-

A paniolo astride his horse

mental sound of popular Hawaiian music. There are now ranches all over the state. Hawai'i Island has annual rodeos at Honoka'a, Waimea, Na'ālehu, and Waikoloa. Maui's *paniolo* host a parade and rodeo on July 4 in Makawao *(see p105)*.

and Mānā Hale, an 1840s New England-style saltbox with a rich *koa*-wood interior. The latter, the original family home, contains a display of Parker family photographs.

🏛 Keck Observatory Center

65-1120 Māmalahoa Hwy (Hwy 19).
📞 *(808) 885-7887.* ⬜ *Mon–Fri.*
⬤ *public hols.* ♿

🏛 Parker Ranch Visitor Center

Parker Ranch Shopping Center, Māmalahoa Hwy (Hwy 19). 📞 *(808) 885-7655.* ⬜ *daily.* ⬤ *public hols.*
🎥 ♿

🎪 Historic Parker Ranch Homes

Off Māmalahoa Hwy (Hwy 190). 📞 *(808) 885-5433.* ⬜ *daily.* ⬤ *public hols.* 🎥 ♿ *(partial access only.)*

Waipi'o Valley ⑮

Hawai'i Co. ℹ *Big Island VB, West Hawai'i, (808) 886-1655.*

IF ANY PARTICULAR SPOT could be designated the spiritual heartland of ancient Hawai'i, it would have to be Waipi'o, or the "Valley of the Kings." The largest of seven enormous amphitheater valleys that punctuate this windward stretch of coast, Waipi'o measures 1 mile (1.5 km) wide at the sea and extends nearly 6 miles (10 km) inland. Its steep walls, laced with waterfalls, including the stupendous Hi'ilawe cascade, rise as high as 2,000 ft (600 m). Waipi'o Stream slices the lush valley floor, courses through

fertile taro fields, and empties into the rough sea across a wide black-sand beach.

The road from the stunning lookout at the end of Highway 240 down to the valley floor is only a mile (1.5 km) long, but its steepness limits access to four-wheel-drive vehicles; on foot the trip takes about 30 minutes. Shuttle tours, even one in a mule-drawn surrey, are available at the tiny village of Kukuihaele, and nearby stables offer horseback trips.

In precontact days, Waipi'o supported a population of over 10,000. A sacred place, the valley contained a number of important *beiau*, including a *pu'uhonua* (place of refuge) equal to the one at Hōnaunau *(see pp116–17)*. The valley was Kamehameha the Great's boyhood playground. It was here that he received the sponsorship of his terrifying war god Kūkā'ilimoku; he also defeated his cousin and rival Keoua in the valley. Today, Waipi'o's few inhabitants cultivate taro, lotus, avocado, breadfruit, and citrus, and earnestly protect Hawai'i's ancient spirit.

ENVIRONS: The nearby town of **Honoka'a** was once the thriving capital of the Hāmākua Sugar Company's plantations. The company folded in 1994, however, and the now quiet town offers a strip of secondhand stores and antique shops.

Isolated Waipi'o Valley, historically a sacred site and now a favorite of hikers and nature lovers

The route serving Mauna Loa weather station, off Saddle Road

Saddle Road ⑯

Hawai'i Co. Hwy 200 from Waimea to Hilo. ⓘ *HVCB, Hilo, (808) 961-5797.*

To drive the 55-mile (89-km) Saddle Road linking Hilo and Waimea is to drive along the shoulders of giants. The jumbled peaks of **Mauna Kea** rise to the north, while broad **Mauna Loa** looms to the south, the road following the trough where the two mountains collide. Some car rental companies ban drivers from taking the Saddle Road, an "unimproved" two-lane highway, but the road is better than they make out. As long as you drive at a reasonable speed, and in daylight, this is not a hazardous trip.

Drivers get a close-up look at the ecological forces at work on the island's interior – the cool rain forests of Hilo district, dominated by '*ohi'a* trees, *koa*,

and huge ferns; the subalpine lava fields at the road's 6,500-ft (2,000-m) summit; and the vast, parched grasslands on the Waimea side. The road serves two sizable military installations, and much of the traffic is generated by them.

The highest vantage point from which to view the imposing terrain is a weather station situated 11,000 ft (3,350 m) above sea level. It is reached along a narrow paved road that begins near the summit of Saddle Road and climbs for 17 miles (27 km) up Mauna Loa. The 45-minute drive is hard work (loosening the gas tank cap helps to prevent vapor lock at this altitude), but the reward is the spectacular view across Saddle Road to Mauna Kea. Starting at the weather station, an extremely rugged trail – a four- to six-hour hike – leads to the crater on the summit of Mauna Loa, at 13,677 ft (4,169 m).

Mauna Kea ⑰

Hawai'i Co. Off Saddle Road (Highway 200) at mile marker 28. ⓘ *HVCB, Hilo, (808) 961-5797.*

Midway between Hilo and Waimea, an unmarked but well-paved road climbs up Mauna Kea, winding through a native *mamane* forest that has been severely damaged by the predations of wild goats and sheep. The road rises so steeply that most cars crawl up the 15-minute drive to the **Onizuka Center for International Astronomy**.

Here, a small visitor center, named after the Kona-born astronaut who died in the 1986 explosion of the space shuttle *Challenger*, offers the solace of shelter with refreshments. It also has informative displays about the ecology of Mauna Kea and a video about its observatories. There are impressive views, too, but the panorama is better still from the summit. Driving to the very top of Mauna Kea is impossible, however, without a four-wheel-drive vehicle. The alternative is to go on foot. The 4,600-ft (1,400-m) climb is a tough 6-mile (10-km) hike.

The route to the summit takes in several remarkable sites: the **Mauna Kea Ice Age Natural Area Reserve**, with a quarry where the ancient Hawaiians obtained the rock used for making their axlike tools, or adzes; **Moon Valley**, where *Apollo* astronauts practiced driving their lunar rover in the 1960s; **Lake Waiau**, the third-highest lake in the US; and **Pu'u Poli'ahu**, the legendary abode of Pele's sister Poli'ahu, the goddess of snow.

Mauna Kea is crowned with a cluster of astronomical domes, including the **W.M. Keck Observatory**. Research teams from the US, Canada, France, and the UK are based here, collecting new information about the cosmos.

🏛 **Onizuka Center for International Astronomy**
6 miles (10 km) N of mile marker 28 off Saddle Road (Hwy 200). **Visitor Center** 📞 *(808) 961-2180.* 🕐 *Thu–Sun.* ♿ 📷 *call ahead for observatory tours.*

Mauna Kea, a giant post-shield stage volcano (*see pp10–11*), viewed from Mauna Loa weather station

Hāmākua Coast ⓲

Hawai'i Co. Hawai'i Belt Rd (Hwy 19), Waipi'o Valley to Hilo. 🚗 *Honoka'a, Laupāhoehoe, Honomū, and Pepe'ekeo.* 🅸 *HVCB, Hilo, (808) 961-5797.*

THE VERDANT CLIFFS lining the island's windward coast are stunning company on the drive along the Hawai'i Belt Road (Hwy 19). With dozens of side roads begging investigation, you can easily spend a day traveling the 55 miles (89 km) between Waimea and Hilo.

High in the hills south of Honoka'a is **Kalōpā State Recreation Area**. This has a native forest nature trail and a small arboretum of Hawaiian and introduced plants. Twelve miles (19 km) farther on is **Laupāhoehoe Point**, a lush lava outcrop that juts into the pounding sea, providing stupendous views along the coast. A sizable village once existed here but was destroyed by the 1946 tsunami (*see p125*).

At **Kolekole Beach County Park**, south of mile marker 15, a delightful stream tumbles into the ocean, making this a popular picnic and swimming spot.

🍴 Kalōpā State Recreation Area

Off Hawai'i Belt Rd (Hwy 19), 2 miles (3 km) S of Honoka'a. 🅲 *Division of State Parks, (808) 974-6200.* 🅾 *daily.* 🅰

'Akaka Falls State Park ⓳

Hawai'i Co. Highway 220, 3.5 miles (5.5 km) W of Honomū. 🚗 *Honomū.* 🅲 *Division of State Parks, (808) 974-6200.* 🅾 *daily.*

TWO OF THE STATE'S most hypnotic waterfalls have been packaged for easy viewing at 'Akaka Falls State Park, in the hills above the Hāmākua Coast. A loop trail, taking less than half an hour, links the 400-ft (120-m) **Kahūnā Falls** to **'Akaka Falls**, an unbroken cascade of 420 ft (130 m). At the main lookout, the roar of water almost drowns out the incessant clicking of cameras.

The waterfalls apart, the breezy 66-acre park alone is worth the visit. Paths wind

THE W.M. KECK OBSERVATORY

Mauna Kea, due to its elevation, the clear air, and the absence of light and air pollution, is the best observatory site in the world – enabling the telescopes at its summit to observe the universe with minimal distortion. Keck I (built in 1992) and Keck II (1996), sitting like a pair of huge eyes on the mountain top, have four times the imaging power of the world's next largest telescope in California. Instead of just one monolithic mirror, each observatory has a mosaic of flexible mirror segments computer-guided to focus in unison.

The twin globes of the W.M. Keck Observatory on Mauna Kea

through a rich blend of trees, vines, bamboo, ginger, orchids, and other exotic plants, accompanied by the cooling sounds of rushing streams.

The access road veers off Highway 19 at the welcoming old sugar town of **Honomū**, which has dwindled from its 1930s population of 3,000 to just over 500 today. The residents have kept the small main street alive, with the **Ishigo General Store and Bakery** (established 1910) and several other weathered wooden buildings serving as cafés and gift shops. The **Honomū Henjoji Mission**, a temple of the Buddhist Shingon Esoteric

Gracefully cascading 'Akaka Falls, set back above the Hāmākua Coast

sect, was founded in the 1920s and has a sanctuary richly ornamented in black lacquer and gold. The signs inviting visitors in are sincerely meant.

卍 Honomū Henjoji Mission

28-1668 Government Main Road, Honomū. 🅲 *(808) 963-6308.* 🅾 *call ahead for details.*

Pepe'ekeo Scenic Drive ⓴

Hawai'i Co. Off Hawai'i Belt Road (Hwy 19), 4 miles (6.5 km) N of Hilo. 🚗 *Pepe'ekeo.* 🅸 *HVCB, Hilo, (808) 961-5797.*

THIS 4-MILE (6.5-km) scenic detour off the Hawai'i Belt Road plunges into a moist riot of tropical growth, crossing a dozen waterfall-fed streams and shaded by enormous vine-draped palms and mango, banana, and *hala* trees.

Halfway along the drive, at beautiful Onomea Bay, the **Hawai'i Tropical Botanical Garden** has trails meandering through a patch of rain forest that includes a lily pond and a vast array of tropical plants.

🌺 Hawai'i Tropical Botanical Garden

2 miles (3 km) from either end of the drive. 🅲 *(808) 964-5233.* 🅾 *daily.* 🅾 *Jan 1, Thanksgiving, Dec 25.* 🅿

Hilo ㉑

With 38,000 residents, significant shipping and fishing industries out of its large bay, and a campus of the University of Hawai'i, Hilo rightfully deserves its designation as the state's second city. In spirit, though, "rainy old Hilo" couldn't be more different from sunny, urban Honolulu. The downtown buildings, many of them beautifully restored, were mostly constructed in the early 1900s; the streets are quiet, the pace is slow, and the atmosphere is low-key. In fact, the frantic currents of modern commerce have bypassed Hilo.

Exploring Hilo

Nature itself has checked the city's progress in two ways: the fact that rain falls 278 days of the year has not endeared Hilo to sun-worshiping vacationers; and, as though even more water were needed, the sea pounded Hilo with two destructive tsunamis in 1946 and 1960. The city has since retreated from the sea, turning the waterfront area into enormous green parks.

The Hawaiian Telephone Company building

Hilo has a friendly, relaxed, and ethnically diverse personality. The population is largely Japanese and Filipino in ancestry, and the stores and eating places reflect that heritage. The Merrie Monarch Festival, the state's most prestigious *hula* competition, takes place here every year in the week following Easter. The plentiful rain makes Hilo a natural garden, suited to orchids and anthuriums. This is a city not so much for "tourists" as for visitors.

Downtown

Many of the brightly colored, restored buildings of the old business district, clustered next to the Wailuku River, are listed with the National Register of Historic Places. Look out for the **Hawaiian Telephone Company building**, which combines aspects of the traditional Hawaiian house (*hale*) and Californian mission architecture; its designer, C.W. Dickey, is credited with developing Hawaiian Regional Architecture. A walking tour brochure is available from the Hawai'i Visitors and Convention Bureau and Lyman House.

🏠 Farmers' Market

Corner of Mamo St and Kamehameha Ave. ⬤ *Wed & Sat.*
On two mornings a week the junction of Mamo Street and Kamehameha Avenue turns into a multilingual open-air marketplace. Farmers bring exotic produce such as squash blossoms, ice cream bananas, cut orchids, and mats woven from *lauhala* (leaves of the pandanus plant). Stroll around and pick up a fresh breakfast.

🏠 Suisan Fish Auction

85 Lihiwai St. ⬤ *Mon–Sat.* ♿
Every day except Sunday, Hilo fishermen display their catch at this bayside auction house. The starting bell rings between 7 and 8am, and the haggling (in pidgin) for *'ōpakapaka, mahimahi, 'ahi,* and other locally caught fish is fast and soon finished. The public can watch from a roped-off area.

Fresh catch sold to the highest bidder at the Suisan Fish Auction

🏛 Wailoa Visitor Center

In Wailoa River State Park, Piopio St.
📞 *(808) 933-0416.* ⬤ *Mon–Sat.*
⬤ *public hols.* ♿
This octagonal gallery sits on a wide lawn where the Japanese quarter used to be – the town refused to rebuild here after the tsunami of 1960. Downstairs there is a photographic display showing the appalling destruction caused by the tsunami's giant waves. The rest of the gallery is dedicated to temporary exhibitions.

🏛 Lyman Museum and Mission House

276 Haili St. 📞 *(808) 935-5021.*
⬤ *Mon–Sat.* ⬤ *Jan 1, Jul 4, Thanksgiving, Dec 25.* 📷 ♿ *museum only.*
Lyman House was the home of the the Reverend David and Sarah Lyman, missionaries who settled in Hilo in the early 1830s. It is preserved as though the Lymans were still in residence, with Victorian curios, a cradle, and quilts. The complex also includes a

People and produce at the lively Farmers' Market

TSUNAMIS IN HILO

In 1946 an Alaskan earthquake triggered a tsunami that hit the unsuspecting Hawaiian Islands on the morning of April 1. Waves 56 ft (17 m) high tore Hilo's bayfront buildings off their foundations and swept them inland, killing 96 people. In 1960, another tsunami struck with a vengeance. Originating off the coast of Chile, it slammed Hilo on May 23 with three successive waves, causing damage worth $23 million. In spite of warnings, many locals refused to retreat, and 61 died.

Great devastation in the aftermath of the 1946 tsunami

modern museum housing a varied collection of Hawaiiana, including a display of volcanic geology and artifacts from the years of immigration, such as a *braginha* – the Portuguese precursor to the *'ukulele*.

♣ Waiākea Peninsula
Banyan Drive.

Jutting into Hilo Bay, Waiākea Peninsula supports a nine-hole golf course, a row of high-rise hotels, and the 30-acre

Lili'uokalani Gardens. The latter is a Japanese park that blends fish ponds with small pagodas and arched bridges. A footbridge crosses to tiny **Coconut Island**, now a park and popular fishing spot but once a place of healing; the Hawaiians called it Moku Ola (Island of Life). **Banyan Drive** loops the peninsula under the dense shade of huge banyans planted by celebrities such as Amelia Earhart and Babe Ruth.

🐦 Rainbow Falls
Waiānuenue Avenue, 2 miles (3 km) W of Downtown.

Rainbow ("Waiānuenue") Falls earns its name when the morning sun filters through the mist generated by the 80-ft (24-m) waterfall, creating beautiful rainbows. The hollow at the base of the falls is the legendary home of Hina, Maui's mother. The surrounding trails provide a range of lookouts.

🏖 The Eastern Beaches
Kalaniana'ole Ave.

Kalaniana'ole Avenue, which follows the east side of Hilo Bay, passes a number of beach parks interlaced with large fish ponds. **James Kealoha Beach Park** (also called Four Mile Beach) offers excellent snorkeling and swimming on its sheltered eastern side; fishermen often cast their nets on the Hilo side, which is also a popular but challenging winter surfing hangout. Another good swimming spot is **Richardson Ocean Park**, which nature has sculpted into protected, lagoonlike pools.

A fisherman throwing his net into the rough waters off James Kealoha Beach Park

Pāhoa's old Akebono Theater, now a popular spot for concerts

Pāhoa ㉒

Hawai'i Co. 🏘 *1,100.* 🚗 ⓘ *HVCB, Hilo, (808) 961-5797.*

Tʜᴇ ᴍᴀɪɴ sᴛʀɪᴘ of Pāhoa, the central town of the Puna district, offers a double surprise – "Wild West"-style buildings with raised boardwalks and low awnings that have been reinterpreted along psychedelic themes. Shops sell hemp products, espresso coffee, and New Age books. The recently refurbished **Akebono Theater** (built in 1917) has been kept alive to host a busy schedule of rock and reggae concerts.

Three miles (5 km) southeast of Pāhoa, a state-sponsored geothermal energy project has attempted to derive electricity from the heat of the world's most active volcano. However, a public outcry over environmental damage has embroiled the project in legal controversy.

Kapoho ㉓

Hawai'i Co. ⓘ *HVCB, Hilo, (808) 961-5797.*

Iɴ 1960, ᴛʜᴇ ᴛᴏᴡɴ of Kapoho was destroyed by lava that spewed from a fire fountain 2,600 ft (795 m) wide. Today, the eerie devastation can be crossed on a 2-mile (3-km) cinder road leading to **Cape Kumukahi**, where a lighthouse was inexplicably spared when the flow parted. Volcanic activity in Kapoho is a source of local legends: one tells of a

local chief who challenged a beautiful young woman to a sled race down Kapoho Crater and found to his shock that he was competing with the volcano goddess, Pele, riding on a wave of lava.

In 1790, one such wave surged through a nearby forest, leaving *'ōhi'a* trunks sheathed in black stone. Today, only the hollowed-out casts, or "lava trees," remain, but new trees have grown back. Together they make up the **Lava Tree State Monument**, a shady park with a trail around the casts. This serene spot will be best enjoyed if you bring your mosquito repellent.

Lava tree cast

🌲 Lava Tree State Monument
Highway 132, 2.5 miles (4 km) E of Pāhoa. 🟥 *Division of State Parks, (808) 974-6200.* 🔵 *daily.* ♿

Clidemia hirta (Koster's curse) growing in a lava tree cast

Puna Lava Flows ㉔

Hawai'i Co. Hwy 137 SW of Kapoho for 14 miles (23 km). ⓘ *HVCB, Hilo, (808) 961-5797.*

Nᴀʀʀᴏᴡ ʜɪɢʜᴡᴀʏ 137 traces the Puna coastline along the base of Kīlauea's East Rift Zone. Here, the dense foliage occasionally breaks into solidified lava flows, mute reminders that Puna residents live by the grace of Madam Pele's fury.

At **Ahalanui Beach Park**, a natural thermal spring in a coconut grove has been adapted into a 60 ft (18 m) wide seaside swimming pool. With a sandy bottom and waves crashing against the pool's edge, this is the best place to swim in the district.

Isaac Hale Beach Park features camping, a small boat ramp, and a rugged beach with a respectable surf break. **MacKenzie State Recreation Area**, a cliff-top campsite set in an ironwood forest, gives access to an old Hawaiian coastal trail and a long lava tube.

Southwest of here the Puna coastal road ends with shocking abruptness where the roadway, and indeed the entire countryside, has been obliterated by congealed piles of lava. In 1990, this flow erased the town of Kalapana and a much-loved black-sand beach called Kaimū.

🏖 Ahalanui Beach Park
Hwy 137, 1 mile (1.5 km) NE of junction with Pāhoa-Pohoiki Rd. 🔵 *daily.*
🏖 Isaac Hale Beach Park
Junction of Hwy 137 and Pāhoa-Pohoiki Rd. 🔵 *daily.*
🌲 MacKenzie State Recreation Area
Hwy 137, 2 miles (3 km) S of junction with Pāhoa-Pohoiki Rd. 🔵 *daily.*

Volcano Village ㉕

Hawai'i Co. 🏘 *1,500.* 🚗 ⓘ *HVCB, Hilo, (808) 961-5797.*

Cᴜᴛ ɪɴᴛᴏ ᴛʜᴇ *'ōhi'a* rain forest of Mauna Loa's high windward slopes, this village lies just a mile (1.5 km) outside the entrance to **Hawai'i**

The beautiful black beach at Punalu'u Beach Park, southwest of Pāhala

Volcanoes National Park *(see pp128–9)*. The village has a general store and a gas station (the only one in the area) and makes a good provisioning stop before entering the park.

Environs: Just 2 miles (3 km) west of the park entrance, a small road leads northwest to **Volcano Golf and Country Club**, which has an 18-hole public golf course and an inexpensive restaurant. At the end of the road a winery *(see p177)* gives tastings of its unique wines, which include a guava Chablis.

A short drive east of Volcano Village are **Akatsuka Orchid Gardens**, where visitors can take a self-guided tour of the sumptuous orchid collection.

🌸 **Akatsuka Orchid Gardens**
Hawai'i Belt Rd (Hwy 11), 5 miles (8 km) E of Volcano Village. [(808) 967-8234. ◯ *daily.* ● *public hols.* ♿

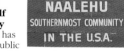

NAALEHU
SOUTHERNMOST COMMUNITY
IN THE U.S.A.
Road sign in Na'alehu

Ka'ū District ㉖

Hawai'i Co. ⊞ *Pāhala, Punalu'u, Nā'ālehu and Wai'ōhinu.* ℹ *HVCB, Hilo, (808) 961-5797.*

THE LONG SOUTHERN arc of the Hawai'i Belt Road (Hwy 11) between Volcano Village and Kailua-Kona traverses the vast and sparsely populated Ka'ū district. Three very small towns are located here. Agricultural **Pāhala**, where macadamia nuts, sugarcane, and oranges are grown, is a quiet place where the only commotion might be the occasional crowing of roosters. **Na'alehu**, the most southerly town in the United States, is Ka'ū's largest town, with a few small shops. Tiny **Wai'ōhinu** is known for a monkeypod tree that Mark Twain planted in 1866. The original tree fell in a storm in 1957 but has since grown again from shoots.

The gem of the south coast is **Punalu'u Beach Park**, where a pure black sand beach is crowded with coconut trees. Visitors may camp here and at **Whittington Beach Park**, 5 miles (8 km) farther south.

🏕 **Punalu'u Beach Park**
Off Hwy 11, 5 miles (8 km) SW of Pāhala. ◯ *daily.* [*Dept of Parks and Recreation, Hilo, (808) 961-8311.*

Ka Lae ㉗

Hawai'i Co. S Point Rd, off Hwy 11, 6 miles (10 km) W of Wai'ōhinu. ℹ *HVCB, Hilo, (808) 961-5797.*

ALSO KNOWN AS South Point, Ka Lae is as far south as you can travel in the United States. Constant fierce winds drive against a battered grassland that gives way finally to a rocky shoreline. Halfway along the 11-mile (18-km) access road, three rows of enormous, propeller-driven electricity generators emit a repetitive music of almost maddening whistles. It all feels suitably like the ends of the earth.

Although the powerful waves are daunting, these have long been prime fishing grounds. The mooring holes that ancient Hawaiians drilled into the coastal rocks so that they could keep their canoes safe while they went fishing are still visible – providing some of the earliest recorded evidence of Polynesian settlement.

A four-wheel-drive road runs 2.5 miles (4 km) northeast, to **Green Sands Beach**, which is composed of olivine sand.

Wind-powered electricity generators along the road to Ka Lae

Hawai'i Volcanoes National Park ㉘

Petroglyph at Pu'u Loa, near the coast

THE NATIONAL PARK encompasses about a quarter of a million acres, including the 13,677-ft (4,169-m) summit of Mauna Loa, 150 miles (240 km) of hiking trails, and vast tracts of wilderness that preserve some of the world's rarest species of flora and fauna. But it is Kīlauea Caldera and the lava flows of its furious East Rift Zone that draw most visitors. Two roads – Crater Rim Drive, which loops around the caldera, and Chain of Craters Road, which descends through the recent outpourings – form a gigantic drive-through museum. The present eruption started in 1983 and produces slow-moving lava that poses no threat to visitors. However, you should stay out of closed areas; no one knows how long the flow will continue or where it will next erupt.

Lava fountains spewing from Kīlauea during the 1983 eruption

Kīlauea Overlook
Jaggar Museum
MAUNA LOA
NĀ'ĀLEHU
Hawai'i Belt Road
Crater Rim Drive
Crater Rim Trail

KĪLAUEA CALDERA

★ Halema'uma'u Overlook
Once a boiling lake of lava, the crater below still steams with sulfurous fumes. This is the home of Pele, the volcano goddess (see p14).

HALEMA'UMA'U CRATER
Halema'uma'u Trail
Crater Rim Drive

PROFESSOR JAGGAR (1871–1953)

Thomas A. Jaggar was a pioneer in the young science of volcanology. A professor of geology at Massachusetts Institute of Technology, he founded the Hawaiian Volcano Observatory (now part of the Jaggar Museum) at Kīlauea Caldera in 1912. Four years later, he and Honolulu publisher Lorrin Thurston persuaded Congress to preserve the area as a national park. Professor Jaggar developed techniques for collecting volcanic gases and measuring ground tilt, seismic activity, and lava temperatures. The work he initiated has made Kīlauea one of the best understood volcanoes in the world.

Professor Jaggar working at his desk in 1916

| 0 meters | 500 |
| 0 yards | 500 |

STAR FEATURES

★ Halema'uma'u Overlook

★ Thurston Lava Tube

Kīlauea Iki Overlook

In 1959 the crater below this overlook filled with bubbling lava, shooting fire fountains 1,900 ft (580 m) into the air. Today a hiking trail crosses the cool crater floor to give a close-up view.

⑪ **Military Camp**

Steam Vents

Kīlauea Visitor Center and Volcano Art Center

Volcano House Hotel

Sandalwood Trail

Crater Rim Drive

VOLCANO VILLAGE

HILO

Crater Rim Trail

emi'uma'u Trail

KĪLAUEA IKI CRATER

Kīlauea Iki Trail

yron Ledge Trail

Devastation Trail

Chain of Craters Road

KEANAKĀKO'I CRATER

EAST RIFT ZONE

Crater Rim Trail

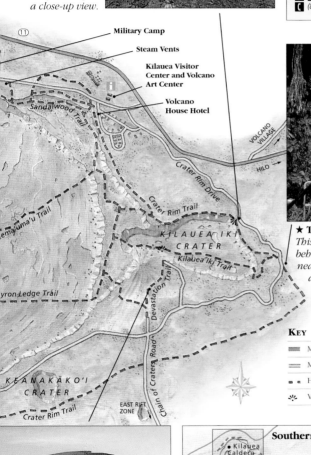

★ Thurston Lava Tube

This huge tunnel was left behind when a subterranean river of lava drained away. An easy trail runs through the tube and a grove of giant ferns.

KEY

▰▰▰	Major road
▬▬▬	Minor road
▪ ▪	Hiking trail
⚶	Vista

Devastation Trail

This short walk passes through the ghostly remains of a rain forest wiped out by ash falling from Kīlauea Iki's 1959 eruption.

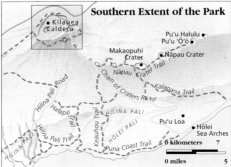

Southern Extent of the Park

Kīlauea Caldera

Pu'u Halulu

Pu'u 'Ō'ō

Makaopuhi Crater

Nāpau Crater

Nāpau Crater Trail

Chain of Craters Road

Kalapana Trail

Hilina Pali Road

Halapē Trail

Keauhou Trail

HILINA PALI

Pu'u Loa

HŌLEI PALI

Hōlei Sea Arches

Hilina Pali Trail

Puna Coast Trail

HILINA PALI

| 0 kilometers | 7 |
| 0 miles | 5 |

KAUA'I

I T IS NO COINCIDENCE *that the oldest of the major Hawaiian islands is also the most beautiful. Wind and water have had six million years to carve Kaua'i into a stunning array of pleated cliffs and yawning chasms, while the rich topsoil of the "Garden Island" is cloaked in a spectacular mantle of emerald green vegetation. With its sandy beaches and large coral reefs, Kaua'i is Hawai'i's most irresistible destination.*

The outline of the volcano that created Kaua'i has all but vanished, leaving a roughly circular island on which no place is more than a dozen miles (19 km) from the ocean. Although its highest point barely exceeds 5,000 ft (1,500 m), the interior remains a forbidding, waterlogged wilderness, and Kaua'i's 56,500 inhabitants are distributed fairly evenly around the coastal lowlands.

Settled by a separate wave of Polynesian voyagers – possibly the small, legendary *Menehune (see p135)* – and never conquered by the other islands, Kaua'i has its own proud history. It was here that Captain Cook first landed, and here too that the sandalwood and sugar industries were established. A trail of ancient temples can still be seen along the Wailua River on the east shore, and former plantation towns from Hanalei in the north to Hanapēpē in the south lend the island a small-town charm.

The capital Līhu'e is surprisingly sleepy, while resorts such as Princeville and Po'ipū are rare pockets of modern luxury in an otherwise timeless rural landscape.

Scenery is Kaua'i's greatest attraction. The North Shore, in particular, is stunning, with a succession of gorgeous beaches to the east and the soaring Nā Pali Coast to the west. High above lies Kōke'e State Park, where trails command views of the valleys and lace through the rain-soaked Alaka'i Swamp, home to rare flora and fauna. The road to the park climbs the flanks of mighty Waimea Canyon, an ever-changing panoply of colors.

In 1992, Kaua'i was devastated by Hurricane Iniki, which killed three people and damaged over 70 percent of the island's homes. Facilities and infrastructure have now fully recovered, and the island is back to normal.

Workers picking taro, a traditional Hawaiian crop cultivated in Kaua'i's Hanalei Valley

◁ The soaring cliffs of the Nā Pali Coast, accessible only by rugged trail, or by boat or helicopter tour

Exploring Kaua'i

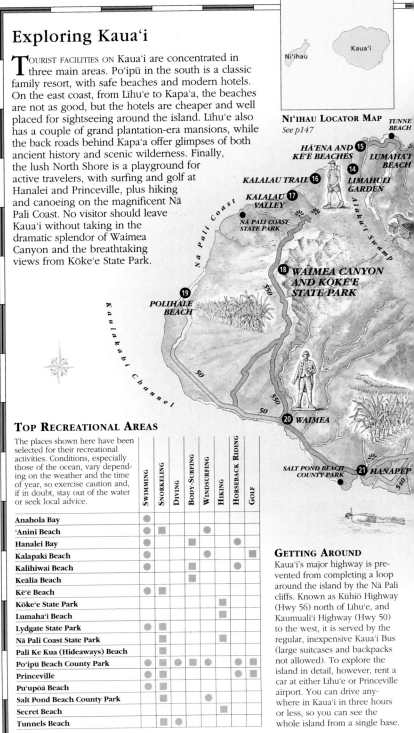

TOURIST FACILITIES ON Kaua'i are concentrated in three main areas. Po'ipū in the south is a classic family resort, with safe beaches and modern hotels. On the east coast, from Līhu'e to Kapa'a, the beaches are not as good, but the hotels are cheaper and well placed for sightseeing around the island. Līhu'e also has a couple of grand plantation-era mansions, while the back roads behind Kapa'a offer glimpses of both ancient history and scenic wilderness. Finally, the lush North Shore is a playground for active travelers, with surfing and golf at Hanalei and Princeville, plus hiking and canoeing on the magnificent Nā Pali Coast. No visitor should leave Kaua'i without taking in the dramatic splendor of Waimea Canyon and the breathtaking views from Kōke'e State Park.

NI'IHAU LOCATOR MAP
See p147

Ni'ihau

Kaua'i

TUNNELS
BEACH

HA'ENA AND ⑮
KE'E BEACHES

LUMAHA'I
BEACH

KALALAU TRAIL ⑯

⑭
LIMAHULI
GARDEN

KALALAU ⑰
VALLEY

NĀ PALI COAST
STATE PARK

⑱ WAIMEA CANYON
AND KŌKE'E
STATE PARK

⑲
POLIHALE
BEACH

⑳ WAIMEA

SALT POND BEACH
COUNTY PARK

㉑ HANAPEP

TOP RECREATIONAL AREAS

The places shown here have been selected for their recreational activities. Conditions, especially those of the ocean, vary depending on the weather and the time of year, so exercise caution and, if in doubt, stay out of the water or seek local advice.

	SWIMMING	SNORKELING	DIVING	BODY-SURFING	WINDSURFING	HIKING	HORSEBACK RIDING	GOLF
Anahola Bay	●							
'Anini Beach	●	■			●			
Hanalei Bay	●			■			●	
Kalapaki Beach	●				●			■
Kalihiwai Beach	●			■			●	
Keālia Beach				■				
Ke'e Beach	●	■						
Kōke'e State Park						■		
Lumaha'i Beach						■		
Lydgate State Park	●	■						
Nā Pali Coast State Park		■				■		
Pali Ke Kua (Hideaways) Beach		■						
Po'ipū Beach County Park	●	■	●	■	●		●	■
Princeville	●	■					●	■
Pu'upōā Beach	●	■						
Salt Pond Beach County Park	■				●			
Secret Beach						■		
Tunnels Beach		■	●					

GETTING AROUND

Kaua'i's major highway is prevented from completing a loop around the island by the Nā Pali cliffs. Known as Kūhiō Highway (Hwy 56) north of Līhu'e, and Kaumuali'i Highway (Hwy 50) to the west, it is served by the regular, inexpensive Kaua'i Bus (large suitcases and backpacks not allowed). To explore the island in detail, however, rent a car at either Līhu'e or Princeville airport. You can drive anywhere in Kaua'i in three hours or less, so you can see the whole island from a single base.

HANALEI BAY
PU'UPŌĀ BEACH
PALI KE KUA BEACH
'ANINI BEACH
KALIHIWAI BEACH
SECRET BEACH

9 **KĪLAUEA POINT**

11 *PRINCEVILLE*

12
HANALEI

10
KALIHIWAI

56

ANAHOLA BAY
8 *ANAHOLA*

6
*MOUNT
ʻAIʻALEʻALE*

DONKEY BEACH
KEĀLIA BEACH

ʻŌPAEKAʻA FALLS

7 *KAPAʻA*

5 *SLEEPING GIANT*

580
4 *KINGʻS HIGHWAY*

3 *FERN GROTTO*   *LYDGATE STATE PARK*

WAILUA FALLS **2**

56

1 *LĪHUʻE*
KALAPAKĪ BEACH

50   58

*HULĒʻIA
NATIONAL
WILDLIFE
REFUGE*

*MENEHUNE
FISH POND*

ALLERTON GARDEN
2   *KŌLOA*

POʻIPŪ

*ŌʻIPŪ BEACH
OUNTY PARK*
23

K a u a ʻ i   C h a n n e l

0 kilometers	10
0 miles	5

Cloud-capped Mount Waiʻaleʻale, the wettest place on earth

SIGHTS AT A GLANCE

SEE ALSO

KEY

▭	Major road
▭	Minor road
▭	Dirt or four-wheel-drive road
▭	Scenic route
=	River or stream
☆	Vista

Remote Polihale Beach, with the soaring Nā Pali cliffs behind

Līhu'e ➊

ALTHOUGH LĪHU'E is Kaua'i's administrative and business center, it amounts to little more than a plantation village. It was built in the mid-19th century to serve the Līhu'e Sugar Mill, whose rusting machinery still dominates the downtown area. Līhu'e's multi-ethnic heritage, which stems from plantation days, is reflected in some of the shops and restaurants here. Within a few miles of central Līhu'e lie several more attractive areas. The oceanfront district, now recovered from the hammering it took from Hurricane Iniki in 1992, is especially appealing. Though the Kaua'i Marriott Resort dominates Kalapakī Beach, visitors can also enjoy a safe swim or a surfing lesson.

Hamura Saimin Stand, an Oriental diner in central Līhu'e (see p175)

Exploring Līhu'e

The outskirts of town offer hidden delights. To the west, pristine Hule'ia Stream has been set aside as a wildlife sanctuary, overlooked by a splendidly forbidding ridge of green mountains. To the east lies the barely distinct community of Hanamā'ulu, where a pleasant little beach, sadly too polluted for swimming, lines a sweeping crescent bay.

🏛 Kaua'i Museum

4428 Rice Street. 📞 (808) 245-6931. 🕐 Mon–Sat. 🌑 Jan 1, Labor Day, Jul 4, Thanksgiving, Dec 25. 🎟 🚻
This two-part museum relates the island's history from the earliest times. The Wilcox Building centers on a collection of traditional artifacts gathered by the missionary Wilcox family, including huge *koa*-wood bowls and *kāhili*, feathered standards once used as a sign of royalty in Hawai'i. The newer Rice Building tells *The Story of Kaua'i*, with displays ranging from dangerous ancient weapons to videos on geology. Dioramas show how the island might have looked before European contact, and the arrival of immigrants from

around the world is chronicled, with an emphasis on the harsh conditions endured by early plantation workers. A gift shop sells books and crafts, and the museum has its own café.

⛩ Grove Farm Homestead

Nāwiliwili Road. 📞 (808) 245-3202. 🕐 Mon, Wed & Thu. 🌑 public hols. **Donation.** 🎟 *by appointment.*
No settlement existed on the site of modern Līhu'e until 1864, when George Wilcox, the son of early missionaries, established the Grove Farm Plantation. Hawai'i's sugar business was then in its first boom, and although water was scarce, Wilcox prospered by developing a network of irrigation channels that reached deep into the mountains.

He lived on until the 1930s, content with a humble cottage. It was his heirs who built the imposing mansion, paneled throughout in dark, heavy *koa*-wood, that now forms the centerpiece of the Grove Farm Homestead. As well as

the rather formal house and cramped servants' quarters, the two-hour guided tour takes in Wilcox's lush and beautifully scented private orchard. Phone a week in advance for a place on the tour; you will not be let in without a reservation.

🏖 Kalapakī Beach

Off Wa'apā Road (Hwy 51), at Kaua'i Marriott Resort.
Līhu'e became Kaua'i's main port during the 1920s, when a new deepwater harbor was dredged in Nāwiliwili Bay. While the breakwaters and harbor installations appeal only to avid fishermen, the gently sloping white sands of Kalapakī Beach just to the east are highly inviting.

The safest beach in the area, it is one of the finest for family use on the entire island, and as such is home to the top-class Kaua'i Marriott Resort *(see p161)* and a handful of restaurants. Expert surfers swirl right out into the bay, but the inshore waters are sheltered enough for children. The western limit of the beach is marked by the mouth of Nāwiliwili Stream. On the far side, the palm-fringed lawns of Nāwiliwili Beach County Park are ideal for picnics.

⛩ Kilohana Plantation

3-2087 Kaumuali'i Hwy (Hwy 50), 1.5 miles (2.5 km) W of Līhu'e. 📞 (808) 245-5608. 🕐 *daily.* 🚻 *ground floor.*
The grand house known as Kilohana Plantation was, like Grove Farm Homestead, built by the plantation-owning Wilcoxes. Dating from the

The shady *koa*-wood veranda at Grove Farm Homestead

Late 19th-century carriage used for tours at Kilohana Plantation

VISITORS' CHECKLIST

Kaua'i Co. 🏠 5,500. ✈ 2 miles
(3 km) E. 🚌 Rice St, (808) 241-
6410. 🚻 HVCB, 4334 Rice St,
Suite 101, (808) 245-3971. 🎭
Kaua'i-Tahiti Fete (mid-Aug).

1930s, its resemblance to an English country estate makes it the perfect home for one of Kaua'i's most elegant restaurants *(see p175)*, as well as a small mall of expensive craft shops and galleries. Hurricane Iniki cleared away many of the trees on the property so that the mansion now commands superb views of Kilohana mountain inland. Horse-drawn carriages tour the adjacent cane fields – now cultivated more for show than for profit – and you can take longer wagon tours into the backcountry.

♤ Menehune Fish Pond
Hulemalū Road, 1.5 miles (2.5 km) S of Lihu'e. ● *to the public.*
West of Nāwiliwili Harbor, a minor road ascends a small headland to enter an idyllic pastoral landscape that comes as a surprise so close to Lihu'e. Beneath a highway lookout, the tranquil Hule'ia Stream makes a sharp right-angle turn. Ancient Hawaiians exploited this natural bend by constructing a 900-ft (275-m) dam of rounded boulders to create the Alakoko ("Rippling Blood") Fish Pond. Skilled fish farmers,

the Hawaiians used it to fatten mullet for the royal table; as the fish grew, they could no longer pass through the latticed sluices that had allowed them to enter the enclosure.

This ancient structure is more commonly referred to as the Menehune Fish Pond, its prehistoric stonemasonry being credited, as so often in Hawai'i, to the little *Menehune*. These mythical figures are described by popular legend as hairy dwarfs already hard at work in Hawai'i when the first Polynesian settlers arrived. Now privately owned, the fish pond can be seen only from afar.

Unless you rent a kayak, the same goes for the **Hule'ia National Wildlife Refuge** just upstream, where former taro and rice terraces are set aside for the exclusive use of a raucously grateful population of waterbirds.

Wailua Falls ❷

Kaua'i Co. Mā'alo Road (Hwy 583), 5 miles (8 km) N of Lihu'e. 🚌 *Lihu'e.*

Sugarcane still grows in an unbroken swath north from central Lihu'e, as far as the south fork of the Wailua River. The one winding road through the fields, which branches left from the main highway a mile (1.5 km) north of Lihu'e, leads directly to the 80-ft (24-m) Wailua Falls.

From the roadside parking lot you can admire the white cascade as it tumbles from a sheer ledge. After heavy rain the river also bursts from a couple of natural tunnels hollowed into the rock wall below. Reaching the pool below the falls is difficult and dangerous because the hillside is all but vertical and very muddy. The intrepid will find a slippery path lined with knotted ropes five minutes' walk back down the road.

The twin cascade of Wailua Falls, seen from a roadside overlook

The ruins of Poli'ahu Heiau, a sacrificial temple on the King's Highway

beach. Only vestiges survive here of the mighty stone walls of the **Hikinaakalā Heiau** (the name means "Rising of the Sun"), where worshipers would greet the dawn. Across the highway farther inland, Kaua'i's largest temple, **Malae Heiau**, lies buried beneath a tree-covered mound.

North of the river, a short way up Kuamo'o Road (Hwy 580), **Holoholokū Heiau** was, by contrast, so small that it could be entered only on all fours. Even so, it was the site of Kaua'i's first human sacrifices. Farther up the road lies a pair of boulders known as the **Birthing Stones**; only chiefs whose mothers gave birth while wedged between them could ever rule Kaua'i. A mile (1.5 km) farther up Kuamo'o ("lizard") Ridge, on a flat promontory with wide views, the stone walls of **Poli'ahu Heiau** remain in place, guarded by swaying coconut palms.

Half a mile (800 m) more and the ground to the right drops away to swift 'Ōpaeka'a ("rolling shrimp") Stream, which tumbles over the broad **'Ōpaeka'a Falls**. It is a fine spectacle, but do not go closer than the roadside lookout.

Lydgate State Park
Leho Drive, off Kūhiō Hwy (Hwy 56), just S of Wailua River.

Sleeping Giant ⑤

Kaua'i Co. 1.5 miles (2.5 km) NW of Wailua. Waipouli.

THE EAST SHORE'S principal residential district nestles 3 miles (5 km) in from the ocean, behind the undulating ridge of Nounou Mountain.

Fern Grotto ③

Kaua'i Co. Wailua River. Smith's Motor Boat Service, (808) 821-6892; Wai'ale'ale Boat Tours, (808) 822-4908; from Wailua Marina, off Kūhiō Hwy (Hwy 56). Waipouli. daily.

ALTHOUGH A SANDBAR makes it impossible to sail up the Wailua River from the ocean, a constant procession of pleasure barges sets out from a marina upstream for the 2-mile (3-km) excursion to the Fern Grotto. This large cave behind a fern-draped rock face is famous for its beauty, but since Hurricane Iniki struck in 1992, it has been looking more bedraggled and less romantic than you might expect. A paved path, lined with lush foliage, leads up to the grotto, where you may end up being serenaded with the *Hawaiian Wedding Song* – about three couples per day get married here. The hour-long narrated cruise gives you a chance to enjoy some attractive scenery, with a sing-along on the return trip.

King's Highway ④

Kaua'i Co. Waipouli. HVCB, Lihu'e, (808) 245-3971.

THE WAILUA VALLEY was the seat of power in ancient Kaua'i, and the nearby shoreline remains the island's main population center. A trail of sacred sites known as the King's Highway ran from the ocean to the remote peak of Mount Wai'ale'ale. It started just south of the Wailua River in what is now **Lydgate State Park**, a deservedly popular

Sleeping Giant ridge, its profile reminiscent of a reclining figure

This long, low hillock is more commonly known as Sleeping Giant, thanks to an outline resembling a huge human figure lying flat on its back.

Three distinct hiking trails climb from its east, west, and south sides. They are reached from Kūhiō Highway (Hwy 56), Kāmala Road (Hwy 581), and Kuamoʻo Road (Hwy 580) respectively. They converge to follow the alarmingly narrow crest, arriving at a meadow-like clearing in the forest at the top. This prime picnic spot offers panoramic views up and down the coastline, as well as westward to the sequence of parallel ridges that stretch inland. You can continue up the giant's head from here, but be extremely careful; the ridge is very steep in places and prone to rock slides.

Mount Waiʻaleʻale ➏

Kauaʻi Co. 11 miles (18 km) W of Wailua.

WITHIN SPITTING distance of Kapaʻa's sunny beaches lies one of the wettest places on earth – Mount Waiʻaleʻale, or "overflowing water." An average of 440 in (1,100 cm) of rain each year cascades in huge waterfalls down its green-velvet walls. The summit, wreathed in almost perpetual mists, was the last call on the sacred King's Highway; the ancients would follow knife-edge ridges to reach a mountain-top *heiau* (temple).

These days, unless you take a helicopter tour, you can glimpse Waiʻaleʻale only from below. Follow Kuamoʻo Road (Hwy 580) past ʻŌpaekaʻa Falls and the Keahua Forestry Arboretum, and if the clouds clear you will be confronted by astonishing views of a sheer, pleated cliff face. Dirt roads lead through the forest to its base, where the Wailua River thunders down from the 5,148-ft (1,570-m) peak. These roads are dangerous, if not impassable, after heavy rain.

1920s rain gauge once used on Mt. Waiʻaleʻale

The curving expanse of Donkey Beach, popular with nudists and surfers

Kapaʻa ➐

Kauaʻi Co. 🏠 8,200. 🚗 🛈 HVCB, Lihuʻe, (808) 245-3971.

TOURIST DEVELOPMENT along Kauaʻi's East Shore, also known as the Coconut Coast, is mostly concentrated into the 5-mile (8-km) coastal strip that stretches north of the Wailua River. Maps mark distinct communities at Wailua and Waipouli, but the only real town here is Kapaʻa, farther north. Though most of the false-front buildings that line its wooden boardwalks now hold tourist-related businesses such as restaurants, souvenir stores, or equipment rental outlets, it still maintains the look of a late 19th-century plantation village. The fringe of sand at the ocean's edge is divided into a number of not particularly noteworthy beach parks.

ENVIRONS: The first of the more appealing beaches north of Kapaʻa is tucked out of sight half a mile (800 m) from the highway and is reached by a forest trail that drops to the right not far past mile marker 11. This uncrowded, pretty stretch of sand is known as **Donkey Beach**, thanks to the beasts of burden that used to work in the adjacent sugar fields and were turned loose to graze along the beach's edges in the evenings. In their absence wildflowers have flourished in the meadows, but there are still no trees to provide shade for sunbathers, many of whom take advantage of this remote spot to go entirely naked. The surf here is generally too rough to allow swimming, but is a rendezvous for expert surfers.

Anahola ➑

Kauaʻi Co. 🏠 1,200. 🚗 🛈 HVCB, Lihuʻe, (808) 245-3971.

THE SMALL, scattered village of Anahola overlooks the sweeping, palm-fringed curve of Anahola Bay, an ancient surfing site. North of town, just inland of the highway, is the picturesque **Anahola Baptist Church**. Set against a beautiful mountain backdrop, the church makes a lovely photograph.

Nearby Anahola Beach is often relatively empty, despite its combination of beautiful setting, safe swimming, and convenient access. Reached by a spur road that loops down from Kūhiō Highway (Hwy 56) shortly after mile marker 13, the beach faces the most sheltered section of Anahola Bay. The area nearest the showers is reserved for family swimming, while the slightly more turbulent waters farther north are enjoyed by local surfers.

In recent years, Hawaiian activists have staged protests on the beach. They argue that the state has failed to meet its obligation to provide native Hawaiians with affordable housing in the area. However, their campaigns have not been directed against tourists.

An inviting stretch of golden sand at secluded Secret Beach, near Kīlauea Point

Kīlauea Point ⑨

Kaua'i Co. Kilauea Róad, off Kūhiō Highway (Hwy 56), 10 miles (16 km) NW of Anahola. 🚗 *Kilauea*. 🛈 *HVCB, Lihu'e, (808) 245-3971.*

THE HAWAIIAN name Kilauea ("much spewing") applies not only to the southernmost volcano on Hawai'i Island but also to the northernmost spot on the Hawaiian archipelago, Kaua'i's Kilauea Point. Here the name refers not to spouting lava, but rather to the raging waves that foam around the base of this rocky promontory. Together with a couple of tiny offshore islets, the splendidly windswept cliff top has been set aside as the **Kīlauea Point National Wildlife Refuge**, a sanctuary for Pacific seabirds. Displays in the refuge's well-equipped visitor center enable amateur birdwatchers to pick out frigatebirds, Laysan albatrosses, and various tropic birds.

A short walk beyond the visitor center leads to the red and white **Kīlauea Lighthouse**, which marks the beginning of Kaua'i's North Shore. When erected in 1913, the lighthouse

HAWAII VISITORS BUREAU MARKER

KILAUEA LIGHTHOUSE

Colorful official marker for the lighthouse

held the largest clamshell lens in the world, but that has now been supplanted by a much smaller and barely noticeable structure on its far side. As you approach the tip of the headland, extensive views open up to the west beyond Secret Beach and Princeville to the Nā Pali cliffs. The exposed oceanfront slopes to the east, meanwhile, are flecked with thousands of white seabirds and can be explored on ranger-led walking tours.

ENVIRONS: The most dramatic views of Kilauea Lighthouse and, in winter especially, of the mighty waves that pound northern Kaua'i, are from the vast but little-visited shelf of glorious yellow sand known as **Secret Beach**. To reach it, turn right onto Kalihiwai Road, half a mile (800 m) west of the Kilauea turn-off, then follow a red-dirt track that cuts away almost immediately to the right. From its far end, a narrow trail zig-zags through the woods, coming out after ten minutes at a luscious tropical cove. Even in the summer, when the mile (1.5 km) of coarse sand at least doubles in width, the sea tends to be too rough for swimming. However, it is worth walking

the full length of the beach to see the white surf as it crashes against the black lava rocks that poke from the sand, and the glorious waterfall at the far end, nearest the lighthouse.

🦆 Kīlauea Point National Wildlife Refuge
Kilauea Point. 📞 *(808) 828-1413.* ⭕ *daily.* ● *Jan 1, Thanksgiving, Dec 25.* 🎫 ♿

Kalihiwai ⑩

Kaua'i Co. 🏠 *450.* 🛈 *HVCB, Lihu'e, (808) 245-3971.*

FROM KŪHIŌ HIGHWAY (Highway 56), two successive turnings, a mile and a half (2.5 km) apart, are called Kalihiwai Road. The two parts of the road through this small settlement were connected until a tsunami washed away the bridge over the Kalihiwai River in 1957. The last few hundred yards of the eastern segment, just before the mouth of the river, run alongside the lovely **Kalihiwai Beach**. Shielded behind a grove of ironwood trees, this beach offers fine surfing and body-surfing as well as swimming. Kūhiō Highway crosses the river about half a mile (800 m) back from the ocean; glance inland from the bridge at this point to spot the beautiful, wide **Kalihiwai Falls**.

ENVIRONS: The second (western) segment of Kalihiwai Road quickly dead-ends at the Kalihiwai River, with no beach on this side. However, an unmarked spur road to the left, halfway down this segment, leads to quiet **'Anini Beach**. Here, between 3 miles (5 km) of golden sand and the coral reef that lies 200 yds (180 m) offshore, shallow turquoise waters provide the safest swimming on Kaua'i's North Shore. There is also excellent snorkeling on the coral reef itself, as well as an idyllic campsite set among the trees. The large lawns on the inland side of the road host polo matches on summer Sunday afternoons, often with boisterous crowds cheering on the players.

The Princeville Hotel, set amid golf courses and ocean views

The mouth of the Kalihiwai River with Kalihiwai Beach behind

Princeville ⓫

Kaua'i Co. 🏄 *1,250.* ✈ 🚌
ℹ HVCB, Lihu'e, (808) 245-3971.

THE FORMER SUGAR plantation and livestock ranch of Princeville, set on the rolling meadows of a headland above Hanalei Bay, was sold off in the 1960s to be developed as Kaua'i's most exclusive resort. Its centerpiece, the opulent **Princeville Hotel** *(see p161)*, occupies a prime site near the remains of an earthwork fort built by the German adventurer George Schäffer in 1816 *(see p146)*. Its long-range views of the North Shore mountains are now shared by two golf courses, as well as several more hotels, condominiums, vacation homes, and a small shopping mall.

Below the bluffs, Princeville boasts some delightful little beaches. The best of the bunch, **Pu'upoā Beach**, is reached by trails that drop from both the Princeville Hotel and the Hanalei Bay Resort next door. Its wide sands offer dramatic views across Hanalei Bay, as well as over the wetlands to the peaks that tower behind Hanalei *(see p140)*, and there's excellent family swimming in the shallow waters. Pu'upoā Beach stretches as far as the mouth of the Hanalei River, so rented kayaks can easily be paddled upstream. Princeville-based surfers and snorkelers flock to **Pali Ke Kua Beach**, also known as Hideaways Beach, by way of a trail down from the tennis courts of the Pali Ke Kua condominiums.

KAUA'I IN THE MOVIES

The fabulous scenery of Kaua'i has served as an exotic backdrop in countless Hollywood blockbusters, from a Caribbean paradise in *Islands in the Stream* (1977) to South America in *Raiders of the Lost Ark* (1981) and Vietnam in *Uncommon Valor* (1983). Ever since Esther Williams performed one of her trademark aquatic ballets in Hanalei Bay in *Pagan Love Song* (1950), the island has starred alongside the big screen's biggest names. Frank Sinatra's war-torn Pacific-island beach in *None but the Brave* (1965) was Pila'a Beach, east of Kilauea. Meanwhile, Elvis Presley's greatest box-office hit, *Blue Hawaii* (1961), climaxed with a gloriously kitsch wedding ceremony at the Coco Palms Resort. The remote Honopū Valley on the Nā Pali coast stood in as Skull Island in the 1976 remake of *King Kong* and, before Hurricane Iniki put an abrupt end to proceedings, much of *Jurassic Park* (1993) was shot in Hanapēpē Valley. Kaua'i is probably best remembered, however, for its role in the smash-hit Rodgers and Hammerstein musical *South Pacific* (1958). Of the movie's show-stopping songs, *Some Enchanted Evening* was filmed at Hanalei Bay, and, most famous of all, Mitzi Gaynor sang *I'm Gonna Wash That Man Right Out of My Hair* at Lumaha'i Beach.

Publicity poster of Elvis Presley in *Blue Hawaii*

Hanalei ⑫

Kaua'i Co. 🏘 500. 🚌
ℹ HVCB, Lihu'e, (808) 245-3971.

ONLY ONE SPOT in all the islands bears the name Hanalei, or "crescent bay." Nowhere deserves it more than the placid half-moon inlet, fringed with golden sand and cradled by soaring green cliffs, that lies just west of Princeville.

The flat valley floor of the Hanalei River was in ancient times a prime area for growing taro. Later turned into a patchwork of rice paddies by Chinese settlers, it is once again dominated by taro, planted under the auspices of the **Hanalei National Wildlife Refuge** to re-create the preferred habitat of the state's increasingly endangered waterbirds. Crisscrossed by irrigation channels and scattered with inaccessible islands that poke from the mud, it is home to an ever-changing population of coots, herons, stilts, and transient migratory birds. The valley's lush, green landscape is best seen from a lookout on Kūhiō Highway (Hwy 56), just west of the Princeville turnoff.

The slender bridge across the Hanalei River is the first of a series of one-lane bridges that slow North Shore traffic to a virtual crawl, thereby helping to protect the region from the ravages of overdevelopment. The village of **Hanalei** on the far side is a relaxed place, still recognizably a plantation settlement but kept busy these days catering to the needs of a year-round community of surfers and Nā Pali adventurers.

The taro fields of Hanalei Valley, seen from a highway overlook

A trio of awe-inspiring mountains forms a magnificent backdrop – Hīhīmanu to the east, Māmalahoa to the west, and, in the center, the sublime Nāmolokama, furrowed with over 20 waterfalls that combine to form Wai'oli Stream.

At first glance **Hanalei Bay** might look like an ideal harbor, but so many ships have come to grief on its submerged reefs that only shallow-draft pleasure yachts now use the old jetty on its eastern side. Conditions for swimmers using the 2-mile (3-km) strand west of the jetty depend on the state of the reef; although there are several attractive spots for sunbathing or camping, swimming is only really advisable from Waikoko Beach at the western end, beyond the mouth of the Wai'oli Stream. Expert surfers, untroubled by these issues, set off from Wai'oli Beach, or "Pinetrees Park," nearer the center of the bay, to practice their art amid the waves that break at the bay's entrance.

Hanalei's most visible relic of the past is the missionary complex, set on landscaped lawns west of the town center and backed by high, tree-clad mountains. The town's earliest Christian edifice, **Wai'oli Church**, was put up in 1841. Dwarfed beneath a tall, sloping roof, this large wooden structure now functions as a social hall, set back to the right of its successor, the 1912-vintage **Wai'oli Hui'ia Church**. With its vivid green shingles, shimmering stained glass, and gray-capped belfry, all nestled beneath a spreading palm tree, Wai'oli Hui'ia is without a doubt the loveliest building on Kaua'i. Tucked away behind it, the **Wai'oli Mission House** was home to several generations of missionaries, including the Wilcoxes (see p134), whose descendants lived here until the late 1970s. Although the original furnishings have disappeared, period replacements enable the guided tours to give visitors a vivid sense of 19th-century Hanalei.

🏠 **Wai'oli Mission House**
Kūhiō Hwy (Hwy 56). 📞 (808) 245-3202. 🕐 Tue, Thu & Sat. 🔴 public hols. **Donation.** ♿ ground floor only.

Lumaha'i Beach ⑬

Kaua'i Co. Off Kūhiō Highway (Hwy 56), 2 miles (3 km) W of Hanalei. 🚌 Hanalei.

IMMEDIATELY BEYOND Hanalei Bay, a small roadside pull-off marks the top of a steep, muddy trail down to the spell-binding Lumaha'i Beach. Thanks to its appearance in the movie *South Pacific (see p139)*, this has a reputation as the most romantic beach in all Hawai'i. Its golden sands always seem to hold at least one pair of lovers, but the beaches are long and broad enough to maintain the illusion of privacy. Except on very calm days, rolling in the surf is not a good idea.

The striking facade of Wai'oli Hui'ia Church

The mountain peak of Bali Hai may have dominated the beach on screen, but that was due to technical trickery; in fact it's a tiny outcrop called Makana at the end of a ridge, 4 miles (6.5 km) farther west.

Limahuli Garden ⑭

Kaua'i Co. Kūhiō Hwy (Hwy 56), 6 miles (10 km) W of Hanalei. **(** *(808) 826-1053.* **◯** *Tue–Fri & Sun.* **●** *Jan 1, Thanksgiving, Dec 25.* **⚐ ⚑**

THE LUSH Limahuli Garden is located a quarter of a mile (400 m) before the end of Kūhiō Highway, in a steep, high valley on its inland side. In ancient times, the Limahuli Valley was a self-sufficient *ahupua'a* (a wedge-shaped division of land running from mountain to sea). Since then, it has barely been occupied, with the exception of the notorious "Taylor Camp," an ocean-front commune that survived from 1969 to 1977 on land owned by Elizabeth Taylor's brother.

Part of the valley remains in sufficiently pristine condition to have been set aside as a botanical sanctuary, protecting both indigenous Hawaiian plants and species brought to the islands by early Polynesian settlers. The preserve is run by the National Tropical Botanical Garden, whose aim is to preserve the native species and increase their numbers.

Visitors are permitted to explore only a 17-acre portion that begins at the road and stretches inland, supporting

reconstructed ancient taro terraces that climb the well-watered hillside. A network of trails allows one to meander through a mixed forest of unusual trees, such as the Polynesian-introduced *kukui* or candlenut, once prized for its oil, and the native *'ōhi'a 'ai* or mountain apple. The higher slopes command wonderful views of the coastline below, as well as giving glimpses of the jagged Nā Pali cliffs to the west. Inland, the strangely eroded mountains loom above slender Limahuli Stream, overshadowing the off-limits Limahuli Preserve.

Hā'ena and Kē'ē Beaches ⑮

Kaua'i Co. Off Kūhiō Hwy (Hwy 56), 7 miles (11 km) W of Hanalei.

TWO SEPARATE beach parks with similar names are located near the end of the highway along the North Shore. The first one, **Hā'ena Beach County Park**, offers a pleasant campsite in a coconut grove where the shoreline is too exposed for safe swimming. Ten minutes' walk east from here is **Tunnels Beach**, whose extensive reef is one of Kaua'i's most popular snorkeling sites. The name refers not to the beautiful coral formations but to the tubular waves that lure the surfers here in winter. Immediately west of here, the second park, **Hā'ena State Park**, is mostly inaccessible to

Snorkeling at Tunnels Beach

casual visitors, having been set aside more to spare this section of coast from development than to make it available for public use. **Kē'ē Beach**, at the end of the road but still within the state park, is one of the most beautiful of all the North Shore beaches, its glowing yellow sands all but engulfed by rampant tropical vegetation. The turquoise inshore lagoon provides an irresistible cooling-off spot for hikers back from the Kalalau Trail *(see pp142–3)*, as well as a much-loved swimming and snorkeling site. However, the often-turbulent waters around and beyond the reef hold perils for the unwary.

Many legends attach themselves to this remote beach, including one that identifies it as the original birthplace of *hula*. Pele the volcano goddess *(see p14)* is said to have been enticed here in a dream by the sweet music of the young Kauaian warrior Lohi'au. Upon waking, she sent her sister Hi'iaka to bring Lohi'au to her, but these two promptly fell in love. Beneath the undergrowth, near the start of the Kalalau Trail, crumbling walls mark the site of Lohi'au's home, while the raised headland just west of the beach holds the remains of Hawai'i's first *hālau hula* (*hula* school). Here, Hi'iaka passed on the art of *hula* to eager devotees from all the islands.

Hibiscus at Limahuli Garden

Limahuli Garden's taro terraces, where the crop is grown in the traditional way

Kalalau Trail ⑯

T HE PRECIPITOUS CLIFFS of the Nā Pali Coast make it impossible for the road to continue west of Kē'ē Beach, but hardy hikers can follow the narrow Kalalau Trail 11 more miles (18 km) to isolated Kalalau Valley. One of the most dramatic hikes in the world, it threads its way through a landscape of almost primeval vastness and splendor. While this is not an expedition to undertake lightly, a half-day round trip to Hanakāpī'ai Valley is within most capabilities and provides an unforgettable wilderness experience. The trail gets progressively drier as it heads west, so the initial stretches are the muddiest, with the densest vegetation. Negotiating this tangled forest of *hala* (pandanus) trees often requires scrambling over rock falls, or picking your way among slippery tree roots.

Start of the trail ①
The trail climbs steeply from the trailhead at the end of Kūhiō Highway, affording spectacular views of the rugged coastline.

Makana Peak ②
On special occasions, the ancient Hawaiians tossed flaming logs into the night sky from this peak. Crowds would gather in boats on the sea below to watch this early form of fireworks.

Ke Ahu A Laka ③
This was once Hawai'i's most celebrated *hālau hula* (*hula* school), where students could spend several years learning their art. The ancient temple nearby is thought to have been used for graduation ceremonies.

Hanakāpī'ai Valley ④
In summer, a pristine sandy beach replaces the pebbles found in winter at the mouth of Hanakāpī'ai Valley. This shore has a high rate of drownings, and swimming is extremely dangerous.

End of the trail ⑨
For the last 5 miles (8 km), the trail clings perilously to a sandstone cliff that turns to dust at every step, thanks to the goats that have eaten the vegetation that should bind the soil together. The view of Kalalau Valley is the reward for the long hike.

Tips for Hikers

There is no food or safe drinking water along the trail. To camp in Hanakāpi'ai, Hanakoa, or Kalalau valleys, you must obtain permission in advance from the State Parks office, 3060 'Eiwa St, Lihu'e, HI 96766, (808) 274-3444. It is also possible to enjoy the North Shore coastline by boat or helicopter. For a full list of tour operators, contact the HVCB, Lihu'e, (808) 245-3971.

Kē'ē Beach
Kūhiō Hwy

Hanakāpi'ai Falls ⑤
An energetic hour's hike inland, through a long-abandoned coffee plantation, ends up at this towering waterfall.

Pā Ma Wa'a ⑥
This vertical 800-ft (240-m) cliff stands above a protected little cove welcomed by weary canoers. The boulder at the top marks the highest point on the Kalalau Trail.

Hanging Valleys ⑦
Between Hanakāpi'ai and Hanakoa, the trail dips into a number of "hanging valleys," where the streams have yet to cut their way down to sea level.

Hanakoa Valley ⑧
The campsite here is set amid the ruins of ancient taro terraces (see p109), with no access to the sea. The mighty 2,000-ft (600-m) cascade at the head of the valley is just 600 yds (550 m) away – a short but muddy climb.

0 kilometers 2
0 miles 1

KEY

- - Hiking trail

▬ Road

⚹ Vista

Ko'olau the Leper (far right) with his family

Kalalau Valley ⑰

Kaua'i Co. ℹ HVCB, Lihu'e, (808) 245-3971.

U NLESS YOU PERSEVERE through the last difficult stretch of the Kalalau Trail, the majestic amphitheater of Kalalau Valley can be seen only from afar. Most visitors view it by boat or helicopter tour, or from the two lookouts at the end of Kōke'e Road (see pp144–5).

For well over 1,000 years this isolated valley was home to a thriving community of taro farmers. In the years after European contact, however, disease and the lure of the city thinned out the population, the last permanent inhabitant leaving in 1919. Later, Kalalau became a cattle ranch and was then briefly colonized by hippies who sneaked in during the 1960s. Attempts to evict them resulted in the creation of the Nā Pali Coast State Park, which now controls access and limits places at Kalalau's idyllic camp site.

The valley's pinnacles made a perfect refuge for the infamous Ko'olau the Leper, as immortalized by Jack London (see p15) in his story of the same name. Ko'olau, a cowboy from Waimea, fled into the valley in the 1890s rather than face exile and death at Moloka'i's dreaded leper colony (see pp86–7). Ko'olau's wife eventually left Kalalau alone, after both her husband and son had died of leprosy.

Birds of Kaua'i

The innermost recesses of the Nā Pali valleys, and the bogs and ravines that stretch across the top of Kaua'i, are cloaked with dense rain forest. This unique environment is the last natural sanctuary for the island's native flora and fauna. Before human contact with Hawai'i, only a handful of bird species lived here – probably descendants of wind-blown stragglers lucky to find dry land. Encountering endemic plants with curved flowers, many birds developed curved bills for sipping nectar; others acquired short, strong beaks for crushing seeds and nuts. Forest birds extinct elsewhere in the state still cling to life in the 'ōhi'a forests of the Alaka'i Swamp. Honeycreepers abound here, the most common being the bright-red 'i'iwi, with its black wings and salmon-colored sickle-shaped bill; the 'apapane, similarly colored but with a short, black bill; and the diminutive yellow 'anianiau. Also conspicuous is the gregarious rust-colored 'elepaio, which follows hikers through the forest.

Most prominent on the Nā Pali Coast are the soaring tropicbirds, while in the drier Kōke'e State Park, honking nēnē appear at the lookouts together with Kaua'i's most ubiquitous bird, the moa, or red jungle fowl – a showy wild chicken.

The tiny 'anianiau

Red-billed tropicbird

Moa, red jungle fowl

Waimea Canyon and Kōke'e State Park ⑱

W AIMEA CANYON, known as the "Grand Canyon of the Pacific," was created by an earthquake that almost split Kaua'i in two. Over time, heavy rains have helped form a gorge 3,000 ft (915 m) deep that is still eroding at a frightening pace, as landslides slash away layers of rich green vegetation and the Waimea River washes tons of red mud daily into the ocean.

Most visitors see the canyon from the lookouts dotted along the rim, along Kōke'e Road, but hiking trails enable the more adventurous to explore in greater depth. At the north end of Waimea Canyon is Kōke'e State Park, laced through by more hiking trails and including the most accessible part of the daunting Alaka'i Swamp. The road finally ends at two stunning overlooks 4,000 ft (1,220 m) above the Nā Pali Coast.

View from Waimea Canyon Drive showing eroded, exposed earth

Kōke'e State Park Headquarters
Information and maps are available here, and the staff advises on hiking conditions.

Kōke'e Museum has informative displays on local wildlife and history, and at the lodge next door you can buy gifts and simple meals.

★ Waimea Canyon Lookout
Despite being the lowest of the lookouts, this offers the definitive canyon views: north into the gorges cut by the Waiahulu and Po'omau streams, and south to Waimea itself on the distant shoreline.

STAR FEATURES
★ Alaka'i Swamp
★ Pu'u O Kila Lookout
★ Waimea Canyon Lookout

Iliau Nature Loop
Reached from mile marker 9, this roadside trail is named after the iliau plant, which is endemic to this part of Kaua'i. Native plants along the loop are labeled.

Waimea

Kalalau Trail
(see pp142–3)

Kalalau Lookout

Kalalau Trail

Valley Trail

Kaluapuhi Trail

Pihea Trail

Alaka'i Swamp Trail

Pihea Trail

Ditch Trail

Mōhihi Trail

Kohua Ridge Trail

Koaie Canyon Trail

Waimea Canyon Trail

↓ Waimea

Kilohana Lookout

VISITORS' CHECKLIST

Kaua'i Co. Kōke'e Road (Highway 550). ☎ *Kaua'i Division of State Parks, (808) 274-3444.* **Kōke'e State Park** ○ *daily.* **Kōke'e Museum** ☎ *(808) 335-9975.* **Donation.** ○ *daily.* 🏠 **Kōke'e Lodge** ☎ *(808) 335-6061.* 🔲 *Cabins available for rent.*

★ Pu'u O Kila Lookout
The main body of the magnificent Kalalau Valley (see p143) opens out at this spectacular lookout. The shore is inaccessible from here.

Pihea Trail switchbacks down for 4 miles (6.5 km) to emerge at an exposed headland high above Nu'alolo Valley.

Alaka'i Swamp Trail is a makeshift boardwalk leading to the cliffs above Wainiha Valley, with views to Hanalei.

★ Alaka'i Swamp
This bowl-like depression is drenched by up to 500 in (1,270 cm) of rain per year. Much of that water goes to feed Kaua'i's myriad waterfalls, but the rest is trapped by an underlying layer of nonporous volcanic rock. Part rainforest, part mist-draped bog, the Alaka'i Swamp boasts some of Hawai'i's rarest birds, such as the 'i'iwi, or honeycreeper.

Kukui Trail
An extension of the Iliau Nature Loop, this trail heads sharply down into the canyon as far as the Waimea River – a relatively easy, rewarding trip.

KEY

▬▬	Major road
▭▭	Minor road
▭▭	Dirt or four-wheel-drive road
▪ ▪	Hiking trail
〰	River
✻	Vista
🏠	Picnic area

0 kilometers 2
0 miles 1

Polihale Beach ⑲

Kaua'i Co. 5 miles (8 km) beyond the end of Kaumuali'i Hwy (Hwy 50).

THE WESTERNMOST region of Kaua'i, shielded from the ocean winds in the rain shadow of the central mountains, is characterized by long, flat expanses of sand. A sizable chunk has been taken over by the US military, whose sophisticated installations include systems that would give early warning of another attack on Pearl Harbor.

Skirt the security fences by following the dirt roads inland, and 15 miles (24 km) northwest of Waimea you come to the vast expanse of Polihale Beach. The surf is far too ferocious for swimming, but it's a wonderful place for a walk, with the cliffs of the Nā Pali Coast rising to the north. Head west from the end of the road and you'll reach the dunes known as the **Barking Sands**, whose hollow grains are said to groan and howl when disturbed by wind or a heavy footfall.

Waimea ⑳

Kaua'i Co. 1,900. HVCB, Lihu'e, (808) 245-3971.

WAIMEA IS AMONG Kaua'i's more historic towns. It was here in 1778 that the crewmen of Captain Cook's third Pacific voyage – after pausing to shoot a Hawaiian – became the first Europeans to set foot on Hawaiian soil. Cook stated that "I never saw Indians so much astonished," while he himself was amazed to find the natives speaking a Polynesian language similar to those in the far-off South Seas. A statue of Cook graces the town center.

However, perhaps mindful of the mixed results of Cook's visit, including rampant venereal disease, the beach where he landed is named not in his honor but after Lucy Wright, Waimea's first native teacher. Situated west of the Waimea ("reddish water") River, it is

Statue of Captain Cook in Waimea

made up largely of mud washed down from Waimea Canyon. A plaque marks the site of Cook's first landfall.

Just across Waimea River, a headland holds what's left of **Russian Fort Elizabeth**. This star-shaped edifice was built by an adventurer, George Schäffer, in 1816. A German doctor, pretending to be a naturalist but working as a spy for the Russian-American Company, he had gained the confidence of Kaumuali'i, the chief of Kaua'i, and decided to double-cross his employers. He and Kaumuali'i hatched a plot to conquer the archipelago and divide it between the Tsar of Russia and the chief. Within a year, fooled into thinking that the US and Russia were at war, Schäffer fled the islands. His fort served the government for 50 more years but is now dilapidated.

Hanapēpē ㉑

Kaua'i Co. 1,400. HVCB, Lihu'e, (808) 245-3971.

HALFWAY BETWEEN Waimea and Po'ipū, Hanapēpē makes an intriguing detour off Kaumuali'i Highway (Hwy 50). Although taro was once grown in the valley, the village owes its late 19th-century look to the Chinese laborers who farmed rice here after serving out their contracts on sugar plantations.

Later Hanapēpē was all but abandoned, but several of its timber-frame buildings have now reopened as galleries and craft shops, and there are several attractive restaurants.

Allerton Garden ㉒

Kaua'i Co. (808) 742-2623. Kalāheo. Mon–Sat. Thanksgiving, Dec 25. with prior notification. by appointment, at visitor center across from Spouting Horn parking lot, Lāwa'i Road, Po'ipū.

LAWA'I VALLEY stretches back from the pretty little cove of Lāwa'i Kai, 2 miles (3 km) west of Po'ipū. Occupied in antiquity by taro farmers and later used by Chinese immigrants to grow rice, the valley became Queen Emma's favorite retreat in the 1870s. In the 1930s, it was bought by the Allertons, a Chicago banking family, and a plot near the sea was exquisitely landscaped to create Allerton Garden.

Bequeathed to the National Tropical Botanical Garden by the last of the Allertons in 1987, the valley was devastated by Hurricane Iniki in 1992. It will be some time before either the Allertons' oceanfront home or Queen Emma's cottage are fully restored, but the Allerton Garden is once more a showpiece. Unlike its counterpart at Limahuli (see p141), it aims to delight the eye rather than concentrate on native plants.

Visitors are transported from the visitor center near Po'ipū to the otherwise inaccessible site in low-roofed, open-sided

The pool and pavilion of the Diana Fountain at Allerton Garden

vintage limousines known as Hilo sampans, and from there tour the garden on foot. The Allertons conceived the design as a series of separate "rooms," and each section, such as the serene Diana Fountain or the Italianate Art Deco Mermaid Fountain, has its own character. The plants are the real stars, however, from dazzling heliconias and bromeliads to assorted tropical fruits in the orchards. Species familiar as house plants in chillier climes revel in the opportunity to run riot, while graceful palms line the placid stream that glides through the heart of the valley.

Serious botanists will appreciate the chance to see rare species in the nursery, including *Kanaloa kahoolawensis*, a woody shrub whose only two known wild specimens were first identified on Kaho'olawe *(see p102)* during the 1980s. Prior reservation is required for the tour, and children under five are not admitted. A visitor center, surrounded by 10 acres of gardens near the parking lot, was opened in 1997.

Po'ipū **㉓**

Kaua'i Co. 🏠 *1,000.* 🚌 *2 a day.* **ℹ** *HVCB, Lihu'e, (808) 245-3971.*

Sprawling to either side of the mouth of the Waikomo Stream, at the southern tip of Kaua'i, Po'ipū remains the island's most popular beach

Spouting Horn sending up a jet of water

resort. In 1992, Hurricane Iniki ripped the roofs off its plush oceanfront hotels and filled their lobbies with sand and ruined cars. Give or take the odd derelict property, Po'ipū is now back to normal: a strip of hotels, condos, and restaurants.

The prime spot in the center of the beach is **Po'ipū Beach Park**, complete with vigilant lifeguards and a kids' playground. There's safe swimming directly offshore, and great snorkeling around the rocks at its western end. To the east, **Brennecke's Beach** is more of a haunt for young surfers, while farther along, beyond Makahū'ena Point, the shoreline becomes a wilderness of sand dunes. The fossilized

bones of long-extinct flightless birds known as Māhā'ulepū have been found in this area, and several native plant species survive here and nowhere else.

Environs: Po'ipū itself is a modern creation, but the rudimentary jetty at the mouth of Waikomo Stream has been in use since the mid-19th century. Known as Kōloa Landing, it was built to serve Hawai'i's first sugarcane plantation, established 2 miles (3 km) inland at **Kōloa** in 1835. Kōloa now plays second fiddle to Po'ipū, but with its wooden boardwalks and false-fronted stores, it's a pleasant place for a stroll. A huge sugar mill dominates the area a mile (1.5 km) east of town. Built in 1913, it finally shut down in 1996.

The coastal road west of Po'ipū ends after only a mile (1.5 km) at **Spouting Horn**, a natural blow-hole in a ledge of black lava a few steps back from the sea. The waves that break against the rock are channeled underground and then forced up in fountains of white spume that can reach a height of 50 ft (15 m) before raining down onto the usual crowd of spectators. It is very dangerous to approach closer than the roadside lookout.

Ni'ihau, the "Forbidden Island"

Lying 15 miles (24 km) southwest of Kaua'i, but just visible from the coast at Waimea, Ni'ihau is the smallest populated island in the chain, with 250 inhabitants. Owned by the Gay and Robinson families – descendants of Elizabeth Sinclair, who paid Kamehameha V $10,000 for the island in 1864 – it is little affected by tourism. You can visit only by a costly helicopter tour that avoids the inhabited areas *(see p197)*. It has no hotel, airport, or cars.

Although Ni'ihau's original inhabitants were furious at the sale of their homeland to an outsider, the isolation has since turned the island into the last stronghold of Hawaiian culture – Hawaiian is still the first language here. When not tending cattle for the Ni'ihau Ranch, locals support themselves with fishing, farming, and threading necklaces of the delicate *pūpū* (shells) that wash up on the beaches.

With annual rainfall of just 12 in (300 mm) Ni'ihau is able to support only minimal agriculture. The only town, Pu'uwai ("heart"), is on the west coast, a grid of dirt roads dotted with bungalows and colorful gardens.

Ni'ihau's west coast and the tiny town of Pu'uwai

TRAVELERS' NEEDS

WHERE TO STAY

FROM THOUSAND-ROOM, oceanfront mega-resorts to a treehouse for two in Hawai'i Island's Waipi'o Valley, the accommodation possibilities in Hawai'i are as numerous as they are diverse. The price range, too, is vast. As the beach is the main attraction for most visitors, the hotels closest to the ocean are considered most desirable and are usually the most pricey. Air-conditioning is

Bellhop at Mauna Lani

standard, though some smaller and older properties provide ceiling fans instead. In addition to resort hotels, there are many dozens of smaller hotels, condominiums, inns, and bed & breakfasts, all with lower rates. Many of the inns and B&Bs are charming and distinctive and stress personalized service; some, like the Old Wailuku Inn at Ulupono on Maui, are historic properties.

CHAIN AND BOUTIQUE HOTELS

MOST OF HAWAI'I's large resort hotels are run by well-known chains such as **Hilton**, **Hyatt**, and **Sheraton**. Some are so self-contained and offer such a variety of activities that many visitors choose never to leave the property. If you prefer elegance and gracious service, however, head for gems like the Halekūlani in Waikīkī *(see p153)* or Maui's Four Seasons Resort *(see p158)*.

Less pricey options include local chains such as **Aston Hotels & Resorts**, **Outrigger Hotels Hawai'i**, and **Marc Resorts Hawai'i**, as well as smaller, individual establishments that stress service over amenities. The latter, known as "boutique" hotels, are popular with inter-island travelers.

CONDOMINIUMS

A CONDOMINIUM UNIT or "condo" – an apartment, really – is an ideal choice for a family or travelers who would prefer to spend their money

on sightseeing and activities rather than on accommodations and dining. On O'ahu, they are mostly in high-rise buildings *mauka* (inland) of Waikīkī. On the neighboring islands, they are generally in low-rise complexes often located on or near the beach.

Condos range in size from studios to three-bedroom units suitable for up to eight adults or a family. They have kitchens and are stocked with everything from china to beach towels. Most condo units are privately owned and may be booked directly, through companies such as **Sunquest Vacations** on Hawai'i Island, **Kaua'i Vacation Rentals** on Kaua'i, and **Destination Resorts Hawai'i** on Maui *(see p158)*. Condos in smaller complexes can be booked through the building's resident manager. Housekeeping service varies, but is normally provided every three or four days.

Front Desk at Kaua'i's Princeville Hotel *(see p161)*

INNS AND B&Bs

HAWAI'I's FEW INNS are worth seeking out as an alternative to the big hotels. Because they are small and do not offer the amenities of the resorts, their staff pride themselves on service and attention to detail. Maui's Lahaina Inn, a restored Victorian-era masterpiece, is a stunning example *(see p157)*.

In recent years hundreds of B&Bs (bed & breakfasts) have sprung up all over Hawai'i. Many are just a room in someone's home; others are charming cottages. If a B&B is your style, contact **Hawai'i's Best Bed & Breakfasts**, which represents the top 100 in the state. Other associations include **All Islands Bed & Breakfast** and **Bed & Breakfast Hawai'i**.

CAMPING AND HOSTELS

CAMPSITES range in setting from beachfront park to volcanic crater. All county and state parks require permits, available for a small fee from **County Departments of Parks and Recreation** or the **State Department of Land and Natural Resources**. Some parks have basic cabins, which are inexpensive, but usually

Water activities at the Hilton Waikoloa Village Resort *(see p160)*

◁ **Vacationers enjoying the sea and sun at one of Hawai'i's golden sand beaches**

Idyllic seaside camp site at ʻAnini Beach on Kauaʻi's North Shore

booked months in advance, especially on weekends. The main islands also have hostels, with dormitory accommodations and some private rooms. Contact the Hawaiʻi Visitors and Convention Bureau for more information *(see p191).*

PRICES AND BOOKING

HAWAIʻI HAS accommodations to match every desire and wallet. Prices are highest from December to April, and lowest in May, June, September, and October. One of the more economical options is to stay in a condo. A one-bedroom unit, which can easily fit a family of four, costs between $150 and $250 per night. Some inns and B&Bs have double rooms for under $100 a night.

Cabin in Haleakalā National Park

It is simplest to book accommodations through your travel agent. The Hawaiʻi Visitors and Convention Bureau can help, as can resort and B&B reservation services. You can also book directly; most have phone numbers that are toll-free in the US – they are preceded by area code (800) or (888).

Bungalow bedroom at Mauna Lani on the Kohala Coast *(see p160)*

HIDDEN EXTRAS

ALL ACCOMMODATIONS are subject to a combined sales and room tax of 11.42 percent. Most places allow children to share with parents at no extra charge, but check beforehand. Phone calls and faxes from hotel rooms are more expensive than normal rates, and many hotels in Honolulu charge a daily rate for parking. Extra costs can include things like towel "rental" and items from your minibar. To avoid surprises at check-out, ask beforehand. Tipping is not mandatory, but average tips for staff are as follows: $2–3 a day for housekeepers; $1–2 for bell-hops and parking attendants.

VISITORS WITH DISABILITIES

ALL HOTELS and many smaller properties have at least some rooms with disabled access; many ensure access to public areas as well. The Commission on Persons with Disabilities *(see p191)* publishes the *Aloha Guide to Accessibility,* which has a list of the most accessible hotels.

TRAVELING WITH CHILDREN

FAMILIES WITH CHILDREN should choose a large resort with children's activities, or a condo. Most of the hotels with activities charge for the care, but some of the top hotels offer a fantastic service at no additional charge.

Choosing a Hotel

THESE HOTELS have been selected across a wide price range for their excellent facilities and locations. Where room rates span more than one price category, we have given the lowest. Figures in parentheses indicate the number of suites available. The chart lists the hotels by area; the color-coded thumb tabs indicate the areas covered on each page. For restaurant listings see pages 166–75.

	CREDIT CARDS	OCEAN VIEW	CHILDREN'S PROGRAM	GOOD RESTAURANT
HONOLULU AND WAIKĪKĪ				
WAIKĪKĪ: *The Breakers Hotel.* **Map 4 D4.** $$ 250 Beach Walk, HI 96815. ((808) 923-3811, (800) 426-0494. FAX (808) 923-7174. A 1950s vintage, Hawaiian-style oasis, amid towering neighbors, that prides itself on Hawaiian hospitality. Tropical flowers and a patio surround the swimming pool. Kitchenette in every room. **Rooms:** 49 (15)	AE MC V			
WAIKĪKĪ: *Hawaiiana Hotel.* **Map 4 D4.** $$ 260 Beach Walk, HI 96815. ((808) 923-3811, (800) 367-5122. FAX (808) 926-5728. Built in 1955, these low-rise buildings provide a tropical Hawaiian setting. Kona coffee and pineapple juice are served by the pool each morning. Hawaiian entertainment two nights a week. **Rooms:** 93	AE MC V D JCB			
WAIKĪKĪ: *Island Colony Hotel - A Marc Suite.* **Map 4 E4.** $$ 445 Seaside Ave, HI 96815. ((808) 923-2345, (800) 922-7866. FAX (808) 921-7105. A simple, no-frills hotel on a busy street off Kalākaua Avenue, near the Ala Wai Canal. Short walk to the heart of Waikīkī. **Rooms:** 271 (76)	AE MC V, D JCB			
WAIKĪKĪ: *Outrigger Waikiki Tower.* **Map 4 D5.** $$ 200 Lewers Street, HI 96815. ((808) 922-6424, (800) 688-7444. FAX (808) 923-7437. A pleasant enough hotel for the price, less than half a block from Waikīkī Beach. Four restaurants and three bars. **Rooms:** 439	AE MC V, D JCB	●		●
WAIKĪKĪ: *Queen Kapi'olani Hotel.* **Map 4 F5.** $$ 150 Kapahulu Ave, HI 96815. ((808) 922-1941, (800) 367-5004. FAX (808) 596-0158. Overlooking Kapi'olani Park and Diamond Head, this simple high-rise is a good value. Relatively quiet location, half a block from Kūhiō Beach, and close to the zoo, aquarium, and the rest of Waikīkī. **Rooms:** 315	AE MC V D JCB	●		●
WAIKĪKĪ: *Royal Garden at Waikiki.* **Map 4 D4.** $$ 440 'Olohana St, HI 96815. ((808) 943-0202, (800) 367-5666. FAX (808) 945-7407. This boutique hotel is truly a breath of luxurious fresh air. Half a block from the Ala Wai Canal, it is fairly quiet with beautifully appointed rooms and baths, and an excellent restaurant, Cascada. **Rooms:** 201 (19)	AE MC V D JCB		■	●
WAIKĪKĪ: *Aston Waikiki Beachside Hotel.* **Map 4 E5.** $$$ 2452 Kalākaua Ave, HI 96815. ((808) 931-2100, (800) 922-7866. FAX (808) 922-8785. An elegant boutique hotel with lavishly appointed small guest rooms and public areas. Attentive service and complimentary breakfast. **Rooms:** 79	AE MC V, D JCB	●		
WAIKĪKĪ: *Aston Waikiki Sunset.* **Map 4 F4.** $$$ 229 Paoakalani Ave, HI 96815. ((808) 922-0511, (800) 922-7866. FAX (808) 923-8580. Located just a block from the beach and two from the zoo, this all-suite hotel has a pool, tennis court, and minigrocery on site. **Suites:** 377	AE MC V, D JCB			
WAIKĪKĪ: *Hawaiian Regent Hotel.* **Map 4 F5.** $$$ 2552 Kalākaua Ave, HI 96815. ((808) 922-6611, (800) 367-5370. FAX (808) 921-5222. This 5-acre resort beside Kūhiō Beach has two towers with attractively decorated rooms, some of which offer spectacular views. Six restaurants, two swimming pools, and many shops. **Rooms:** 1,291 (12)	AE MC V D JCB	●	■	●
WAIKĪKĪ: *The Outrigger Reef on the Beach.* **Map 4 D5.** $$$ 2169 Kālia Road, HI 96815. ((808) 923-3111, (800) 688-7444. FAX (808) 924-4957. This attractive, beachfront hotel is a good choice as a mid-price option. Nightly Hawaiian entertainment in the lounge. **Rooms:** 837 (46)	AE MC V D JCB	●		
WAIKĪKĪ: *Outrigger Waikiki on the Beach.* **Map 4 E5.** $$$ 2335 Kalākaua Ave, HI 96815. ((808) 923-0711, (800) 688-7444. FAX (808) 921-9749. The flagship of the Outrigger chain, this oceanfront hotel has eight restaurants and five lounges. The Society of Seven, one of Honolulu's most popular cabaret acts, performs here. **Rooms:** 496 (34)	AE MC V D JCB	●		

Price categories for a standard double room for one night in tourist season (Dec–Apr), including taxes:

$ under $85
$$ $85–$150
$$$ $150–$250
$$$$ $250–$400
$$$$$ over $400

CREDIT CARDS
Indicates which credit cards are accepted: *AE* American Express; *MC* MasterCard; *V* VISA; *D* Discover; *JCB* Japanese Credit Bureau.

OCEAN VIEW
Indicates that oceanfront guest rooms are available, or rooms with spectacular views of the ocean.

CHILDREN'S PROGRAM
Hotel can provide cribs, babysitting service, children's menu, special children's activities, or facilities such as video or game room.

GOOD RESTAURANT
Recommended restaurant within the hotel complex, offering good food, often in an attractive setting or with a lovely view.

WAIKĪKĪ: *Pacific Beach Hotel.* **Map 4 F5.** $$$
2490 Kalākaua Ave, HI 96815. ((808) 922-1233, (800) 367-6060. FAX (808) 922-8061.
The main attraction at this twin-tower hotel across from Kūhiō Beach is the three-story aquarium – you can even dine beside it at the Oceanarium Restaurant. Pool, spa, tennis, and shopping on site. *Rooms: 822 (8)*
Credit Cards: AE MC V D JCB · *Ocean View* · *Children's Program* · *Good Restaurant*

WAIKĪKĪ: *Radisson Waikīkī Prince Kūhiō.* **Map 4 F4.** $$$
2500 Kūhiō Ave, HI 96815. ((808) 922-0811, (888) 557-4422. FAX (808) 923-0330.
Considered the best of the Outrigger line, this hotel is a block from the beach and two from Kapiʻolani Park, but seems a long way from the Waikīkī crowds. Lovely rooms with marble baths. *Rooms: 619 (6)*
Credit Cards: AE MC V D JCB · *Ocean View* · *Children's Program* · *Good Restaurant*

WAIKĪKĪ: *Waikīkī Beachcomber Hotel.* **Map 4 E5.** $$$
2300 Kalākaua Ave, HI 96815. ((808) 922-4646, (800) 622-4646. FAX (808) 923-4889.
In the most congested part of Waikīkī, the attractions here are the proximity to the beach, the Royal Hawaiian Shopping Center, and International Market Place, plus Don Ho, who performs here *(see p181).* *Rooms: 491 (6)*
Credit Cards: AE MC V JCB · *Ocean View* · *Good Restaurant*

WAIKĪKĪ: *Waikīkī Joy Hotel.* **Map 4 D4.** $$$
320 Lewers Street, HI 96815. ((808) 923-2300, (800) 922-7866. FAX (808) 924-4010.
One of the smaller boutique hotels, with very pleasant rooms and interesting "extras," including Jacuzzi tubs, state-of-the-art stereo systems, and a karaoke studio. Lewers Street can be noisy. *Rooms: 47 (47)*
Credit Cards: AE MC V D JCB · *Good Restaurant*

WAIKĪKĪ: *Waikīkī Parc Hotel.* **Map 4 D5.** $$$
2233 Helumoa Rd, HI 96815. ((808) 921-7272, (800) 422-0450. FAX (808) 923-1336.
This friendly, intimate hotel offers affordable luxury, a great location, and two excellent restaurants. Guests here enjoy signing privileges at the Halekūlani, the Waikīkī Parc's "sister" hotel. *Rooms: 298*
Credit Cards: AE MC V D JCB · *Ocean View* · *Good Restaurant*

WAIKĪKĪ: *Halekūlani.* **Map 4 D5.** $$$$
2199 Kālia Rd, HI 96815. ((808) 923-2311, (800) 367-2343. FAX (808) 926-8004.
The Halekūlani is the epitome of elegance. Everything is perfect – the manicured tropical grounds, the tasteful decor, the superb cuisine at La Mer, and the beautiful, orchid-design pool. *Rooms: 412 (44)*
Credit Cards: AE MC V JCB · *Ocean View* · *Children's Program* · *Good Restaurant*

WAIKĪKĪ: *Hyatt Regency Waikīkī.* **Map 4 E5.** $$$$
2424 Kalākaua Ave, HI 96815. ((808) 923-1234, (800) 233-1234. FAX (808) 923-7839.
Located in the center of Waikīkī, this impressive resort consists of two 40-story towers joined by an elaborate atrium with an intriguing but very noisy waterfall. Several quality restaurants. *Rooms: 1,212 (18)*
Credit Cards: AE MC V D JCB · *Ocean View* · *Children's Program* · *Good Restaurant*

WAIKĪKĪ: *The Royal Hawaiian.* **Map 4 D5.** $$$$
2259 Kalākaua Ave, HI 96815. ((808) 923-7311, (800) 325-3589. FAX (808) 924-7098.
This elegant Waikīkī landmark, built in 1927, is affectionately known as the Pink Palace *(see pp50–51).* *Rooms: 526 (54)*
Credit Cards: AE MC V, D JCB · *Ocean View* · *Children's Program* · *Good Restaurant*

WAIKĪKĪ: *Sheraton Moana Surfrider.* **Map 4 E5.** $$$$
2365 Kalākaua Ave, HI 96815. ((808) 922-3111, (800) 325-3535. FAX (808) 923-0308.
This stunning "First Lady of Waikīkī," whose central part was built in 1901, combines modern comforts with high elegance and grandeur *(see p52).* Don't miss tea on the Banyan Veranda. *Rooms: 747 (46)*
Credit Cards: AE MC V D JCB · *Ocean View* · *Children's Program* · *Good Restaurant*

WAIKĪKĪ: *Sheraton Waikīkī Hotel.* **Map 4 D5.** $$$$
2255 Kalākaua Ave, HI 96815. ((808) 922-4422, (800) 325-3535. FAX (808) 923-8785.
If you like to be right in the middle of the action, this huge hotel fronting a tiny beach may be just the place for you. The top floor offers a spectacular panoramic view. *Rooms: 1,722 (130)*
Credit Cards: AE MC V D JCB · *Ocean View* · *Children's Program* · *Good Restaurant*

WAIKĪKĪ: *Aston Waikīkī Beach Tower.* **Map 4 F5.** $$$$$
2470 Kalākaua Ave, HI 96815. ((808) 926-6400, (800) 922-7866. FAX (808) 926-7380.
All-suite luxury hotel with large *lanai,* across from the beach. No restaurant or activities, but concierge service is available. *Suites: 96*
Credit Cards: AE MC V, D JCB · *Ocean View*

For key to symbols see back flap

<table>
<tr><td>

Price categories for a standard double room for one night in tourist season (Dec–Apr), including taxes:

$ under $85
$$ $85–$150
$$$ $150–$250
$$$$ $250–$400
$$$$$ over $400

</td><td>

CREDIT CARDS
Indicates which credit cards are accepted: *AE* American Express; *MC* MasterCard; *V* VISA; *D* Discover; *JCB* Japanese Credit Bureau.

OCEAN VIEW
Indicates that oceanfront guest rooms are available, or rooms with spectacular views of the ocean.

CHILDREN'S PROGRAM
Hotel can provide cribs, babysitting service, children's menu, special children's activities, or facilities such as video or game room.

GOOD RESTAURANT
Recommended restaurant within the hotel complex, offering good food, often in an attractive setting or with a lovely view.

</td></tr>
</table>

	CREDIT CARDS	OCEAN VIEW	CHILDREN'S PROGRAM	GOOD RESTAURANT
GREATER HONOLULU: *Ala Moana Hotel.* **Map 3 A4.** **$$** 410 Atkinson Drive, HI 96814. (808) 955-4811, (800) 367-6025. FAX (808) 944-2974. Located near the popular Ala Moana Beach Park, the Hawai'i Convention Center, and the Ala Moana Center, this 36-story hotel has eight restaurants, including the well-known Nicholas Nickolas. *Rooms: 1,102 (67)*	AE MC V D JCB	●		●
GREATER HONOLULU: *Hawaiian Monarch Hotel.* **Map 3 C3.** **$$** 444 Niu Street, HI 96815. (808) 949-3911, (800) 535-0085. FAX (808) 955-3506. Modern high-rise on Waikīkī's western edge with good views. Three blocks from the beach and five from the Ala Moana Center. *Rooms: 439*	AE MC V, D JCB	●		●
GREATER HONOLULU: *Inn on the Park.* **Map 3 C4.** **$$** 1920 Ala Moana Boulevard, HI 96815. (808) 946-8355, (800) 367-5004. FAX (808) 946-4839. At Waikīkī's entrance, this hotel is closer to the shops than the beach but is a good value place to stay. *Rooms: 238*	AE- MC V JCB	●		
GREATER HONOLULU: *Pagoda Hotel and Terrace.* **Map 3 A3.** **$$** 1525 Rycroft St, HI 96814. (808) 941-6611, (800) 367-6060. FAX (808) 955-5067. Popular with locals, the Pagoda offers rooms that are unadorned but a good value. The hotel is set in beautiful water gardens; a "floating" Chinese restaurant serves quality fare. *Rooms: 200; Apartments: 160*	AE MC V D JCB			
GREATER HONOLULU: *Doubletree Alana Waikīkī Hotel.* **Map 3 C4.** **$$$** 1956 Ala Moana Boulevard, HI 96815. (808) 941-7275, (800) 367-6070. FAX (808) 949-0996. A favorite with islanders, this is one of the best boutique hotels and is near that shoppers' mecca, the Ala Moana Center. Attractively appointed, functional rooms. *Rooms: 268 (45)*	AE MC V D JCB	●		●
GREATER HONOLULU: *The 'Ilikai/Hotel Nikko Waikīkī.* **Map 3 B4.** **$$$** 1777 Ala Moana Boulevard, HI 96815. (808) 949-3811, (800) 245-4524. FAX (808) 947-0892. Convenient for Waikīkī beaches and Ala Moana Center and Beach Park. The main attractions are Sarento's Italian restaurant, a tennis center, and a laser arena for playing tag. *Rooms: 696 (52)*	AE MC V D JCB	●		●
GREATER HONOLULU: *Mānoa Valley Inn* **$$$** 2001 Vancouver Drive, HI 96822. (808) 947-6019. FAX (808) 946-6168. Set in beautiful grounds minutes from Waikīkī, this 1915 home is showing signs of wear but it still retains its old-fashioned charm. Some rooms share a bath. *Rooms: 7 Cottage: 1*	MC V			
GREATER HONOLULU: *The New Otani Kaimana Beach Hotel* **$$$** 2863 Kalākaua Ave, HI 96815. (808) 923-1555, (800) 356-8264. FAX (808) 922-9404. On beautiful Sans Souci beach, this boutique hotel has small but nicely appointed rooms and two seaside restaurants – the Japanese Miyako and the Hau Tree Lānai, which serves delicious breakfasts. *Rooms: 102 (22)*	AE MC V D JCB	●	■	●
GREATER HONOLULU: *Hawai'i Prince Hotel Waikīkī.* **Map 3 A4.** **$$$$** 100 Holomoana St, HI 96815. (808) 956-1111, (800) 782-9488. FAX (808) 946-0811. Every room at this marina-front hotel faces the ocean, but there are no *lānai*. Popular with Japanese tourists, it is near the Ala Moana Center and has two highly regarded restaurants. *Rooms: 464 (57)*	AE MC V JCB	●		●
GREATER HONOLULU: *Hilton Hawaiian Village.* **Map 3 C4.** **$$$$** 2005 Kālia Road, HI 96815. (808) 949-4321, (800) 445-8667. FAX (808) 947-7898. More like a small city than a hotel, the Hilton has it all – a beach, three pools, over 100 shops, and 20 lounges and restaurants, most notably the Golden Dragon and award-winning Bali-by-the-Sea. *Rooms: 2,182 (363)*	AE MC V D JCB	●	■	●
GREATER HONOLULU: *Kāhala Mandarin Oriental, Hawai'i* **$$$$** 5000 Kāhala Ave, HI 96816. (808) 739-8888, (800) 367-2525. FAX (808) 739-8800. The modern, stylish Kāhala is fronted by a great swimming beach and is within reach of 20 public golf courses. The hotel's famous lagoon is home to two bottlenose dolphins. *Rooms: 342 (29)*	AE MC V D JCB	●	■	●

O'AHU

KAHUKU: *Turtle Bay Condominiums* $$
56-565 Kamehameha Hwy, PO Box 248, HI 96731. (808) 293-2800.
FAX (808) 293-2169. Sharing grounds with the Hilton (below), these condos are perfect for families who want to escape the hustle and bustle of Waikiki. The golf course is adjacent; the beach is nearby. **Units: 52**
AE MC V D JCB

KAHUKU: *Turtle Bay Hilton Golf and Tennis Resort* $$$
57-091 Kamehameha Hwy, HI 96731. (808) 293-8811,
(800) 445-8667. FAX (808) 293-9147. The only full-service resort on the gorgeous North Shore. Amenities include a championship golf course, a tennis complex, riding, and water sports. **Rooms: 461 (24)**
AE MC V D JCB

KAILUA: *Lanikai Bed & Breakfast* $$
1277 Mokulua Drive, HI 96734. (808) 261-1059, (800) 258-7895. FAX (808) 262-2181. Comfortable rooms in chic neighborhood across from lovely Lanikai Beach. Continental breakfast. Warm, knowledgeable hosts. **Rooms: 1 (1)**
MC V

KAILUA: *Pat's Kailua Beach Properties* $$
204 S Kalāheo Avenue, HI 96734. (808) 261-1653. FAX (808) 261-0893. The O'Malleys have homes in beautiful residential areas of Kailua and Lanikai. Simple, comfortable, Hawaiian-style lodgings. **Homes: 30**
AE MC V

KĀNE'OHE: *Ali'i Bluffs Windward Bed & Breakfast* $
46-251 'Iki'iki St, HI 96744. (808) 235-1124, (800) 235-1151. FAX (808) 235-1124. This European-style B&B is a short drive from O'ahu's best beach. The wonderful hosts have filled the house with antiques and art. **Rooms: 2**

KĀNE'OHE: *Schrader's Windward Marine Resort* $$$
47-039 Lihikai Drive, HI 96744. (808) 239-5711, (800) 735-5711. FAX (808) 239-6658. A quiet rural setting on a peninsula with lots of personalized attention. You can fish right from your *lānai*. One to three bedrooms with kitchenettes are available. **Rooms 22**
AE MC V D

SUNSET BEACH: *North Shore Vacation Homes* $$$
59-229C Ke Nui Rd, Hale'iwa, HI 96712. (808) 638-7289, (800) 678-5263. FAX (808) 638-8736. Hawaiian-style beach houses in a quiet North Shore neighborhood. Large *lānai* and all the comforts of home. **Homes: 4**
MC V

WAIMEA: *Kē Iki Hale* $$$
59-579 Kē Iki Rd, Hale'iwa, HI 96712. (808) 638-8229. FAX (808) 638-8229. Extremely basic, comfortable beach cottages run by a local resident. Serene, old-fashioned, family-style Hawai'i. **Rooms: 4 (8)**
MC V

MOLOKA'I AND LĀNA'I

KALUAKO'I (MOLOKA'I): *Kaluako'i Hotel and Golf Club* $$
Kaluako'i Road, PO Box 1977, HI 96770. (808) 552-2555, (888) 552-2550. FAX (808) 552-2821. Moloka'i's only full-fledged resort and 18-hole golf course offers warmth and comfort but none of the glitz of the mega-resorts. The rooms are in two-story redwood structures. **Rooms: 89 (14)**
AE MC V D JCB

KALUAKO'I (MOLOKA'I): *Kaluako'i Villas* $$
1131 Kaluako'i Road, PO Box 350, HI 96770. (808) 552-2721, (800) 367-5004. FAX (808) 552-2201. In the Kaluako'i Resort area on Kepuhi Beach. Soft colors and rattan furniture. No telephones or air-conditioning. **Units: 42**
AE MC V

KALUAKO'I (MOLOKA'I): *Paniolo Hale Resort Condominiums* $$
Lio Place, PO Box 190, HI 96770. (808) 552-2731, (800) 367-2984. FAX (808) 552-2288. Individually owned studio and one- and two-bedroom condos within the Kaluako'i Resort. No air-conditioning. **Units: 23**
AE MC V

KALUAKO'I (MOLOKA'I): *Ke Nani Resort* $$$
Kaluako'i Road, PO Box 289, HI 96770. (808) 552-2761, (800) 535-0085. FAX (808) 552-0045. Also within Kaluako'i Resort, these one- and two-bedroom condos are a short walk from Kepuhi Beach. Full kitchens, private *lānai*, and other home comforts. No air-conditioning. **Units: 120**
AE MC V D JCB

KAUNAKAKAI (MOLOKA'I): *Hotel Moloka'i* $$
Mile marker 2, Kamehameha V Hwy, PO Box 1020, HI 96748. (808) 553-5347, FAX (808) 553-5047. This oceanfront, Polynesian-style hotel is a favorite with islanders, offering simple, comfortable lodgings and warm service. Enjoy seaside dining at the Holo Holo Kai Restaurant. **Rooms: 42**
AE MC V JCB

For key to symbols see back flap

Price categories for a standard double room for one night in tourist season (Dec–Apr), including taxes:

$ under $85
$$ $85–$150
$$$ $150–$250
$$$$ $250–$400
$$$$$ over $400

CREDIT CARDS
Indicates which credit cards are accepted: *AE* American Express; *MC* MasterCard; *V* VISA; *D* Discover; *JCB* Japanese Credit Bureau.

OCEAN VIEW
Indicates that oceanfront guest rooms are available, or rooms with spectacular views of the ocean.

CHILDREN'S PROGRAM
Hotel can provide cribs, babysitting service, children's menu, special children's activities, or facilities such as video or game room.

GOOD RESTAURANT
Recommended restaurant within the hotel complex, offering good food, often in an attractive setting or with a lovely view.

	Credit Cards	Ocean View	Children's Program	Good Restaurant
KAUNAKAKAI (MOLOKA'I): *Wavecrest Resort* $$ Mile marker 13, Kamehameha V Hwy, HCO1 Box 541, HI 96748. (808) 558-8103, (800) 535-0085. FAX (808) 558-8206. This low-key, seaside complex of one- and two-bedroom suites is the closest accommodation possible to the gorgeous east end of Moloka'i. No telephones or air-conditioning. 🔲🔲🔲🔲🔲 **Units:** 126	AE MC V	●		
KAUNAKAKAI (MOLOKA'I): *Moloka'i Shores Suites* $$$ Mile marker 1, Kamehameha V Hwy, PO Box1037, HI 96748. (808) 553-5954, (800) 535-0085. FAX (808) 553-5954. These comfortable oceanfront one and two-bedroom condos are minutes from town. The lawn offers views of Lāna'i and winter whale-watching. No telephones or air-conditioning. 🔲🔲🔲🔲🔲 **Suites:** 102	AE MC V, D JCB	●		
LĀNA'I CITY (LĀNA'I): *Hotel Lāna'i* $$ 828 Lāna'i Ave, PO Box 520, HI 96763. (808) 565-4700, (800) 795-7211. FAX (808) 565-6450. Built by the Dole Pineapple Company in 1923 for "important guests," this hotel reflects Hawai'i's plantation era. Guests can use facilities at the other two Lāna'i resorts for free. 🔲🔲🔲🔲🔲 **Rooms:** 10 **Cottage:** 1	AE MC V			●
LĀNA'I CITY (LĀNA'I): *The Lodge at Kō'ele* $$$$ Keōmuku Hwy, PO Box 310, HI 96763. (808) 565-7300, (800) 321-4666. FAX (808) 565-3868. Reminiscent of an elegant country estate with high, beamed ceilings and stone fireplaces, the exquisite Lodge offers superb rooms, excellent food, and a top-quality golf course. 🔲🔲🔲🔲🔲🔲🔲 **Rooms:** 88 (14)	AE MC V JCB		▣	●
MĀNELE BAY (LĀNA'I): *Mānele Bay Hotel* $$$$ Off Mānele Road (Hwy 440), PO Box 310, HI 96763. (808) 565-7700, (800) 321-4666. FAX (808) 565-2483. Set above beautiful Hulopo'e Bay, this gilt-edged, elegant resort blends Mediterranean and plantation styles. Delicious food, lush grounds, and a superb golf course. 🔲🔲🔲🔲🔲🔲🔲🔲 **Rooms:** 224 (26)	AE MC V JCB	●	▣	●

MAUI

	Credit Cards	Ocean View	Children's Program	Good Restaurant
HĀNA: *Blair's Original Hāna Plantation Houses* $ PO Box 249, HI 96713. (808) 923-0772, (800) 228-4262. FAX (808) 248-8240. Each of these houses has its own special charm with outdoor showers, antiques, and flowers. This is old-style Hawai'i at its very best – friendly and peaceful. 🔲🔲🔲🔲🔲 **Units:** 9	MC V	●		
HĀNA: *'Ekena* $$ Kalo Road, PO Box 728, HI 96713. (808) 248-7047. FAX (808) 248-7047. Perfect for visitors seeking total peace and relaxation, this beautiful hillside home is fully equipped with all necessities. Wraparound balconies offer fabulous 360° views. 🔲🔲🔲🔲🔲 **Units:** 2		●		
HONOKŌWAI: *Aston at Papākea Resort* $$$ 3543 Lower Honoapi'ilani Road, HI 96761. (808) 669-4848, (800) 922-7866. FAX (808) 665-0662. These spacious, low-rise condos are situated in a quiet seaside area north of Kā'anapali, and offer jacuzzis and tennis courts among their facilities. 🔲🔲🔲🔲🔲🔲🔲 **Units:** 364	AE MC V, D JCB	●		
KĀ'ANAPALI: *Aston Kā'anapali Shores* $$$ 3445 Honoapi'ilani Highway, HI 96761. (808) 667-2211, (800) 922-7866. FAX (808) 661-0836. High-rise, beachfront condos ranging from simple studios to luxurious two-bedroom suites. Jet spas, sauna, floodlit tennis courts. Beach Club restaurant serves three meals a day. 🔲🔲🔲🔲🔲🔲🔲 **Units:** 463	AE MC V D JCB	●	▣	
KĀ'ANAPALI: *Kā'anapali Beach Hotel* $$$ 2525 Kā'anapali Parkway, HI 96761. (808) 661-0011, (800) 262-8450. FAX (808) 667-5978. Great hospitality has earned this low-rise property a reputation as Maui's most Hawaiian hotel. Authentic foods, craft classes, and botanical tours are some of the special touches. 🔲🔲🔲🔲🔲🔲🔲 **Rooms:** 416 (14)	AE MC V D JCB	●	▣	●

KĀʻANAPALI: *Royal Lahaina Resort* $$$
2780 Kekaʻa Drive, HI 96761. (808) 661-3611, (800) 447-6925. FAX (808) 661-6150.
This well-established beachside hotel prides itself on its sense of culture; an award-winning *lūʻau* (see p164) is presented nightly. Great Sunday brunch at the Royal Ocean Terrace. Ten tennis courts. *Rooms: 566 (26)*
AE MC V D JCB

KĀʻANAPALI: *The Whaler on Kāʻanapali Beach* $$$
2481 Kāʻanapali Parkway, HI 96761. (808) 661-4861, (800) 367-7052.
FAX (808) 661-8315. Distinctive, white twin towers right on the beach, with ocean-front pool. Good shopping nearby. *Units: 360*
AE MC V

KĀʻANAPALI: *Hyatt Regency Maui Resort* $$$$
200 Nohea Kai Drive, HI 96761. (808) 661-1234, (800) 233-1234.
FAX (808) 667-4498. Luxury resort with lush grounds. Special features include "Tour of the Stars" – a fascinating astronomy show – and the unashamedly romantic Swan Court restaurant. *Rooms: 784 (31)*
AE MC V D JCB

KĀʻANAPALI: *Maui Marriott Beach Resort* $$$$
100 Nohea Kai Drive, HI 96761. (808) 667-1200, (800) 763-1333.
FAX (808) 667-8300. Modern oceanfront resort, with facilities including a fitness center, swimming pools, whirlpools, and tennis courts. *Rooms: 701 (19)*
AE MC V D JCB

KĀʻANAPALI: *Sheraton Maui* $$$$
2605 Kāʻanapali Parkway, HI 96761. (808) 661-0031, (800) 782-9488.
FAX (808) 661-0458. The Sheraton is perched on top of Black Rock, 80 ft (24 m) above the beach. Special touches include native plants and furnishings made from *koa* wood and *kapa* (see p18). *Rooms: 510 (45)*
AE MC V D JCB

KĀʻANAPALI: *The Westin Maui* $$$$
2365 Kāʻanapali Parkway, HI 96761. (808) 667-2525, (800) 228-3000.
FAX (808) 661-5764. Luxury beachfront resort with five pools featuring waterfalls, slides, and a swim-through grotto. *Rooms: 733 (28)*
AE MC V, D JCB

KAPALUA: *Kapalua Bay Hotel* $$$$
1 Bay Drive, HI 96761. (808) 669-5656, (800) 367-8000. FAX (808) 669-4694.
Elegant, understated, oceanfront resort with lovely beaches and good restaurants. Shops next door. *Rooms: 191 (3); Villas: 15*
AE MC V, D JCB

KAPALUA: *The Ritz-Carlton Kapalua* $$$$
1 Ritz-Carlton Drive, HI 96761. (808) 669-6200, (800) 241-3333. FAX (808) 665-0026.
Luxury hotel with superb golf courses and white-sand beaches nearby. The Grill has island cuisine and live jazz. *Rooms: 490 (58)*
AE MC V, D JCB

KĪHEI: *Kamaʻole Sands Condominium* $$
2695 S Kīhei Road, HI 96753. (808) 874-8700, (800) 367-5004. FAX (808) 879-3273.
Popular complex ranging from studios to three-bedroom units set in tropical gardens across from the beach. Four tennis courts. *Units: 440*
AE MC V

KĪHEI: *Mana Kai Maui Resort* $$
2960 S Kīhei Road, HI 96753. (808) 879-1561, (800) 367-5242. FAX (808) 874-5042.
Modest, eight-story resort on a long, white-sand beach, excellent for swimming and snorkeling. Rental car included. *Rooms: 126*
AE MC V

KĪHEI: *Maui Coast Hotel* $$$
2259 S Kīhei Road, HI 96753. (808) 874-6284, (800) 895-6284. FAX (808) 875-4731.
Modern hotel in central Kīhei with a great location – across from the beach and close to shops and restaurants. *Rooms: 151 (115)*
AE MC V, D JCB

KĪHEI: *Maui Lū Resort* $$
575 S Kīhei Road, HI 96753. (808) 879-5881, (800) 922-7866. FAX (808) 879-4627.
Simple, comfortable accommodations. The beach is nearby and close to many shops and restaurants. *Rooms: 120*
AE MC V, D JCB

KULA: *Bloom Cottage and House* $$
229 Kula Highway (Hwy 37), HI 96790. (661) 393-0550. FAX (661) 393-5015.
On the slopes of Haleakalā, close to upcountry Maui's sights. Four-poster bed; Hawaiian quilts; *koa*-wood furniture. *Cottage: 1; House: 1*
AE MC V, D JCB

LAHAINA: *Lahaina Inn* $$
127 Lahainaluna Road, HI 96761. (808) 661-0577, (800) 669-3444.
FAX (808) 667-9480. Lovingly restored to Victorian elegance, this small inn has individually decorated rooms with private *lānai* on which breakfast is served. David Paul's Lahaina Grill is downstairs (see p172). *Rooms: 9 (3)*
AE MC V D JCB

For key to symbols see back flap

Price categories for a standard double room for one night in tourist season (Dec–Apr), including taxes:
$ under $85
$$ $85–$150
$$$ $150–$250
$$$$ $250–$400
$$$$$ over $400

CREDIT CARDS
Indicates which credit cards are accepted: *AE* American Express; *MC* MasterCard; *V* VISA; *D* Discover; *JCB* Japanese Credit Bureau.

OCEAN VIEW
Indicates that oceanfront guest rooms are available, or rooms with spectacular views of the ocean.

CHILDREN'S PROGRAM
Hotel can provide cribs, babysitting service, children's menu, special children's activities, or facilities such as video or game room.

GOOD RESTAURANT
Recommended restaurant within the hotel complex, offering good food, often in an attractive setting or with a lovely view.

	CREDIT CARDS	OCEAN VIEW	CHILDREN'S PROGRAM	GOOD RESTAURANT
LAHAINA: *Puamana* $$ 34 Pua'ilima Place, HI 96761. ☎ (808) 667-2712, (800) 669-6284. FAX (808) 661-5875. Private, beachfront community of individually owned and decorated units south of Lahaina, with three pools. Partial air-conditioning. *Units:* 230	AE MC V D			
LAHAINA: *Lahaina Shores Beach Resort* $$$ 475 Front Street, HI 96761. ☎ (808) 661-4835, (800) 628-6699. FAX (808) 661-4696. This six-story plantation-style resort with fully equipped kitchens is the only beachfront hotel in town. Close to shops. *Rooms:* 184 (15)	AE MC V			
MAKAWAO: *Olinda Country Cottages & Inn* $$ 2660 Olinda Road, HI 96768. ☎ (808) 572-1453, (800) 932-3435. FAX (808) 573-5326. Uphill from Makawao, at an elevation of 4,000 ft (1,200 m) and on a road shaded by towering eucalyptus trees, this Tudor-style inn and private cottage are furnished with fine antiques. Awesome views. *Rooms:* 2 (1); *Cottages:* 2		●		
MĀKENA: *Maui Prince Hotel* $$$$ 5400 Mākena Alanui, HI, 96753. ☎ (808) 874-1111, (800) 321-6248. FAX (808) 879-8763. An oasis far from the crowds, with comfortable ocean-view rooms, lovely grounds, and a great beach. Prince Court, one of three restaurants, offers a wonderful Sunday brunch. *Rooms:* 291 (19)	AE MC V JCB	●	■	●
NĀPILI: *Nāpili Kai Resort* $$$ 5900 Honoapi'ilani Road, HI 96761. ☎ (808) 669-6271, (800) 367-5030. FAX (808) 669-5740. Low-rise complex with airy rooms on fabulous Nāpili Bay. Under a unique arrangement, employees' children are taught Hawaiian culture and present a weekly show. *Rooms:* 111 (51)	AE MC V	●	■	
NĀPILI: *Outrigger Nāpili Shores Resort* $$$ 5315 Lower Honoapi'ilani Road, HI 96761. ☎ (808) 669-8061, (800) 688-7444. FAX (808) 669-5407. The units at this family-oriented complex overlook Nāpili Bay, one of Maui's best beaches. The Orient Express offers Thai and Chinese cuisine as well as a sushi bar. *Units:* 98	AE MC V D JCB	●		●
WAILEA: *Destination Resorts Hawai'i* $$$ 555 Kaukahi St, HI 96753. ☎ (808) 879-1595, (800) 367-5246. FAX (808) 874-3554. Individually owned and decorated units near the beach and golf courses, in six different condominium "villages." Fully-equipped kitchens, housekeeping service, swimming pools, and barbecue areas. *Units:* 276	AE MC V JCB	●		
WAILEA: *Four Seasons Resort Maui at Wailea* $$$$ 3900 Wailea Alanui, HI 96753. ☎ (808) 874-8000, (800) 334-6284. FAX (808) 874-2222. A handsome resort with elegant grounds, airy rooms, resplendent baths, and impeccable service. The fine dining room, Seasons, serves creative Hawai'i Regional Cuisine (see p162). *Rooms:* 301 (79)	AE MC V D JCB	●	■	●
WAILEA: *Kea Lani Hotel, Suites & Villas* $$$$ 4100 Wailea Alanui, HI 96753. ☎ (808) 875-4100, (800) 882-4100. FAX (808) 875-1200. With an exterior reminiscent of an Arabian palace, this all-suite hotel offers beautiful lodgings and lovely grounds, just steps from the beach. Fine in-house dining; five golf courses nearby. *Suites:* 413; *Villas:* 37	AE MC V D JCB	●	■	●
WAILEA: *Outrigger Wailea Resort* $$$$ 3700 Wailea Alanui, HI 96753. ☎ (808) 879-1922, (800) 688-7444. FAX (808) 875-4878. The first hotel in Wailea, this grand old "lady" sits on extensive, tropically landscaped, oceanfront grounds. The renowned Hawaiian hospitality brings guests back year after year. Casual restaurant. *Rooms:* 466 (50)	AE MC V D JCB	●		●
WAILEA: *Renaissance Wailea Beach Resort* $$$$ 3550 Wailea Alanui, HI 96753. ☎ (808) 879-4900, (800) 992-4532. FAX (808) 874-5370. Set on gorgeous grounds, this well-established beachfront hotel provides extensive sports facilities. Restaurants include the Maui Onion, which serves the best Maui onion rings on the island. *Rooms:* 335 (10)	AE MC V D JCB	●	■	●

WAILEA: *Grand Wailea Resort, Hotel & Spa* $$$$$
3850 Wailea Alanui, HI 96753. **[** *(808) 875-1234, (800) 888-6100.* **FAX** *(808) 879-4077.*
Built in 1991 as Hawai'i's most expensive resort, it is all grandeur and glamour.
There are three pools – including a 2000-ft (600-m) river pool – a huge spa, and
a $30-million art collection. 🎴 🎴 🎴 🎴 🎴 🎴 🎴 🎴 🎴 🎴 🎴 *Rooms: 728 (52)*

	AE			
	MC	●	■	●
	V			
	D			
	JCB			

WAILUKU: *Old Wailuku Inn at Ulupono* $$
2199 Kaho'okele St, HI 96793. **[** *(808) 244-5897, (800) 305-4899.* **FAX** *(808) 242-9600.*
Personalized service is the hallmark of this gracious central Maui inn, built as
a grand private home in 1924. Each room carries the theme of a local flower.
The gourmet breakfast is delicious. 🎴 🎴 🎴 🎴 🎴 *Rooms: 7. 2 night minimum*

	AE
	MC
	V
	D
	JCB

HAWAI'I ISLAND

HILO: *Hawai'i Naniloa Hotel* $$
93 Banyan Drive, HI 96720. **[** *(808) 969-3333, (800) 367-5360.* **FAX** *(808) 969-6622.*
Located on lovely Banyan Drive, the Naniloa is as luxurious as it gets in Hilo.
There are two pools, a health spa, and a restaurant on the property, and a nine-
hole golf course across the street. 🎴 🎴 🎴 🎴 🎴 🎴 🎴 🎴 🎴 *Rooms: 318 (7)*

	AE		
	MC	●	●
	V		
	JCB		

HILO: *Hilo Hawaiian Hotel* $$
71 Banyan Drive, HI 96720. **[** *(808) 935-9361, (800) 367-5004.* **FAX** *(808) 961-9642.*
The views from the guest rooms here are the best in Hilo. Amenities include a
swimming pool, restaurant, and shops. 🎴 🎴 🎴 🎴 🎴 🎴 🎴 *Rooms: 265 (18)*

	AE		
	MC	●	●
	V, D		
	JCB		

HILO: *Hilo Seaside Hotel* $$
126 Banyan Way, HI 96720. **[** *(808) 935-0821, (800) 560-5557.* **FAX** *(808) 969-9195.*
Built in the 1950s, the Seaside offers basic, very clean, inexpensive accommodations and friendly, Hilo-style service. 🎴 🎴 🎴 🎴 🎴 🎴 🎴 *Rooms: 135*

	AE
	MC
	V, D
	JCB

HILO: *Uncle Billy's Hilo Bay Hotel* $$
87 Banyan Drive, HI 96720. **[** *(808) 935-0861, (800) 367-5102.* **FAX** *(808) 935-7903.*
A low-rise, family-style Polynesian resort with a nightly *hula* show, where you
can experience Hilo as local residents do. 🎴 🎴 🎴 🎴 🎴 🎴 🎴 *Rooms: 143*

	AE		
	MC	●	●
	V		
	D		

HŌLUALOA: *Hōlualoa Inn* $$$
76-5932 Māmalahoa Highway (Hwy 180), PO Box 222, HI 96725. **[** *(808) 324-1121,*
(800) 392-1812. **FAX** *(808) 322-2472.* On the slopes of Mount Hualālai, this charming
inn with open-air design and eucalyptus floors has great views of the Kona
coast. The breakfast coffee is grown on the estate. 🎴 🎴 🎴 *Rooms: 4 (2)*

	AE	
	MC	●
	V	

KAILUA-KONA: *King Kamehameha's Kona Beach Hotel* $$
75-5660 Palani Road, HI 96740. **[** *(808) 329-2911, (800) 367-6060.* **FAX** *(808) 329-4602.*
Excellent location, fronted by a small, white-sand beach and adjacent to the
Kailua-Kona pier. Hawaiian hospitality and first-rate *lū'au (see p164).* Sacred
heiau (temple) on the grounds. 🎴 🎴 🎴 🎴 🎴 🎴 🎴 🎴 *Rooms: 445 (15)*

	AE		
	MC	●	●
	V		
	D		
	JCB		

KAILUA-KONA: *Royal Kona Resort* $$
75-5852 Ali'i Drive, HI 96740. **[** *(808) 329-3111, (800) 774-5662.* **FAX** *(808) 329-7230.*
Historic resort with Hawaiian details, including *koa*-wood rails, fish-hook
chandeliers, and hand-carved headboards. Kamehameha the Great's stone
bathtub lies beyond the swimming pool. 🎴 🎴 🎴 🎴 🎴 🎴 🎴 🎴 *Rooms: 442*

	AE		
	MC	●	●
	V		
	D		
	JCB		

KAILUA-KONA: *Kona Village Resort* $$$$$
Queen Ka'ahumanu Hwy, PO Box 1299, HI 96745. **[** *(808) 325-5555, (800) 367-5290.*
FAX *(808) 325-5124.* This uniquely relaxing resort north of Kailua-Kona consists of *hale* (houses) in various Pacific styles. No phones or televisions; superb
service and food – all meals included. 🎴 🎴 🎴 🎴 🎴 🎴 🎴 🎴 *Hale: 125*

	AE	
	MC	●
	V	
	JCB	

KEAUHOU: *Kanaloa at Kona Condominiums* $$$
78-261 Manukai Street, HI 96740. **[** *(808) 322-9625, (800) 688-7444.*
FAX *(808) 322-3818.* Low-rise complex on Keauhou Bay. Three pools, lighted tennis
courts, and Edward's restaurant *(see p174).* 🎴 🎴 🎴 🎴 🎴 🎴 🎴 🎴 *Suites: 166*

	AE		
	MC	●	●
	V, D		
	JCB		

KEAUHOU: *Keauhou Beach Hotel* $$$
78-6740 Ali'i Drive, HI 96740. **[** *(808) 322-3441, (800) 922-7866.* **FAX** *(808) 322-3117.*
Adjacent to Kahalu'u Beach, where there is great snorkeling, this Hawaiian-
style resort includes the open-air Kuakini Terrace, which offers buffets and
popular Hawaiian entertainment. 🎴 🎴 🎴 🎴 🎴 🎴 🎴 🎴 *Rooms: 305 (6)*

	AE		
	MC	●	●
	V		
	D		
	JCB		

KOHALA COAST: *The Royal Waikoloan* $$$
69-275 Waikoloa Beach Drive, HI 96738. **[** *(808) 886-6789, (800) 688-7444.*
FAX *(808) 886-7852.* Within the Waikoloa Resort with access to sports facilities and
shops. Pleasant, comfortable rooms. 🎴 🎴 🎴 🎴 🎴 🎴 🎴 🎴 *Rooms: 535 (10)*

	AE		
	MC	●	●
	V, D		
	JCB		

For key to symbols see back flap

Price categories for a standard double room for one night in tourist season (Dec–Apr), including taxes:

$ under $85
$$ $85–$150
$$$ $150–$250
$$$$ $250–$400
$$$$$ over $400

CREDIT CARDS
Indicates which credit cards are accepted: *AE* American Express; *MC* MasterCard; *V* VISA; *D* Discover; *JCB* Japanese Credit Bureau.

OCEAN VIEW
Indicates that oceanfront guest rooms are available, or rooms with spectacular views of the ocean.

CHILDREN'S PROGRAM
Hotel can provide cribs, babysitting service, children's menu, special children's activities, or facilities such as video or game room.

GOOD RESTAURANT
Recommended restaurant within the hotel complex, offering good food, often in an attractive setting or with a lovely view.

	CREDIT CARDS	OCEAN VIEW	CHILDREN'S PROGRAM	GOOD RESTAURANT
KOHALA COAST: *Hāpuna Beach Prince Hotel* $$$$ 62-100 Kauna'oa Drive, HI 96743. ☎ (808) 880-1111, (800) 882-6060. FAX (808) 880-3142. This stylish but low-key resort nestles beside the island's best beach. Every room faces the ocean. 🖩 🎱 ⚓ 🏊 🍴 🛁 P ♿ 🛥 *Rooms: 314 (36)*	AE MC V JCB	●	■	●
KOHALA COAST: *Mauna Kea Beach Hotel* $$$$ 62-100 Mauna Kea Beach Drive, HI 96743. ☎ (808) 882-7222, (800) 882-6060. FAX (808) 882-5700. The island's first big resort, built in 1965, legendary Mauna Kea feels like a spacious private estate. ⚓ 🏊 🍴 🛁 P ♿ 🛥 *Rooms: 300 (10)*	AE MC V, D JCB	●	■	●
KOHALA COAST: *Mauna Lani Bay Hotel and Bungalows* $$$$ 68-1400 Mauna Lani Drive, HI 96743. ☎ (808) 885-6622, (800) 367-2323. FAX (808) 885-1484. Huge rooms, or bungalow with own pool and butler. Canoe-House restaurant. 24 🖩 🎱 ⚓ 🏊 🍴 🛁 P ♿ 🛥 *Rooms: 340 (10); Bungalows: 5*	AE MC V, D JCB	●	■	●
KOHALA COAST: *Hilton Waikoloa Village Resort* $$$$$ 425 Waikoloa Beach Drive, HI 96738. ☎ (808) 886-1234, (800) 445-8667. FAX (808) 886-2902. Set amid sprawling grounds, this is the giant of the Kohala resorts. Golf, tennis courts, and six restaurants. Swim with the dolphins at the "Dolphin Encounter." 🖩 🎱 ⚓ 🏊 🍴 🛁 P ♿ 🛥 *Rooms: 1,185 (56)*	AE MC V D JCB	●	■	●
KOHALA COAST: *The Orchid at Mauna Lani* $$$$$ 1 North Kanikū Drive, HI 96743. ☎ (808) 885-2000, (800) 845-9905. FAX (808) 885-5778. One of the three Mauna Lani hotels, this beautiful property includes a 36-hole golf course. 24 🖩 🎱 ⚓ 🏊 🍴 🛁 P ♿ 🛥 *Rooms: 483 (54)*	AE MC V, D JCB	●	■	●
VOLCANO VILLAGE: *Chalet Kīlauea-The Inn at Volcano* $$ Wright Rd & Laukapu Rd, PO Box 998, HI 96785. ☎ (808) 967-7786, (800) 937-7786. FAX (808) 967-8660. Set at an altitude of 4,000 feet (1,200 m), this 1945 cedar-wood home has plush, individually decorated rooms. 🖩 🎱 ⚓ 🛁 P 🛥 *Rooms: 2 (4)*	AE MC V, D JCB			
VOLCANO VILLAGE: *Kilauea Lodge* $$ Old Volcano Road, PO Box 116, HI 96785. ☎ (808) 967-7366. FAX (808) 967-7367. Built as a YMCA camp in 1938, the refurbished lodge is a mile (1.5 km) from Volcanoes National Park. Fine restaurant. 🖩 🎱 P 🛥 *Rooms: 11; Cottages: 2*	MC V			●
WAIMEA: *Kamuela Inn* $ Kawaihae Road (Hwy 19), PO Box 1994, HI 96743. ☎ (808) 885-4243. FAX (808) 885-8857. This comfortable inn in quaint Waimea is near the wonderful Merriman's Restaurant *(see p174)*. Book in advance. 🎱 ⚓ 🛁 P 🛥 *Rooms: 21 (11)*	AE MC V, D JCB			
WAIMEA: *Waimea Gardens Cottage* $$$ PO Box 563, HI 96743. ☎ (808) 885-4550, (800) 262-9912. FAX (808) 885-0559. This property beside a mountain stream was owned by a Hawaiian family for more than seven generations. It includes part of the original 100-year-old bathhouse. 🖩 ⚓ P 🛥 *Cottages: 2. 3 night minimum*				
WAIPI'O VALLEY: *Waipi'o Treehouse* $$$$ Off Highway 240, PO Box 5086, Honoka'a, HI 96727. ☎ (808) 775-7160. This amazing lodging is for adventurers only. It is almost inaccessible, so you will be escorted in and out. Bring everything you need. 🎱 *Treehouse: 1; Cottage: 1*	MC V			

KAUA'I

HANALEI: *Hanalei Valley Vacation Cottages* $ PO Box 1038, HI 96714. ☎ (808) 826-9828. FAX (808) 826-1119. This beautiful cottage surrounded by tropical foliage is furnished with 1940s- and 50s-style Hawaiiana. Outdoor shower; helpful hosts. 🖩 ⚓ P 🛥 *Cottages: 2*				
HANALEI: *Hanalei Colony Condominium Resort* $$$ 5-7130 Kūhiō Hwy, PO Box 206, HI 96714. ☎ (808) 826-6235, (800) 628-3004. FAX (808) 826-9893. This peaceful seaside property is the "Last Resort" before the road's end. Full kitchens; no air-conditioning or TV. 🖩 🎱 ⚓ 🏊 P 🛥 *Units: 46*	AE MC V	●		

KAPA'A: *Kaua'i Coast Resort at the Beachboy* $$
4-484 Kūhiō Hwy, HI 96746. (*(808) 822-3441, (800) 922-7866.* FAX *(808) 822-0843.*
Fronting a long stretch of beach, this property offers modern rooms and proximity to shops and restaurants. *Rooms: 152*
AE, MC, V, D, JCB

KAPA'A: *Kaua'i Coconut Beach Resort* $$$
Coconut Market Place, Mile marker 7, Kūhiō Hwy, HI 96746. (*(808) 822-3455,* *(800) 222-5642.* FAX *(808) 822-1830.* The only seaside resort on the Coconut Coast with a full range of amenities. It is convenient for shopping and sightseeing, and boasts Kaua'i's best *lū'au (see p164). Rooms: 277 (30)*
AE, MC, V, D, JCB

KŌKE'E STATE PARK: *Kōke'e Lodge* $
Kōke'e Road (Hwy 550), PO Box 819, HI 96796. (*(808) 335-6061.*
If you like mountain hiking trails, breathtaking scenery, and a cabin with a wood-burning stove, book here well in advance. The cabins are plain but have all the necessities. Home-style restaurant. *Cabins: 12*
MC, V, D

KŌLOA: *Victoria Place Bed & Breakfast* $$
3459 Lāwa'i Loa Lane, PO Box 930, HI 96765. (*(808) 332-9300.* FAX *(808) 332-9465.*
Lovely rooms and tropical breakfast. The knowledgeable owner can send you to hidden beaches, restaurants, and shops. *Rooms: 4*

LĪHU'E: *Aston Kaha Lani Resort* $$$
4460 Nehe Road, HI 96766. (*(808) 822-9331, (800) 922-7866.* FAX *(808) 822-2828.*
A few minutes north of town, this low-rise complex offers a range of condos in a quiet setting beside the beach. The attractive units have fully-equipped kitchens. Free tennis and outdoor barbecues. *Units: 74*
AE, MC, V, D, JCB

LĪHU'E: *Aston Kaua'i Beach Villas* $$$
4330 Kaua'i Beach Drive, HI 96766. (*(808) 245-7711, (800) 922-7866.*
FAX *(808) 245-5550.* Just outside town in a beautifully landscaped setting, this comfortable property is right on the beach. Guests can use facilities at the Outrigger Kaua'i Beach next door. *Units: 150*
AE, MC, V, D, JCB

LĪHU'E: *Outrigger Kaua'i Beach* $$$
4331 Kaua'i Beach Drive, HI 96766. (*(808) 245-1955, (888) 805-3843.*
FAX *(808) 246-9085.* Built in 1986, this luxury beachfront hotel offers a "super" pool featuring caves, waterfalls, and fountains. Also on site are a whirlpool spa, tennis courts, and two restaurants. *Units: 341*
AE, MC, V, D, JCB

LĪHU'E: *Kaua'i Marriott Resort & Beach Club* $$$$
3610 Rice Street, HI 96766. (*(808) 245-5050, (800) 228-9290.* FAX *(808) 245-5049.*
Fronting Nāwiliwili Bay, this luxury resort enjoys a quarter-mile (400 m) of white-sand beach and the largest pool in Hawai'i. Restaurants include the casual Duke's Canoe Club *(see p175). Rooms: 345 (11)*
AE, MC, V, D, JCB

PO'IPŪ: *Po'ipū Kai Condominium Resort* $$$
1941 Po'ipū Road, HI 96756. (*(808) 742-7400, (800) 367-8020.* FAX *(808) 742-9121.*
Six low-rise condo clusters – each with a pool – offer spacious, individually owned units with access to two beaches. *Units: 200*
AE, MC, V, D, JCB

PO'IPŪ: *Hyatt Regency Kaua'i Resort & Spa* $$$$
1571 Po'ipū Road, HI 96756. (*(808) 742-1234, (800) 233-1234.* FAX *(808) 742-1557.*
The lobby at this opulent oceanfront resort is richly decorated with *koa* wood; the open-air design evokes 1920s Hawai'i. Five dining options, a magnificent spa, and many shops. *Rooms: 602 (37)*
AE, MC, V, D, JCB

PRINCEVILLE: *Hanalei Bay Resort & Suites* $$$
5380 Honoiki Road, PO Box 220, HI 96714. (*(808) 826-6522, (800) 827-4427.*
FAX *(808) 826-6680.* Perched above Hanalei Bay, this gem is rated in the Condé Nast Traveler Magazine Top 30 Tropical Resorts worldwide. Lagoon pool with waterfalls, tennis courts, superb golf nearby. *Rooms: 182 (49)*
AE, MC, V, D, JCB

PRINCEVILLE: *Princeville Hotel and Resort* $$$$
5520 Ka Haku Road, PO Box 3069, HI 96722. (*(808) 826-9644, (800) 826-4400.*
FAX *(808) 826-1166.* This elegant resort, built on a bluff facing Hanalei Bay, offers exquisite panoramas. Spacious rooms; splendid dining. Golf, tennis, and in-house movie theater. *Rooms: 242 (10)*
AE, MC, V, D, JCB

WAIMEA: *Waimea Plantation Cottages* $$$
9400 Kaumuali'i Hwy, PO Box 367, HI 96796. (*(808) 338-1625, (800) 922-7866.*
FAX *(808) 338-2338.* Step back into old Hawai'i at these wonderfully restored plantation cottages set in a coconut grove at the gateway to Waimea Canyon. Ceiling fans and period furniture. *Cottages: 48*
AE, MC, V, D, JCB

For key to symbols see back flap

WHERE TO EAT

FROM LOCAL-STYLE drive-ins to elegant dining rooms, the opportunities for eating well in Hawai'i are endless. In addition to hundreds of restaurants of every description, there are informal outlets – such as street stalls, delis, and coffeehouses – that sell delicious, cheap food, which is perfect for a quick bite between bouts of sightseeing. In large shopping malls, food courts offer a wide,

Sign for Papaya's in Kapa'a *(see p175)*

surprisingly good array of ethnic and American food, and for those with late-night cravings, some supermarkets and convenience stores offer food 24 hours a day. There are many open-air restaurants, and indoor places are usually air-conditioned. Unless you stick to the mainstream fast-food outlets, you cannot fail to taste the full range of exotic flavors that influence cooking in Hawai'i.

Banyan Court Bar at the Sheraton Moana Surfrider Hotel *(see p153)*

MEAL TIMES

SOME VISITORS to Hawai'i may be surprised by the state's early meal times. You will find places open for breakfast at 5am; lunch starts at 11am; and dinner begins at 5pm and is often over by 9pm. Many local-style establishments do not serve dinner and close by 2pm.

Cocktail hour begins early, too, around 4pm. Most hotels and restaurants serve *pūpū* (Hawaiian-style hors d'oeuvres) with the drinks, sometimes at no additional charge.

Many restaurants are closed on Sunday or Monday, but hours and closing days often change. You should phone if you have your heart set on a particular restaurant (it is a good idea to book anyway).

HAWAI'I REGIONAL CUISINE

THE DAYS OF Hawai'i as a gastronomic wasteland are long gone – thanks, in no small part, to the advent of the Hawai'i Regional Cuisine

movement. Peter Merriman *(see p174)* is widely acknowledged as leader of a pack of chefs who were determined to put Hawai'i on the culinary map. Other chefs, including Roy Yamaguchi on O'ahu *(see p168)*, Mark Ellman on Maui *(see p172)*, and Jean-Marie Josselin on Kaua'i *(see p175)*, quickly followed suit – until a core group of 12 chefs formed a nonprofit organization dedicated to the promotion of Hawai'i Regional Cuisine.

The cuisine takes its ingredients directly from local farms and the surrounding Pacific, but its influences come from the many ethnic groups that make up Hawaiian society. The results – dishes such as breadfruit vichysoisse, tempura of Keāhole baby lobster, and Kona coffee cheesecake, as well as the upsurge of interest in Hawaiian cooking – have been of benefit to everyone,

from local producers to the dining public. Whichever name you use – Hawai'i Regional, Island Regional, East Meets West, or Pacific Rim – this new cuisine makes the most of what the islands have to offer.

LOCAL FOOD

THOSE DISHES collectively known as "local food" are as diverse as the population that has created them. This style of cooking is filling, inexpensive, and unbeatable in the eyes of local people and those who acquire a taste for it.

The "plate lunch" is the most traditional local-style meal and consists of a meat or poultry main course – such as *teriyaki* beef, two scoops of sticky rice, and a scoop of macaroni or potato salad heaped onto a paper plate or molded tray. These lunches are dispensed from street carts or diners,

Chef Roy Yamaguchi at his restaurant in Honolulu *(see p168)*

David Paul's Lahaina Grill on Front Street, Lahaina *(see p172)*

and there are often dozens of food choices – of Japanese, Chinese, Korean, Filipino, and even American origin. Expect to pay in the region of $5–8.

Poi (a gray paste made from pounded taro root and definitely an acquired taste); *kālua* pork (from a whole pig baked in leaves, especially at *lū'au*); sweet potato; *limu* (seaweed); and *laulau* (fish, pork, and taro leaf stems wrapped in *ti* leaves and then steamed) are all easy-to-find Hawaiian staples.

You will see sushi everywhere, and *bento* is a Japanese version of the plate lunch, served cold. *Saimin*, a Japanese-style bowl of broth brimming with pork, fish cake, green onions, and noodles, is popular for breakfast, lunch, or dinner. Another common dish is *manapua*, the local version of Chinese steamed buns filled with seasoned pork.

Local sweet treats include shave ice (or "snow cones"), scrapings of ice flavored with syrup, and crack seed – dried fruits and chewy candies seasoned with Chinese five-spice known as *li hing mui*.

Mock-Victorian Burger King, Waikiki

FAST FOOD AND TAKE-OUT MEALS

HAWAI'I IS part of the United States, after all, so don't be surprised to find Burger King, McDonald's, Pizza Hut, Taco Bell, and the rest. However, you will find things on the menu that are particular to Hawai'i: most notably *saimin*, sticky rice and Portuguese sausage. Local-style fast food is sold at numerous drive-ins throughout Hawai'i, and at the many branches of Zippy's on O'ahu; most of the Zippy's outlets are open 24 hours. Another local company, L & L Drive-In, is expanding fast and has many outlets on O'ahu, too.

Few restaurants will not do food to take out. Many groceries and supermarkets have delis and salad, Chinese food, or *bento* bars offering take-out meals. Health food stores often have food bars, too. All these places are good for picnic food – Hawai'i being ideal picnicking territory.

Delivery, on the other hand, is rarely available in Hawai'i. Your choices will be limited to large chains like Pizza Hut and Domino's Pizza.

COFFEEHOUSES

JUST LIKE ON the US mainland, coffeehouses have opened up all over the islands. The difference in Hawai'i is that they are not chains, and they feature aromatic home-grown Kona coffee *(see p115)*.

Most coffeehouses sell delicious pastries, mostly home-baked, and many provide light meals as well.

ALCOHOL

MOST RESTAURANTS have bars and wine lists offering a good choice from around the world. Restaurants without a bar will usually allow patrons to bring in their own beer or wine, and there is rarely a charge for opening the bottle.

VEGETARIANS

ALTHOUGH THERE ARE only a few vegetarian restaurants in Hawai'i, many places have a vegetarian section on their menu and will accommodate vegetarians with a plate of steamed vegetables and rice or a vegetarian pasta dish. All you have to do is ask.

CHILDREN

HAWAI'I IS an extremely child-friendly place, and the only restaurants that do not welcome children with open arms are the few very formal dining rooms – mostly located in fancy resort hotels. But even here, children should never be turned away.

Many restaurants provide a children's menu, with small portions of the food kids love, such as pizzas and burgers.

ETIQUETTE

MANY RESTAURANTS are non-smoking, and those that are not provide separate smoking and nonsmoking sections. Many have air-conditioning.

A standard restaurant tip is 15 percent of the check. Depending upon the service and style of restaurant, you may wish to tip more or less than this.

Casual dress is acceptable in all but the most formal of Hawai'i's restaurants, and then jackets are usually requested rather than required.

Local-style diner on Hawai'i Island

Hawai'i's Varied Cuisine

HAWAI'I'S WATERS teem with fish, and seafood lovers will savor the excellent local varieties caught daily just for island restaurants and then prepared in dozens of creative ways by the new breed of chefs. But fish is not the only choice. One of the great benefits of Hawai'i's multi-ethnicity is the incredible array of cuisines available – Chinese dim sum, Japanese sushi, Korean ribs, Thai summer rolls, Portuguese pastries, Mexican tacos, French escargots, Italian pasta, good old American meat and potato dishes, and much more.

Market stand in Chinatown

American fare, exemplified by a traditional breakfast of eggs-over-easy, bacon, fried potatoes, and toast and jelly, is widely available throughout Hawai'i.

Portuguese pastries come in a variety of forms. One of the favorites is the doughnut-style malasada.

Marinated, grilled beef

Sticky rice

Kim chee

***Japanese sushi** is usually raw fish thinly sliced, wrapped around sweetened rice, and served with wasabi (green horseradish) and pickled ginger.*

***Korean** kim chee, or pickled cabbage, is a popular addition to marinated beef or chicken dishes, together with sticky rice.*

HAWAIIAN LŪ'AU

Traditional Hawaiian *lū'au* (feasts) are held to mark special occasions with friends and family, as they have been for centuries. The main event is the preparation of the *kālua* pig, which is baked slowly in an *imu* (underground oven). A pit is dug in the ground and filled with hot coals and banana and *ti* leaves, onto which the pig is laid. It is then covered with more leaves and earth and left to bake for up to eight hours. *Laulau* – bundles of beef, pork, chicken, or fish with taro leaf stems wrapped in *ti* leaves – are also baked in the *imu*. Another staple of *lū'au* is *poi*, a thick purple-gray paste made from pounded taro root *(see p109)* and eaten with the fingers. *Lomi-lomi* salmon – thinly sliced raw salmon marinated with tomatoes and green onions – is often included as a side dish. For dessert, a coconut pudding

Laulau   Sweet potato   Kālua pig

Haupia   Taro   Breadfruit, or 'ulu

called *haupia* is served. Nowadays, there are also dishes from Hawai'i's ethnic groups, creating a delicious choice of *lū'au* foods.

Steamed dumpling

Soy sauce

Shrimp toast

Minced pork dumpling

Mini spring roll

Chinese dim sum is an assortment of deep-fried, steamed, and baked dumplings, filled with beef, pork, fish, or vegetables, that are dipped in soy sauce and eaten with chopsticks.

Chef Sam Choy

SIGNATURE DISHES

Recently, many Hawai'i chefs have developed "signature dishes" – their own specialties made of fresh local ingredients. They include Sam Choy's delicious seafood *laulau*, Beverly Gannon's Hunan rack of lamb, David Paul Johnson's *kālua* duck, and Roy Yamaguchi's original chocolate soufflé. These and many other must-try items are usually highlighted on menus.

Thai green curry, available in varying degrees of spiciness, is accompanied by rice, making a delicious, filling meal.

Juicy char-grilled steak is a popular dinner choice, served here with fresh asparagus and roast potatoes.

Pepper sauce

Cucumber

Seared 'ahi tuna

Yellow and red peppers

Teriyaki beef, chicken, or fish may be stir-fried in a wok with vegetables and seasonings or grilled over charcoal.

'Ahi tuna may be served rare with a creamy pepper sauce or with a peppered coating and a soy-based sauce.

TROPICAL FRUIT

Hawai'i has an abundance of year-round fresh fruit, from tropical star fruit and guavas to coconuts, pineapples, and bananas.

Lychee

Guava

Avocado

Mango

Bananas

Breadfruit

Papaya

Coconut

Pineapple

Choosing a Restaurant

THE RESTAURANTS in this guide have been selected across a range of price categories for their exceptional food, good value, and interesting location. Some are one of a chain, with branches in other locations. Entries are arranged alphabetically within price category by area. Color-coded thumb tabs indicate the regions covered on each page.

	CREDIT CARDS ACCEPTED	OUTDOOR TABLES	HRC	GOOD WINE LIST	LATE NIGHT MENU

HONOLULU AND WAIKĪKĪ

DOWNTOWN HONOLULU: *Legend Seafood.* **Map 1 A2.** $$
Suite 108, 100 N Beretania Street. (808) 532-1868.
The huge menu at this Chinese restaurant includes a fabulous assortment of dim sum. Locals flock here on weekend mornings. 🅿 🍸 🚶 ♿
Credit cards: AE MC V JCB

DOWNTOWN HONOLULU: *Indigo.* **Map 1 A2.** $$
1121 Nu'uanu Avenue. (808) 521-2900.
Indigo is set in a gentrified area on the edge of Chinatown. The food is Asian and innovative, if a little inconsistent; service is good. 🍸 🚶 ♿
Credit cards: MC V, D JCB — Outdoor Tables ●, Good Wine List ●

DOWNTOWN HONOLULU: *Gordon Biersch.* **Map 1 A3.** $$$
1 Aloha Tower Drive (at Aloha Tower Marketplace). (808) 599-4877.
Gordon Biersch has the distinction of being Hawai'i's very first "brew pub." Lagers are brewed on the premises. Specialties include garlic fries and ribeye steak *pūlehu*-style (grilled over hot coals). ★ 🎵 🅿 🍸 🚶 ♿
Credit cards: AE MC V D JCB — Outdoor Tables ●, HRC ■, Good Wine List ●, Late Night Menu ■

DOWNTOWN HONOLULU: *Sunset Grill.* **Map 1 B4.** $$$
500 Ala Moana Boulevard (at Restaurant Row). (808) 521-4409.
This popular San Francisco-style bistro offers American food with an international twist. An open kitchen lets you see the chefs at work. 🅿 🍸 🚶 ♿
Credit cards: AE MC V, D JCB

DOWNTOWN HONOLULU: *Palomino Euro Bistro.* **Map 1 A3.** $$$$
66 Queen Street (at Harbor Court). (808) 528-2400.
At mezzanine level in the heart of Downtown, this casual but elegant restaurant has a view of the harbor. Specializes in cracker-thin pizzas, spit-roasted chicken, and homemade *tiramisu.* 🅿 🍸 🚶 ♿ 🍴 *lunch Sat & Sun.*
Credit cards: AE MC V D — Good Wine List ●, Late Night Menu ■

DOWNTOWN HONOLULU: *Ruth's Chris Steak House.* **Map 1 B4.** $$$$
500 Ala Moana Boulevard (at Restaurant Row). (808) 599-3860.
Beef, obviously, is the main event here. Regardless of which cut you order, the meat will be of excellent quality and perfectly cooked. The menu also includes seafood, chicken, and large side orders. 🅿 🍸 🚶 ♿
Credit cards: AE MC V JCB — Outdoor Tables ●, Good Wine List ●

WAIKĪKĪ: *Kyotaru Restaurant.* **Map 4 D4.** $
2154 Kalākaua Avenue. (808) 924-3663.
Bright, casual, and offering great value, Kyotaru is the perfect place for the uninitiated to taste Japanese cuisine – sushi, tempura, and teriyaki. 🅿 🚶 ♿
Credit cards: MC V D

WAIKĪKĪ: *Trattoria.* **Map 4 D5.** $$
2168 Kālia Road (in the Edgewater Hotel). (808) 923-8415.
The ambience is pure Italian with frescoes on the walls and ceilings. Steak, lobster, and fresh fish are offered along with northern Italian dishes. Early birds can enjoy a variety of inexpensive pasta dishes. 🅿 🍸 🚶 ♿
Credit cards: AE MC V D JCB — Outdoor Tables ●, Good Wine List ●

WAIKĪKĪ: *Duke's Canoe Club.* **Map 4 E5.** $$$
2335 Kalākaua Avenue (in the Outrigger Waikīkī). (808) 922-2268.
Just steps from Duke Kahanamoku's favorite surfing spot *(see p53)*, this is part restaurant, part bar, part museum, and one of the most popular hang-outs in town. Varied menu of steak, fish, and salads. ★ 🎵 🅿 🍸 🚶 ♿
Credit cards: AE MC V D — Outdoor Tables ●, Good Wine List ●

WAIKĪKĪ: *Matteo's.* **Map 4 D4.** $$$
364 Seaside Avenue (in the Marine Surf Hotel). (808) 922-5551.
Local residents consistently vote this Waikīkī landmark the best Italian restaurant in the city. The interior is conducive to quiet, romantic dining. Noteworthy Caesar salad and delicious specialty coffees. 🅿 🍸 🚶 ♿
Credit cards: AE MC V D JCB — Good Wine List ●

WAIKĪKĪ: *La Mer at the Halekūlani.* **Map 4 D5.** $$$$$
2199 Kālia Road. (808) 923-2311.
French-influenced dishes, such as fresh fish *en croûte*, are impeccably prepared and presented at this highly rated restaurant. The ocean view is magnificent. Wine manager Randolph Ching is a master. 🅿 🍸 ♿
Credit cards: AE MC V JCB — Good Wine List ●

Price categories for a three-course meal, with a glass of wine, including tax and service charges:

$ under $20
$$ $20–$30
$$$ $30–$45
$$$$ $45–$60
$$$$$ over $60

CREDIT CARDS ACCEPTED
AE American Express; *MC* MasterCard; *V* VISA; *D* Discover; *JCB* Japanese Credit Bureau.
OUTDOOR TABLES
Tables for eating outdoors, often with a good view.
HRC (HAWAI'I REGIONAL CUISINE)
Gourmet food incorporating fresh island ingredients with influences from Hawai'i's different ethnic groups.
GOOD WINE LIST
Denotes a wide range of good quality wines.
LATE NIGHT MENU
Light meals and snacks available until late.

	Price	CREDIT CARDS ACCEPTED	OUTDOOR TABLES	HRC	GOOD WINE LIST	LATE NIGHT MENU
GREATER HONOLULU: Eggs 'N' Things. Map 3 C4. ✔ 1911-B Kalākaua Avenue. ((808) 949-0820. Locals line up in eager anticipation of the luscious omelettes, pancakes, crepes, and eggs Benedict served at this Honolulu institution. Open from 11pm to 2pm, it is also great if you're prone to midnight cravings. P 👤	$					■
GREATER HONOLULU: Hale Vietnam Restaurant 1140 12th Avenue. ((808) 735-7581. A giant, laughing Buddha greets you at this Kaimuki neighborhood restaurant. Authentic Vietnamese food: fresh, light, and flavorful. 🍸 👤	$	MC V D			●	
GREATER HONOLULU: Makai Market Food Court. Map 3 A4. 1450 Ala Moana Boulevard (at Ala Moana Center). ((808) 955-9517. Huge seating area surrounded by kiosks offering every conceivable type of food from pizza to Korean barbecue, Japanese *bentos,* and salads. P 🍸 ♿	$					
GREATER HONOLULU: Ono Hawaiian Foods 726 Kapahulu Avenue. ((808) 737-2275. Second only to a *tūtū's* (grandmother's) kitchen, this small eating place is great for Hawaiian dishes such as *poi, laulau,* and *lomi-lomi* salmon. ● *Sun.*	$			■		
GREATER HONOLULU: California Pizza Kitchen. Map 3 A4. 1450 Ala Moana Boulevard (at Ala Moana Center). ((808) 941-7715. Whether it is Thai, barbecue, Italian, or just salad you want, this pizzeria can sate any desire with its exciting, original combinations. P 🍸 👤 ♿	$$	AE MC V, D JCB			●	
GREATER HONOLULU: The Contemporary Café 2411 Makiki Heights Drive. ((808) 523-3362. A perfect complement to the Contemporary Museum, this cozy café has a short menu of tasty soups, salads, and sandwiches. P 👤 ♿ ● *Mon.*	$$	AE MC V	●			
GREATER HONOLULU: Dixie Grill BBQ and Crab Shack. Map 2 D4. 404 Ward Avenue. ((808) 596-8359. As close as it gets in Hawai'i to a Southern roadhouse. "Mess of crabs" and "two-pound bust-your-belly burger" are huge. P 🍸 👤 ♿	$$	AE MC V, D JCB	●			
GREATER HONOLULU: Keo's. Map 3 C4. 2028 Kūhiō Avenue (in the Ambassador Hotel). ((808) 951-9355. Keo Sananikone's name is synonymous with Thai food in Hawai'i. Specialities include the stir-fried shrimp with peanut sauce and delicious lemon-grass chicken. P 🍸 👤 ♿	$$	AE MC V, D JCB			●	
GREATER HONOLULU: Scoozee's. Map 2 E5. 1200 Ala Moana Boulevard (at Ward Centre). ((808) 597-1777. Thick tomato sauces, crusty Italian bread, and huge portions help to explain Scoozee's popularity. Filled with business people at lunch. P 🍸 👤 ♿	$$	AE MC V JCB	●		●	
GREATER HONOLULU: Swiss Inn 5730 Kalaniana'ole Hwy (at Niu Valley Shopping Center). ((808) 377-5447. Casual atmosphere, continental specialties, and excellent value have made the Swiss Inn a firm favorite with island families. P 🍸 👤 ♿ ● *Mon, Tue.*	$$	AE MC V, D JCB			●	
GREATER HONOLULU: 3660 On the Rise 3660 Wai'alae Avenue. ((808) 737-1177. This unassuming restaurant in a refurbished building was a pioneer in the gentrification of the wonderful Kaimuki neighborhood. Creative island cuisine with a European flair; don't miss the desserts. P 🍸 👤 ♿ ● *Mon.*	$$$	AE MC V D JCB		■	●	
GREATER HONOLULU: Alfred's at Century Center. Map 3 B3. 3rd Floor, 1750 Kalākaua Avenue. ((808) 955-5353. Alfred Vollenweider has long impressed his customers with updated European classics. Signature items include *'ōpakapaka* (pink snapper) in champagne sauce and entrecôte café de Paris. P 🍸 👤 ♿ ● *Sun, Mon.*	$$$	MC V D JCB			●	

For key to symbols see back flap

Price categories for a three-course meal, with a glass of wine, including tax and service charges:

- $ under $20
- $$ $20–$30
- $$$ $30–$45
- $$$$ $45–$60
- $$$$$ over $60

CREDIT CARDS ACCEPTED
AE American Express; *MC* MasterCard; *V* VISA; *D* Discover; *JCB* Japanese Credit Bureau.

OUTDOOR TABLES
Tables for eating outdoors, often with a good view.

HRC (HAWAI'I REGIONAL CUISINE)
Gourmet food incorporating fresh island ingredients with influences from Hawai'i's different ethnic groups.

GOOD WINE LIST
Denotes a wide range of good quality wines.

LATE NIGHT MENU
Light meals and snacks available until late.

Restaurant	Price	Credit Cards Accepted	Outdoor Tables	HRC	Good Wine List	Late Night Menu
GREATER HONOLULU: *Café Sistina.* Map 2 F2. 1314 S King Street. (808) 596-0061. Northern Italian chef/owner Sergio Mitrotti produces masterpieces not only on the plates but also on the walls. Fine reproductions of Renaissance paintings adorn every surface. A unique dining experience.	$$$	AE MC V, D JCB			●	
GREATER HONOLULU: *Donato's Ristorante e' Carpacceria* Suite 102, 4614 Kilauea Avenue. (808) 738-5655. Contemporary decor, authentic regional Italian cuisine, plus a specialty gourmet market make this new restaurant a rising star.	$$$	AE MC V, D JCB			●	
GREATER HONOLULU: *Kincaid's Fish, Chop & Steakhouse.* Map 2 D5. 1050 Ala Moana Boulevard (at Ward Warehouse). (808) 591-2005. Kincaid's offers excellent food and first rate service. A terrific place to take a break from shopping. Extremely busy around noon.	$$$	AE MC V, D JCB		■	●	■
GREATER HONOLULU: *Kyo-ya Japanese Cuisine.* Map 3 C4. 2057 Kalākaua Avenue. (808) 947-3911. The setting and service typify the serenity of traditional Japanese dining. The food and presentation are always excellent. lunch Sun.	$$$	AE MC V, D JCB			●	
GREATER HONOLULU: *The Pineapple Room.* Map 3 A4. 1450 Ala Moana Boulevard (at Ala Moana Center). (808) 945-8881. Warm and inviting, with a woodburning oven in the exhibition kitchen. Don't pass up the signature dish: pineapple crabcakes.	$$$	AE MC V, D JCB		■	●	
GREATER HONOLULU: *Roy's Restaurant* 6600 Kalaniana'ole Highway. (808) 396-7697. This is where Hawai'i Regional Cuisine, originally called Pacific Rim, began. Chef Roy Yamaguchi calls this tasty food Euro-Asian.	$$$	AE MC V, D JCB	●	■	●	
GREATER HONOLULU: *Ryan's Grill.* Map 2 E5. 1200 Ala Moana Boulevard (at Ward Centre). (808) 591-9132. This lively favorite calls itself a "go anytime, order anything" bistro. Dishes range from juicy burgers to fresh fish grilled over *kiawe* wood.	$$$	AE MC V	●		●	■
GREATER HONOLULU: *Sam Choy's Breakfast, Lunch and Crab* 580 N Nimitz Highway. (808) 545-7979. Sam Choy, one of the founders of Hawai'i Regional Cuisine (HRC), is the state's official culinary ambassador. This huge warehouse turns out tasty dishes of crab, lobster, clams, oysters, fish, and even meat.	$$$	AE MC V, D JCB		■	●	
GREATER HONOLULU: *Sam Choy's Diamond Head Restaurant* Suite 201, 449 Kapahulu Avenue. (808) 732-8645. This is another of Sam's fabulous restaurants. The amazing service and generous portions of beautifully presented food make this one of the happiest dining experiences in the islands.	$$$	AE MC V, D JCB	●	■	●	
GREATER HONOLULU: *Singha Thai Cuisine.* Map 3 C4. 1910 Ala Moana Boulevard. (808) 941-2898. With Royal Thai dancers performing each evening, award-winning Singha Thai is an exotic haven. Magnificent dishes.	$$$	AE MC V, D JCB	●		●	
GREATER HONOLULU: *Alan Wong's Restaurant.* Map 3 B2. 3rd Floor, 1857 S King Street. (808) 949-2526. Considered by many to be the best restaurant in town, this is owned by an HRC original, who fashions innovative dishes out of traditional Hawaiian ingredients. Friendly staff make up for the odd location.	$$$$	AE MC V JCB		■	●	
GREATER HONOLULU: *John Dominis Restaurant.* Map 1 C5. 43 'Āhui Street. (808) 523-0955. This beautiful restaurant has lava walls and an interior waterway. The mainly older diners relish the fresh fish, tiger shrimps, and lobster.	$$$$	AE MC V JCB			●	■

GREATER HONOLULU: *Nick's Fishmarket Restaurant.* **Map 3 C4.** $$$$
2070 Kalākaua Avenue. ((808) 955-6333.
Since 1970, this award-winning restaurant has served up superb seafood.
Specialties include lobsters from around the world. 🎵 P Y 🕴 &
AE MC V, D JCB

GREATER HONOLULU: *A Pacific Café Oʻahu.* **Map 2 E5.** $$$$
1200 Ala Moana Boulevard (at Ward Centre). ((808) 593-0035.
Hawaiʻi Regional Cuisine right on the cutting edge. Try the wok-charred
mahimahi (dolphin fish) or the Mongolian-style lamb. 🎵 P Y 🕴 &
AE MC V D

OʻAHU

HALEʻIWA: *Kua ʻAina Sandwich* ✓ $
66-214 Kamehameha Highway (Hwy 83). ((808) 637-6067.
If you love burgers and fries, try this humble surfer hangout on Oʻahu's
North Shore. A local landmark, it has the best food in town. P 🕴 &

KAʻAʻAWA: *Crouching Lion Inn* $$
51-666 Kamehameha Highway (Hwy 83). ((808) 237-8511.
Built in 1934, this impressive building has several dining areas and ocean
views. Specialties include Slavonic steak and *kālua* pork. P Y 🕴 &
AE MC V, D JCB

KAILUA: *Casablanca Restaurant* $$
19 Hoʻolaʻi Street. ((808) 262-8196.
Both a Moroccan-Mediterranean bistro and traditional Khima Room with low
tables. Tasty lamb brochettes, couscous, and chicken in honey. P 🕴 &
MC V

KAILUA: *Buzz's Original Steakhouse* $$
413 Kawailoa Road. ((808) 261-4661.
Buzz's offers ocean views and steak, fish, and lamb dinners. Delicious *kiawe*-
broiled steak and lobster, teriyaki ribs, and famous salad bar. P Y &

MOLOKAʻI AND LĀNAʻI

KAUNAKAKAI (MOLOKAʻI): *Kanemitsu Bakery* $
79 Ala Malama Street. ((808) 553-5855. Open only until 11:30am.
As locals maintain, if you haven't been to Kanemitsu's, you haven't been to
Molokaʻi. Sweet breads baked daily. Local-style breakfast and lunch. P 🕴

KAUNAKAKAI (MOLOKAʻI): *Molokaʻi Pizza Café* $
Wharf Road (at Kahua Shopping Center). ((808) 553-3288.
This bright, efficiently run restaurant is perfect for families. Salads and ice
cream treats round out a mostly pizza menu. Ethnic daily specials. P 🕴

KALUAKOʻI (MOLOKAʻI): *ʻŌhiʻa Lodge* $$$
Kaluakoʻi Hotel and Golf Club, Kepuhi Beach. ((808) 552-2555.
This is as fine as the dining gets on Molokaʻi, with large portions of tasty
ribs, chicken, and fresh Hawaiian fish. Very friendly service. 🎵 P Y 🕴
AE MC V, D JCB

MAUNALOA (MOLOKAʻI): *Village Grill Restaurant* $$$
Maunaloa Highway. ((808) 552-0012.
Ranch-style restaurant features stonegrill cooking. Great steaks, shrimp,
and prime rib. *Paniola* decor is tastefully done. P Y 🕴 &
AE MC V

LĀNAʻI CITY (LĀNAʻI): *Blue Ginger Café* $
409 7th Street. ((808) 565-6363.
Reminiscent of a 1950s' kitchen with oilcloth table coverings and home
cooking, including fried noodles and fish. A local gathering place. 🕴

LĀNAʻI CITY (LĀNAʻI): *Tanigawa's* $
419 7th Street. ((808) 565-6537.
Basic, local-style home cooking, such as fried chicken and teriyaki beef.
The aromas from the grill mingle with the lively conversation. P

LĀNAʻI CITY (LĀNAʻI): *The Formal Dining Room* $$$$
The Lodge at Kōʻele, Keōmuku Road. ((808) 565-7300.
With decor as stunning as the rest of the property, this sumptuous dining
room offers delicious breakfast, lunch, and dinner selections. Don't miss
the chicken sandwich and the unbelievable pineapple cider. P Y 🕴 &
AE MC V JCB

MĀNELE BAY (LĀNAʻI): *ʻIhilani Dining Room* $$$$$
Mānele Bay Hotel, off Mānele Road (Hwy 440). ((808) 565-2296.
The most luxurious dining experience on Lānaʻi. Everything is impeccable –
the Mediterranean gourmet food, the service, the ambience. P Y &
AE MC V, D JCB

For key to symbols see back flap

<table>
<tr><td colspan="2">Price categories for a three-course meal, with a glass of wine, including tax and service charges:

$ under $20
$$ $20–$30
$$$ $30–$45
$$$$ $45–$60
$$$$$ over $60</td><td>CREDIT CARDS ACCEPTED
AE American Express; MC MasterCard; V VISA; D Discover; JCB Japanese Credit Bureau.

OUTDOOR TABLES
Tables for eating outdoors, often with a good view.

HRC (HAWAI'I REGIONAL CUISINE)
Gourmet food incorporating fresh island ingredients with influences from Hawaii's different ethnic groups.

GOOD WINE LIST
Denotes a wide range of good quality wines.

LATE NIGHT MENU
Light meals and snacks available until late.</td></tr>
</table>

		CREDIT CARDS ACCEPTED	OUTDOOR TABLES	HRC	GOOD WINE LIST	LATE NIGHT MENU
MAUI						
HAʻIKŪ: *Paʻuwela Café* 375 West Kuiʻaha Road, #37. *(808) 575-9242.* Owned by the Speeres – a pastry chef and her chef-instructor husband – this café serves fresh, delicious food and excellent pastries. 🅿 🚹 ♿	$		●	■		
HAʻIKŪ: *Trattoria Haʻikū* Corner of Kokomo Rd & Haʻikū Rd (at Haʻikū Marketplace). *(808) 575-2820.* At this welcoming trattoria you'll find traditional Italian food interpreted with fresh local ingredients and home-grown herbs. Splashing fountains and warm decor. 🅿 🍷 ♿ ⬤ Mon.	$$$	AE MC V	●		●	
HĀLIʻIMAILE: *Hāliʻimaile General Store* 900 Hāliʻimaile Road. *(808) 572-2666.* This beautifully refurbished 1929 store, in the middle of a pineapple plantation on the slopes of Haleakalā, offers fabulous, hearty food. 🅿 🍷 🚹 ♿	$$$$	AE MC V		■	●	
HĀNA: *Hāna Ranch Restaurant* Hāna Ranch Center, off Hāna Highway (Hwy 360). *(808) 248-8255.* Whether in the light-wood dining room or outside amid the serenity of Hāna, the food is excellent, prepared simply with local ingredients. 🅿 🍷 🚹	$$$	AE MC V, D JCB	●			
KĀʻANAPALI: *Hula Grill* 2435 Kāʻanapali Parkway (at Whalers Village). *(808) 667-6636.* This is an enchanting replica of a 1940s Hawaiian beach house sitting right on Kāʻanapali Beach. Lunch, dinner, and cocktails are served. ⭐ 🎵 🅿 🍷 🚹 ♿	$$$	AE MC V	●	■	●	■
KĀʻANAPALI: *Leilani's on the Beach* 2435 Kāʻanapali Parkway (at Whalers Village). *(808) 661-4495.* Great for "people-watching" – the beach is so close you'll find sand in your shoes. Try the smoked fish and the ice-cream drinks. 🎵 🅿 🍷 🚹 ♿	$$$	AE MC V D	●		●	■
KAHANA: *Roy's Kahana Bar & Grill* 4405 Honoapiʻilani Hwy (Hwy 30) (at Kahana Gateway). *(808) 669-6999.* Roy Yamaguchi, Hawaii's best known chef and the champion of Euro-Asian cuisine, has restaurants on four of the islands. The food is consistently good, but diners are often rushed at these busy restaurants. 🅿 🍷 🚹 ♿	$$$	AE MC V D JCB		■	●	
KAHANA: *Roy's Nicolina* 4405 Honoapiʻilani Hwy (Hwy 30) (at Kahana Gateway). *(808) 669-5000.* Located right next door to Roy's Kahana Bar & Grill, Nicolina started out as its casual cousin but has quickly evolved into an almost identical twin. The obvious choice when the other is busy. 🅿 🍷 🚹 ♿	$$$	AE MC V, D JCB		■	●	
KAHULUI: *Class Act Restaurant* 310 Kaʻahumanu Avenue (at Maui Community College). *(808) 984-3480.* Book ahead for the fabulous, eclectic food prepared by students. The college's kitchen is open for lunch only (11am–12:30pm) and, obviously, only during the school year. 🅿 ♿ ⬤ Thu, Sat–Tue.	$		●	■		
KAHULUI: *Koho's Grill & Bar* 275 Kaʻahumanu Avenue (at Kaʻahumanu Center). *(808) 877-5588.* This great-value family-style restaurant provides an alternative to the center's fast-food court. Excellent burgers, salads, and plate lunches. 🅿 🍷 🚹 ♿	$$	AE MC V				
KAPALUA: *Sansei Seafood Restaurant & Sushi Bar* 115 Bay Drive (at the Kapalua Shops). *(808) 669-6286.* Two chefs – one Japanese, one American – create incredible Japanese-based Pacific Rim cuisine. It may be a little out of the way but it is well worth the trip. 🅿 🍷 🚹 ♿	$$$	AE MC V, D JCB			●	■

KAPALUA: *The Plantation House Restaurant* $$$$
2000 Plantation Club Drive (in the Plantation Course Clubhouse). 📞 *(808) 669-6299*.
Chef Alex Stanislaw truly shines at dinner, blending his Mediterranean
heritage with fresh local bounty. The views are astounding. 🅿 🍸 🔆 ♿
AE MC V

KIHEI: *Maui Tacos* $
2411 S Kihei Road (at Kama'ole Beach Center). 📞 *(808) 879-5005*.
Part of a growing chain, this tiny restaurant serves gourmet Mexican fast
food. Mark Ellman creates fresh, healthful, and delicious food. 🅿 ♿

KIHEI: *Stella Blues Café* $$
1215 S Kihei Road (at Long's Center). 📞 *(808) 874-3779*.
This bright café/deli serves fresh, well-prepared, no-nonsense food.
Vegetarian selections, takeouts, and picnics are available. 🅿 🔆 ♿
MC V D

KIHEI: *The Greek Bistro* $$$
2511 S Kihei Road. 📞 *(808) 879-9330*.
Tasty, authentic Greek food in pleasant open-air surroundings. The special
bistro potatoes are an absolute must. For the indecisive, the Greek sam-
pler platter, called "Feast of the Gods," is a great choice. 🅿 🍸 🔆 ♿
AE MC V, D JCB

KIHEI: *A Pacific Café Maui* $$$$
1279 S Kihei Road (in Azeka Place II Shopping Center). 📞 *(808) 879-0069*.
This is the second in HRC chef Jean-Marie Josselin's growing list of loca-
tions. The food is fantastic and as creative as the striking surroundings.
A tandoori oven and open kitchen form the centerpiece. 🅿 🍸 ♿
AE MC V D JCB

LAHAINA: *Cheeseburger In Paradise* $
811 Front Street. 📞 *(808) 661-4855*.
Juicy burgers, golden fries, and crispy onion rings, plus ocean views and perfect service, make this one of Hawai'i's favorite restaurants. 🎵 🍸 🔆 ♿
AE MC V D

LAHAINA: *Village Pizzeria* $
505 Front Street. 📞 *(808) 661-8112*.
If you love the aromas and tastes of a New York-style, Italian pizza place
you'll feel at home here. Delicious pizza, by the pie or slice. 🅿 🍸 🔆 ♿
AE MC V D

LAHAINA: *Hard Rock Café – Maui* $$
900 Front Street (at Lahaina Center). 📞 *(808) 667-7400*.
Part of the rock-and-roll theme chain with a few island twists. Menu includes
barbecue ribs, salads, and sandwiches. Fun, noisy, good value. 🅿 🍸 🔆 ♿
AE MC V, D JCB

LAHAINA: *Kobe Japanese Steak House* $$
136 Dickenson Street. 📞 *(808) 667-5555*.
Here you will find one of the best sushi bars on Maui, plus knife-wielding
teppanyaki chefs who provide the entertainment while cooking dinner
before your eyes. 🅿 🍸 🔆 ♿
AE MC V, D JCB

LAHAINA: *Woody's* $$
839 Front Street. 📞 *(808) 661-8788*.
Under a new name, Woody's serves Island-American favorites, including
a superb *ceviche* (raw fish in lime juice). Great ocean views. 🍸 🔆 ♿
AE MC V, D JCB

LAHAINA: *Chart House* $$$
1450 Front Street. 📞 *(808) 661-0937*.
This is one of a highly successful statewide chain established by two
world-class surfers. The prime rib, steak, and seafood have made it a
household name. The coconut crunchy shrimp is a must. 🅿 🍸 🔆 ♿
AE MC V D JCB

LAHAINA: *I'o* $$$$
505 Front Street. 📞 *(808) 661-8422*.
This new restaurant features HRC and a modern, funky look. Dress is casual
chic, and fine dining is the order of the day. 🅿 🍸 🔆 ♿
AE MC V, D JCB

LAHAINA: *Kimo's* $$$
845 Front Street. 📞 *(808) 661-4811*.
This long-established restaurant offers oversized portions of fresh fish or fine
steak. Great service and a location lapped by calm waters. 🎇 🎵 🍸 🔆 ♿
AE MC V D

LAHAINA: *Longhi's* $$$
888 Front Street. 📞 *(808) 667-2288*.
Created by "a man who loves to eat" (Bob Longhi), this is a Maui insti-
tution. The orange juice and coffee alone are worth the trip for breakfast.
Specials include *'ahi* (tuna) Torino and shrimp amaretto. 🅿 🍸 🔆 ♿
AE MC V D JCB

Price categories for a three-course meal, with a glass of wine, including tax and service charges:

$ under $20
$$ $20–$30
$$$ $30–$45
$$$$ $45–$60
$$$$$ over $60

CREDIT CARDS ACCEPTED
AE American Express; *MC* MasterCard; *V* VISA; *D* Discover; *JCB* Japanese Credit Bureau.

OUTDOOR TABLES
Tables for eating outdoors, often with a good view.

HRC (HAWAI'I REGIONAL CUISINE)
Gourmet food incorporating fresh island ingredients with influences from Hawaii's different ethnic groups.

GOOD WINE LIST
Denotes a wide range of good quality wines.

LATE NIGHT MENU
Light meals and snacks available until late.

Restaurant	Price	Credit Cards Accepted	Outdoor Tables	HRC	Good Wine List	Late Night Menu
LAHAINA: Gerard's Restaurant 174 Lahainaluna Road (at the Plantation Inn). (808) 661-8939. French food is served with European flair and Hawaiian *aloha* in a charming country setting. Gerard Reversade remains true to his classical roots while incorporating island ingredients into his original recipes.	$$$	AE MC V D JCB	●		●	
LAHAINA: David Paul's Lahaina Grill 127 Lahainaluna Road. (808) 667-5117. Voted "Best Maui Restaurant" four times by *Honolulu* magazine readers, this oasis among the bustle of town provides oft-changing menus. Try the superb *kālua* duck, Tequila shrimp, or triple berry pie.	$$$$$	AE MC V D JCB		■	●	
LAHAINA: Old Lahaina Lū'au 1251 Front Street. (808) 667-1998. The next best thing to a Hawaiian family party, this *lū'au (see p164)* has won many awards for authenticity. Great show and traditional food, including *poi*, *kālua* pig, *mahimahi*, and *lomi-lomi* salmon.	$$$$$	AE MC V	●			
LAHAINA: Pacific'O Restaurant 505 Front Street. (808) 667-4341. Creative, eye-catching cuisine focusing on fresh fish and other island ingredients. Great beachfront location. Very good service.	$$$$	AE MC V JCB	●	■	●	
MA'ALAEA: The Waterfront Restaurant 50 Hau'oli Street. (808) 244-9028. Several types of local fish prepared in as many as nine different ways are presented each evening at this oceanside landmark. Other choices include a selection of game. Experienced staff and excellent wine list.	$$$$	AE MC V D JCB	●			
MAKAWAO: Casanova Italian Restaurant and Deli 1188 Makawao Avenue. (808) 572-0220. Delicious early-morning omelettes and cappuccino, or tasty picnic lunches at the deli; authentic Italian specialties in the restaurant.	$$	MC V D JCB			●	■
MAKAWAO: Makawao Steak House 3612 Baldwin Avenue. (808) 572-8711. In this 1927 wooden building on Makawao's main street you'll find good home-style cooking – hot bread and creamy butter, substantial salads, and big portions of meat (or fish), potatoes, and vegetables.	$$$	MC V				
NAPILI: Koho's Grill & Bar 5095 Nāpilihau Street (at Nāpili Plaza). (808) 669-5299. Serving the same terrific lunch and dinner menus as its older sister in Kahului *(see p170)*, this branch offers the added bonus of a game room – enjoy darts, pool, or pinball with the consistently good food.	$$	AE MC V JCB				
PĀ'IA: Charley's Restaurant and Saloon 142 Hāna Highway (Hwy 36). (808) 579-9453. Before the long and winding road to Hāna, stop here for what many consider the best and biggest breakfasts on Maui. The burgers and pizzas are great, too. Charley is the big, black-and-white Great Dane.	$$	AE MC V D				
PĀ'IA: Mama's Fish House 799 Poho Place. (808) 579-8488. Dining with Mama in her famous beach house provides a living memory of Maui in picture-perfect Kū'au, just east of Pā'ia. Creatively prepared fresh fish served with island accompaniments, and fantastic desserts.	$$$$	AE MC V D JCB		■	●	
PUKALANI: Upcountry Café 7-2 Āewa Place. (808) 572-2395. "Local-style with modern flair" may be the best way to describe the food at this popular upcountry spot. Big breakfasts, satisfying plate lunches, and excellent dinners prepared in simple, delicious ways.	$	AE MC V				

WAILEA: *Joe's Bar & Grill* $$$$
131 Wailea Iki Place (at the Wailea Tennis Center). ((808) 875-7767.
"Home Cooking from Paradise" is the motto at Joe and Beverly Gannon's
casual, open-air restaurant. Delicious fare and huge portions. **P Y ᛟ &**

| AE |
| MC |
| V, D |
| JCB |

WAILEA: *The Seawatch Restaurant* $$$$
100 Wailea Golf Club Drive. ((808) 875-8080.
Each table at this stunning restaurant in the Wailea Gold Course Clubhouse
has a spectacular view. Fresh Hawaiian fish and great wine list. **P Y ᛟ &**

| AE |
| MC |
| V |

WAILUKU: *A Saigon Café* $
1792 Main Street. ((808) 243-9560.
Incredibly flavorful food, with plenty for vegetarians. Try the sweet and
sour soup, Vietnamese burrito, rice in a clay pot, or stuffed tofu. **P Y ᛟ &**

| MC |
| V |

WAILUKU: *Tokyo Tei* $$
1063 Lower Main Street, #C101. ((808) 242-9630.
Popular with local people, this tiny place offers tasty, affordable food. The
vegetable tempura and teriyaki pork and fish are excellent. **P Y ᛟ &**

| MC |
| V |

HAWAI'I ISLAND

HILO: *Bear's Coffee* $
106 Keawe Street. ((808) 935-0708.
Hilo's hippest little place where locals gather to "talk story," read the paper,
and enjoy coffee, tasty breakfasts of Belgian waffles, or quick lunches,
such as Greek salad or a burrito supremo. **P ᛟ & ●** *Lunch: Sun.*

| MC |
| V |
| JCB |

HILO: *Café 100* $
969 Kīlauea Avenue. ((808) 935-8683.
Café 100 has been serving plate lunches of food such as beef teriyaki,
beef curry, *laulau*, or *kālua* pig to folks in Hilo for more than 50 years, at
outdoor picnic-style tables. Very friendly, very local. **P ᛟ & ●** *Sun.*

HILO: *Ken's House of Pancakes* $
1730 Kamehameha Avenue. ((808) 935-8711.
This 24-hour diner is best known for its incredible, all-day breakfasts –
exceptional omelettes, potent coffee, and warm, friendly service. **P ᛟ &**

| AE |
| MC |
| V |
| D |

HILO: *Nihon Restaurant & Cultural Center* $$
123 Lihiwai Street. ((808) 969-1133.
Japanese in design, Nihon gives you culture with your sushi. The upstairs
dining room offers a beautiful view of Hilo Bay and Liliʻuokalani
Gardens. The food is authentic and delicious. **P Y ᛟ & ●** *Sun.*

| AE |
| MC |
| V |
| D |
| JCB |

HILO: *Restaurant Miwa* $$
1261 Kīlauea Avenue (at Hilo Shopping Center). ((808) 961-4454.
In a corner of the shopping center is this neighborhood Japanese restau-
rant. Stark and clean with light-wood tables and a sushi bar. **P Y ᛟ &**

| AE |
| MC |
| V, D |
| JCB |

HILO: *Café Pesto* $$$
308 Kamehameha Avenue. ((808) 969-6640.
A 1910 building that has survived more than one tsunami, this casual café in
a lovely setting near Hilo Bay offers creative pizzas and pasta. **Y ᛟ &**

| AE |
| MC |
| V, D |
| JCB |

HILO: *Harrington's Restaurant* $$$
135 Kalanianaʻole Avenue. ((808) 961-4966.
Set on Reed's Pond, this romantic, nautical restaurant has a varied menu,
including Slavic steak and fresh catch meunière style. **♬ P Y ᛟ &**

| MC |
| V |

KAILUA-KONA: *Kona Ranch House* $$
75-5653 ʻOloli Street. ((808) 329-7061.
An early 20th-century ranch house, Hawaiian style. Steak, seafood, and
salads robust enough to satisfy everyone. **P Y ᛟ & ●** *dinner.*

| AE |
| MC |
| V, D |
| JCB |

KAILUA-KONA: *Oodles of Noodles* $$$
Suite 102, 75-1027 Henry Street. ((808) 329-9222.
Over 40 noodle dishes are offered at this sophisticated spot by an HRC
original, Amy Ferguson-Ota. **P Y ᛟ &**

| AE |
| MC |
| V, D |
| JCB |

KAILUA-KONA: *Sam Choy's Restaurant* $$$
73-5576 Kau Hola Street. ((808) 326-1545.
Despite the industrial location, Sam's original restaurant, birthplace of his
seafood *laulau*, is a must. Bring your own wine. **P ᛟ & ●** *Sun, Mon pm.*

| MC |
| V |
| D |

For key to symbols see back flap

Price categories for a three-course meal, with a glass of wine, including tax and service charges:

$ under $20
$$ $20–$30
$$$ $30–$45
$$$$ $45–$60
$$$$$ over $60

CREDIT CARDS ACCEPTED
AE American Express; *MC* MasterCard; *V* VISA; *D* Discover; *JCB* Japanese Credit Bureau.
OUTDOOR TABLES
Tables for eating outdoors, often with a good view.
HRC (HAWAI'I REGIONAL CUISINE)
Gourmet food incorporating fresh island ingredients with influences from Hawaii's different ethnic groups.
GOOD WINE LIST
Denotes a wide range of good quality wines.
LATE NIGHT MENU
Light meals and snacks available until late.

	Credit Cards Accepted	Outdoor Tables	HRC	Good Wine List	Late Night Menu
KAILUA-KONA: *Jameson's By the Sea* $$$ 77-6452 Ali'i Drive. (808) 329-3195. Ocean views and outdoor dining right on the water's edge at this popular island-style restaurant. Specialties include baked stuffed shrimp, poached 'ōpakapaka (pink snapper) and homemade chiffon pies.	AE MC V D JCB	●		●	
KAILUA-KONA: *Kona Inn Restaurant* $$$ 75-5744 Ali'i Drive (at Kona Inn Shopping Village). (808) 329-4455. Good choice for open-air dining in the heart of Kailua. This historic property was built by the Inter-Island Steam Navigation Company in 1928 and has kept a nautical theme. Straightforward fish, steak, and chicken.	AE MC V	●		●	■
KAILUA-KONA: *Restaurant La Bourgogne* $$$ 77-6400 Nālani Street, #101. (808) 329-6711. Classic French country cuisine served in a country inn setting. Chef/owner Ron Gallaher lovingly re-creates the foods of Burgundy using local ingredients. With only ten tables, reservations are strongly advised. Sun.	AE MC V D JCB			●	
KAILUA-KONA: *Huggo's* $$$$ 75-5828 Kahakai Road. (808) 329-1493. Built in 1919, this torch-lit dining room is so close to the ocean you can feed the fish from your table. Fish and beef specialties.	AE MC V, D JCB	●	■	●	
KEAUHOU: *Edward's at Kanaloa* $$$ 78-261 Manukai Street. (808) 322-1003. Small dining patio with the Pacific as backdrop. At dinner, the celebrated chef offers tasty dishes such as lobster salad or rack of lamb.	AE MC V, D JCB	●			
KOHALA COAST: *The Canoe House* $$$$$ 68-1400 Mauna Lani Drive (grounds of Mauna Lani Bay Hotel). (808) 885-6622. The Canoe House combines a magnificent open-air setting with impressive Pacific Rim cuisine and conjures up images of Hawai'i in a simpler time. A *koa* canoe hangs from the ceiling. Marvelous sunset views.	AE MC V D JCB	●		●	
WAIMEA: *Merriman's Restaurant* $$$$ Kawaihae Road (Hwy 19) and Opelo Road (in Opelo Plaza). (808) 885-6822. Recognized as the "Pied Piper of Hawai'i Regional Cuisine," Peter Merriman searches relentlessly for new, local ingredients to use in his food. He has even been known to dive for sea urchins to put in his soup.	AE MC V JCB		■	●	

KAUA'I

	Credit Cards Accepted	Outdoor Tables	HRC	Good Wine List	Late Night Menu
ANAHOLA: *Duane's Ono Char-Burgers* $ Kūhiō Highway (Hwy 56). (808) 822-9181. A sigh of relief was heard throughout the islands when this roadside stand was repaired following Hurricane Iniki. Arguably Hawaii's best burgers.		●			
HANAMĀ'ULU: *Hanamā'ulu Restaurant & Teahouse* $$ 3-4291 Kūhiō Highway (Hwy 56). (808) 245-2511. Off the beaten track but a local landmark. Unusually, both Japanese and Chinese food are served. Typical Japanese teahouse. Mon.	MC V	●			
HANAPĒPĒ: *Green Garden Restaurant* $ Kaumuali'i Highway (Hwy 50). (808) 335-5422. This Kaua'i landmark has glorious tropical foliage both inside and out. The plate lunches are delicious and extremely inexpensive. Do not leave without trying the *liliko'i* (passion fruit) chiffon pie. Tue.	AE MC V	●			
KAPA'A: *The Eggbert's* $ 4-484 Kūhiō Highway (Hwy 56) (at Coconut Marketplace). (808) 822-3787. After taking a battering from Hurricane Iniki, this delightful restaurant is back in a new location. Design your own version of the eggs Benedict and two- or three-egg omelettes that made Eggbert's famous.	MC V	●			

KAPAʻA: *Kountry Kitchen* $
1485 Kūhiō Highway (Hwy 56). ((808) 822-3511.
Customers rave about the banana pancakes at this homey restaurant with
its floral wallpaper and antiques. **P ⚥ ●** *dinner.*
MC
V

KAPAʻA: *Papaya's* $
4-831 Kūhiō Highway (Hwy 56) (at Kauaʻi Village). ((808) 823-0190.
This is pretty much the only place for "health" food on Kauaʻi. Everything
is fresh and inexpensive. Seating is under umbrellas outside. **P ⚥ ●** *Sun.*
MC
V
D

KAPAʻA: *A Pacific Café* $$$$
4-831 Kūhiō Highway (Hwy 56) (at Kauaʻi Village). ((808) 822-0013.
The first of renowned chef Jean-Marie Josselin's restaurants. Innovative
dishes, such as wok-charred *mahimahi* or seared scallops, served in a
comfortable, tropical dining room decked with local art. **P Ψ ⚥ ⚥**
AE
MC
V
D
JCB

KĪLAUEA: *The Kīlauea Bakery & Pau Hana Pizza* $
2484 Keneke Street (at Kong Lung Center). ((808) 828-2020.
Tom and Katie Pickett have made a name for themselves with extraordinary
breads, coffee, and pizzas. Arrive early for best bread selection. **P ●** *Sun.*
MC
V

LĪHUʻE: *Hamura Saimin Stand* $
2956 Kress Street. ((808) 245-3271.
Many feel this restaurant makes Hawaiʻi's best noodles. Customers sit at
a counter, and even on the hottest day, the *saimin* is indescribably delicious.

LĪHUʻE: *Kauaʻi Chop Suey* $
3501 Rice Street (at Pacific Ocean Plaza). ((808) 245-8790.
This cash-only, neighborhood-style restaurant has an extensive Chinese
menu; takeouts also available. Another local favorite. **P ⚥ ●** *Mon.*

LĪHUʻE: *Tip Top Café & Motel* $
3173 ʻAkāhi Street. ((808) 245-2333.
This spotlessly clean, oversized dining room has 1950s-style booths and
orchids on every table. Breakfasts and lunches are hearty. **P ⚥ ⚥ ●** *Mon.*
MC
V

LĪHUʻE: *Café Portofino* $$
3501 Rice Street (at Pacific Ocean Plaza). ((808) 245-2121.
You could be forgiven for thinking you're in the Mediterranean here. The
tile floors, brocade chairs, soft pink and gray linens, and modern Northern
Italian cuisine create the feeling of an Italian villa. **♫ P Ψ ⚥ ⚥**
AE
MC
V
D
JCB

LĪHUʻE: *Gaylord's at Kilohana* $$$
3-2087 Kaumualiʻi Highway (Hwy 50). ((808) 245-9593.
Located at Kauaʻi's legendary plantation estate, Gaylord's offers gracious
open-air dining with unhurried service and a menu ranging from pasta to
prime rib. Explore the grounds of the mansion *(see p134).* **P Ψ ⚥ ⚥**
AE
MC
V, D
JCB

LĪHUʻE: *Duke's Canoe Club* $$$
3500 Rice Street (in the Kauaʻi Marriott Hotel). ((808) 246-9599.
As in Honolulu, this "museum" to Duke Kahanamoku offers big portions
of well-prepared American fare in an open-air setting. **★ ♫ P Ψ ⚥ ⚥**
AE
MC
V, D
JCB

LĪHUʻE: *JJ's Broiler* $$$
3416 Rice Street (at Anchor Cove Shopping Center). ((808) 246-4422.
The aroma of steak sizzling on the grill permeates the air. JJ's offers island
hospitality and generous helpings. The ocean view is great. **P Ψ ⚥ ⚥**
MC
V
D

POʻIPŪ: *Casa Di Amici* $$$
2301 Nalo Road. ((808) 742-1555.
This open-air restaurant offers a distinctive combination of International
Eclectic recipes and fresh island ingredients. **♫ P Ψ ⚥ ⚥**
MC
V

POʻIPŪ: *ROY'S POʻIPŪ BAR AND GRILL* $$$
2360 Kiahuna Plantation Drive. ((808) 742-5000.
With a menu just like the ones at other Roy's locations *(see p170),* this
vibrant restaurant also features an exhibition kitchen in full view behind
a glass wall. Slightly erratic service but wonderful food. **P Ψ ⚥ ⚥**
AE
MC
V
D
JCB

POʻIPŪ: *The Beach House* $$$$
5022 Lāwaʻi Road. ((808) 742-1424.
Now under new ownership, this upgraded restaurant is just steps from the
ocean. Fantastic views, excellent service, and great regional cuisine
featuring fresh fish. **P Ψ ⚥ ⚥**
AE
MC
V
D

For key to symbols see back flap

SHOPPING IN HAWAI'I

PINEAPPLES, MACADAMIA nuts, Kona coffee, alohawear, T-shirts, tropical flowers – these are the things that top visitors' shopping lists, and they are easy to find. Traditional Hawaiian crafts, such as *kapa* cloth, pandanus baskets, and Ni'ihau shell *lei*, are harder to find and usually more costly – but unique, beautiful, and

Hilo Hattie fashion house logo

worth the hunt. You will find many things that look like they could be made in Hawai'i but actually come from Taiwan, Hong Kong, or the Philippines. If you are determined to purchase "the real thing," be sure to check carefully. The addresses and telephone numbers of all the shops mentioned in the text are given on page 179.

Sleek and pristine interior of the Ala Moana Center, within easy access of Waikiki

WHERE TO SHOP

WHILE SHOPPING CENTERS do not dominate the landscape as they do in parts of the United States, they are still a common feature of Hawai'i's main towns. They usually contain a great variety of shops, from department stores to craft shops. Most are open-air.

The biggest are on O'ahu, such as the **Royal Hawaiian Shopping Center** and the **Ala Moana Center** in Honolulu. Maui's **Whalers Village**, located within the Kā'anapali resort area, contains some interesting shops, but the island's biggest mall is Kahului's **Ka'ahumanu Center**. The best choice in Hilo is at the **Prince Kūhiō Plaza**, while **Kaua'i Village**, a plantation-style mall on Kaua'i, is one of the island's smaller and more pleasant malls.

Supermarkets, grocery shops, Longs Drugs stores, and discount shops such as ABC Stores and K-Mart have the best prices for things like macadamia nuts, jam, and coffee. These are the best places for cheap souvenirs, too. Museum shops are often good for Hawaiian crafts.

Anyone who likes secondhand shops should enjoy scouring shops and home sales for collectibles (or "Hawaiiana") from old aloha shirts to vintage postcards, at bargain prices. The islands are big on secondhand shops and "garage sales," too, in which people sell secondhand goods in their garages. Check the Friday edition of the newspapers for weekend garage sales. The papers also give details of crafts fairs and market days.

WHEN TO SHOP

YOU CAN SHOP 24 hours a day, seven days a week if you wish – some supermarkets and convenience stores never close.

Malls and large stores are normally open from 10am to 9pm, Monday to Saturday, and often on Sunday (but the hours are usually shorter). Small stores open from about 9am to 5 or 6pm, Monday to Saturday, and are closed on Sundays.

HOW TO PAY

TRAVELERS' CHECKS in US dollars and credit cards are accepted more or less everywhere in Hawai'i (*see p194*). However, it is a good idea to carry at least some cash for purchases at roadside stands and small, family-run stores.

Remember that sales tax of 4.17 percent is added to every purchase made in Hawai'i, and that this tax will be added to the total bill by the cashier.

FRUIT AND FLOWERS

MANY VISITORS take the fresh flavors and aromas of Hawai'i home with them. You can take coconuts, pineapples, and papayas (but no other fruit) through customs, as long as they are passed by the **US Department of Agriculture (USDA)** inspection.

It is best to buy such fruit prepackaged at airport shops or other reputable stores that specialize in "take home" fruits. There are many of these stores in Hawai'i, such as the **Maui Tropical Plantation & Country Store** near Wailuku. Someone at your hotel should know the best place on any particular island. These same places sell sterile cuttings and

Roadside stand selling tropical Hawaiian fruit in Hāna on Maui's windward coast

seeds of tropical plants that have been passed by USDA. You can have your purchases delivered to the airport from which you are leaving or sent directly to your home address.

You can export all fresh flowers, subject to agricultural inspection, apart from jade vines, gardenias, and *maunaloa*. Hawai‘i Island is the best place for anthuriums, while you should buy protea and exotics in Maui. You can export *lei*, but most last only a very short time; check with the florist or *lei*-maker, because some *lei* are very attractive when dried. Alternatively, you could consider buying a nonperishable *lei* made of nuts, feathers, seeds, or shells, for example *(see p19)*. The best places to buy flower *lei* are the small shops in Honolulu's Chinatown, but the stands at Honolulu International Airport have a good selection, too.

Macadamia nuts, in easy-to-pack cans

If you are unsure whether or not you'll be able to take a particular item home with you, check first by telephoning the USDA.

FOOD AND DRINK

ALTHOUGH MANGOES, guava, and *liliko‘i* (passion fruit) are not permitted out of the islands, chutneys, jams, jellies, and other products made with these fruits are great buys.

World-famous Kona coffee comes from Hawai‘i Island, but coffee is now grown on Maui and Kaua‘i too. All coffees are available in whole-bean or ground, flavored, instant, and decaffeinated varieties.

Macadamia nuts also come in many forms, from dry-roasted and salted to honey-flavored or chocolate-covered. Adventurous gastronomes may like to try taro chips and "crack seed" – preserved and seasoned nuts, fruits, seeds, and sweets. All these products are sold at supermarkets, grocery stores, convenience stores, and specialty shops throughout the islands. **Shirokiya** (Honolulu), a Japan-based department store, also sells a great variety of unusual prepared food.

Hawai‘i has two wineries. The **Tedeschi Winery** on Maui makes a couple of good red table wines, one sparkling wine, and, its most famous product, Maui Blanc – a light pineapple wine. The **Volcano Winery** on Hawai‘i Island is producing some interesting wines from various tropical fruits while waiting for its grapevines to mature.

ART

LIKE GAUGUIN, many artists have followed their muse to the Pacific. Unlike Gauguin, the majority are not very good. There are literally dozens of "galleries," mostly in tourist shopping areas. Some specialize in sales of very expensive work that has no investment value – in spite of what the resident "consultants" tell you. If you need advice, someone at your hotel should be able to direct you to a reliable source; museums can often be of help, too.

There is some wonderful art to be found in Hawai‘i. And much of it – in the form of lithographs, posters, and even cards – is affordable. Dietrich Varez of Volcano (on Hawai‘i Island), for example, lovingly creates earth-brown linoleum block prints depicting local legends. They are glorious, easy to find, and cheap, at about $20 apiece. You will find his work in the **Volcano Art Center**. Another reputable gallery on Hawai‘i Island is **Studio 7** in Hōlualoa.

The **Viewpoints Gallery** in Makawao (Maui) is a collective representing some fine local artists.

One of the many art galleries on Front Street in Lahaina, Maui

You can also rely on good quality at the **Village Gallery** and **Lahaina Arts Society** in Lahaina, and there is usually interesting work in the **Nohea Gallery** in Honolulu.

COLLECTIBLES

JUST ABOUT ANYTHING Hawaiian from the 1940s to the 1970s is now considered collectible: postcards, Matson steamship menus, even kitsch ceramic *hula* girls, and especially old aloha shirts known as "silkies."

You'll find such things in the little shops on Wailuku's Market Street and in "antique" shops such as **Bailey's Antiques** and **Aloha Antiques & Collectibles** in Honolulu, and **The Only Show in Town** in Kahuku (O‘ahu); **Hula Heaven** in Kona and **Seconds to Go** in Honoka‘a (Hawai‘i Island); the **Pā‘ia Trading Company** on Maui; and **Islander Trading Co.** on Kaua‘i. It may be more fun hunting in second-hand stores and garage sales.

Display of blown-glass vases and other objects in a Maui gallery

Man weaving a coconut-leaf hat on a Hawai'i Island street

CRAFTS

Hawai'i teems with artisans. Hand-crafted bowls of mango, monkeypod, or *koa* wood make beautiful presents and mementos. You can also buy *koa* hair ornaments, chopsticks, and key chains. Wooden objects can be found in craft shops in most big towns.

Hawai'i also has many expert weavers. Coconut leaf is often used, but *hala* (pandanus) is better quality. Mats, bags, and hats are all popular buys. Ceramic bowls, vases, and plates are also popular. **Following Sea** in Honolulu is a good bet for these.

It is virtually impossible to buy vintage Hawaiian quilts (most are family heirlooms), but new quilts, and even quilt kits, are easy to find. Try **Maui Crafts Guild** in Pa'ia or the **Gallery of Great Things** on Hawai'i Island. Hawaiian *kapa* (bark cloth) is hard to find. Most *kapa* goods for sale are from Samoa or Tonga.

Combing the crafts fairs is a fun way to see what is available. Museum shops are also good sources, as are the many specialty shops, including **Cook's Discoveries** on Hawai'i Island, **Ola's Hanalei** on Kaua'i, and its sister store on Maui, **Ola's Makawao**.

JEWELRY

Costume jewelry is made from everything you can think of – ceramic, paper, plastic, metals, and more – and can be found at crafts fairs.

Fine jewelry made of pearls, coral, jade, silver, and gold is sold in department stores and in the dozens of specialty shops, such as **The Gallery Ltd** in Kahului and Kaua'i's **Jim Saylor Jewelers**. "Heritage jewelry," Victorian gold jewelry with names and designs inscribed in black enamel, is popular. It is also expensive, so be sure to buy from a reliable dealer.

The most precious pieces of Hawaiian jewelry available are Ni'ihau shell *lei*. The shops on Kaua'i are the best places to buy them, but be sure to do some advance research. A simple choker may cost as little as $25, while museum-quality, multi-strand, waist-length *lei* typically cost thousands of dollars.

Shopping bag from Liberty House

BOOKS AND MUSIC

The big bookstores, such as **Barnes & Noble** (O'ahu), **Waldenbooks** (everywhere), and **Borders** (O'ahu, Maui, Kaua'i, and Hawai'i Island), have the best choice of books about Hawai'i, with everything from novels to cook books. Borders also carries excellent selections of Hawaiian music. **Native Books & Beautiful Things**, in Honolulu, has a wide range of Hawaiian-language books.

Most music stores, whether locally based **Tempo Music** or gigantic **Tower Records**, sell both traditional and contemporary Hawaiian music.

Tempo Music shop logo

CLOTHES AND FABRIC

The days of tourists strolling down the street dressed in matching polyester *mu'umu'u* and aloha shirts seem to have gone. Even the state's biggest producer of alohawear, **Hilo Hattie**, now sells attractive cotton or cotton-blend island fashions in its many fashion centers. **Sig Zane Designs** (Hilo), and **Reyn's** and **Liberty House** (both are statewide department stores) stock some stunning Hawaiian-style clothing in the latest fashions, colors and subtle prints. **Mamo Howell** is big in the world of Hawaiian couture, but you might want to think about whether you will be able (or want) to wear your expensive *mu'umu'u* back home.

Sarongs are popular beachwear among local women and men. They are sold everywhere and cost $10–35, depending on the fabric and design. Most places offer tips on how to wear what is basically a couple of yards of material finished on all four sides.

Hawai'i is a great place to stock up on swimsuits, and it must be the T-shirt capital of the world, too. T-shirts are sold everywhere, emblazoned with every imaginable design and logo. **Crazy Shirts**, with two dozen stores statewide, is considered by many to stock both the highest quality shirts and the best choice of designs.

Sarongs displayed outside a shop on O'ahu's North Shore

DIRECTORY

SHOPPING CENTERS

Ala Moana Center
1450 Ala Moana Blvd,
Honolulu, O'ahu.
Map 3 A4.
((808) 955-9517.

Ka'ahumanu Center
275 Ka'ahumanu Ave,
Kahului, Maui.
((808) 877-4325.

Kaua'i Village
4-831 Kūhiō Hwy,
Kapa'a, Kaua'i.
((808) 822-4904.

Prince Kūhiō Plaza
111 E Pū'ainakō St,
Hilo, Hawai'i Island.
((808) 959-3555.

Royal Hawaiian Shopping Center
2201 Kalākaua Ave,
Waikīkī, O'ahu. **Map** 4 D5.
((808) 922-0588.

Whalers Village
2435 Kā'anapali Parkway,
Kā'anapali, Maui.
((808) 661-4567.

FRUIT AND FLOWERS

Maui Tropical Plantation & Country Store
1670 Honoapi'ilani Hwy,
Wailuku, Maui.
((808) 244-7643.

US Department of Agriculture (USDA)
Honolulu International
Airport, Honolulu, O'ahu.
((808) 861-8490.

FOOD AND DRINK

Shirokiya
Ala Moana Center,
Honolulu, O'ahu.
Map 3 A4.
((808) 973-9111.

Tedeschi Winery
'Ulupalakua, Maui.
((808) 878-6058.

Volcano Winery
35 Pi'imauna Drive,
Volcano, Hawai'i Island.
((808) 967-7479.

ART

Lahaina Arts Society
Old Lahaina Courthouse,
Lahaina, Maui.
((808) 661-0111.

Nohea Gallery
Ward Warehouse,
1050 Ala Moana Blvd,
Honolulu, O'ahu.
Map 2 D5.
((808) 596-0074.

Studio 7
Māmalahoa Hwy,
Hōlualoa, Hawai'i Island.
((808) 324-1335.

Viewpoints Gallery
3620 Baldwin Ave,
Makawao, Maui.
((808) 572-5979.

Village Gallery
120 Dickenson St,
Lahaina, Maui.
((808) 661-4402.

Volcano Art Center
Hawai'i Volcanoes National
Park, Hawai'i Island.
((808) 967-7565.

COLLECTIBLES

Aloha Antiques & Collectibles
926 Maunakea St, Hono-
lulu, O'ahu. **Map** 1 A2.
((808) 536-6187.

Bailey's Antiques
517 Kapahulu Ave,
Honolulu, O'ahu.
((808) 734-7628.

Islander Trading Company
Coconut Marketplace,
Kapa'a, Kaua'i.
((808) 822-3333.

Hula Heaven
Kona Inn Shopping Village,
Kailua-Kona, Hawai'i Island.
((808) 329-7885.

The Only Show in Town
56-901 Kamehameha Hwy,
Kahuku, O'ahu.
((808) 293-1295.

Pā'ia Trading Company
106 Hāna Hwy,
Pā'ia, Maui.
((808) 579-9472.

Seconds to Go
Mamani St and
Rickard Place,
Honoka'a, Hawai'i Island.
((808) 775-9212.

CRAFTS

Cook's Discoveries
64-1066 Māmalahoa Hwy,
Waimea, Hawai'i Island.
((808) 885-3633.

Following Sea
Kahala Mall,
4211 Wai'alae Ave,
Honolulu, O'ahu.
((808) 734-4425.

Gallery of Great Things
Parker Square,
Waimea, Hawai'i Island.
((808) 885-7706.

Maui Crafts Guild
43 Hāna Hwy,
Pā'ia, Maui.
((808) 579-9697.

Ola's Hanalei
5016 Kūhiō Hwy,
Hanalei, Kaua'i.
((808) 826-6937.

Ola's Makawao
1156 Makawao Ave,
Makawao, Maui.
((808) 573-1334.

JEWELRY

The Gallery Ltd
60 E Wakea St, #115
Kahului, Maui.
((808) 661-0696.

Jessica's Gems
Whalers Village
Kā'anapali, Maui.
((808) 661-4223.

Jim Saylor Jewelers
1318 Kūhiō Hwy,
Kapa'a, Kaua'i.
((808) 822-3591.

BOOKS AND MUSIC

Barnes & Noble
Kahala Mall,
4211 Wai'alae Ave,
Honolulu, O'ahu.
((808) 737-3323.

Borders
Ward Centre, 1200 Ala
Moana Blvd, Honolulu,
O'ahu. **Map** 2 E5.
((808) 591-8995.

Native Books & Beautiful Things
222 Merchant St, Honolulu,
O'ahu. **Map** 1 A3.
((808) 599-5511.

Tempo Music
Ka'ahumanu Center,
Kahului, Maui.
((808) 871-8317. Call
for the nearest branch.

Tower Records
611 Ke'eaumoku St,
Honolulu, O'ahu.
Map 2 F3.
((808) 941-7774. Call
for the nearest branch.

Waldenbooks
Kahala Mall, 4211 Wai'alae
Ave, Honolulu, O'ahu.
((808) 737-9550. Call
for the nearest branch.

CLOTHES AND FABRIC

Crazy Shirts
Ala Moana Center,
Honolulu, O'ahu.
Map 3 A4.
((808) 973-4000. Call
for the nearest branch.

Hilo Hattie
700 N Nimitz Hwy,
Honolulu, O'ahu.
((808) 535-6500. Call
for the nearest branch.

Liberty House
Ala Moana Center,
Honolulu, O'ahu.
((808) 941-2345. Call
for the nearest branch.

Mamo Howell
Ward Warehouse,
1050 Ala Moana Blvd,
Honolulu, O'ahu.
Map 2 D5.
((808) 592-0616.

Reyn's
Ala Moana Center,
Honolulu, O'ahu.
Map 3 A4.
((808) 949-5929. Call
for the nearest branch.

Sig Zane Designs
122 Kamehameha Ave,
Hilo, Hawai'i Island.
((808) 935-7077.

ENTERTAINMENT IN HAWAI'I

MUSIC, SONG, AND DANCE are as important to Hawaiians as the food that they eat and the air they breathe. From the musicians strumming in virtually every hotel lounge to the Merrie Monarch Festival (known as the "Olympics of *hula*"), Hawai'i is alive with the sounds of music. Besides Hawaiian rhythms, all kinds of

Hawaiian *hula* dancer

music from country to rock, jazz, and reggae can be enjoyed, and world-class places stage both rock and classical concerts, opera, and even Broadway musicals.

You can dance the night away in nightclubs in Honolulu and certain parts of Maui, but you should be prepared for somewhat earlier nights in most parts of the state.

Hawaiian tourist magazines, a good source of information

PRACTICAL INFORMATION

THE FRIDAY EDITION of *The Honolulu Advertiser* has the most complete entertainment listings; the neighboring islands' newspapers also have entertainment sections once a week. Local radio stations and posters plastered all over town are other sources, along with free local newspapers such as *Honolulu Weekly*. Your hotel should have up-to-date listings.

TICKET OUTLETS

IT IS BEST TO BUY tickets in advance for major events such as the Broadway shows that are occasionally put on in Honolulu. You can charge tickets to a major credit card for many events by telephoning **Ticket Plus**.

If you're buying tickets in person, there is sure to be a convenient ticket outlet near your hotel for almost any event; check with the hotel's guest services department. Music stores sell most concert tickets, for example.

Local people are not known for making plans a long way in advance, so there are usually tickets to be had at the door for smaller events.

If you want to attend the really big shows – the Merrie Monarch Festival in April or February's NFL Pro Bowl, for example – you should plan your holiday around them. Tickets for these must be purchased months in advance. You should also note that hotel rooms are at a premium during particularly big events.

HAWAIIAN MUSIC, HULA, AND LU'AU

A GREAT DEAL of the Hawaiian entertainment that is most popular with visitors – from the sounds of traditional chants and slack-key guitar *(kī hō'alu)* to traditional foods and *hula* costumes – has been "adjusted" for Western tastes. However, as a result of the cultural renaissance that has occurred in the state over the last decade, traditional Hawaiian entertainment is now accessible to anyone who wishes to experience it. Virtually every hotel offers Hawaiian music of some description on a regular, if not daily, basis, and many put on *hula* shows, too. Such performances are usually free.

The **Waikīkī Shell** in Kapi'olani Park is a magnificent outdoor spot that hosts many concerts of Hawaiian music and *hula* throughout the year.

"The Shell" is also home to the free **Kodak Hula Show**, a Waikīkī institution held three times a week. This show was begun by Kodak in 1939, and over the decades it has given many tourists the chance to watch and photograph *hula*.

Small shows staged at island shopping centers are often the most authentic. They usually feature students of Hawaiian music and dance from *hālau hula* (*hula* schools) and are almost always free.

For a unique treat, enjoy the remarkable talent of the two Brothers Cazimero, whose extraordinary voices and skill on the guitar and bass combine to produce one of Honolulu's best shows. Check the listings in the newspapers or tourist magazines for details of shows.

Most of the major hotels offer *lū'au* – the traditional feasts of the islands *(see p164)*. Prices

The impressive sight of a traditional Hawaiian feast or *lū'au* in Lahaina, Maui

Colorful pageant at the Polynesian Cultural Center on O'ahu *(see p78)*

are approximately $45–50 for adults and half that for kids. On O'ahu, try the **Paradise Cove Lū'au** in 'Ewa, about 25 miles (40 km) from Waikīkī; tickets include the bus from town. The best place to go on Maui is, without doubt, **Old Lahaina Lū'au**, in a lovely setting overlooking the ocean.

The only waterfront *lū'au* in Kailua-Kona (Hawai'i Island) is held at **King Kamehameha's Kona Beach Hotel**, while the one at secluded **Kona Village Resort** is well known as the most authentic on the islands. On Kaua'i, be sure to make reservations in advance for the **Tahiti Nui Lū'au** in Hanalei, which takes place every Friday night and is perhaps Hawai'i's most "local-style" – that is, most boisterous – *lū'au*.

You can also enjoy a more authentic and inexpensive experience by checking the local newspaper for fundraisers and other *lū'au* put on by civic groups. If you get really lucky and are invited to a big Hawaiian family party, accept the invitation. You will have the experience of a lifetime.

POLYNESIAN SHOWS

THESE SHOWS are Hawai'i's real extravaganzas, and usually include a *lū'au*-style meal as well as exhibitions of music and dance from Pacific islands like Tahiti, Samoa, Tonga, and Fiji. All the islands have them. While they may vary in scale, Polynesian shows are broadly similar in content – never failing to deliver women wearing grass skirts.

The **Polynesian Cultural Center** in Lā'ie (O'ahu) stages several shows daily, including "*Mana!*," an evening show featuring a cast of over 100, and the newest and most Hawaiian show, the *Ali'i Lū'au*. An alternative on O'ahu is **Creation: A Polynesian Odyssey**, staged at the Sheraton Princess Ka'iulani Hotel in Waikīkī.

The Hyatt Regency Maui offers **Drums of the Pacific**, and the *lū'au* at the **Royal Lahaina Resort** features a Polynesian show. Finally, you can also try the show at the **Hilton Waikoloa Village Resort** on Hawai'i Island.

NIGHTLIFE

H AWAI'I IS, traditionally, an early-to-bed, early-to-rise place. Night owls will find enough to do in Honolulu, especially in Waikīkī, and there is a fair amount happening on Maui – mostly in Lahaina. But do not expect a great deal in the way of exciting nightlife on Hawai'i Island, Kaua'i, or any of the smaller islands.

However, many bars and hotel lounges provide live entertainment, and karaoke bars abound on all the islands. On any night of the week, especially on O'ahu and Maui, you can choose from rock, pop, jazz, country, reggae, or Hawaiian music – either live or played by a DJ.

In Honolulu, you will find everything from entertainment legend **Don Ho** – whose

offering of strictly middle-of-the-road songs appeals mainly to the older generations – to **Magic of Polynesia**, a multimedia extravaganza with outstanding music. Mimickry also features in the lively Las Vegas-style show put on by the **Society of Seven**, a group of veterans who have been on the circuit for more than 25 years; they appear at the Outrigger Waikīkī hotel.

Frank DeLima, a master of playful, ethnic comedy, appears regularly throughout the islands, and he is often joined by Kaua'i singer Glenn Medeiros. Consult the listings in the newspapers and tourist magazines for places and times of performances.

Big international names from Tony Bennett to Sting and legendary rock bands like the Eagles appear at major O'ahu places such as the spectacular **Hawai'i Theatre**, the **Neal Blaisdell Concert Hall**, and the **Aloha Stadium**.

Maui's top spot is the impressive $31-million **Maui Arts & Cultural Center**, with several different auditoriums for concerts, plays, and art-house films. **Casanova Italian Restaurant** in Makawao occasionally brings in big-name talent, such as Willie Nelson, Los Lobos, and Richie Havens, as well as great local bands. All the resort hotels have music daily somewhere on the property – a restaurant, club, lounge, or lobby.

Waikīkī's dance clubs stay open into the small hours, some until 4am. Among the most popular places is **Wave Waikīkī**, a large club where fairly progressive rock bands play every night except Mondays. Another place is the **Ocean Club** at Downtown Honolulu's Restaurant Row. Revelers can also dance the night away at **Tsunami**, a high-tech disco in the Grand Wailea Resort on Maui.

On Kaua'i, and on the Kona and Kohala side of Hawai'i Island, the resort hotels provide the best evening entertainment; many of them have nightclubs.

Admission tickets for major events

The Honolulu Boy Choir, well known for performances throughout Oʻahu

THEATER

FOR ANYTHING OTHER than small community theater, Honolulu is the place to be. At least a couple of Broadway musicals show up each year, usually at the **Neal Blaisdell Concert Hall**. Past shows include *Les Miserables*, *Cats*, and *Phantom of the Opera*. The **Mānoa Valley Theatre** presents local productions of the cream of Broadway and off-Broadway. Hawaiʻi's oldest company, the **Diamond Head Theatre**, offers a mixed bag of performances each season, as does the **Kumu Kahua Theatre** – some of whose shows are written locally.

On weekends, at any time of year, it should be possible to see a performance by at least one of Maui's four community theater groups – the Maui Academy of Performing Arts, Maui Community Theatre, the Baldwin Theater Guild, and Studio Hāmākua Poko. Most often the place is one of the two theaters inside the **Maui Arts & Cultural Center** in Kahului, although the Maui Community Theater uses the lovingly restored **ʻĪao Theater** in historic Wailuku.

Hawaiʻi Island has several community theater groups, too: Akebono Theater, Aloha Community Players, and Hilo Community Players. The lovely **Kahilu Theatre** in upcountry Waimea is a wonderful spot.

On the Garden Isle, the Kauaʻi Community Players offer an almost continuous program of performances throughout the year. There's a beautiful new performing arts center on the campus of **Kauaʻi Community College**.

OPERA, CLASSICAL MUSIC, AND DANCE

THE STATE'S resident opera company, **Hawaiʻi Opera Theatre**, stages three or four operas from January to April. These are held in Honolulu's **Neal Blaisdell Concert Hall**, which is also often the place for Oʻahu's main series of classical concerts, staged by the **Honolulu Symphony Orchestra** between October and May. You should also look out for performances by the **Hawaiʻi Youth Symphony Association**, made up of student musicians from all the islands. The **Honolulu Boy Choir** has a good reputation, too. Each year they give a concert at the Ala Moana Center to open the Christmas season. They also give moving performances on Christmas Eve and Christmas Day at the Royal Hawaiian Hotel in Waikīkī.

Every year at least one of the mainland's most reputable ballet companies travels across the Pacific to perform in Hawaiʻi, usually at the Neal Blaisdell Concert Hall. The **Hawaiʻi Ballet Theatre** – the islands' oldest ballet troupe – presents the *Nutcracker Suite* every

Sign for the top cultural place on Maui

winter for the holiday crowds, plus another ballet in summer. The **Honolulu Dance Theatre** performs unique works that combine dance with theater.

The **Maui Symphony Orchestra** performs in a number of places, giving a series of concerts at the **Maui Arts & Cultural Center**. This center also hosts some of the performances organized every year by the **Maui Philharmonic Society** – ranging from Big Band music to ethnic dance and classical ballet. The places vary with each particular show.

The Kapalua Music Festival takes place every June in West Maui's Kapalua resort, with a series of classical concerts performed over two weekends.

FILMS AND FILM FESTIVALS

A LARGE and, for the most part, free film festival, the **Hawaiʻi International Film Festival**, takes place each November. Scores of films are shown at various theaters on Oʻahu (some of which charge admission in the first week, and on the neighboring islands the second week; even tiny communities are included.

New films normally open in Honolulu at the same time as on the mainland. In addition to the many spots that specialize in big Hollywood movies, the **University of Hawaiʻi**, community colleges, and other venues present art-house, foreign, and classic films on a regular basis. Check the Friday edition of *The Honolulu Advertiser* for the latest listings.

You can go to the movies on the neighboring islands, too, but the choice there is a great deal more limited. It was only a few years ago that Maui got its first multiplex cinema. The **Maui Arts & Cultural Center** presents seasons of foreign and art-house films. On the neighboring islands, there are special showings of non-blockbuster films, often presented by community colleges, civic organizations, and various nonprofit groups.

DIRECTORY

TICKET OUTLETS

Ticket Plus
(808) 526-4400.

MAJOR VENUES

Aloha Stadium
99-500 Salt Lake Blvd,
'Aiea, O'ahu.
(808) 486-9300.

Hawai'i Theatre
1130 Bethel Street,
Honolulu, O'ahu.
Map 1 A2.
(808) 528-0506.

**Maui Arts &
Cultural Center**
One Cameron Way,
Kahului, Maui.
(808) 242-7469.

**Neal Blaisdell
Concert Hall**
777 Ward Avenue,
Honolulu, O'ahu.
Map 2 D3.
(808) 591-2211.

Waikīkī Shell
2805 Monsarrat Avenue,
Kapi'olani Park,
Honolulu, O'ahu.
(808) 591-2211.

HAWAIIAN MUSIC, HULA, AND LŪ'AU

**King
Kamehameha's
Kona Beach Hotel**
75-5660 Palani Road,
Kailua-Kona,
Hawai'i Island.
(808) 329-2911.

Kodak Hula Show
Waikīkī Shell,
Honolulu, O'ahu.
(808) 627-3379.

Kona Village Resort
Queen Ka'ahumanu Hwy,
Ka'ūpūlehu-Kona,
Hawai'i Island.
(808) 325-5555.

Old Lahaina Lū'au
1251 Front Street,
Lahaina, Maui.
(808) 667-1998.

Paradise Cove Lū'au
92-1089 Ali'inui Drive,
'Ewa, O'ahu.
(808) 973-5828.

Tahiti Nui Lū'au
5-5134 Kūhiō Highway,
Hanalei, Kaua'i.
(808) 826-6277.

POLYNESIAN SHOWS

**Drums of the
Pacific**
Hyatt Regency Maui,
200 Nohea Kai Drive,
Kā'anapali, Maui.
(808) 667-4420.

**Hilton Waikoloa
Village Resort**
425 Waikoloa Beach Drive,
Kohala Coast,
Hawai'i Island.
(808) 886-1234.

**Polynesian
Cultural Center**
55-370 Kamehameha Hwy,
Lā'ie, Oahu.
(808) 293-3333.

**Royal Lahaina
Resort**
2780 Keka'a Drive,
Kā'anapali, Maui.
(808) 661-3611.

**Creation: A Poly-
nesian Odyssey**
Sheraton Princess
Ka'iulani Hotel,
120 Ka'iulani Ave,
Waikīkī, O'ahu. **Map** 4 E4.
(808) 931-4660.

NIGHTLIFE

**Casanova Italian
Restaurant**
1188 Makawao Avenue,
Makawao, Maui.
(808) 572-0220.

Don Ho
Waikīkī Beachcomber
Hotel, 2300 Kalākaua Ave,
Waikīkī, O'ahu.
(808) 923-3981.

Magic of Polynesia
Waikīkī Beachcomber
Hotel, 2300 Kalākaua Ave,
Waikīkī, O'ahu.
Map 4 E5
(808) 971-4321.

Ocean Club
Restaurant Row,
500 Ala Moana Blvd,
Honolulu, O'ahu.
Map 1 B4.
(808) 526-9888.

Society of Seven
Outrigger Waikīkī Hotel,
2335 Kalākaua Avenue,
Waikīkī, O'ahu.
Map 4 E5.
(808) 923-7469.

Tsunami
Grand Wailea Resort,
3850 Wailea Alanui Drive,
Wailea, Maui.
(808) 875-1234.

Wave Waikīkī
1877 Kalākaua Avenue,
Waikīkī, O'ahu.
Map 3 B3.
(808) 941-0424.

THEATER

**Diamond Head
Theatre**
520 Makapu'u Avenue,
Honolulu, O'ahu.
(808) 734-0274.

'Iao Theater
68 N Market Street,
Wailuku, Maui.
(808) 244-8680.

Kahilu Theatre
67-1185 Māmalahoa Hwy,
Waimea, Hawai'i Island.
(808) 885-6017.

**Kaua'i Community
College Performing
Arts Center**
3-1901 Kaumuali'i Hwy,
Lihu'e, Kaua'i.
(808) 245-8270.

**Kumu Kahua
Theatre**
46 Merchant Street,
Honolulu, O'ahu.
Map 1 A3.
(808) 536-4441.

**Mānoa Valley
Theatre**
2833 E Mānoa Road,
Honolulu, O'ahu.
(808) 988-6131.

OPERA, CLASSICAL MUSIC, AND DANCE

**Hawai'i Ballet
Theatre**
Leeward Community
College Theater,
96-045 Ala Ike Street,
Pearl City, O'ahu.
(808) 422-9772.

**Hawai'i Opera
Theatre**
987 Waimanu St,
Honolulu, O'ahu.
Map 2 E4.
(808) 596-7372.

**Hawai'i Youth
Symphony
Association**
Suite 201, 1110 University
Avenue, Honolulu, O'ahu.
Map 4 D1.
(808) 941-9706.

**Honolulu Boy
Choir**
Suite 1901, 615 Pi'ikoi
Street, Honolulu, O'ahu.
Map 2 E3.
(808) 596-7464.

**Honolulu Dance
Theatre**
3041 Mānoa Road,
Honolulu, O'ahu.
(808) 988-3202.

**Honolulu
Symphony
Orchestra**
Suite 202, 650 Iwilei Rd,
Dole Cannery, Honolulu,
O'ahu. **Map** 1 B5.
(808) 538-8863.

**Maui
Philharmonic
Society**
J Walter Cameron Center,
95 Mahalani Street,
Wailuku, Maui.
(808) 244-3771.

**Maui Symphony
Orchestra**
PO Box 1033,
Wailuku, Maui.
(808) 877-2167.

FILMS AND FILM FESTIVALS

**Hawai'i
International
Film Festival**
Suite 745, 1001 Bishop
Street, Honolulu, O'ahu.
Map 1 A3.
(800) 752-8193.

**University of
Hawai'i**
2444 Dole Street,
Honolulu, O'ahu.
Map 4 D1.
(808) 956-7235.

OUTDOOR ACTIVITIES

With its hot climate, Hawai'i is a great place for outdoor activities, many of which are focused on the ocean. All over the islands you will find people surfing, swimming, paddling, windsurfing, or fishing at all hours of the day. The abundance of coral and exotic marine life is a big attraction for divers and snorkelers, too. On land, there are many attractive,

Hawai'i's colorful yellow tang fish

well-maintained hiking trails, as well as paths for horseback riding, which provide a great way to enjoy the islands' fine scenery. Golf courses also make the most of the landscape and have turned the state into a golfer's mecca. Dotting the islands are dozens of courses, ranging from affordable public links to some of the world's most challenging professional courses.

Snorkeler enjoying a close encounter with a trumpet fish

SNORKELING

HAWAI'I IS GREAT snorkeling territory. Darting butterfly fish, rainbow parrotfish, bright yellow tangs, and sea turtles are all common sights. A few choice spots include Shark's Cove and Hanauma Bay on O'ahu, Maui's Honolua Bay and offshore Molokini, and Hawai'i Island's Kahalu'u Bay.

Early morning is the best time to observe the fish. Some snorkel sites are dangerous during high wave action, so check the conditions first.

For equipment rental at good prices, **Snorkel Bob's** has outlets on O'ahu, Maui, Kaua'i, and Hawai'i Island.

SCUBA DIVING

DIVING IS VERY POPULAR in Hawai'i. The leeward sides of the islands have the best dive sites, most of which are accessible only by boat.

The Lāna'i Cathedrals, off the south coast of Lāna'i, are spectacular formations honeycombed with passageways. Maui's Honolua Bay is loaded

with green sea turtles and has an interesting wall of live coral. The Mākaha Lava Tubes off the Wai'anae Coast of O'ahu are another sea turtle haunt. Red Hill, off Hawai'i Island's Kona Coast, is an exotic landscape of lava formations.

Some good dive operators are: **Bubbles Below** (Kaua'i), **Extended Horizons** (Maui), **Dive Makai Charters** (Hawai'i Island) and **Captain Bruce's Scuba Charters** (O'ahu).

SWIMMING

THE WATERS OFF Hawai'i are cool and inviting. Maui and O'ahu have the best beaches, particularly Maui's Kā'anapali Coast and the southern and windward shores of O'ahu, where the surf is usually gentle. World-famous Waikīkī Beach is one of the best

swimming spots, but locals generally prefer nearby Sans Souci. On O'ahu's windward side both Kailua Beach and Lanikai Beach are mellow and uncrowded with lovely, clear water. Hawai'i Island's Mauna Kea Beach is also good.

If you enjoy serious wave action, look out for Hawai'i's "rough-water" swimming contests, such as the demanding summer North Shore Roughwater Swim Series on O'ahu. The ocean is dangerous. Safety tips for anyone entering the water are given on page 192.

SURFING, BODY-SURFING, AND WINDSURFING

ATHLETES FROM around the globe flock to Hawai'i to test their mettle at some of the world's best surf breaks. With 7 miles (11 km) of excellent surf spots between Hale'iwa and Sunset Beach, O'ahu's North Shore is the surfing capital of the world, and site of the annual Triple Crown contest (see p21). But there is a cornucopia of world-class surf breaks around the rest of the O'ahu coast, and also on the coasts of Maui and Kaua'i.

Waikīkī's gentle rollers are ideal for beginners. Beach boys offer surfing lessons, just like in the old days, and boards can also be rented here. Chun's Reef on O'ahu's North Shore

Surfer taking a break between rides on the Hawaiian surf

Novices being given a windsurfing lesson at Kailua Beach Park on Oʻahu

is a good place for beginners. **Surf-n-Sea** rents boards here and also offers lessons.

The Lahaina Breakwall, east of Lahaina, is another popular spot for beginners. You can rent surfboards from **Honolua Surfco**, **Local Motion**, and other Maui surf shops. The **Nancy Emerson School of Surfing** offers lessons; **Windsurf Kauaʻi** rents boards and offers lessons on Kauaʻi. Call the **Surf News Network** for general information.

You can surf all year, but the waves reach their peak from November through April, when the north shore of any island can be dangerous for experienced surfers – let alone beginners. The power of the ocean in Hawaiʻi is beyond description and many visitors get into trouble after paddling out into big surf. The best advice is "Never surf alone."

Body-surfing, in which riders wearing flippers lie flat on a bodyboard or boogie board *(see p20)*, is also popular. At Oʻahu's Makapuʻu and Sandy Beach, waves crash onto a shallow sandy shorebreak, and body-surfers shoot through the tube barely ahead of the lip of the wave. Point Panic in Honolulu is also a favorite spot. All three of these places are dangerous, but for spectators they are fantastic.

Beginners can get their fins wet at Oʻahu's Bellows Beach and Waikīkī Beach, Maui's Wailea Beach, and Kauaʻi's Shipwreck Beach. To rent bodyboards, try **Planet Surf** in Waikīkī, **Local Motion** in Lahaina, and **Progressive Expressions** on Kauaʻi.

Windsurfing has a big following. The sport's hub is Maui's North Shore, Hoʻokipa Beach being the top spot for acrobatics. On Oʻahu, Kailua Bay suits all ability levels, and Diamond Head's constant winds and breaking waves make it a windsurfer's delight. Windsurfers replace surfers at Sunset Beach when the wind blows strongly.

Lessons and equipment are available from: **Naish Hawaiʻi** (Oʻahu), which is owned and run by world-champion windsurfer Robbie Naish; **Extreme Sports Maui** or **Hi-Tech Surf Sports**, both on Maui; and **Windsurf Kauaʻi** in Hanalei, on Kauaʻi.

KAYAKING, CANOEING, AND SAILING

K AYAKING IS all the rage in Hawaiʻi. Favorite spots include Oʻahu's Kailua Bay and Kauaʻi's Wailua River. The kayak is also one of the preferred ways to visit Kauaʻi's magnificent Nā Pali Coast. Kayaks can be rented from **Go Bananas** and **Twogood Kayaks Hawaiʻi** (Oʻahu), **Tradewind Kayaks** (Maui), and **Outfitters Kauaʻi** (Kauaʻi).

Traditional Hawaiian canoe paddling in outrigger canoes is popular, too. The October Bankoh Nā Molokaʻi Hoe race *(see p23)* is the most important contest of its kind in the world. Regattas are held on weekends in several places, but the sport is run by tightly knit clubs, making it hard to participate. However, Waikīkī

beach boys will take you out to ride the waves in an outrigger near the Moana Hotel *(see p52)*.

Hawaiʻi is a major stopping-place for boats crossing the Pacific, and the state has a strong seafaring tradition of its own. Two of the world's biggest regattas, the Kenwood Cup and the Trans Pacific Race, take place in Hawaiʻi.

Kāneʻohe Bay on Oʻahu is the best place for small boat sailing, though Waikīkī is also suitable. The **Hawaiʻi Yacht Club** and **Waikīkī Yacht Club** take on experienced deckhands for Honolulu's weekly Champagne Race (so named because the winners are given champagne). Races are held on Friday afternoons.

FISHING

H AWAIʻI IS FAMOUS for its deep-sea fishing – above all on the Kona Coast, where record catches are often made of Pacific blue marlin, yellow-fin tuna, and other gamefish. This area is the best for trips, but charters can be arranged on all the islands. **Sea Verse** operates in Honolulu while **Blue Hawaiʻi Sportfishing** is based in Kailua-Kona, Hawaiʻi Island. On Maui, you can arrange fishing trips with **Hinatea Charters** and **Aerial Sportfishing Charters**. *Hawaiʻi Fishing News* is a good source of infomation.

Hawaiʻi's long shoreline offers lots of surf casting for smaller fish, such as snapper and giant *ulua* (jack). Take care if you fish; conditions in the best surf-casting places can be hazardous.

Women kayak training on the gentle waters of Waikīkī's Ala Wai Canal

Cyclist on a scenic bike ride through Waikīkī's Ala Moana Park, away from the multitudes at the beach

CYCLING AND MOUNTAIN BIKING

NARROW SHOULDERS and variable road quality make Hawai'i a poor place for bike riding. Mountain biking trails are limited too, but those that do exist are of good quality. Trails above Pūpūkea on O'ahu's North Shore are very popular, with ocean views and challenging riding.

South of Kula on Maui, in the Polipoli Springs Recreation Area, several miles of trails snake through ravines and forests of eucalyptus and giant ferns. An easier but extremely popular adventure is the sunrise descent down Haleakalā, a 38-mile (61-km) stretch starting in Haleakalā National Park *(see pp106–7)* that contains 21 switchbacks and superb views.

For quality mountain bike rentals, try **Barnfield's Raging Isle Sports** in Hale'iwa, O'ahu, or **Haleakalā Bike Co**, **West Maui Cycle and Sports**, or **South Maui Bicycles** on Maui.

HIKING

AN EXTENSIVE NETWORK of state and national parks crisscrossed by trails makes Hawai'i great hiking territory. The terrain ranges from barren volcanic desert to lush fern rain forest with waterfalls and cool swimming holes.

There are trails to suit everyone in terms of both accessibility and difficulty. Two of the finest are Kaua'i's Kalalau Trail along the stunning, rugged Nā Pali Coast *(see pp142–3)* and the Kaupō Trail, which descends from Haleakalā's volcanic moonscape to the lush rain forest of the Kīpahulu Valley *(see p109)*.

Clubs and environmental groups, including the **Sierra Club**, **Nature Conservancy**, and the **Hawai'i Nature Center**, organize hikes on a number of islands. Some of the state, national, and county parks have campsites for longer stays *(see p151)*.

Changing weather conditions can be a serious hazard when hiking; flash floods in narrow ravines are common, and hikers disappear with alarming regularity. It is dangerous to hike alone. Before you set off, leave word of your plans and your expected time of return with a friend or someone at the hotel. Pack water, a flashlight, warm clothes, and a blanket in case you become stranded.

Hiker enjoying the wild scenery of Haleakalā National Park, Maui

GOLF

WITH 75 COURSES, Hawai'i is a golfer's heaven. The number of courses and good climate ensure that Hawai'i also has more top professional golf tournaments than any other part of the US. **Ko'olau Golf Club** on O'ahu was designated "the toughest golf course in America" by the US Golfing Association.

Maui is considered the best island for golf. The three courses at the **Kapalua Resort** are gorgeous, with long fairways and tall evergreens running down to the sea. On Kaua'i, both **Prince Golf Course** and the course at **Po'ipū Bay Resort** are world-class, with stunning views.

Greens fees range from under $30 on the municipal courses to $100-plus for a round on a plush resort course. Try to book a few days – or even weeks – in advance. Waikīkī's **Ala Wai Golf Course**, for example, is so popular that it is inaccessible to most people.

Golfers at Princeville Golf Course, one of Hawai'i's top clubs

OTHER ACTIVITIES

HAWAI'I'S MILD CLIMATE lends itself to all warm weather activity. In-line skating and jogging are common pastimes, particularly on O'ahu, where paved paths circle Ala Moana and Kapi'olani Parks. There are public tennis courts on the four major islands, though they are often very busy.

Horses can be rented on all islands, and many places also arrange tours. Two good trails are along the Moloka'i cliffs and in Maui's Kīpahulu Valley. Horses or rides can be organized through the following: **CJM Country Stables**, **Mauna Kea Resorts Stables**, **Moloka'i Mule Ride**, and **Paniolo Riding Adventures**.

DIRECTORY

SNORKELING

Snorkel Bob's
702 Kapahulu Avenue,
Honolulu, O'ahu.
☎ (808) 735-7944.

75-5831 Kahakai Road,
Kailua-Kona,
Hawai'i Island.
☎ (808) 329-0770.

5425 Lower
Honoapi'ilani Road,
Lahaina, Maui.
☎ (808) 669-9603.

3236 Po'ipū Road,
Kōloa, Kaua'i.
☎ (808) 742-2206.

SCUBA DIVING

Bubbles Below
6251 Hauaala Road,
Kapa'a, Kaua'i.
☎ (808) 822-3483.

**Captain Bruce's
Scuba Charters**
East and West O'ahu.
☎ (808) 373-3590.

**Dive Makai
Charters**
PO Box 2955,
Kailua-Kona,
Hawai'i Island.
☎ (808) 329-2025.

**Extended
Horizons**
PO Box 10785,
Lahaina, Maui.
☎ (808) 667-0611.

SURFING, BODY-SURFING, AND WINDSURFING

**Extreme Sports
Maui**
397 Dairy Road,
Kahului, Maui.
☎ (808) 871-7954.

**Hi-Tech Surf
Sports**
425 Kōloa Street,
Kahului, Maui.
☎ (808) 877-2111.

Honolua Surfco
845 Front Street,
Lahaina, Maui.
☎ (808) 661-8848.

Local Motion
1295 Front Street,
Lahaina, Maui.
☎ (808) 661-7873.

Naish Hawai'i
155 Hāmākua Drive,
Suite A, Kailua, O'ahu.
☎ (808) 262-6068.

**Nancy Emerson's
School of Surfing**
PO Box 463,
Lahaina, Maui.
☎ (808) 873-0264.

**Planet Surf
Waikīkī**
159 Ka'iulani Avenue,
Waikiki, O'ahu.
☎ (808) 924-9050.

**Progressive
Expressions**
5420 Kōloa Road,
Kōloa, Kaua'i.
☎ (808) 742-6041.

Surf-n-Sea
62-595 Kamehameha Hwy,
Hale'iwa, O'ahu.
☎ (808) 637-9887.

Surf News Network
Daily updates on water
conditions, weather, etc.
Surfline:
☎ (808) 596-7873.

Windsurf Kaua'i
PO Box 323,
Hanalei, Kaua'i.
☎ (808) 828-6838.

KAYAKING, CANOEING, AND SAILING

Go Bananas
799 Kapahulu Avenue,
Honolulu, O'ahu.
☎ (808) 737-9514.

Hawai'i Yacht Club
1739-C Ala Moana Blvd,
Suite C, Honolulu, O'ahu.
☎ (808) 944-9666.

Outfitters Kaua'i
2827A Po'ipū Rd,
Kōloa, Kaua'i.
☎ (808) 742-9667.

Paragon Charters
RR4, Box 43,
Kula, Maui.
☎ (808) 244-2087.

Tradewind Kayaks
PO Box 9,
Kīhei, Maui.
☎ (808) 879-2247.

**Twogood Kayaks
Hawai'i**
345 Hahani Street,
Kailua, O'ahu.
☎ (808) 262-5656.

Waikīkī Yacht Club
1599 Ala Moana Blvd,
Honolulu, O'ahu.
☎ (808) 955-4405.

FISHING

**Aerial Sportfishing
Charters**
PO Box 831,
Lahaina, Maui.
☎ (808) 667-9089.

**Blue Hawai'i
Sportfishing**
PO Box 390387,
Kailua-Kona,
Hawai'i Island.
☎ (808) 322-3210.

**Hawai'i Fishing
News**
6650 Hawai'i Kai Drive,
Suite 201,
Honolulu, O'ahu.
☎ (808) 395-4499.

Hinatea Charters
Slip 27, Lahaina Harbor,
Lahaina, Maui.
☎ (808) 667-7548.

Sea Verse
Kewalo Basin, Slip C,
Honolulu, O'ahu.
☎ (808) 591-8840.

CYCLING AND MOUNTAIN BIKING

**Barnfield's Raging
Isle Sports**
66-250 Kamehameha Hwy,
Building B,
Hale'iwa, O'ahu.
☎ (808) 637-7707.

Haleakalā Bike Co
810 Ha'ikū Rd, Suite 120,
Ha'ikū, Maui.
☎ (808) 575-9595.

**South Maui
Bicycles**
1993 S Kihei Road, #5,
Kīhei, Maui.
☎ (808) 874-0068.

**West Maui Cycle
and Sports**
840 Waine'e Street,
Lahaina, Maui.
☎ (808) 661-9005.

HIKING

**Hawai'i Nature
Center**
2131 Makiki Heights Drive,
Honolulu, O'ahu.
☎ (808) 955-0100.

**Nature
Conservancy**
1116 Smith St, Suite 201,
Honolulu, O'ahu.
☎ (808) 537-4508.

Sierra Club
PO Box 2577,
Honolulu, O'ahu.
☎ (808) 538-6616.

GOLF

Ala Wai Golf Course
404 Kapahulu Avenue,
Waikiki, O'ahu.
☎ (808) 733-7387.

Kapalua Resort
300 Kapalua Drive,
Lahaina, Maui.
☎ (808) 669-8814.

Ko'olau Golf Club
45-550 Kionaole Road,
Kāne'ohe, O'ahu.
☎ (808) 236-4653.

Po'ipū Bay Resort
2250 Ainako Street,
Kōloa, Kaua'i.
☎ (808) 742-8711.

Prince Golf Course
PO Box 3040,
Princeville, Kaua'i.
☎ (808) 826-5000.

HORSEBACK RIDING

**CJM Country
Stables**
1731 Kelaukia Street,
Kōloa, Kaua'i.
☎ (808) 742-6096.

**Mauna Kea Resorts
Stables**
Pukalani Road
Kamuela, Hawai'i Island.
☎ (808) 885-4288.

Moloka'i Mule Ride
PO Box 200, Moloka'i.
☎ (808) 567-6088.

**Paniolo Riding
Adventures**
PO Box 363,
Honoka'a, Hawai'i Island.
☎ (808) 889-5354.

SURVIVAL
GUIDE

PRACTICAL INFORMATION

Tourism is Hawai'i's most important industry. From the bright lights of Waikīkī and Honolulu to the remote waterfalls of Maui's Hāna district, the islands offer something for everyone – whatever the budget. There is no escaping the fact that paradise can be expensive: the cost of living in the state is thought to be about 40 percent higher than that in the rest of the US. For those planning a money-is-no-object vacation, all kinds of luxuries await. But visitors on a more modest budget can have an equally memorable trip. Hawai'i is a great destination all year round, but you will enjoy better prices if you choose to visit in the off season – between April and December. At any time of year, however, many of the islands' biggest attractions are free, and many others, including national parks and larger museums, charge only low admission prices.

FOREIGN VISITORS

The conditions for entering Hawai'i are the same as for entering other parts of the US. Citizens of the UK, most western European countries, New Zealand, Australia, and Japan need a valid passport but no visa, as long as they stay for less than 90 days, have a return ticket, and enter the US on an airline or cruise line in the visa waiver program (which includes all the major carriers). Canadian citizens require only proof of residence. Citizens of all other countries need a valid passport and a tourist visa, which can be obtained from a US consulate or embassy.

No inoculations are required unless you come from, or have stopped in, an area suffering from an epidemic, particularly cholera or yellow fever.

Hawai'i has two main languages: English and Hawaiian (see p208). You may see signs written in Hawaiian but will rarely hear it spoken. Many people in the tourist industry also speak Japanese.

VISITOR INFORMATION

Visitor information desks at all island airports provide maps and guides, and major hotels usually have a knowledgeable and helpful guest services desk. All islands also have a tourist information center – either a branch of the **Hawai'i Visitors and Convention Bureau** (HVCB), or another visitor association. If

you need information before leaving home, contact the nearest branch of the HVCB. See the list opposite.

OPENING HOURS

Most businesses are open on weekdays from 9am to 5pm (for banking hours see p194). Shopping malls and many stores are open from 10am to 9pm Monday to Saturday; other stores close earlier, between 5 and 7pm. Sunday shopping is more limited, but some supermarkets, convenience stores, and gas stations are open 24 hours a day, seven days a week.

Although the opening hours of attractions vary, most places admit visitors daily, except on major public holidays.

ALCOHOL AND SMOKING LAWS

The legal drinking age in Hawai'i is 21. It is illegal to drink in any of the state or national parks or to carry an open container of alcohol in your vehicle. Grocery stores, supermarkets, and convenience stores sell beer, wine, and spirits, all of which can be bought seven days a week.

Smoking is prohibited in public buildings, elevators, shops, and theaters. Most restaurants are divided into smoking and non-smoking sections.

Old-fashioned Surrey horses and carriage on Waipi'o Valley Wagon Tour (see p121)

SPECIAL VACATIONS AND GUIDED TOURS

If you want to explore Hawai'i's natural beauty, but prefer to leave the organizing to someone else, there are a number of companies specializing in such vacations. These include **American Wilderness Experience**, the **Sierra Club**, and the **Nature Conservancy of Hawai'i**.

In addition, many companies offer guided tours of attractions on individual islands. The largest and most reliable of these firms are **Robert's Hawai'i** and **Pleasant Island Holidays**. They offer packages that include inter-island flights, accommodations, bus tours, and car rental. Your hotel's guest services desk should be knowledgeable about guided tours of specific attractions and be able to give you advice on making arrangements.

A bottle of local wine

◁ **Multicolored surfboards for rent on Waikīkī Beach**

WEDDINGS

GETTING MARRIED in Hawai'i is relatively simple, and you do need not be a US citizen. The bride and groom must obtain a marriage license from the **Department of Health**. Contact the **HVCB** or any other visitor association for more information on outfits that organize weddings.

ELECTRICITY

ELECTRICITY FLOWS at the standard US 110–120 volts. To operate 220-volt appliances, you will need a voltage converter and a plug adapter with two flat, parallel prongs. Most hotel rooms have coffee- or tea-making facilities and sockets for shavers; some also provide hair dryers.

Standard American plug

ETIQUETTE, TIPS, AND TAXES

HAWAI'I IS A friendly, casual place where hugs and kisses on the cheek are common greetings. It may appear that islanders are never in a hurry, so prepare yourself for Hawai'i's leisurely pace.

Clothing is casual, too: pack sandals, sneakers, shorts, and casual evening wear. If you visit in winter, or plan to scale mountains, you should take long pants and a sweater or jacket, plus sturdy shoes.

It is customary to tip good service. The standard restaurant tip is 15 percent of the check; you should tip taxi drivers 10–15 percent of the fare; baggage handlers at least $1 per piece of luggage; and valet parking attendants $2.

Hawai'i has a 4.17 percent sales tax on all goods and services and an additional hotel tax of 7.24 percent.

SINGLE TRAVELERS

SMALL HOTELS, bed-and-breakfasts, and campsites are the best bet for single travelers. Guided tours are good ways to meet people. Islanders will often "adopt" a single traveler, so you may even end up a guest at a big family party.

SENIOR CITIZENS

SENIOR CITIZENS (those age 62 and over) can claim discounts at many attractions, including national parks, and at some hotels, restaurants, and shops, upon presentation of their photo ID. Always ask about discounts, and check local publications or contact the **Department of Parks and Recreation** (see p151) for special events.

CHILDREN

HAWAI'I IS great for families. Most hotels allow children to share a room with their parents at no extra charge, and many also have family suites. Larger hotels often have kids' programs and babysitters. Restaurants are child-friendly, and even if there's no special menu they often provide youngsters with a hamburger or even a peanut butter and jelly sandwich.

VISITORS WITH DISABILITIES

HAWAI'I WELCOMES visitors with disabilities. Most hotels and restaurants, and many attractions, have wheelchair ramps, reserved parking, and specially equipped toilets. The **Disability and Communication Access Board** issues the *Aloha Guide to Accessibility*, with information on access to beaches, parks, shopping centers, and attractions. They also give details about support services.

Parking for people with disabilities

DIRECTORY

HAWAI'I VISITORS AND CONVENTION BUREAU OFFICES

Australia
c/o The Sales Team, Suite 2, Level 2, 34 Burton St, Milsons Point, NSW 2061.
📞 (612) 9955-2619.

Canada
Suite 104, 1260 Hornby St, Vancouver, BC V6Z 1W2.
📞 (604) 669-6265.

New Zealand
c/o Walshes World, 3rd Floor, Dingwall Building, 87 Queen St, Auckland.
📞 (649) 379-3708.

United Kingdom
PO Box 208, Sunbury-on-Thames, Middlesex TW16 5RJ.
📞 (020) 8941-4009.

Hawai'i (head office)
Suite 801, Waikiki Business Plaza, 2270 Kalākaua Ave, Honolulu, O'ahu, HI 96815.
📞 (808) 923-1811.

SPECIAL VACATIONS AND GUIDED TOURS

American Wilderness Experience
📞 (800) 444-0099.

Nature Conservancy of Hawai'i
📞 (808) 537-4508.

Pleasant Island Holidays
📞 (808) 922-1515.

Robert's Hawai'i
📞 (808) 539-9400.

Sierra Club
📞 (415) 977-5522.

VISITORS WITH DISABILITIES

Disability and Communication Access Board
919 Ala Moana Blvd, Room 101, Honolulu, O'ahu, HI 96814.
📞 (808) 586-8121.

WEDDINGS

Department of Health
Marriage License Office, 1250 Punchbowl St, Honolulu, O'ahu, HI 96813.
📞 (808) 586-4545.

Health and Personal Security

Lifeguard sign, Kūhiō Beach

DESPITE BEING in the tropics, Hawai'i carries remarkably few health risks (it boasts the highest life expectancy in the US). No immunizations are necessary, there are no land snakes to worry about, and only a few nasty creepy-crawlies. You should be aware of certain potential dangers if you go hiking or camping, but generally it is the sun and the ocean that pose the biggest threats to your health. Hawai'i does not have a serious crime problem, but you should take the normal precautions and use your common sense.

OCEAN SAFETY

THE PACIFIC OCEAN is as powerful as it is beautiful. Whether or not you are an experienced swimmer, pay careful attention to the conditions of the sea. If you have not surfed before, do not try it without proper instruction.

Always ask the lifeguard on duty about the state of the ocean, and heed the posted warnings. If you aren't used to identifying dangerous currents, avoid unguarded beaches. Note that some beaches can be perfectly safe in summer but very dangerous in winter.

When you're in the water, swim facing away from the beach. So-called rogue waves arrive as if from nowhere and can sweep you out to sea. Should you get carried out by a rip current, try to swim with it until it dissipates – usually 50–100 yds (45–90 m) from shore. Never swim alone,

watch out for surfers, and keep a very close eye on children. Always check for rocks, coral, and other potential dangers below the surface. You are advised to wear protective foot gear such as reef slippers whenever possible.

Should you happen to cut yourself on coral, clean the cut thoroughly with antiseptic. If you step on a sea urchin, the spine is likely to break off, leaving a tip embedded in your skin.

Signs warning of currents, dangerous shore break, and big surf

This will dissolve in several days, but applying vinegar may speed up the process.

Jellyfish are fairly common in Hawai'i. You're most likely to see them washed up on the shore. Their stings vary from mild to severe, the worst being that of the Portuguese

man-of-war. If you are stung by a jellyfish, the best remedy is to apply a paste of vinegar and meat tenderizer.

Encounters with sharks are very rare; should you see one, simply swim back to shore as quickly and quietly as you can.

SUN, HEAT, AND OTHER NATURAL HAZARDS

WHETHER YOU'RE FAIR or dark-skinned, it is vital to protect yourself against the harsh Hawaiian sun. Be sure to wear a hat and sunglasses, and use plenty of sun block. You should consider wearing a T-shirt if you plan to snorkel for more than just a short time.

Introduce yourself to the sun gently after you first arrive, and at any stage try to stay out of the sun between 11am and 2pm, when the rays are at their strongest; even on overcast days, the ultraviolet rays penetrate the clouds. Heat can be a danger too. Drink plenty of fluids and avoid being out in high temperatures for long periods without breaks to let your body cool down.

Mosquitoes do not carry malaria, but they can still be a real nuisance. Black widow spiders and scorpions are a potential danger to be aware of if you are planning to hike or camp in the wilds.

PERSONAL SAFETY

ALTHOUGH NOT completely free of crime, Hawai'i is still a remarkably safe place. Violent crime is rare.

Use common sense. Hitch-hiking is illegal; avoid hiking alone, and being in dark or remote areas at night. If in doubt, ask your hotel whether or not a particular area is safe.

Carry minimal cash when you go out, and do not take your passport unless you need to change travelers' checks. Leave your best jewelry at home, and other valuables in a safe – either in your room or at the hotel front desk.

THE FOLLOWING ARE PROHIBITED:
Alcoholic Beverages   Animals
Ball Playing   Camping
Flying Disc   Littering

Lifeguard on duty at Kūhiō Beach Park, Waikīkī

Fire engines in the station, ready for an emergency call

The main possibility of theft is from a rented vehicle. Never leave any valuables in the car; thieves are skilled at dealing with door and trunk locks.

LOST PROPERTY

EVEN THOUGH you have only a slim chance of retrieving stolen property, you should report all stolen items to the police. Keep a copy of the police report for when you make your insurance claim.

Most credit cards have toll-free numbers for reporting a loss, as do Thomas Cook and American Express for lost travelers' checks. If you lose your passport, contact your embassy or consulate.

TRAVEL INSURANCE

TRAVEL INSURANCE cover of a minimum of $1 million is highly recommended, mainly because of the high cost of medical treatment. Make sure the policy covers emergency medical care, accidental death, trip cancellation, and loss of baggage or documents.

MEDICAL TREATMENT

EVEN THE SMALLEST towns in Hawai'i have some kind of medical center, although the facilities on Moloka'i and Lāna'i are not as extensive as those on the main islands. As you would expect, Honolulu's medical services are the best equipped in the state.

Ask at your hotel if you need a doctor, dentist, or any other healthcare professional. All medical care is expensive: even a simple visit to a doctor can cost over $100. Hospitals take most credit cards, but doctors and dentists will usually want to be paid in cash. Visitors without insurance documents may need to pay in advance.

Anyone on prescription drugs should take along a supply and ask their doctor for a copy of the prescription in case more is needed. Pharmacies are plentiful (Long's Drugs has branches on all the islands), and you can buy some medicines in supermarkets and convenience stores.

Suntan lotions and sun block, on sale in stores all over Hawai'i

DRINKING WATER

IT IS GENERALLY SAFE to drink the tap water, although in some areas, such as upcountry Maui and parts of Hawai'i Island, the water is susceptible to pollution from acid rain.

You should carry bottled water on long drives and all hikes. Never drink the water in freshwater streams or pools. A bacterial disease called leptospirosis, carried by rats and mice, can be picked up either by drinking untreated water or by exposing cuts or abrasions to fresh water.

EMERGENCIES

IN AN EMERGENCY, the police, ambulance, or fire services can be reached by dialing 911. For emergencies in the water, call the **Coast Guard, Search and Rescue** direct if there is no lifeguard. There is also a 24-hour **Suicide and Crisis Line**.

If you need emergency cash, arrange to transfer it from your bank at home, or use American Express's **Moneygram** service.

DIRECTORY

LOST CREDIT CARDS AND TRAVELERS' CHECKS

American Express
(800) 528-4800 (cards).
(800) 221-7282 (checks).

Diners Club
(800) 234-6377.

MasterCard
(800) 826-2181.

Thomas Cook
(800) 223-7373 (checks).

VISA
(800) 336-8472.

MEDICAL TREATMENT

Hilo Medical Center
1190 Waiānuenue Avenue.
(808) 974-4700.

Kona Community Hospital
Kealakekua, Kona.
(808) 322-9311.

Lāna'i Community Hospital
7th Street, Lāna'i City.
(808) 565-6411.

Maui Medical Center
221 Mahalani Street, Wailuku.
(808) 244-9056.

Moloka'i General Hospital
Kaunakakai.
(808) 553-5331.

Queen's Medical Center
1301 Punchbowl St, Honolulu.
(808) 538-9011.

Wilcox Memorial Hospital
3420 Kūhiō Highway, Lihu'e.
(808) 245-1100.

EMERGENCY NUMBERS

All Emergencies
911 to alert police, fire, and medical services.

Coast Guard, Search and Rescue
(808) 541-2450.

Moneygram
(800) 926-9400.

Suicide and Crisis Line
(808) 521-4555.

Banking and Communications

Keypad on a bank's cash dispenser

MONEY MATTERS in Hawai'i are similar to those in the rest of the US. So, don't even think about taking any currency other than US dollars. And since credit cards and travelers' checks are the most common form of currency, it is easy to avoid carrying lots of cash around. Communications are straightforward too, and the postal services are very good given Hawai'i's isolation.

BANKING

ALL BANKS ARE open Monday to Friday from 8:30am to 3:30pm, and many stay open until 6pm on Fridays. A few offer longer weekday hours and also open on Saturdays.

The two largest banks – First Hawaiian Bank and Bank of Hawai'i – have many branches throughout the islands. Other banks with branches on all the islands include American Savings Bank, Central Pacific Bank, and Territorial Savings.

CREDIT CARDS

ANYONE WITHOUT a credit card may feel like a social outcast in Hawai'i. Credit cards can be used to pay for almost anything – from admission tickets to hospital bills. It is also standard practice for car rental companies and hotels to take an imprint of your card as security; rental companies may require a sizable cash deposit from visitors who do not have a credit card.

The most widely accepted cards are VISA and MasterCard. American Express, Diners Club, Discover, and JCB are also commonly accepted. The credit card companies have special numbers to call if you lose your card *(see p193)*.

With a credit card you can also withdraw cash from ATMs (Automatic Teller Machines), found at most banks and many shopping malls. The main ATM systems are Cirrus and Plus which accept MasterCard, VISA, and various bank cards.

TRAVELERS' CHECKS

TRAVELERS' CHECKS are the safest form of currency to carry with you, since lost or stolen checks can be easily refunded. In many instances, you can use them as if they were cash: US dollar travelers' checks are accepted as payment by many businesses. Change will be given in cash.

To exchange your checks into cash directly, go to a bank. Note that travelers' checks in other currencies will be of no use at all.

Public pay phone, owned and operated by GTE Hawaiian Tel

TELEPHONE CALLS

MAKING TELEPHONE CALLS in Hawai'i is easy. The area code for the state is 808. You don't need to use the area code when making local calls (i.e., within one island). Inter-island calls count as long distance, and the number must be preceded by 1-808 when dialing. Calls to other area codes must be preceded by 1.

It costs 35 cents to make a local call from public phones. Otherwise, the charge varies according to the time of day and the distance. The cheapest rates are from 11pm to 8am Monday to Thursday, and from 11pm Friday to 8am Monday.

The cost of calls made from a hotel room is much higher than the normal rate. Most hotels should have a pay phone in the lobby that you can use.

Given that you'll need lots of change to make long-distance calls from a pay phone, you may want to buy a phone card (usable on touch-tone phones). Many businesses have toll-free phone numbers, preceded by 1-800 or 1-888 rather than 1-808. These are toll-free only from within the United States.

Directory assistance for the island you're on is 1-411; for the others it's 1-808-555-1212.

HAWAI'I TIME

Hawai'i has a time zone all of its own – known as Hawai'i Standard Time (HST). The West Coast of the US mainland is two hours ahead of Hawai'i, and the time difference increases by one hour each time you move east into a new time zone. Unlike the rest of the US, Hawai'i does not put its clocks forward for summer daylight saving, so some of the time differences listed below increase by one hour when the respective countries switch to summer time. In the Northern Hemisphere this is generally from March or April to October.

City and Country	Hours + HST	City and Country	Hours + HST
Athens (Greece)	+12	Moscow (Russia)	+13
Auckland (New Zealand)	+22	New York (US)	+5
Beijing (China)	+18	Paris (France)	+11
Berlin (Germany)	+11	Perth (Australia)	+18
Chicago (US)	+4	Rome (Italy)	+11
Dublin (Ireland)	+10	Sydney (Australia)	+20
Hong Kong (China)	+18	Tokyo (Japan)	+19
London (UK)	+10	Toronto (Canada)	+5
Los Angeles (US)	+2	Vancouver (Canada)	+2
Madrid (Spain)	+11	Washington D.C. (US)	+5

POSTAL SERVICES

POST OFFICES ARE usually open from 8:30am to 4:30pm, Monday to Friday, and on Saturday morning. Smaller post offices may have shorter hours. Mailboxes can be found on the streets of all major cities and towns. You can also purchase stamps and send mail from your hotel's front desk.

Sending a letter within the US costs the same, regardless of the destination. The time it takes for ordinary mail to reach the US mainland from Hawai'i depends on where you mail the letter. From Honolulu it should not take more than four days. Since all mail goes via Honolulu, allow a week for mail mailed on the other islands – and longer for mail to the rest of the world.

If you use Express Mail or one of the various private courier services such as UPS or FedEx, allow for an extra day or two if you are sending from or waiting to receive on an outer island.

US stamps with tropical plants

NEWSPAPERS AND MAGAZINES

HAWAI'I HAS TWO statewide daily newspapers – the *Honolulu Advertiser* (morning) and *The Honolulu Star-Bulletin* (afternoon). Hawai'i Island, Maui, and Kaua'i each has at least one daily paper, as well as weeklies. National newspapers, such as the *Wall Street Journal*, *USA Today*, and *The New York Times*, as well as the *San Francisco Chronicle* and *Los Angeles Times*, are easy to find in Honolulu and in many of the larger hotels on the other islands.

Hawai'i's main daily newspapers

Various local magazines are worth looking out for, such as *Honolulu*, which is monthly, or *Hawai'i* and *Aloha*, both bimonthly general interest magazines. You will also find free visitor publications at the airports, on street corners in Waikīkī, and at many shopping malls on the other islands.

TELEVISION AND RADIO

ALL THE MAIN US television networks – ABC, CBS, PBS, NBC, and FOX – have local affiliate stations; check local listings on each island for the channel numbers. There are also a few interesting home-grown cable stations.

You can tune into dozens of local and state radio stations, but don't expect to pick up much if you are surrounded by volcanoes.

RECOMMENDED READING

IF YOU WANT TO read up on the islands, there are many titles to choose from. *Shoal of Time* by Gavan Daws (University of Hawai'i Press) is an entertaining history of the islands, though you may prefer James Michener's epic, *Hawaii* (Random House) – a historical novel that is considered by many to be essential reading. *Paradise News* (Penguin), a novel by David Lodge, also makes a good vacation read. Or try Jack London's *Stories of Hawaii* (Mutual). *Hawaii: A Natural History* by Sherwin Carlquist (Doubleday) is all you will need on the flora and fauna, while *Hawaiian Mythology* by Martha Beckwith (University of Hawai'i Press) contains all the most important legends.

RELIGIOUS SERVICES

THANKS TO Hawai'i's rich cultural mix, a wide range of religious services – from Catholic to Buddhist – can be found in Honolulu, and the choice is only slightly more limited on the other islands.

Sidewalk sign warning against the effects of careless dumping on local marine life

Ask at your hotel or at the local visitor information center about services, or check in the Friday or Saturday editions of the local paper for details.

If you visit native Hawaiian religious sites, be sure to treat them with the utmost respect. It is best not to leave your own offerings, and you should not move or remove anything under any circumstances.

RESPECT FOR THE LAND

THE LAND, OR *'āina* ("that which feeds"), is the most important element of the local culture. Traditional Hawaiians believe that humans are merely stewards of the land, put here to protect and nurture it, not to exploit it. They believe that every natural object, from a whale to a grain of sand, has life and a soul. You should therefore treat everything in nature with great respect.

Do not remove anything from its home; if you pick up a shell to look at it, for example, remember to put it back where you found it. Littering is both offensive and illegal.

CONVERSION CHART

US Standard to Metric
1 inch = 2.54 centimeters
1 foot = 30 centimeters
1 mile = 1.6 kilometers
1 ounce = 28 grams
1 pound = 454 grams
1 US quart = 0.947 liter
1 US gallon = 3.8 liters

Metric to US Standard
1 centimeter = 0.4 inch
1 meter = 3 feet 3 inches
1 kilometer = 0.6 mile
1 gram = 0.04 ounce
1 kilogram = 2.2 pounds
1 liter = 1.06 US quarts

TRAVEL INFORMATION

ONE OF THE world's most popular tourist destinations, Hawai'i entertains more than six million visitors a year (which is about six times its resident population). A few steamship lines include Hawai'i on their itineraries, but most visitors arrive by air. This will usually get you as far as Honolulu, but that's only the start. (As residents and regular visitors will undoubtedly inform you, if you've seen only O'ahu, you haven't really seen Hawai'i.) Travel from one island to another is done mainly by air, although there are a handful of ferry services (plus some luxury cruises). As for exploring individual islands, the only reliable way to get around is by car; public transportation is minimal except on O'ahu.

Hawaiian Airlines plane in flight

FLYING TO HAWAI'I

GIVEN THAT SO many visitors go to Hawai'i, there are a vast number of flights, mainly to Honolulu. Most people fly via the US or Canada, and there are many good connections from Los Angeles and other West Coast cities. United Airlines, American Airlines, and Air New Zealand all fly direct from Europe, but normally you'll need to change planes.

The more you shop around the better air fare you'll get. There are literally dozens of deals available, and it's worth taking the time to do some research, or to trust a reliable travel agent to do it for you.

There are various ways to cut the cost of your fare. Most importantly, the cheapest deals are generally available in off-peak months – namely May, June, September, and October. So-called discounted fares often come with advance purchase requirements and other restrictions, particularly involving cancellations. Be sure to check these carefully before you purchase the ticket to avoid unpleasant surprises at the last minute.

Most airlines also offer cheaper deals if you travel to arrive on a weekday. It's better to arrive in Hawai'i during the week anyway, since local residents often fly between islands on weekends, making airport (and hotel check-in) crowds even larger than normal. Weekend reservations may also be difficult to come by at short notice.

The Hawaiian Islands are the earth's most isolated landmass, so be prepared for a long flight; the shortest flight time is about five hours – from Los Angeles. From Europe, expect up to 18 hours traveling.

Logo for Aloha Airlines, one of the main inter-island carriers

HAWAI'I'S AIRPORTS

HAWAI'I'S TRANSPORTATION hub is **Honolulu International Airport**, 10 miles (16 km) west of Waikīkī, on O'ahu. Its two terminals handle about 1,000 international, domestic, and inter-island flights daily.

Kahului Airport is Maui's major airport, with inter-island and several mainland flights daily. A few flights from Kahului make up some of the eight daily connections to tiny **Hāna Airport** on Maui's east coast. **Kapalua-West Maui Airport**, 6 miles (10 km) north of Lahaina, has just one runway (and no telephone). The airport serves the Kā'anapali and Kapalua resort areas.

On Moloka'i, little **Ho'olehua Airport** is situated 8 miles (13 km) northwest of the island's main town, Kaunakakai. It sees 20 inter-island flights per week and is open only when a flight is about to arrive or depart. There's also a tiny airstrip on the Kalaupapa Peninsula.

Only inter-island carriers use **Lāna'i Airport**, with its one-room terminal 4 miles (6.5 km) southwest of Lāna'i City.

Keāhole-Kona Airport, near Kailua-Kona on Hawai'i Island, has the state's prettiest terminal; its check-in counters and snack bars are housed in small thatched huts. It handles mostly inter-island services, as does **Hilo International Airport**, 3 miles (5 km) east of downtown Hilo. **Waimea-Kohala Airport**, in the grasslands south of Waimea, services Trans Air flights only.

Lihu'e Airport, just a few miles east of Kaua'i's capital, sees the occasional United Airlines long-haul flight. Kaua'i's North Shore is served by **Princeville Airport** (no telephone), with flights to and from Maui, Moloka'i and Lāna'i via Honolulu.

Plane taxiing on the runway at Honolulu International Airport

Departure building at Keāhole-Kona Airport on Hawai'i Island

PACKAGE TOURS

THERE ARE lots of package tours to Hawai'i to choose from. These include air and hotel costs, car rental, inter-island travel, and often some activities and meals. Try to book tours through a reliable travel agent since prices and itineraries vary enormously.

Local travel agents, inter-island airlines, Robert's Hawai'i, and Pleasant Island Holidays *(see p191)* all offer packages and sometimes discounts on activities and meals. Both deals and itineraries change often, so check close to your departure date or make arrangements when you get to Hawai'i.

INTER-ISLAND AIR TRAVEL

NO ONE SHOULD VISIT Hawai'i without exploring beyond Honolulu and O'ahu. You can book excursions to the outer islands before you leave home, but this can also be done after you arrive.

Four airlines offer an inter-island service. The two largest are **Hawaiian Airlines** and **Aloha Airlines**. The average round-trip price between any two islands with either of these carriers is $194.

The other two carriers are small commuter lines. **Island Air** connects Honolulu with Maui's Kahului and Kapalua-West Maui airports, Moloka'i,

Travel magazines for individual Hawaiian islands

and Lāna'i, and charges the same fares as Aloha Airlines. **Trans Air** runs inter-island flights from Honolulu to Waimea-Kohala (Hawai'i Island) and Moloka'i, with fares from $104 to $164.

Ni'ihau Helicopters runs a tour of the private island of Ni'ihau *(see p147)*. This pricey tour (over $250 per person) touches down at a couple of beaches and is the only way to visit the island. The helicopter leaves two times a day from Hanapēpē on Kaua'i.

CUSTOMS AND AGRICULTURAL INSPECTIONS

FOREIGN VISITORS to Hawai'i, who stay at least 72 hours, have the following duty-free allowance: 1 liter of wine or alcohol; 200 cigarettes or 100 cigars (as long as they are not Cuban), or 4.4 lbs (2 kg) of smoking tobacco; and $100 worth of gifts. You are forbidden from bringing in foodstuffs or plants from any foreign country.

Every piece of luggage, regardless of its destination, is subject to an agricultural inspection when you leave. You can take only certain produce and flowers out of the islands, so you must be sure to ask about this when you purchase them. On the other hand, no such restrictions are imposed on the export of processed foods.

Public Transportation, Cars, and Ferries

Birds on the highway

IT IS UNDENIABLE THAT if you don't have a car your horizons will be rather limited in Hawai'i. Having your own vehicle provides both freedom of movement and the chance to be spontaneous (most locals keep a swimsuit and towel in their car because they never know when the beach will look too good to resist). Those dependent on public transportation will be able to reach few destinations beyond the confines of cities with an airport. Some of Hawai'i's most spectacular landscapes are out of bounds even to four-wheel-drive vehicles; this is when hikers can come into their own.

Waikīkī Trolley, plying the streets and sights of Honolulu

PUBLIC TRANSPORTATION

O'AHU IS ALONE in having a good public transit system. Called **TheBus**, its fleet of buses will take you almost anywhere on the island for $1. Luggage isn't allowed, so these buses are not very useful for the airport.

Other companies, the Waikīkī Trolley and Aloha Tower Trolley among them, serve Honolulu and Waikīkī, with a hop-on, hop-off service to major sights. Elsewhere, public transportation is minimal. Kaua'i and Hawai'i Island have limited bus service, and Moloka'i has none.

Route map for O'ahu buses

TAXIS AND SHUTTLES

TAXIS CAN USUALLY be found at most airports and outside major hotels, but the only place where you'll find it relatively easy to hail a cab is in Honolulu. Elsewhere, you'll need to call a taxi by phone. There are no taxis in Hāna or Kalaupapa, and Lāna'i boasts

only a limited service operated by the **Lāna'i City Service**.

Be sure to ask up front what the fare will be. Approximate one-way fares from various airports into town are: $20 from Honolulu airport to Waikīkī; $15 from Hilo airport into downtown Hilo; $25 from Keāhole-Kona to Kona; $55 from Kahului to Kā'anapali; $6 from Ho'olehua to Kaunakakai; $8 from Lihu'e airport into Lihu'e, and $18 north to Kapa'a.

Buses and shuttles (vans) serve some airports and resorts – often free for resort guests. On O'ahu, **Airport Waikīkī Express** operates a shuttle bus service between Honolulu airport and Waikīkī for about $8 per person. Both **Trans-Hawaiian** and **SpeediShuttle** link Maui's Kahului airport with the island's resorts. Fares are $13–32, depending on the destination.

CAR RENTAL

YOU MUST BE 21 (25 in some cases), have a valid driver's license and a credit card to rent a vehicle in Hawai'i. Most companies rent cars, vans, and four-wheel-drive vehicles. The large rental companies – **Alamo**, **Avis**, **Budget**, **Dollar**, **Hertz**, **National** – all have desks at the main airports. The **Lāna'i City Service** also has a range of vehicles for rent.

It is best to book a car before you leave home, if only to get the car you want. Rates start at about $35 per day, but there are discounts for weekly rental, and you can get good deals if you book via some airlines.

You must pay $3 tax per day, and you can also add $10–18 per day by taking out Loss Damage Waiver (LDW). This protects you from Hawai'i's "no fault" policy, which means that in the event of an accident, you are responsible for damage done to the rental car, regardless of fault. Your own insurance policy or credit card may cover rental cars, so check. Most rental contracts forbid even four-wheel-drive vehicles from using unpaved roads.

Cars should be returned with a full tank; fill it beforehand to avoid the high gas prices charged by the rental agencies.

MOTORCYCLING AND BIKING

MOPEDS AND motorcycles can be rented on all the four main islands. It is not mandatory to wear a helmet, but it's a good idea to do so.

You can rent bicycles easily too. People seem to use them mainly for getting about town rather than for touring.

Car rental pick-up area at the airport

RULES OF THE ROAD AND SAFETY

SEAT BELTS are mandatory in Hawai'i, and children under three must sit in approved car seats. Pedestrians always have right of way, and you can turn right after a full stop at a red light unless otherwise stated.

Distances between gas stations can be long, so it's a good idea to keep the tank at least half full. Always check the weather, as many roads wash out during or after heavy rains.

Local people are seldom in a hurry, so allow plenty of time for any journey. Also, residents never use their horns, so on narrow roads check your mirrors regularly and pull over to let cars pass. If you break down, call the rental company.

When you ask for directions, people will often give you landmarks to follow. On O'ahu you'll hear "Go diamondhead" (southeast) or "Go ewa" (northwest), and on all the islands you'll hear the words *mauka* ("toward the mountain") and *makai* ("toward the sea"). Many signs are in Hawaiian, so if you are getting help ask to be shown the way on a map.

PARKING

IT'S FAIRLY EASY to find free parking in Hawai'i, except in metropolitan Honolulu. Be sure to heed all signs. If there's no free parking, use a parking garage instead; you can often get your parking ticket validated by a restaurant, shopping center, or attraction and so park at little or no charge. Valet parking is provided at all major hotels and many restaurants.

Expeditions inter-island ferry in Lāna'i's Mānele Bay

FERRIES

HAWAI'I HAS JUST one ferry route, which crosses the 'Au'au Channel to link Maui with Lāna'i. **Expeditions** runs several daily ferries on this crossing, and in the winter the service doubles as a whale-watching cruise. The ferries depart from Lahaina Harbor and dock at Mānele Bay on Lāna'i about an hour later. The fare is about 50 percent less than the equivalent air fare. The crossing can be rough.

CRUISES

IN THE OLD DAYS, *hula* dancers and *lei* greeters would line Honolulu's piers to welcome the cruise ships. Times have changed. Several luxury lines stop in Hawai'i as part of a broader itinerary. They include **Crystal Cruises**, **Princess Cruises**, **Cunard**, **Holland America Line**, and **Royal Caribbean International**.

In addition, there are cruises around the islands. The SS *Independence* departs from Honolulu on Saturdays for a seven-day trip to Kaua'i, Maui, and Hawai'i Island. Contact **American Hawai'i Cruises** for more information.

Floodlit cruise ship dominating the Honolulu oceanfront

General Index

Acknowledgments

DORLING KINDERSLEY would like to thank the following people whose contributions and assistance have made the preparation of this book possible.

CONTRIBUTORS

GERALD CARR is Professor of Botany at the University of Hawai'i, Manoa and a resident of O'ahu. BONNIE FRIEDMAN runs a public relations firm on Maui, contributes regularly to Hawaiian publications, and volunteers at a Hawaiian language immersion school. RITA GOLDMAN is a freelance writer and editor who has lived on Maui since 1978. CLEMENCE MCLAREN is a Honolulu-based writer and teacher. MELISSA MILLER, a native of Honolulu, is a poet, storyteller, grant writer, and nonprofit consultant. ALEX SALKEVER is a Hawai'i-based journalist specializing in sports. STEPHEN SELF is Professor of Geology at the University of Hawai'i, Manoa and a resident of O'ahu. GREG WARD, an established travel writer who has written extensively on the Hawaiian islands, is also the author of *Hawaii: The Rough Guide*. PAUL WOOD, freelance writer, editor, writing teacher, and long-term resident of Maui, is the author of *Four Wheels Five Corners: Facts of Life in Upcountry Maui.*

DESIGN AND EDITORIAL

Stephen Bere, Hilary Bird for preparing the index, Louise Bolton, Arwen Burnett, Barbara Carr for fact checking, Jane Ewart, Fay Franklin, Emily Green, Emily Hatchwell, Des Helmsley, Kim Kemp, Georgina Matthews, Simon Melia, Robert Mitchell, Lee Redmond, Mary Sutherland, Greta Walker for initial research, and Stewart Wild for proofreading.

SPECIAL ASSISTANCE

Alana Waikiki, Aston Wailea Resort, Sheryl Toda and Tracey Matsushima at Bishop Museum, Four Seasons Resort Maui at Wailea, Elizabeth Anderson at Haleakala National Park, Richard Rasp at Hawai'i Volcanoes National Park, Julie Blissett at HVCB (UK), Sharon Brown at Kalaupapa National Historical Park, Geraldine Bell at Pu'uhonua O Hōnaunau National Historical Park, Stouffer Renaissance Wailea Beach Resort, Bill Haig and Linda Matsunaga at TheBus, the State Parks Administrator at Waimea Canyon and Koke'e State Park, and RM Towill Corporation for artwork reference.

ADDITIONAL SPECIAL PHOTOGRAPHY

Philip Dowell, DK Studio/Steve Gorton, Frank Greenaway, Dave King, John Heseltine, Neil Mersh, Andrew McKinney, David Murray and Jules Selmes, Roger Philips, Clive Streeter, Andrew Whittuck, and Jerry Young.

PHOTOGRAPHY PERMISSIONS

Dorling Kindersley would like to thank the following for their kind permission to photograph at their establishments and for their assistance with photography: Sharon Clark at the Hawai'i Film Office, George Applegate HVCB Big Island, Connie Wright at the HVCB Moloka'i, Department of Interior and the National Park Service 106–7, 116–117 and 128–129 and all other churches, museums, restaurants, hotels, shops, galleries, and other sights too numerous to thank individually.

PICTURE CREDITS

t = top; tl = top left; tlc = top left center; tc = top center; trc = top right center; tr = top right; cla = center left above; ca = center above; cra = center right above; cl = center left; c = center; cr = center right; clb = center left below; cb = center below; crb = center right below; bl = bottom left; b = bottom; bc = bottom center; bcl = bottom center left; br = bottom right; d = detail

Works of art have been reproduced with permission of the following copyright holders:
Stage design for L'Enfant et les Sortileges 1981, courtesy Tradhart, © David Hockney 1981: 59b.

The publisher would like to thank the following individuals, companies, and picture libraries for their kind permission to reproduce their photographs:

AKG, London: 15t, 33t; Museum of Mankind, London 14c; ALEXANDER AND BALDWIN SUGAR MUSEUM, Maui: 105bl; ALLSPORT UK LTD.: Vandystadt/Sylvain Cazenane 21c; ARCHIVE PHOTOS: 18tr, 32b, 33b.
Courtesy of BAMBOO RIDGE PRESS: cover illustration from *Wild Meat and The Bully Burgers* with kind permission of the artist Cora Yee 15b; BIOFOTOS: Heather Angel 13ca; BISHOP MUSEUM, Honolulu: 30c, 31t, 32c, 56c, 57t, 128b; Charles Furneaux 115cr; engraved by JG Woods 1878 20tr, BRIDGEMAN ART LIBRARY, London: Museum of Mankind, London 18c, 19t; National Library of Australia, Canberra *Captain Cook c1820* by John Webber engraved by Josef Selb c1820 29b; Scottish National Portrait Gallery *Robert Louis Stevenson (1850–94)* 1892 by Count Girolamo Pieri Nerli 15c(d); PAUL J BUKLAREWICZ: 16cl.
GERALD CARR: 12br, 13tc/bc; JEAN LOUP CHARMET: *from Voyage Autours du Monde* by Louis Choris 1822 6–7; 16tr, 28t; BRUCE COLEMAN COLLECTION: Jeff Foot Productions 101b; CORBIS UK LTD: Bettman Archive 32t, /Acme 125t, /UPI 51t, 53b; CULVER PICTURES, INC, New York: 29c, 31c, 31b, 32c, 56tl; CURRENT EVENTS, Kailua-Kona: 115cl.
RON DAHLQUIST: 12c, 21tl, 13br, 70cb, 71tr, 86cb, 96ca, 102b, 103br, 105tr, 107br. ET ARCHIVE, London; National Maritime Museum *Death of Cook* by J Cleavely 29t.
PETER FRENCH: 11b, 12tr, 13tr, 24b, 88t, 115cla, 142b, 144cb, 165tr. CHERYL GILBERT: 115br; RONALD GRANT ARCHIVE: Paramount Pictures *Blue Hawaii* (1961) 139.
ROBERT HARDING PICTURE LIBRARY: Nakamura 148–9; HAWAIIAN HISTORICAL SOCIETY: 14b, *from Voyage Autours du Monde* by Louis Choris 1822 26; HAWAIIAN LEGACY ARCHIVE: 14tl; HONOLULU ACADEMY OF ARTS: Gift of Mrs. C. Montague Cooke, Jr, Charles M. Cooke III and Mrs. Heatin Wrenn in memory of Dr. C. Montague Cooke, Jr 1951 *Nahienaena* Robert Dampier 97t; HONOLULU BOYS CHOIR:182t.
IMAGE BANK, London: 38; INTERNATIONAL COFFEE ORGANISATION, London: 115clb. ©KAUA'I MUSEUM: 143t.
ANTHONY LIMERICK: 96tr, 98t, 103t, 129t/b, 163b, 193t, 194tl/tr, 195t, 197t, 198b.
NASA, Houston: 8c; NATURE PHOTOGRAPHERS: Brinsley Burbidge 12cb/bl, 141c; James Hancock 143cr; Paul Sterry 143cl; PETER NEWARK'S AMERICAN PICTURES: engraved by N Currier 1852 30t; NHPA: Stephen Kraseman 13cb.
PACIFIC STOCK: 28c; Bob Abraham 17b, 22c, 196b; Rita Ariyoshi 178b; Joe Carini 22b; Dana Edmunds 24t; Bill Schlidge 142t; Greg Vaughan 18bl, 19cb, 23b; DOUGLAS PEEBLES: 5tl, 10c, 40ca, 70ca, 72, 81b, 105tl, 121t/b, 130, 145c, 164b, 186b; PHOTO RESOURCE HAWAI'I: David Bjorn 20–1; David Boynton 16bl, 141t; Randy Jay Braun 17c; John Callahan 1, 22t, 25b, 176c; Monte Costa 33ca; Tami Dawson 70t, 147b; David Franzen 45b; Nikiolas Konstantinou 118t; Jon Ogata 145t; Franco Salmoiraghi 71b, 111b, 131b, 119t, 162b; Joe Solem 23t; Jamie Wellner 25t, 196t; Lani Breheme Yamasaki 20c; PHOTO TROFIC: David S Boynton 143b; PICTURES COLOUR LIBRARY: 17t; PLANET EARTH PICTURES: Pete Atkinson 77t; John Lythgoe 151t; PRINCEVILLE HOTEL: 150c; PRIVATE COLLECTION: 7 inset, 14tr, 27b, 30brb, 35 inset, 69 inset, 149 inset, 189 inset. SCOTT ROWLAND: 10b.
SCIENCE PHOTO LIBRARY: Royal Observatory, Edinburgh 110; Soames Summerhays 128tr; THE STOCKMARKET: 16–17; SURFER PUBLICATIONS: Jeff Divine 21b; Tom Servais 20bl/bc/br, 21tr; KEVIN and CAT SWEENEY: 115bla, 184c.
TEDESCHI VINEYARDS: 104tl, 190b; TELEGRAPH COLOUR LIBRARY: S Benbow 184b; Colorific/Jean Paul Nacivet 9t.
BRETT UPRICHARD: 19ca. GREG WARD: 10t, 87t, 142c; NIK WHEELER 180b; WORLD PICTURES: 68–9, 73b.
Front Endpaper: all special photography except DOUGLAS PEEBLES: tl/tlc; SCIENCE PHOTO LIBRARY: Royal Observatory, Edinburgh b.
Jacket: all image special photography except PETER FRENCH; front cr; GETTY IMAGES: Joe Solem front t; PHOTO RESOURCE HAWAI'I: Joe Solem front cra; THE STOCKMARKET: back tl; SURFER PUBLICATIONS: Tom Servais front cl and spine b.

MAPS ERA-Maptech Ltd, Dublin, Ireland.

DORLING KINDERSLEY SPECIAL EDITIONS

DORLING KINDERSLEY books can be purchased in bulk quantities at discounted prices for use in promotions or as premiums. We are also able to offer special editions and personalized jackets, corporate imprints, and excerpts from all of our books, tailored specifically to meet your own needs.

To find out more, please contact:
(in the United Kingdom) – SPECIAL SALES, DORLING KINDERSLEY LIMITED, 9 HENRIETTA STREET, COVENT GARDEN, LONDON WC2E 8PS; TEL. 020 7753 3572;

(in the United States) – SPECIAL MARKETS DEPARTMENT, DORLING KINDERSLEY PUBLISHING, INC., 95 MADISON AVENUE, NEW YORK, NY 10016.

Glossary of Hawaiian Terms

Hawaiian began as an oral language. It was first put into written form by the missionaries who arrived in the 1820s. The teaching and speaking of Hawaiian was banned from the early 1900s, and by the time the native cultural renaissance began in 1978 the beautiful, melodious language was almost totally lost. Immersion programs are beginning to produce a new generation of Hawaiian speakers. Fluent speakers are still few, and native speakers are even more rare. Still, you will hear Hawaiian words liberally sprinkled in conversation and in the islands' glorious music, and see it written on some signs.

SUMMARY OF PRONUNCIATION

The Hawaiian language has just 12 letters: the five vowels plus h, k, l, m, n, p, and w.

unstressed vowels:

a	as in "above"
e	as in "bet"
i	as y in "city"
o	as in "sole"
u	as in "full"

stressed vowels:

ā	as in "far"
ē	as in "pay"
ī	as in "see"
ō	as in "sole"
ū	as in "moon"

consonants:

h	as in "hat"
k	as in "kick"
l	as in "law"
m	as in "mow"
n	as in "now"
p	as in "pin"
w	as in "win" or "vine"

The 'okina (glottal stop) is found at the beginning of some words beginning with vowels or between vowels. It is pronounced like the sound between the syllables in the English "uh-oh."

ali'i	ahlee-ee
liliko'i	leeleekoh-ee
'ohana	oh-hahnah

The kahakō (macron) is a mark found only above vowels, indicating vowels should be stressed.

kāne	**kah**-nay
kōkua	**koh**-koo-ah
pūpū	**poo**-poo

EVERYDAY WORDS

'aina	**aye**-nah	land
aloha	ah-loh-ha	hello; goodbye; love
hale	ha-leh	house
haole	how-leh	foreigner; Caucasian
hula	who-la	Hawaiian dance
kāhiko	**kaa**-hee-koh	old; traditional
kama'āina	kah-mah-**aye**-nah	familiar; resident
kāne	**kah**-nay	man
kapa	kah-pah	bark cloth
keiki	kay-kee	child
kōkua	**koh**-koo-ah	help
kumu	kooh-mooh	teacher
lānai	**luh**-nigh	porch; balcony
lei	layh	garland
lua	looah	bathroom; toilet
mahalo	muh-ha-low	thank you
mu'umu'u	moo-oo-moo-oo	long billowing dress
'ohana	oh-hahnah	family
'ono	oh-noh	delicious
pau	pow	done
puka	poo-kah	hole
wahine	w(v)ah-he-nay	woman
wikiwiki	w(v)eekee-w(v)eekee	quickly

GEOGRAPHICAL AND NATURE TERMS

'a'ā	ah-**aah**	rough, jagged lava
kai	kaee	ocean
koholā	koh-hoh-**laah**	humpback whale
kona	koh-nah	leeward side
ko'olau	koh-oh-lowh	windward side
kukui	kuh-kooh-eeh	candlenut tree
makai	muh-kaee	toward the sea
mauka	mau-kuh	toward the mountains
mauna	mau-nah	mountain
nēnē	**nay-nay**	Hawaiian goose
pāhoehoe	**pah**-hoy-hoy	smooth lava
pali	pah-lee	cliff
pu'u	poo-oo	hill
wai	w(v)hy	fresh water

HISTORICAL TERMS

ahupua'a	ah-hoo-poo-ah-ah	a division of land, from mountains to sea
ali'i	ahlee-ee	chief; royalty
heiau	hey-yow	ancient temple
kahuna	kah-hoo-nah	priest; expert
kapu	kah-poo	forbidden; taboo
kupuna	koo-poo-nah	elders; ancestors
luakini	looh-ah-kee-nee	human sacrifice temple
maka'āinana	mah-kah-**aye**-nanah	commoner
mana	mah-nah	supernatural power
mele	meh-leh	song
mo'o	moh-oh	lizard
oli	oh-leeh	chant
pili	pih-leeh	grass for thatching
pu'uhonua	pooh-ooh-hoh-nuah	place of refuge

FOOD WORDS

'ahi	ah-hee	yellowfin tuna
aku	ah-koo	skipjack; bonito
a'u	ah-oo	swordfish; marlin
haupia	how-peeah	traditional coconut pudding
imu	ee-moo	underground oven
kalo	kah-loh	taro
kālua	**kah**-looah	food baked slowly in underground oven
kiawe	key-ah-veh	wood used for grilling
laulau	lau-lau	steamed filled ti-leaf packages
liliko'i	lee-lee-koh-ee	passion fruit
limu	lee-moo	seaweed
lomi-lomi salmon	low-me low-me	raw salmon pieces with onion and tomato
lū'au	**loo**-ow	Hawaiian feast
mahimahi	muh-hee-muh-hee	dorado; dolphin fish
ono	oh-no	wahoo
opah	oh-pah	moonfish
'ōpakapaka	**oh**-pah-kah-pah-kah	blue snapper
poi	poy	pounded taro root
pūpū	**poo**-poo	appetizer
uku	oo-koo	gray snapper
ulua	oo-looah	jackfish; pompano

PIDGIN

Hawai'i's unofficial conglomerate language is commonly heard on playgrounds, in shopping malls, and backyards throughout Hawai'i. Here are some words and phrases you may hear:

brah	brother, pal
broke da mout'	great food
buggah	pal or pest
fo' real	really
fo' what	why
grinds	food; also to grind
howzit?	how are you?; how is everything?
kay den	okay then
laydahs	later; goodbye
li' dat	like that
li' dis	like this
no can	cannot
no mo' nahting	nothing
shoots!	yeah!
stink eye	dirty look
talk story	chat; gossip

FOR UPDATES TO OUR GUIDES, AND INFORMATION ON
<u>TRAVEL PLANNERS</u>, <u>CITY MAPS</u>
<u>DK EYEWITNESS TRAVEL GUII</u>
<u>PHRASEBOOKS</u>

VISIT US AT
eyewitnesstravel.dk.com

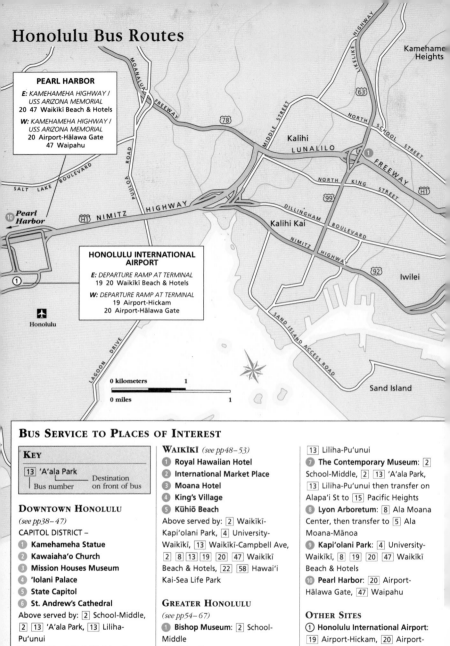

Honolulu Bus Routes

PEARL HARBOR

E: *KAMEHAMEHA HIGHWAY /
USS ARIZONA MEMORIAL*
20 47 Waikīkī Beach & Hotels

W: *KAMEHAMEHA HIGHWAY /
USS ARIZONA MEMORIAL*
20 Airport-Hālawa Gate
47 Waipahu

**HONOLULU INTERNATIONAL
AIRPORT**

E: *DEPARTURE RAMP AT TERMINAL*
19 20 Waikīkī Beach & Hotels

W: *DEPARTURE RAMP AT TERMINAL*
19 Airport-Hickam
20 Airport-Hālawa Gate

Kamehame
Heights

Kalihi

Kalihi Kai

Iwilei

Pearl
Harbor

Honolulu

Sand Island

0 kilometers   1

0 miles   1

Bus Service to Places of Interest

Key

13 'A'ala Park
Bus number   Destination on front of bus

Downtown Honolulu

(see pp38–47)

CAPITOL DISTRICT –

1. **Kamehameha Statue**
2. **Kawaiaha'o Church**
3. **Mission Houses Museum**
4. **'Iolani Palace**
5. **State Capitol**
6. **St. Andrew's Cathedral**

Above served by: 2 School-Middle,
2 13 'A'ala Park, 13 Liliha-
Pu'unui

7. **Fort Street Mall**: 2 School-
Middle, 2 13 'A'ala Park,
13 Liliha-Pu'unui

WATERFRONT –

8. **Aloha Tower and Marketplace**
9. **Hawai'i Maritime Center**

Above served by: 19 Airport-Hickam,
20 Airport-Hālawa Gate, 47
Waipahu

10. **Chinatown**: 2 School-Middle,
2 'A'ala Park, 13 Liliha-Pu'unui,
13 'A'ala Park

Waikīkī *(see pp48–53)*

1. **Royal Hawaiian Hotel**
2. **International Market Place**
3. **Moana Hotel**
4. **King's Village**
5. **Kūhiō Beach**

Above served by: 2 Waikīkī-
Kapi'olani Park, 4 University-
Waikīkī, 13 Waikīkī-Campbell Ave,
2 8 13 19 20 47 Waikīkī
Beach & Hotels, 22 58 Hawai'i
Kai-Sea Life Park

Greater Honolulu

(see pp54–67)

1. **Bishop Museum**: 2 School-
Middle
2. **O'ahu Cemetery**
3. **Royal Mausoleum**
4. **Queen Emma Summer Palace**

Above served by: 4 Nu'uanu-
Dowsett

5. **National Memorial Cemetery
of the Pacific**: 2 School-Middle, 2
13 'A'ala Park, 13 Liliha-Pu'unui
then transfer on Alapa'i St to 15
Pacific Heights

6. **Honolulu Academy of Arts**: 2
School-Middle, 2 13 'A'ala Park,

13 Liliha-Pu'unui

7. **The Contemporary Museum**: 2
School-Middle, 2 13 'A'ala Park,
13 Liliha-Pu'unui then transfer on
Alapa'i St to 15 Pacific Heights

8. **Lyon Arboretum**: 8 Ala Moana
Center, then transfer to 5 Ala
Moana-Mānoa

9. **Kapi'olani Park**: 4 University-
Waikīkī, 8 19 20 47 Waikīkī
Beach & Hotels

10. **Pearl Harbor**: 20 Airport-
Hālawa Gate, 47 Waipahu

Other Sites

① **Honolulu International Airport**:
19 Airport-Hickam, 20 Airport-
Hālawa Gate (hand luggage only)

② **Ala Moana Center**: 8 Ala Moana
Center, 8 Ala Moana Center-Ward
Ave, 19 Airport-Hickam, 20
Airport-Hālawa Gate, 47 Waipahu,
58 Waikīkī-Ala Moana Center

③ **University of Hawai'i**: 4
Nu'uanu-Dowsett

④ **Makiki-Tantalus Trails**: 2 School-
Middle, 2 13 'A'ala Park,
13 Liliha-Pu'unui, then transfer on
Alapa'i St to 15 Pacific Heights